DARK PSYCHOLOGY: 6 BOOKS IN ONE

*Discover the Secrets of Human Behavior,
the Hidden Messages of Body Language,
Learn the Tricks of Mental Manipulation
And Gaslighting to Achieve a Free Life*

Matthew Wallace

The trademarks that are used are without any consent, and the publication of the trademark is without permission or backing by the trademark owner. All trademarks and brands within this book are for clarifying purposes only and are the owned by the owners themselves, not affiliated with this document.

Table Of Contents

Chapter 9: Using Psychology To Re-Program Your Habits

Conclusion

Book 2: How to Analyze People with Dark Psychology?

Introduction

Chapter 1: Analyzing Yourself & Others

Chapter 2: Personality Types & Your Identity

Book 1: Psychology of Human Behavior

The Complete Guide to Behavioral Theories. Discover How to Restructure Your Thinking, Understand Emotions and Develop Emotional Intelligence to Make Your Relationships Successful

Introduction

What scale do you use to understand humans or measure the reason for their actions? The "belief-desire" is the most useful and common denominator. That is, individuals in situations of daily life use both desires and beliefs to understand why others do what they do. For instance, if we were to notice "Bella" going to the cinema, we explain that activity by guessing that Bella believes that the cinema is playing a specific movie and watching it something she desires. This scale can be used flexibly. For instance, if Bella were a film critic, then we might guess her belief-desire situation for watching the film is something other than if Bella were a teenager leaving to see the film with her boyfriend on a date.

Although these scales are very useful for everyday living, a more sophisticated approach is required, a scientifically grounded scale for extensive understanding. A broad variety of distinct paradigms have been generated by the field of psychology, but unluckily, different languages are spoken by these paradigms, and we learn different things regarding the understanding of people from these paradigms. Terms like desires and beliefs are rejected by the supporters of Skinnerian behaviorists. They claim to empirically observe the types of consequences on the frequency of discharged behaviors by the environment. Information processing language is used by cognitive psychologists to explain desires and beliefs. Freudian theorists say that conscious desires and beliefs ultimately play a very small part in explaining the reason behind people's actions. They claim that subconscious forces are the real motivators of human behavior.

I will discuss all of these theories in detail in the following chapters of the book. This will enable you to identify the negative behaviors of others as well as yourself. You will understand the reasons for these actions and where they are rooted in our mindset. What value do these behaviors hold for us, and how can we get rid of behaviors and thoughts that no longer help us. This deep insight into the working f mind will help you to achieve success both in the workplace and in relationships in your life. You will be able to empathize with others as well as with yourself. Instead of cursing yourself for the negative habits, you will able to channel them into more positive ways constructively. So, keep reading if you are interested to know the miracles of the mind and how to use them to favor yourself.

Chapter 1: A Brief History Of Psychology

This chapter provides information regarding the history of psychology and how it evolved as a separate discipline. The modifications that took place and the different thought schools are also discussed in this chapter.

1.1 Psychology In Ancient Greece And Other Civilizations

"A lengthy past but a tiny history."

Ebbinghaus said this as the questions of psychology starts from ancient times (Greece, Egypt, Rome). Psychological topics have been talked about for ages, but there was no separate psychology discipline. Disciplines of natural science and philosophy gave rise to psychology.

Assyrian Tablets

These clay tablets were fire-hardened, and that is why they survived. Written in the shape of the wedge and the system of writing is called cuneiform. They are created by the Mesopotamians. They describe fear regarding found in public without clothes and dreams of death.

Contributions of the Ancients

Ancient philosophers and physicians speculated about the locus of mind and nature, perception and sensation, learning and memory. Their work stood for thousands of years and formed the basis of science and modern psychology. You can find the traces of their work in today's thinking.

Ancient Greek Medicine

Priests performed rituals to give promotion to healing for a fee. The patient was kept in a temple alone. Drugs were used to stop bleeding and relieve pain.

Alcmaeon (500 BC)

He first dissected animal's bodies to observe them objectively. To oppose priests, he formed a medical school and promoted a non-mystical, rational, and observation-dependent medicine. He saw disease and health as harmonious equity. He took a holistic approach to systems of the body.

Hippocrates (460 BC)

Hippocrates also denied the priests' superstition and founded a school of medicine. He said that natural causes are the source of all diseases, and natural methods must be used to treat them. Nature possesses the power to heal. The duty of the physician is to prevent interfering with the healing of nature. He often suggested exercise, music, diet, rest, and link with friends to re-establish natural balance.

Observations done by Hippocrates

The left side of the body is controlled by the right side of the brain and vice versa. He explained symptoms of depression, postpartum depression, paranoia, hysteria, and phobias. He explained in "the nature of man" a theory of 4 senses of humor in correspondence to the 4 elements of earth, water, fire, and air. : blood, phlegm, two biles. Bloodletting to stable humor was regularly practiced during the 1800s. The sign of the bloodletter is a barber pole.

Personality and Humor

If in large quantity:

Yellow Bile = angered easily

Black choleric Bile = peevish

Melancholic Phlegm = apathetic

Dull blood = happy, cheerful, optimistic

The terms bilious, phlegmatic, sanguine (from blood or sanguis) referred to the disparity of the humor and were utilized to describe traits of personality. "Good humor" is a sign of balance of humor.

He explained epilepsy as a sacred disease. Devine meddling resulted from seizures. He denied such concepts and said that a cause would be discovered, which will be physiological. His theory "dry mouth" of thirst explains that when air flows over the throat membranes, it dulls them out, forming a thirst sensation that pushes us to drink.

Hippocrates is seen as the medicine's father, but he contributed to the field of psychology as well. He described the psychological conditions on the basis of their natural causes. He gave treatments that were holistic like Alcmaeon and described problems regarding behavior. He formulated theories that were long-lasting regarding motivation and temperament. He also criticized laws that stopped women from gaining knowledge.

Galen (130 - 200 AD)

Galen combined Rome's Imperial wisdom and formed a library with experiments and personal observation. He wrote a book on the body parts' usefulness. He said that there is nobody part that is superfluous. He asserted the uncertainty of creation without any divine design on this basis.

Galen's Contributions

He described a way of treating issues of the soul in "On the passions and Errors of soul" Diseases come from passions like fear, anger, etc., and you can control them by self-knowledge and understanding. Love for oneself blinds us, and we do not see our own faults. He described a therapeutic relationship first.

Science 1

Measurements are required for science. Observations cannot help us grow unless they are done in a systemic way. You need to repeat the observations, and therefore, the description is supposed to be done in a form that any person can repeat. Measurement is a basic way of studying world properties by giving them a number. Measurement requires mathematics.

Progress in Mathematics

Earlier accomplishments by Egyptians in the field of geometry were refined by Greeks. This served as the base of mathematical theory. Math became the speech of science under the Greeks. Solar eclipses were predicted by math. Mathematical links in the world were related to the order and psychological harmony in the bodily world by Pythagoras.

Science 2 Another science foundation gave the concept that an occurrence can be recognized in words of its parts. Functioning and the combination of fundamental parts may give rise to emergent properties. Biochemistry gives rise to life, which concerns the set of physical elements. An approach from an analytical perspective suggests that by fragmenting down a situation into its chunks, separating them for research, it can be understood better.

Atomism

Democritus told that small atomic pieces in ceaseless motion are the foundation of all matter. Mass of atoms forms the world that works without the requirement of outside forces. This physical world includes the mind of humans. The contents of the mind are the consequence of experience.

Zeno's Paradoxes

This outlook of mind created a problem between the relationship of matter and mind and the dependability of the sensory systems. To show the insufficiency of the senses, paradoxes were invented by Zeno of Elea.

The Humanist Tradition

Plato, Socrates, and Aristotle created epistemology, philosophy's branch that investigates the nature, origin, limits of knowledge for humans, and methods. They study awareness, memory, and learning.

Psychology of Memory by Aristotle

Basic memory principles were developed by Aristotle that have been reused in psychology plenty of times and are key to contemporary theories to this day.

Post-Aristotelian Philosophy

Epicureans added Lucretius and Epicurus and said that sensations kept in memories give rise to all knowledge. Completely materialistic, so the aim of life is to cherish while keeping the pain of others to a minimum.

1.2 Background - Physiology and Philosophy

Even though psychology was not considered a separate field until the end of the 19th century, the history of this field can be found since the time of early Greeks. Rene Descartes, a French scientist in the 1700s, introduced the prospect of dualism. On the basis of this idea, he said that body and mind were 2 separate entities that make the human experience through their interaction. Many ideas, like the relative contributions of nurture vs. nature, have their roots in these ancient philosophical ideas. What is the thing that makes psychology from philosophy, then? Philosophers in early times used methods like logic and observation but psychologists today use scientific methodologies to observe and make conclusions regarding human behavior and thought. Physiology also had a role in the eventual emergence of psychology as an area of science. The research on behavior and the brain in the field of physiology had a huge mark on psychology. This ultimately leads to the application of scientific methodologies to investigate human behavior and thought.

1.3 Psychology appears as an individual discipline

In the middle of the 19th century, Wilhelm Wundt, a German physiologist, was utilizing scientific research techniques to study reaction times. He outlined many connections between physiology and the study of human behavior and thought in his book "Principles of physiological psychology". He opened the first lab of psychology in the world in 1897 at Leipzig University. This is officially considered the beginning of psychology as a distinct field of science. He perceived psychology as an investigation of human consciousness.

He tried to use experimental methods to investigate processes inside the mind. Introspection was a process used by him that is unscientific and unreliable today, but his initial work set the stage for future experimental methods in psychology. Almost 17000 students took lectures at his lab and many more pursued a degree in this field. His influence, however, dwindled later, but his impact on this field cannot be questioned.

1.4 Structuralism

Edward B. Titchener is the founder of structuralism, the first big school of thought in psychology. He was a student of Wundt. We can break the consciousness of humans into tiny parts, according to structuralists. Trained subjects, using introspection, would try to break down their reactions and responses to the simple perceptions and sensations. Structuralism is known for its focus on scientific research but the methods used were subjective, limiting, and unreliable. Structuralism died with Titchener in 1927.

1.5 Functionalism

Psychology thrilled in America from the middle to the end of the 1800s. A major psychologist William James emerged from America during this time. He published a book called the principles of psychology made him the father of psychology in America.

His book was used as a standard text in the field of psychology, and his work leads to the formation of a separate thought school called functionalism. The focus of this school of thought was regarding how behavior really works to aid humans to survive in their environment. Direct observation was the technique used by functionalists to investigate human behavior and the mind.

The focus of both of these schools that emerged, in the beginning, was on human consciousness. The conceptions, however, were majorly different. Structuralists used to break the mental processes down into their tinier parts, while functionalists adhered to the idea that consciousness was more of a continuous process changing all the time. Even though functionalism soon faded as a distinct thought school, later psychologists and theories regarding human behavior and thought were influenced by it.

1.6 Psychoanalysis

Psychologists emphasized the conscious experience of humans up to this point. Sigmund Freud, a physician from Austria, changed the idea of psychology in an unimaginable way. He proposed a theory that focused on the unconscious mind's importance called the theory of personality. His work with patients in the clinical field suffering from hysteria as well as other diseases made him believe that unconscious impulses and experiences during childhood played a role in the development of adult behavior and personality. He explained how these impulses and unconscious thoughts are expressed through mostly slips of tongue and dreams in his book called the psychopathology of everyday life. They are known as Freudian slips. As per Freud, when these unconscious conflicts get extreme or are unbalanced, a human suffers from psychological disorders. This psychoanalytic theory had a huge impact on thought in the 20th century. This theory given by Freud influenced the areas of mental health, popular culture, literature, and art.

1.7 Behaviorism

Psychology had another dramatic change during the start of the 20th century as another thought school called behaviorism came to the surface. This thought school was significantly different from all the other theoretical perspectives. It rejected the focus on both the unconscious and conscious mind. By focusing only on observable behavior, this idea emphasized turning psychology into more of a scientific discipline. Behaviorism had its initial up rise with the work of Ivan Pavlov, a physiologist from Russia. His research on a dog's digestive system uncovered the idea of classical conditioning. This work emphasized the idea that behaviors can be learned through conditioned association. He demonstrated that this conditioning could be utilized in order to form an association between stimulus occurring naturally and environmental stimulus. John B. Watson, a psychologist from America, quickly became one of the biggest advocates of this thought school.

Behaviorism had a huge impact on psychology. This thought school dominated for the coming 50 years, with the introduction of the concept of operant conditioning, B.F. Skinner, a psychologist, furthered the perspective of behaviorism. Operant conditioning showed the impact of reinforcement and punishment on behavior. This thought school eventually fell out of domination in the field of psychology, but the principles are widely used to this day. Therapeutic techniques like behavioral modification, token economies, and behavioral analysis are mostly practiced by professionals to help children utilize new skills and overcome behaviors that are maladaptive.

1.8 The 3rd Force

The start of the 20th century was influenced by behaviorism and psychoanalysis, but during the middle part, another thought school called humanistic psychology came onto the surface. This is also referred to in psychology as the third force. Conscious experiences were emphasized by this theoretical perspective. Carl Rogers, an American psychologist, is considered the father of this thought school. He strongly believed in the power of self-determination and free will, whereas the psychoanalysts focused on unconscious impulses while behaviorists emphasized environmental causes. Abraham Maslow also contributed to the field of humanistic psychology with the theory of the hierarchy of needs for human motivation. He made the suggestion that increasingly complicated needs were the motivation for people. Once people acquire the basic needs, they are motivated to reach for needs of higher levels.

1.9 Cognitive Psychology

A movement called the cognitive revolution started in the 1950s in the field of psychology. Cognitive psychology started replacing behaviorism and psychoanalysis in this time as the dominant outlook on psychology. Observable behaviors were still an interesting aspect for psychologists, but they also started taking an interest in what was looming inside the mind. Cognitive psychology, from that time, has continued to be a dominant area in the field of psychology as researchers keep on studying things like perception, decision making, memory, intelligence, language, and problem-solving. The introductions of techniques of brain imaging like PET scans and MRI have assisted in enhancing the ability of professionals to study workings inside the human brain more closely.

1.10 Psychology Keeps Growing

The field of psychology has gone through immense change over the years, as explained. It has also seen a lot of growth during this period. New perspectives and ideas have always been introduced. Recent research in this field looks at various aspects of the experiences of humans, from the biological impact on behavior to the impact of cultural and social factors on behavior. Psychologists do not focus on any single thought school these days. Instead, they emphasize one single perspective or specialty. They usually draw ideas from a list of theoretical backgrounds. This approach has added new theories and ideas in the field of psychology, which will keep this field growing for many years to come.

1.11 Psychoanalysis and Psychology

Psychoanalysis is considered a combination of therapeutic techniques and psychological theories that have their roots in the theories and work of Sigmund Freud. The core of this analysis is the idea that every person has feelings, memories, desires, and unconscious thoughts.

Basic Tenets

Psychoanalysis says that individuals can gain insight into their present state of mind and undergo catharsis by guiding the unconscious content into conscious awareness. A person can obtain relief from distress with this process. It also suggests that:

- The behavior of a person is controlled by their drives which are unconscious
- Psychological and emotional issues like anxiety and depression are due to the conflicts between the unconscious and conscious mind.
- The incidents of early childhood influence personality development heavily. Personality was mostly developed by the age of 5, according to Freud.
- To protect themselves from the knowledge contained within the unconscious, people utilize defense mechanisms.

Professional analysts can assist a person in bringing some aspects of the unconscious into consciousness through psychoanalytic strategies like free association and dream analysis.

History

Freud was the initiator of psychoanalysis, and he utilized the psychodynamic approach in psychology. According to him, three things: the id, the superego, and the ego formed the mind of humans. The psychosexual stages theory by Freud, dream symbolism, and the unconscious are still known by both laypeople and psychologists. Other people, however, view this work with skepticism. He used case studies and clinical cases to form most of his theories and observations. Therefore, it was difficult to generalize such findings for a large number of people. Still, the theories proposed by him have shaped our thinking regarding how we view the mind of humans as well as the behavior of humans. These theories have strong marks on culture and psychology.

Key Ideas

A number of different ideas and terms are associated with psychoanalysis in relation to the mind, treatment, and personality.

Case Studies

The study of an individual in-depth is known as a case study. It can be of an event or a group as well. Most notable case studies by Freud include Little Hans, Anna O., and Dora. His psychoanalytic theories were heavily influenced by these cases. The professional tries to examine every single aspect of the life of an individual deeply during a case study. This deep study gives the researcher an insight into how the present behavior of an individual is influenced by his history. Although a researcher hopes that the information obtained from a single study can be used to gain an insight in studying other cases, the results are mostly difficult to generalize because the studies are highly subjective. The factors playing a role in one case may be so individualized that others may not relate to it.

1.12 The Unconscious And Conscious Mind

Things that are not in our conscious awareness are in the unconscious mind. It includes secret desires, hidden drives, and childhood memories from the earliest stages of life. Things that might seem socially unacceptable or even unpleasant are contained in the unconscious, as per Freud. These things might be a source of conflict or pain for us, and therefore, we bury them in our unconscious.

Even though these urges, memories, and thoughts are not in our awareness, the way we behave and think is heavily influenced by them. Sometimes, things that are not in our awareness can have an impact on our behavior in ways that are negative and cause psychological distress.

Things that we are aware of are contained in our conscious minds. It also includes things that we can bring into our awareness easily.

Unconscious Mind
- Feelings urges or thoughts that are difficult, socially unacceptable, or even unpleasant.
- Buried for the purpose of avoiding pain or conflict that can be brought up because of them.
- Certain techniques can be used to bring them into our awareness.

Conscious Mind
- Urges, feelings, and thoughts that we can identify or can bring into awareness easily.
- They are not suppressed or hidden.
- Unconscious memories, feelings, or thoughts can influence them.

1.13 Sigmund Freud's Ego, Superego, And Id

The personality of an individual is composed of 3 components, according to Freud. The id, ego, and the superego.

Id

The first element of importance to emerge is called id in the process of shaping personality. It contains the primal urges, unconscious, and the basics.

Ego

The ego is the second element of personality to surface. The requirements of reality are dealt with by this aspect of personality. It assists in countering the id urges and allows us to behave in acceptable and realistic ways. Instead of participating in behaviors that are formed to meet our needs and desires, it compels us to act in ways that are acceptable socially and realistic in nature. Other than just keeping the id demands in check, this element also assists in maintaining a balance between reality and our ideals and basic urges.

Superego

The final element of personality to arise is the superego. It encompasses the values and ideals. The beliefs and values that are instilled in us by society and parents are the force that guides the superego. This force aspires us to act as per these morals.

1.14 The Defense Mechanisms of Ego

The strategies used by the ego are called the defense mechanisms, which it uses to shield itself from anxiety. In order to stop distressing or unpleasant aspects contained in the unconscious from breaching consciousness, these mechanisms act as a protective shield. These mechanisms stop the information from reaching consciousness whenever something inappropriate or overwhelming is experienced. This reduces the distress.

1.15 Neuroscience And Psychology

Neuroscience is all over the front pages in the world of modern science. It has emerged as a key region of exploration because of its own special qualities, plus across plenty of disciplines like psychology. In order to understand the role of neuroscience in psychology, it is important to understand neuroscience. The importance of neuroscience and the connection between body and the mind.

The scientific analysis of the nervous system is called neuroscience. This science studies the function of the nervous system and brain: chemical and biological processes. The working of the brain is being studied since the time of ancient Egyptians, but as a discipline, neuroscience has prospered in recent times. It encompasses the elements of anatomy, human behavior, molecular biology, and more.

Neuroscientific research largely focused on cellular and molecular observations of individual neurons. Neuroscience can give an insight into the anatomy of the brain and our comprehension of psychological, physical, and neurological functioning- particularly, the linking of the brain, mind, and body with the use of the latest computer simulation and imaging tools.

1.16 How Does Neuroscience Help Psychology?

The two sciences may seem to be at odds because neuroscience focuses on physical properties, and the focus of psychology is on their mental equivalents. However, psychology involves the role of neuroscience. Neuroscience and psychology are very less likely to be entirely different fields. Instead, they complement each other in many ways. The questions around behavior and cognition, neuropsychopharmacology, plasticity, and neural development can be answered with the help of these two areas together. Understanding the scientific level of brain functioning and utilizing advanced technology like brain scanners can assist in identifying the correlations between mental states and the brain. Neuroscience has formed advanced methods to investigate the biological processes which underpin behavior. This allows the professionals to intervene regarding mental treatments in a more informed manner.

Chapter 2: Understanding Who We Are?

"Be yourself; all others are already taken" ~Oscar Wilde

To have to study to understand yourself may look counterintuitive in some forms. You must already know that, right? Not really, though.

What we are today is surely due to the help of the experiences that we have had, but this still does not guarantee that we clearly know who we are—what inspires us or what we are looking for in life.

We have developed values and beliefs since our childhood. Some good beliefs and some negative, as a consequence of pressure from our surroundings and the type of environment we have lived in.

2.1 Getting To Know Yourself, What You Like, and What You Want In Life?

I associated fitting into people and achieving great academically with my worth during my childhood.

I had an older sister who performed academically better, and it made me feel like I did not have any worth. This led to decreased self-esteem and issues.

I forced myself to go to school in order to be liked, even though I was extremely ill, in fear that my friends would no longer want me in their group.

All of this seems irrational, but it made complete sense during that time. The school was a symbol of familiarity for me despite all the emotional disorders I experienced. I believed that if I made it to a good university by working hard enough, things would eventually fall into place. So I got good grades by working extremely hard and got an offer from a top university. This was proof for everyone that I was smart enough, but this "proof" felt strangely hollow.

I felt hollow despite believing that achieving all of this would make me feel complete. This is exactly what I dreamed of, and yet it somehow did not feel enough. I started believing that my mind was messed up. After one month at the University of my Dreams, I started hating myself and had doubts about myself. I suffered a nervous breakdown. I spent most of my life thinking and working about the goals which were important to me, only to reach the conclusion that they had no value for me. Instead of having a confidence boost and sense of accomplishment, I spent the month at university feeling like an outsider and a fraud.

I felt as if I did not exist at all when I was at my worst. I had no clue about any of these questions. I had nothing apart from associating myself with negative thoughts. I was diagnosed with depression and anxiety when I left university. I underwent CBT that same year, and it did not help me either.

I felt guilty that therapy was not helping me with my recovery. I would pretend to the doctor that it was helping and lie about it. Despite everything, I was thinking about pleasing others still by acting the way they wanted me to.

The only thing that helped me in my recovery was to take time out for myself and understand myself. I identified through my struggles that I was aiming towards goals that I believed others expected of me all this time.

Some of the thoughts that keep helping me in this struggle and can be worthy of consideration for you as well are as follows:

Understand that it is not up to you to justify what your worth is!

I used to believe that if I accomplish X, then I deserve to accomplish Y. This pattern of thinking is both destructive and completely wrong. It presumes that there exists a hierarchy of an individual's worth. The reality is that every individual is worthy of kindness, respect, and love.

Try to take time out in order to try different things. This will allow you to understand what you like.

I was struck by the thought that I had no clue what I really enjoyed doing after leaving university. If someone had inquired me about this while I was studying at school, I would have answered with so much stuff. The person questioning would have assumed that I was a model student. As if I were a part of public speaking or a debate team. You can enjoy doing that stuff, obviously, but for me, it was just a matter of thinking about what others wanted of me.

I have participated in art classes since then, I was tried cooking, volunteering, creative writing, and exercising, and I am still open to new ideas and things. This has given me an insight into what I really like, and I have had plenty of fun doing so.

Expectations lead to disappointments.

This was one of the most crucial landmarks that I have achieved. To let go of the standard image regarding my life and university was one of the hardest things. These images were fixated in my mind for decades. It was easier to accept things the way they were once I was able to let go of these standard images. I no longer felt as if my whole life was crumbling right in front of my eyes.

2.2 What Is Meant By Identity?

In order to find out the factors which influence the formation of our identity, we must define what identity means in the first place.

- The distinguishing personality or character of a person.
- The relation formed by psychological recognition.
- The determination of staying the same with something asserted or described.
- The uniformity of generic or essential character in distinct instances.

Distinct points of view are highlighted by these 4 definitions. We may have formed an identity inside ourselves on the basis of our psychological recognition. However, differentiating traits that characterize our identity are coordinately subjective from the perspective of other people. We may associate as trustworthy· or confident, while people may tag us as arrogant, unreliable, or meek.

How do we cultivate our identity in our minds, and how is it cultivated in other peoples' minds? We must find our personal potential first, according to psychologists, and then select our life's purpose. After we have recognized how to utilize our abilities, we must seek opportunities to execute them in forms that complete our sense of purpose. We keep developing our identity by recalculating our potential and reorienting our sense regarding purpose.

2.3 Social Identity vs. Personal Identity

There are two types of identity in psychology. Social identity and personal identity. Our self-identity or personal identity is the response regarding one of the most crucial questions all people ask regarding life: Who am I? The way we see ourselves is the concept behind personal identity. This involves variables that can be controlled by us. For example, our interests and decisions. It also includes variables that are not in our control, like race and families.

The way we perceive ourselves is our personal identity, but the way others see us forms our social identity. People identify us from our characteristics inside our career, town, or school. These characteristics will be used by society to identify every person. They will then be positioned in a common group with people that have similar characteristics. Our marital, occupational, behavioral, religious, and financial status can also be used to define some social identities.

Theory of social identity by Henry Tajfel, 1979: This social psychology's framework displays how a piece of a person's identity stems from a feeling of who they're in a collective membership. This notion of social identity was formed in order to contemplate the way one imagines the self-established on groups to which a person belongs socially.

Social Identity Map

Social identity forms the personality of a person. It is a collection of aspects that explain who we're based on our links with groups that explain our identity socially. Three various levels are used to form a simple map of social identity.

Core: Behaviors, attitudes, and elemental traits that make us special as a person, e.g., beliefs, behaviors, values, etc.

Chosen: Characteristics that we can select from to explain our status, skills, and traits, e.g., political affiliation, area of residence, hobbies, occupation, etc.

Given: Conditions or attributes that we do not have any control over, e.g., gender, age, physical characteristics, birth, etc.

2.4 How Is an Identity Created?

What are the factors that have an influence on the formation of identity? Hypothetically, every conscious and unconscious stimulus experienced by us in all of our lives has impacted the way society, and we label and create our identities. Plenty of external and internal factors impact the evolution and formation of identities like family, ethnicity, location, culture, race, interests, media, opportunities, life experiences, personal expression, appearance, and loved ones.

Society

Does the cultivation of our society start from the time we are born? That is not the case in reality. Long prior to our birth, our identity is shaped. The reality is that unselective of the cultures or customs within the society —it has already started forming a person's identity through decades of labeling and characterization based on expected behaviors and traits. Before we are born, these groups, which are pre-determined, are already assembled so we can be categorized.

Most of these extensive traits are formed on looks like skin color and gender. Others include social, religious, ethnicities, and financial statuses. Even aging, a natural phenomenon of life for all women and men, incurs an assumption that is pre-determined. These thoughts, which are pre-determined within our culture, can be harmful or helpful, especially in cases in which elements of the identity of one group are discriminated against or celebrated.

Society can act as a negative and a positive force on our identity. The idea of collectivism, which is used to see ourselves in connection to people within our surroundings, is just as vital as individualism. Having a group that has an identity with similar aspects and either aids us to change or accept the way we identify ourselves is beneficial for all of our lives.

Loved Ones And Family

Our identity is also heavily influenced by our loved ones and family, in addition to the influence of society. We subconsciously or consciously look to our siblings, extended family, and parents as we are exposed to them initially. They serve as the building blocks for our identity. This is a two-way influence as the identities of our loved ones are evolved due to our impact on their lives just as we develop and learn our identity from them.

In our developmental years in the start, we may personify the title of daughter, sister, brother, or son. Variables like the type and size of the family we belong to influence the intensity of our identification with these labels. The level of conflict or support that we get from our family also influences this intensity. In certain instances, the level of conflict or support is impacted by factors in the lives of our parents that make up their identities, like level of education or financial status.

Apart from relationships with family, our romantic and platonic relationships also affect who we are. The size and valence of our idea of self-alter with the seriousness of our relationships. These relationships can influence our self-concept or important facets negatively as well as positively. For instance, losing interest in activities and things that we like or stop staying in touch with cultural or religious attachments.

Ethnicity, Culture, And Race

Culture, race, and ethnicity are among the most complicated and multifaceted factors that have an influence on the formation of identity. These areas of our daily lives are always evolving. While we cannot control ethnicity and race, we can choose to distance or immerse ourselves in the customs, religions, and cultures that we are born into.

Our identities are influenced by these factors from the time we are born, particularly when our loved ones identify intensely with these connections. Our attitudes and behaviors are also influenced by these factors, in addition to forming a basis for our belief system. Each group of cultures may approach problems, show their emotions, or go about their lives in a method that is greatly distinct from another culture.

Many individuals have a deep feeling of pride due to these factors. But, the way our surroundings react to looks like heritage, cultural customs, or skin color can either weaken or strengthen our feeling of pride in that part of our identity. The behaviors and attitudes aimed at us impact the way we act, particularly in the process of our repression or expression of this characteristic of our identity.

Opportunities And Location

Opportunities and location are the things that influence a person's identity. A person is identified by the place where he or she is born, the town or city where they reside, and the community and neighborhood in which they are living. Other circumstances are also a great influence on a person's individuality. These include the economy of the residing area, government, and how we perceive things. Culture and geography also play a major part in a person's creativity, happiness, and productivity.

Contentment with one's own life is based on how well the opportunities are provided by the state or government. If a person feels that he is being isolated or feels lonely or left out, then you will face conflict with your own personality. Different studies have shown that the variables in the surrounding have a large impact on the perspective we have about life in general. However, it does not totally alter the personality but their thought pattern about their own identity.

Media

Media has a direct impact on how a person perceives his own identity and surrounding reality as well. Advertising, movies, TV shows, and all such things have a direct or indirect impact on the perceptions and identity if the message being conveyed is contradictory to what their actual beliefs and perceptions are. Contradictory things are considered to be harmful to self-perception and identity.

In today's world, the internet is one of the major sources of information at hand. Through the internet and social media, we are fed with unwanted comparisons as well as people with similar perceptions or identities. It has the same instant impact as that of friends, family, and the society in which they live.

With the advancement of internet technology, it transforms the personality in total. Therefore, as a result, a virtual personality is developed, which shows the physical characteristics of the person. This personality will hold onto some of the aspects of the true self which a person will not be able to accept completely in reality.

Chapter 3: Anatomy of The Psyche - Limbic System And Emotional Brain

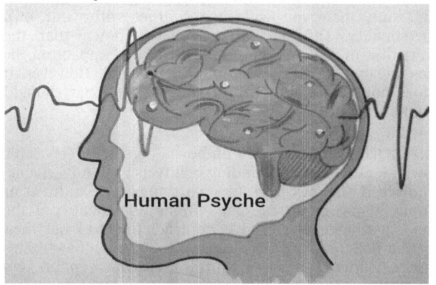

Human Psyche

The brain of humans is among the most complicated systems on the planet. To keep the body working, every single component of the brain has to work in coordination. The central nervous system is formed by spinal cord and the brain. This system, in coordination with the peripheral nervous system, plays the role of controlling functions of the body.

3.1 Our Feelings, Behavior, And Thoughts Are Controlled By Our Brain

There are 3 components of the CNS: The brain, spinal cord, and brain stem.

Psychology looks for an explanation of the behavior and mental processes of humans by investigating the connection between processes inside the mind on a systemic level. As a result, this field is heavily interlaced with the observation of brain.

A person would be able to guess the likely capabilities of animal by observing its brain if he had an understanding of the anatomy of the brain, even he was looking at that specific animal brain for the first time. This is because most of the animals have very similar brains in overall form. The brain has layers in each animal, and common structures are similar. The structures closest to spinal cord—the brain's innermost structures are the oldest components of the brain. These components perform the same activities as they did in the case of our ancestors. Basic functions for survival are regulated by the old brain, including breathing, resting, feeding, and moving, and forms the experiences regarding emotions. Mammals have developed additional brain layers which enable them to carry out functions of higher level, like better memory and better social interactions. Humans have a highly developed cerebral cortex which is the outer layer of the brain. This layer makes us adept at such processes.

3.2 Amygdala

Situated between the 2 cerebral hemispheres and brain stem is an area of the brain called the limbic system. It is responsible for governing memory & emotions. It constitutes the hippocampus, amygdala, and hypothalamus. The amygdala is composed of two clusters of an almond shape. The primary function of the amygdala is the regulation of our reactions to and perceptions of fear and aggression. It works in coordination with other systems of the body that regulate fear like the sympathetic NS, processing smells, stress, and aggression-related neurotransmitters release and facial responses. In a study, Bucy and Klüver (1939) impaired a rhesus monkey's amygdala. This impairing lead to the animal being passive, which was once an angry animal and did not show any aggressive behavior in response to situations of fear. Aggression is also influenced by the amygdala's electrical stimulation in many other animals. In essence to the amygdala's role in making us undergo fear, it also enables us to learn from fear-creating situations. The amygdala enables the brain to memorize details of scenario during a dangerous event so we can avoid such a situation in the near future. (Doyère, Cain, LeDoux and Sigurdsson 2007).

3.3 Cerebral Cortex

In order to survive in the environments, they live, most animals have developed abilities that allow them to adapt to those environments. A few animals have the ability to run very fast, others have developed hard shells, and a few possess acute hearing. Humans do not possess any such abilities, but they are unique in their own way. We are extremely smart and intelligent.

You might believe that the smartness of an organism should be determined by the proportion of their brain weight in comparison to their whole body's weight. But this is not the case. The weight of the brain of an elephant is 1000th to its weight of whole body, but the brain of a whale is just one ten- 100th of its weight of body. Contrary to that, the brain of a human is one- 60th as compared to the weight of its body, the brain of a mouse is one- 40th the weight of its body. Even after such calculations, elephants don't look 10 x smarter as compared to whales & humans obviously look smarter as compared to mice.

The reason behind this intelligence of human beings is not hidden in its size. Cerebral cortex, which is larger in humans as compared to other animals, is the key. It is a bark-like outer layer of the brain that lets humans to learn complex skills, smartly use language, socialize and create tools (Gibson, 2002). Cerebral cortex is folded and wrinkles in humans instead of being smooth, as in the case of many other animals. Wrinkles provide far more size and surface area enables humans to learn, think and remember with increased capacities. The term used for the folding of cortex is corticalization.

Whilst cortex is just around one-10th to 1-inch-thick, and it forms more than eighty percent of the weight of the brain. It contains around 300 trillion synapses and twenty billion cells (Myers, 1999). Billions of glial cells are supporting these neurons, cells that connect to the nerve cells and surround them. They provide nourishment to nerve cells, protect them and absorb any unused neurotransmitters. Glia have different roles, and they come in many forms. For example, myelin sheath is glial cell type that surrounds the axon. The neurons would not be able to perform their function or survive without this sheath (Miller, 2005).

There are two hemispheres of the cerebral cortex. There are 4 lobes of each hemisphere, and the lobes are separated from one another by folds. These folds are called fissures. If you see the cortex beginning at the brain's front, you see frontal lobe. This lobe is responsible for planning, judgment, memory, and thinking. The parietal lobe follows the frontal lobe. It goes from the center of the skull to its back. Its function is to process information regarding touch. At the skull's back lies occipital lobe. Visual information is processed by this lobe. Next to the occipital lobe, almost in mid of the ears, lies temporal lobe. It is basically responsible for language and hearing.

The area of the brain located right ahead of the frontal lobe is called the prefrontal cortex. It plays a role in a variety of complicated tasks such as planning and contributes to the development of personality greatly.

3.4 Prefrontal Cortex

This area of the brain helps individuals to set goals and achieve them. It receives information from a number of brain regions and processes the information in order to adapt accordingly. It contributes to plenty of important functions, like:

- Focusing the attention of a person
- Predicting the results of a person's actions: anticipating happening in the environment
- Planning things for the future
- Adjusting and coordinating complex behaviors
- Controlling impulses and controlling emotional reactions

To understand how these functions link together, let me give you a scenario. Consider a person during a job interview. He has to keep watch on the details mentioned by the interviewer and focus on him as well. If he is asked a difficult question by the interviewer, the person may get edgy. But he can foresee that running away will result in a failure; therefore, he rejects that impulse of fear and asks for an explanation regarding the question. He can think of an answer by gaining more insight into the question asked, and then hopefully; he can ace the interview.

In order to develop the personality of a person, the prefrontal cortex plays a huge role as well. It assists individuals in forming decisions consciously as per their motivations. This can lead to specific inclination in behavior over time, like an individual behaving friendly towards another person in order to become popular. The prefrontal cortex plays a part in choices and complex attitudes that create a personality.

3.5 Development

The last part of brain to develop fully is the prefrontal cortex, as the brain develops in a pattern of starting from the back and ending at the front. This doesn't imply that children don't have a working prefrontal cortex. Instead, the planning and decision-making skills that adults possess are not developed in children until they reach an older age.

The network of neurons in the brain develops way more synapses during adolescence. Communication is increased between brain parts as a result of these new connections. This extension may, however, happen unevenly.

For instance, many 15-year-olds are able to evaluate hypothetical risk like adults. However, the prefrontal cortex of teens has not made as many links with limbic system. To put it into perspective, the area of the brain that enables us to control ourselves cannot communicate with the area of the brain responsible for controlling flight or fight response as well. Thus, the teen may act recklessly under difficult situations, even if they "know better" technically.

The development of the cortex has a lot to do with experiences of life. Teens who have been through a lot of challenges and have experienced a variety of stimuli may mature quickly as compared to others.

3.6 Parts

The wrinkled outer layer of the brain called the cortex forms the prefrontal cortex. A 3rd of this layer is taken up by the prefrontal cortex in adults.

There are different theories regarding the categorization of the prefrontal cortex's different parts. The brain is deeply interconnected, both functionally and physically.

To point at a certain area of the brain and say that this specific function is controlled by this area is very difficult.

According to general functions, we can divide the prefrontal cortex into three main parts.

The Medial Cortex

It plays a role in the motivation and attention of a person. You can think of it as a start button metaphorically. It allows individuals to start an activity at the right time. People become unfocused and apathetic if this area becomes injured. Initiating speech and acting spontaneously can become a problem as well. Focusing on a task can also become a problem once it has begun.

The Orbital Cortex

The area which aids people to ignore distractions and keep their impulses under control is called the orbital cortex. It allows people to keep their strong emotions in check so as to follow the rules of a social gathering. A person once got blown in this area with an iron rod through his skull. He showed plenty of changes in his personality. He became reckless and irritable. He grew prone to crude humor, which was inappropriate. These changes are common, according to research, once this area gets injured.

The Lateral Cortex

The area which helps with the creation and execution of plans is called the lateral cortex. Organizing actions of a person in a specific sequence is also carried out by this area. For example, following the instructions while executing a recipe. The ability of individuals to switch between activities can be disrupted with an injury to this region. The person can also feel difficulty while adapting to modifications in rules.

Chapter 4: Emotions And Psychological State

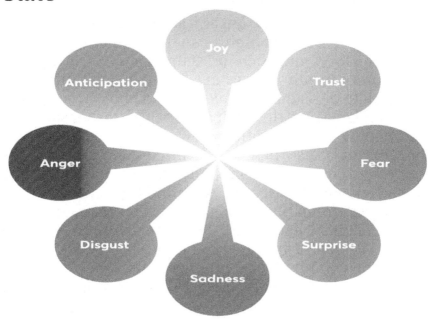

Emotions can have a critical role in shaping our behavior and thinking. The emotions that we feel on day to day basis can force our actions and impact the decisions we make regarding our lives. In order to completely understand emotions, it is vital to recognize the emotion's critical components.

4.1 Emotion Has Three Parts

A subjective (your experience of emotion) component

A physiological (reaction of your body to the emotion) component

An expressive (your behavior in response to the emotion) component

These various elements can have an impact on the purpose and function of the emotional responses.

Emotions can be temporary, like a moment of annoyance over something done by your co-worker. They can also be long-lasting, like suffering from sadness due to the loss of a loved one. But what is the reason behind the experiencing of emotions? What is their role in our lives?

The fundamental emotions, called basic emotions to include fear, disgust, anger, surprise, sadness, and happiness. These emotions can be found throughout human history, and their presence helps us in making judgments rapidly regarding stimuli and form an appropriate decision (LeDoux, 2000). Limbic system, one of oldest areas of the brain, is mainly responsible for determining basic emotions. Thalamus, hypothalamus, and amygdala also play a role in conjunction with the limbic system. These emotions are displayed almost similarly across different cultures because they are determined primarily through evolution (Ekman, 1992; Fridland, Ekman, and Oster, 1987, Elfenbein and Ambady, 2002;). People can, therefore, easily judge facial expressions of individuals of other cultures.

Not all emotions arise from the brain's older parts; we also elucidate our happenings to form a relatively complex exhibition of our emotional encounters. For example, if the amygdala detects that you are falling, it may sense fear, but that feeling may be elucidated totally differently in case of plunging on a ride on roller coaster as compared to falling off an airplane that has malfunctioned.

The cognitive appraisal that accompanies emotions is called cognitive interpretation. They enable us to undergo a complex and much bigger set of emotions called secondary emotions. These emotions are cognitive in large part, but arousal determines our encounters of these emotions as well. They are also determined from their valence— meaning, if they are unpleasant or pleasant feelings.

You might enjoy secondary emotions for some time when you reach a vital goal, maybe an episode of joy, contentment, and satisfaction. But when a friend who is close to you wins an award that you believed you should have won, you might undergo plenty of secondary emotions. Negative in this instance, for example, feeling sad, ashamed, angry, and resentful. You might keep repeating the scenario for months in your mind, going through the same emotions every time you recall that event (Martin and Tesser, 2006).

2 brain pathways parallel the difference between secondary and primary emotions. A slow and a fast pathway (LeDoux, 2000; Damasio, 2000; Ochsner, Gross, Bunge and Gabrieli, 2002). Part of the brain that acts as a gatekeeper during this process is called the thalamus. For example, the fast pathway determines our reaction to the fear emotion which is a basic emotion via limbic system. If we see a car on the highway pulling out next to us, the thalamus sends a signal to amygdala immediately, and we press the pedal for break. Emotions which are secondary are heavily determined through slow pathway via frontal lobes present in cortex. The process of getting jealous while losing a loved one to another person or recollecting our victory in a famous match is much more complicated. Information moves to frontal lobes from the thalamus for integration and cognitive analysis and then reaches the amygdala from there. The emotion's arousal we experience is coupled with a relatively complicated cognitive appraisal, resulting in refined behavioral responses and emotions.

However, you may think of emotions as less important or more frivolous as compared to our relatively rational processes. Both cognition and emotions can assist us in making good decisions. In few instances, we rationally process the benefits and costs of different decisions before we take action, while in other instances, we take actions based on emotions felt by us. Emotions guide our decisions, especially when there is a lot of ambiguity and uncertainty due to conflicting alternatives, making a cognitive analysis hard. We make decisions based on emotions during such cases, and these turn out to be way more accurate as compared to those generated through cognitive processing (Dijksterhuis, Nordgren, Bos and van Baaren, 2006; Damasio, 1994; Wilson and Schooler, 1991; Nordgren and Dijksterhuis, 2009).

4.2 The James-Lange and Cannon-Bard Emotion's Theories

Think of a scenario that happened in the past where you experienced a severe emotional response. Maybe you heard a noise that woke you up during the night time, and you thought that an intruder had entered your house. I am certain that you can recall the reaction as physical in great part. Maybe you recall being flushed, feeling anxious, having difficulty breathing, or heart pounding. You were encountering the emotion's physiological part— arousal— and I am sure that you have experienced same feelings in many situations, maybe when during anger, love, sadness, frustration, and embarrassment.

If you have been through experiences like mine, while you looked at the arousal experienced in situations of strong emotions, you perhaps thought like, "My heart was beating so fast as I was afraid." This interpretation is thought to be correct by some psychologists. The theory proposed by Phillip Bard and Walter Cannon regarding emotions says that the encounter of emotion occurs with the encounter of arousal. According to this theory, an encounter of emotion goes hand in hand with physiological arousal. Therefore, as per this model, heart rate increases simultaneously with awareness of danger.

This idea, however, looks intuitive to experiences of our everyday life; Carl Lange and William James suggested another part of arousal. As per the theory suggested by James-Lang, the arousal experienced by us results in our undergoing of emotion. This theory suggests that emotion and arousal aren't independent, but instead, the emotion relies on arousal.

These theories are supported by research evidence. Fast emotional pathway's operation supports the theory of emotions and arousal occurring together. The experience of emotional stimulus activates the limbic system's emotional circuits. Corresponding reactions which are physical are created quickly by these circuits (LeDoux, 2000). This process is so quick that we think physical arousal and emotion are simultaneous.

Contrary to this, according to the theory of James-Lang, our arousal is stronger as compared to our emotion's experiences. Emotional responses have been reported to be decreased in people with injuries of the spinal cord as their arousal experiences reduce (Hohmann, 1966). The concept that different arousal patterns result in different emotions is also supported. There is more amygdala activation in individuals who view faces which are fearful as compared to those who see joyful or angry faces (Witvliet and Vrana, 1995); we experience flushing and a face (red) on being embarrassed, but this is not the case with other emotions (Britt, Leary, Cutlip, and Templeton, 1992), and experience of compassion leads to release of hormones that are different from when other emotions are experienced.

4.3 2 Factor Theory

The two-factor theory takes a different approach to Lange-James theory, which suggests that different patterns of arousal are associated with different emotions. This theory suggests that every emotion results in a similar experience of arousal. Cognitive assessment of the arousal source differentiates all emotions. This theory suggests that the intensity of arousal determines the experience of emotion, but the situation's cognitive appraisal decides what the emotion will turn out to be. Since both appraisal and arousal are necessary, it can be said that there are two factors of emotions: cognitive factor and an arousal factor (Singer & Schachter, 1962):

Cognition + arousal = emotion

Determining the emotion accurately can be hard for a person in some cases where she or he is experiencing arousal of a higher level. The meaning may not be as clear even though the person is clear about the feeling of arousal. In the case of loving relationships, for example, the arousal is very high, and extreme lows and highs are experienced by partners in the bond. They are in extreme love with one another one day and a big fight abrupt the next day. Individuals may not be certain about they're going through in situations of high arousal. For example, two people in love may be unsure whether what they're feeling is actually hate, love or maybe both simultaneously. Misattribution of arousal is the term used for the tendency to label arousal source incorrectly.

Emotions have the ability to Motivate Us.

You might feel anxious when faced with an exam, thinking about your performance and the impact of the test on your grade. You might study due to these emotional responses. You received motivation by experiencing a particular emotion. This will enable you to do something good regarding your chances of achieving a decent grade.

In our attempt of feeling positive emotions, we also take specific actions and reduce the possibility of feeling emotions that are negative. For example, in order to get a sense of satisfaction, excitement, and commitment, you might look for hobbies or social activities. Contrary to this, you would avoid certain situations that may lead to anxiety, sadness, and boredom.

Emotions allow us to Avoid Danger, Survive and Thrive

Charles Darwin suggested that emotions allow animals and humans to adapt and survive in their environments and reproduce. We are probable to face the irritation source when we are angry. We are prone to flee from threats when we undergo fear. We might reproduce by seeking a mate when we feel the emotion of love. By convincing us to act instantly, emotions play an adaptive role, and our likelihood of success and survival increases by taking action.

Emotions Can assist Us in making Decisions

The decisions we make are heavily influenced by emotions, from our food choices to the leader we choose in political elections. Studies have found that individuals with brain damage hindering their capacity to undergo emotions have a reduced capacity to make choices that are good.

Even in scenarios where we stick with the idea of making decisions with pure rationality and logic, emotions play an important role. Our ability to manage and understand emotions, or emotional intelligence, plays a vital role in our decision-making.

Emotions Allow people around us to Understand Us

In our interaction with other individuals, it is vital to give signs in order to help them recognize whether we are comfortable or not. These signs can be emotional expressions via body language, like various expressions of face connected with the specific emotions we are undergoing.

Stating straightly how we feel can also be an option in some cases. When we inform family members or friends that we are feeling frightened, excited, happy, or sad, we are providing them with vital information that can be used by them to take action.

4.4 Emotions Enable Us To Understand People Around Us

Just like our emotions give others around us a lot of information, we also gain a lot of social information from the emotional expressions of people around us. Social communication is a vital aspect of our relationships and daily life, and it is very important to interpret the emotions of others and react to them in the right manner.

This enables us

To give an appropriate response and form a meaningful and deeper relationship with our family, loved ones, and friends. It enables us to communicate in various social situations in a positive manner, from managing an employee who is hot-headed and dealing with customers.

The scientific study of emotions was done by Charles Darwin. He proposed that in our survival and safety, emotional displays have a major role. If you came across a spitting or a hissing animal, you would get the indication that the animal was defensive and angry.

Understanding the display of emotions of others around us provides us with vital input regarding our response in a specific situation.

Cause behind emotions

Scientists suggest that certain types of thoughts mostly lead to specific emotions. For instance, when a person thinks, "I'm in danger," that individual would feel fear. And, when a person thinks, "I achieved what I aimed for," that individual would feel happy. In case a person thinks, "I lost a valuable thing," that individual would feel sad. At last, when a person thinks, "I was treated unfairly by my friend," that individual would feel angry.

Scientists have found out that questions like these are answered by the thoughts that result in emotions:

Did an unexpected thing happen?

Did an enjoyable thing happen?

Did the thing that happened make things harder or easier for me to achieve my target?

Do I have control over it?

Having control over something implies that you can alter something that you do not prefer. It also implies that you can keep something as it is if you like it.

Will I have the ability to cope with it?

The ability to adjust or find a method to live with something is called coping. A shift in your life that does not bother you in the long period.

Based on the answers to these questions in your mind, you will encounter various emotions when an incident happens. For instance, if your bike malfunctioned, you would probably feel bad if you did not believe you could do something to fix it (implying you do not believe you have the situation under control). And if your friend shifted far away from your place and you believed that you would be able to make new friends, you would probably feel less bad about it. Also, if you believe that not sharing is a wrong thing, then you would get angry with a person not sharing their things.

Has it ever happened to you that you experienced an emotion without knowing the reason? Sometimes emotions are felt by individuals even though they do not sense any thoughts in relation to those emotions. This is rather difficult to understand. But scientists have discovered that emotions can be triggered unconsciously by your brain. This implies that the brain might observe something in your environment and trigger a reaction without you even sensing it. In fact, researchers believe that a lot of stuff done by our brain goes unnoticed by us. These processes are termed unconscious processes. Activities are triggered by your brain without you even realizing it.

For instance, although you do not notice it, a lot of things are controlled in your body by your brain right now, like the activities of your stomach and heart. Suppose you feel an emotion and do not understand why next time, heed close attention to the happenings in your situation and ask the questions stated earlier to yourself. This might aid you in understanding the reason behind your feeling.

4.5 The Process of Feeling An Emotion?

What really happens once an emotion is triggered? Scientists have discovered that it leads to an emotional reaction. The alterations that occur automatically while you are experiencing an emotion (like alterations in your thoughts, alterations in the way you like to act, alterations in activities of body).

There are many different parts of an emotional reaction. One aspect is the changes done by the brain in the body. For instance, when you are angry or afraid, you might sense your heart racing and your lungs working faster by increasing your breathing rate. Or, your eyes might be filled with tears when you turn sad. Your muscles can also be moved automatically with the experience of emotions. For instance, you might smile during happiness, and your voice turns more excited. You might stand somewhat taller as well without even noticing any of these changes.

Thinking differently is another aspect of an emotional reaction. For instance, scientists have discovered that individuals think of sad memories when they are sad, but individuals think of happy memories when they are happy. Similarly, when people feel scared, they look for other threats in their environment. This makes them prone to thinking of other scary situations. Contrary to this, when individuals are happy, they notice things of their preference throughout the day.

Beginning to want to act differently than usual is the last aspect of an emotional reaction. For instance, you ought to fight or yell at someone in case you are angry. Or, an intense desire to run away might arise if you are scared. Or, you might stay at home in your room alone if you are sad.

4.6 Figuring Out The Right Emotion

We usually want to understand emotional reactions after we have undergone the reaction. Has it ever happened to you that you could not decide what emotion you underwent? Our feelings can be confusing a lot of times, and understanding them might require plenty of effort. The reason behind this is that in different situations, the same emotion can be felt differently. For instance, being afraid of a lion can be felt differently than being afraid of giving a speech in front of a large audience. Different emotions can also feel similar sometimes, which can be a source of confused feelings as well. For instance, both fear and anger can result in the fasting of heartbeat, making you shaky.

So you have to find out which emotion you are experiencing during an emotional reaction. For instance, seeing a lion in front of you may result in your heart racing and a strong urge to run away. After you consider different emotions you might be undergoing, you could then make up your mind about "fear" being your best guess. That is, the thought that might cross your mind is, and "I am probably sensing fear in this moment, because I think I could be hurt by this lion whereas, in such a scary condition, the thought of being afraid might not even cross your mind until you take a break after running away and recall the moment. Figuring out the right emotion can be difficult for some individuals as compared to others, according to scientists. People who have difficulty in this regard have a hard time feeling better.

It is vital to practice seeking out what type of feeling you are undergoing by paying importance to your emotions. This will aid you in feeling better quickly by solving your problem when you are going through something bad. It also assists in asking yourself the question about your learning from the times when you have felt scared, angry, or sad and your response in the future to similar situations in case they occur again.

4.7 The Universal Emotions

According to research, there are six classified facial expressions that correspond to different universal emotions: sadness, fear, happiness, disgust, surprise, anger [Black, Yacoob,95]. The interesting thing is that four emotions out of a total of six are negative.

Happiness

Happiness is an emotion that all the people in the world strive for the most. It is usually described as an emotional state which is pleasant and is characterized by joy, contentment, satisfaction, well-being, and gratification. A smile is a facial expression for this emotion. A relaxed stance of body characterizes this state. The tone of speaking becomes pleasant and upbeat during this emotion.

Our approach to the things that are the source of happiness is heavily influenced by culture. For instance, pop culture emphasizes that owning a house or a job that pays great is the source of happiness. The truth behind this is much more complicated, and this emotional state is linked to a variety of aspects of our life. It is a belief since ancient times that health is heavily linked to happiness and modern research confirms this idea. Both mental and physical health is heavily influenced by happiness. Plenty of outcomes like marital satisfaction and increased longevity are linked to happiness. On the other hand, unhappiness can lead to damaging health outcomes. Stress, depression, loneliness, and anxiety, for instance, are a result of unhappiness.

Sadness

A transient state of emotion denoted by feelings of grief, disappointment, disinterest, dampened mood, and hopelessness is sadness. Sadness is an emotion like many other emotions that a lot of people can relate to in life. In some instances, people can suffer from severe and prolonged periods of this emotion, which can result in depression. A number of cues give us the idea of sadness like:

- Crying
- Lethargy
- Quietness
- Dampened mood
- Withdrawal from others

The severity and type of sadness can change on the basis of the root issue, and the way people cope with this emotion can also vary.

People can turn to coping mechanisms due to sadness like self-medicating, avoiding others, fixating on negative thoughts, and losing interest in activities of daily life. This can increase the feelings of this emotion, and the duration of the issue can be prolonged in this way.

Fear

Fear is another strong emotion that has a vital role in man's survival. When you undergo fear as a result of facing something dangerous, you undergo a process known as flight or fight response.

Your respiration and heart rate increase, the muscles turn tense, and the mind turns more alert, informing your body to either stand your ground and fight or flee from the situation and save yourself.

This response aids you in preparing for the dangers of the environment. The expressions used for this sort of emotion can include widening of eyes. It can also involve pulling the chin back. Rapid heart rate and breathing are the physiological reactions of this emotion.

The experience of fear is not the same for every person. Some individuals are more likely to be sensitive in this regard, and certain objects and situations can trigger this emotion easily in such individuals.

The emotional feedback to a threat of immediate nature is called fear, and a similar reaction can be developed to thoughts regarding potential dangers and anticipated threats. This is the general perception regarding anxiety. For instance, social anxiety has an anticipated fear regarding social situations.

Contrary to this, some individuals seek out situations that are fear-provoking. Thrills like extreme sports can induce fear, but some individuals look to thrive and enjoy these feelings.

Exposure therapy involves this idea, in which individuals are exposed to situations and objects which frighten them in a slow manner that is safe and controlled. Eventually, these feelings start to fade away.

Disgust

Disgust is also one of the universal emotions. Retching or vomiting is a physical reaction to this emotion. Turning yourself away from the disgusting object is the body language shown in this emotion. Curling the upper lip and wrinkling of the nose are the facial expressions associated with this emotion.

Plenty of things can be a source of this revulsion sense, like sight, smell, or unpleasant taste. Scientists believe that the reaction to fatal and harmful foods may be the reason behind this emotion's formation. When people taste or smell foods that are rotten, for instance, this emotion is a normal reaction.

Poor hygiene, blood, death, rot, and infection can also cause this response to trigger. This may be a defense mechanism by the body against things that might be a source of transmittable diseases.

Moral disgust can also be experienced by people when they see others participating in acts that they think are immoral, evil, or distasteful.

Anger

Anger is also a powerful emotion identified by feelings of frustration, hostility, antagonism, and agitation towards others. Anger, like fear, can also play a role in the flight or fight response of your body.

You may be compelled to protect yourself by fending off the danger when you see a threat creating feelings of anger. Facial expressions like glaring or frowning are seen during this emotion. A strong stance is seen in body language, and the tone becomes gruffly. Physiological changes like turning red or seating can be seen while a person is undergoing this emotion. Aggressive behaviors like throwing objects, kicking, or hitting can also be seen.

Anger can be beneficial in some cases, even though it is considered a negative emotion. It can help you in a constructive manner by clarifying what you need in a relationship. It can also be a source of motivation in some cases, which can provide a solution to issues that are troubling you by taking action.

Excessive anger can, however, become a problem. It can also become a problem when it is expressed in ways that are not appropriate or harmful and dangerous for others. Such type of anger can take the shape of violence, abuse, or aggression.

There are physical and mental consequences of such excessive anger. This hinders the ability of a person to make decisions rationally and has a negative impact on their physical health as well.

Studies suggest that unchecked anger can lead to diabetes and coronary heart diseases in the longer run. Behaviors that can lead to health risks like aggressive driving, smoking, and alcohol consumption can also be seen in individuals with unchecked anger.

Surprise

Another emotion experienced by humans is called a surprise. It is a brief emotion following an unexpected event marked by a physiological alarm response.

This emotion can be negative, neutral, or positive. A surprise that is unpleasant, for instance, might involve a person waiting for you outside the bathroom to scare you once you come out. A pleasant surprise might involve a scenario where your friends have gathered at your place on your birthday to give you a party. Facial expressions like widening of eyes, raising the brows, and opening of mouth accompany the emotion. Jumping back can be a physical response to this emotion. Verbal reactions like gasping, screaming, or yelling is also seen in individuals undergoing this emotion.

Flight or fight response can be triggered by this emotion as well. When startled, individuals may experience an adrenaline burst that aids the body in preparation for fleeing or fighting.

Human behavior can be heavily impacted by surprise. For instance, studies have shown that surprising events are noticed disproportionately by people.

This is the reason that unusual and surprising events in media tend to stick out in memory comparatively more. Studies have also found that individuals learn more from surprising events. Surprising arguments also influence people more.

4.8 Emotions, Feelings, And Moods

We often use feelings and emotions as interchangeable words, but that is not really the right way. So how can you differentiate between moods, feelings, and emotions?

In simple words, time is the difference. Emotions arise first, and then feelings come once the chemicals of emotion start working in our bodies. The union of feelings results in the formation of moods.

Chemicals released as a reaction to a specific trigger's interpretation by an individual are called emotions. The identification of triggers is done by our brain in approximately 1/4 second, and for the production of chemicals, it takes almost an additional 1/4 second. Emotion chemicals, however, are released in our entire bodies and not only in the brains, and a type of feedback loop is created by our bodies and brains. They last for around 6 seconds.

As we start to combine the emotions, feelings happen. We use the word " feel." for both emotional and physical sensations in English. We can feel cold physically, but it can also be felt emotionally. Feelings are rather "cognitively saturated" as the process of emotional chemicals is in our brains and bodies. A mix of emotions fuels the feeling, and it lasts for a longer period of time as compared to emotions.

Moods are a general thing. A specific incident does not cause them, but instead, multiple inputs result in the formation of moods. Several factors heavily influence the mood: the environment (lighting, weather, individuals around us), mental state (our emotions at the time and where we are focusing attention), and physiology (the way we have been exercising, how fit we are, what we have been eating). Moods can last for minutes or hours and even for days.

Chapter 5: Thought Management And Emotion Regulation

To enhance the positive thinking and aspects does not imply that you have to act all happy and naïve through the difficult or stressful times. To acknowledge your pain is a natural process for the survival and essential element of life as well. Other than recognizing it, you have to experience it thoroughly and then process all your negative emotions in such a manner that it does not come back at you even harder than before.

Two of the most common mistakes made by people while addressing negative emotion are they tend to numb themselves towards that emotion, or they both obsess and ruminate over the concerned issue.

5.1 The Two Methods that Don't Work!

Rumination is like deceiving your own self by being obsessed over the situation or problem that caused you to feel negative. Everything negative is not meant to be sorted by thinking through. It only worsens the situation.

Numbing your emotions comes with the drawback of having a negative impact on the other associated emotions as well. According to Brené Brown, it is impossible for a person to shut off only one emotion at a time. If you try to calm or suppress your anger, it will come at the cost of taking out serenity and happiness along with it. The same is the case with avoidance. For example, if you use alcohol so that you can overcome sadness, then you will never be able to cope with the emotion of sadness.

It's undeniably true that whatever you do in your life or whatever you feel most of the time, there still be some times when you will feel down, and in that time, you will experience anxiety, depression, and stress. They can vary from minor to major and also from person to person. The reason for these feelings or emotions can be anything like the death of a close relative, injury, illness, unemployment, or any such situation. Sometimes the reasons or cause of such feelings are obvious, but at times they can be off without any apparent reason.

It's essential to undergo negative emotions as they will help people to understand and cope with them in a healthy manner. There are several ways to cope with these emotions in difficult times. The main source of help in such situations is social and personal resources. We should engage with these sources or approach them for help rather than just giving up instantly.

5.2 Suppressing And Distorting Negative Outcomes Doesn't Help

The first-hand approach which people implement for negative emotions or feelings could be denial, avoidance, or even suppression. You must have come across people who are visibly anxious, stressed, or even depressed, but they are in denial and are unable to accept it wholeheartedly by being in denial; they are unable to understand that what the actual problem is which needs to be addressed to move on in life with success. The key to coping with these emotions is to accept them and process them in such a manner that you are able to cope with them. People who are living in denial also have difficulty in accepting this bitter reality of having the presence of any issue related to negative emotions or feelings. If a person tries to talk them out of it or try to help them, they would turn your offer or help down that instant. An example of a situation like that is, suppose you have a test, and you have to prepare for it, but you are too anxious or stressed to do so that you try really hard to forget about it completely.

Studies have found that in order to try ignoring the negative feelings and events, there are some difficulties which are faced by people. Ignoring the problems does not help in any way. Even if we are unable to get things done due to depression, unable to have good relationships with people, or being so stressed that it takes a toll on our health, we will not be able to confess these to our own self if we just keep ignoring these things.

Similarly, according to Gross and Levenson, keeping your emotions suppressed for a longer period of time will not be helpful as well. For instance, if you have an exam and that too a big one, then you will have to focus on it completely so that you can suppress it. But in fact, you can never deny or suppress something entirely just by not thinking about it. Also, it may be effective in the short term, but once you are out of this positive thinking pattern energy, negativity will hit you back even harder, and you will experience that once again.

Wegner, along with his colleagues, conducted an experiment that you have to not think about the white bear only for five minutes, but if the thought does pop up in your mind, you will ring a bell, but for participants, it was unable for them to not think about it even though they were instructed. The same thing happens with the individual when they are on a diet, and they will keep thinking about the bar of chocolate that is saved in the fridge or with the person preparing for an exam and not think about all the fun time he has been missing due to studies. These thoughts that you keep on trying to suppress are the ones that have a great negative impact on your day-to-day life and activities.

Trying to keep yourself busy in other activities than focusing on the main problem is yet another poor strategy. We try hard to distract ourselves from the negative feelings by watching tv, book reading, or even cooking, but these things do not work for long. Sometimes people even go to extremes to avoid such feelings or emotions, but to them, it would be more helpful to face them rather than just avoiding the situation. People tend to escape when they feel that there is a difference between their own ideal self and main concepts or when they think that they cannot fulfill other people's expectations.

As per the researcher Roy Baumeister, the behaviors that people adopt for escaping their own self include binge eating, suicide, drug abuse, spiritual ecstasy, and sexual masochism.

Research has also proven that letting your emotions and feelings out is the healthy manner to cope with stress and negativity that is going on in your mind and life. According to James Pennebaker, botting up feelings cannot be of any use. It is best to talk about the things that are bothering you, or you can even write them down. It is beneficial for the person's own well-being.

The experiment was conducted by Beall and Pennebaker. In that experiment, they assigned the people to write about any random topic or the most stressful and traumatic event of their life. Those who wrote about the stressful event of their life were having higher blood pressure than those who wrote about random topics in the experiment. Those having an impact on their health were not likely to visit any health care center. However, something positive did change in them who confronted the negatively impacting event of their life.

The other research was conducted on those whose significant other died last year. Research showed that when they talked about their spouse more often, they were less likely to have an adverse impact on their well-being. Lu and Uysal also concluded that physical pain reduces when a person is more open in expressing himself or herself. Opening up to others comes with its own benefits. It helps the individual to get more information from those the experience is being shared, and they might even help you in difficult times. Along with that, thinking through such situations or writing them can also help an individual to gain the control over their lives.

5.3 Self-Regulation- A Better Approach

It is evident that emotions are a sign of some potential danger. They also help us in making judgments in a shorter period of time, so experiencing them is a positive thing in itself. But one should learn to control them as well so that the result of emotions that is behavior can be in a controlled manner. Self-regulation is something that a person uses his affective and cognitive abilities in reaching his goal, and along with that, regulation of emotions is essential as well.

For becoming the best version of your own self, you have to have the skill of self-regulation. One who has mastered this skill can achieve the goals set for them. For instance, if you are able to have effective self-regulation, then you can perform better in school, in relationships, and even at work, depending on the set goals. When we are unable to do so, then it's the ultimate failure of self-regulation, and they will not be able to succeed in social or personal interactions with others.

Self-control is essential for the best outcomes. A research was conducted by Walter Mischel along with his fellows. In the experiment, self-control was observed. Children of age 4 to 5 years were given the snacks like marshmallows or chocolate chip cookies. They were told that if they wait for a certain period of time, they can have both the snacks, and if not, then they can only get one. Few of them waited and got the reward bigger than those who could not resist the urge to have that snack. They found it so tempting that they were unable to wait for a certain period of time to enjoy the bigger reward. Those who were able to self-regulate their desire of having the snack were rewarded greatly and those who seek immediate satisfaction. The findings showed that these actions for instant rewards are associated with the cognitive abilities of the child. In another study that was conducted on animals showed that such behavior is observed in the animals that were having low serotonin levels in the blood. Low levels of this hormone are also associated with impulsiveness, violence, and suicide as well.

Self-regulation plays a vital role later in life. As per Mischel's study results, children who were able to have self-regulation grew up as having some really positive attributes. These attributes included high achievers, better at socializing, and had the ability to deal with stress and anxiety in a healthy manner. Opposite of it was found in those who were unable to delay the gratification process by instantly opting for the snack. Hence, self-regulation is the main key to success in later life.

5.4 Positive Emotions' Power

If stress is the emotion that is considered negative, there are other emotions to counteract the negative ones. Those emotions would help us to cope with the stress and anxiety and any other negatively impacting emotion. For instance, spending weekends doing fun activities and enjoying the days can give you a sense of pleasure and contentment. Even the thought of weekends can make you feel happy and is enough to lower the burden and stressful thoughts of weekdays. If you are a student, you can be less stressed by having somewhat of a positive attitude towards your routine.

You might have come across the term that whatever you think of becomes a reality. This is how positive thinking patterns help a person to achieve his or her goals. It is always suggested to think of the positive aspects of everything in life, but that does not mean you should suppress the negative emotions and feelings. You must know that how you can pass that phase of emotional turmoil so that it does not last for long. People with a positive attitude are seen to have more control over their life.

Being positive is perceived differently by a different individual. For one, it could be optimized, and for another, it could be self-efficacy. Optimism is referred to as being happy and having a positive approach towards the day to day life. They experience less stress, and even if they do, they are able to handle it appropriately. For self-efficacy, it accounts for a person's own ability to conduct the actions that would lead to the expected outcomes. People who have greater self-efficacy are able to face difficult situations in an effective manner. They are more likely to face the problem through critical thinking and discussion with their fellows or friends. These things ultimately lead to reduced stress levels.

Self-efficacy is the attribute that leads towards a less stressful life. People who are able to alter or change the environment in which they are working or staying also have a positive impact on mental well-being. For instance, people who are working in an office where they are liberated to move the furniture or change the settings of their office a little bit had fewer stress levels than those old people who reside in a nursing home. They are not able to do things as per their own wish and desire. Yet another study showed that if a person is able to control the loud noise in his or her own environment, then he would be less stressed than those who did not even bother to choose the option of minimizing the noise.

As per the researchers, there is another category of people who are self-efficient as well as optimistic. This category is known as hardiness. They are the people who are overall more positive about everything in their life along with the feeling of happiness. They are the ones who use proper tactics to cope with stressful events and are able to have a happy and healthy life.

Different researchers have made statements about each of these characteristics that were found in people to have different impacts in stressful conditions and other aspects of life. For example, optimistic people were seen to recover quickly from injury or illness. People having higher self-efficiency were able to work out regularly and also were able to quit smoking. People of the hardy category were able to tackle difficult situations and events of life in a more comprehensive manner than any other person. Positive thinking has a positive influence on a person in times of stressful events, but still, its impact is minimum if the person is already not in the stressful phase of life.

The researcher Antoni found out that it is possible to learn optimism and to apply it in daily life. He experimented it with the cancer patients who were a pessimist. The results showed that the patient felt less lethargic and weak after the treatment. Similarly, hardiness training is also conducted so that the person can cope with the stressful conditions effectively. It also decreased the stress levels and improved the level of overall satisfaction.

Peterson, with other researchers, found out the impact of positive approaches throughout life. The results showed that those who were more optimistic towards life during the year 1936-1940 in college life led a healthy life for over 50 years and were less likely to die of health issues as compared to those who were less optimistic. The same outcomes were observed in older adults as well.

After having the controlled health correlated factors like economic status, loneliness, and marital status, older adults were observed for the self-efficacy, and positive attitude lived a better and healthy life, and their life span increased up to eight years than those who were more negative towards life and in general. They were also less likely to have unemployment issues and increased income than those who were less optimistic when they were observed after 19 years.

5.5 Cognitive Distortion Types

There are several patterns of distorted thinking that can be catered to with the help of CBT. CBT is the kind of therapy that was developed by Aaron Beck, the psychiatrist, in the 1960s. Ten of the most common types are listed here:

Polarized thinking

This pattern of thinking is called blank & white. It is the type where people are extreme in their thoughts. It's either this or that for them. They usually have a strong belief that either they are going to succeed or they are doomed and a complete failure. This type of thinking pattern is not something to be supportive or useful because life is something that exists among these two extremes.

Overgeneralization

This pattern is associated with applying one outcome to all the relevant situations. For instance, if a person does not score well in one quiz, he will generalize it to be a total failure in that particular subject. Similarly, if one friend betrayed a person, then he or she is going to implement that thing with all the other friends as well. This is linked with PTSD and some other disorders related to anxiety.

Catastrophizing

People with this type of thinking assume things at their worst and even get panicked just by thinking about the dreadful events. For instance, if a person is expected to receive a check and he does not get it on time, then he will keep on thinking of the dreadful scenarios that he will not be able to pay the bills on time and will be evicted out of the house.

This type of thinking usually roots from such experiences, which result in dreadful events.

Personalization

This is associated with severe depression and anxiety. It is associated with taking everything personally, even if it's not. A person with this type of thinking tends to assume that everything that happens is being on purpose or that person is being targeted. For example, if a person got removed from a certain group, he or she would blame themselves for it even if it is not due to them.

Mind reading

When people think that they already know what another person is thinking, then this is called mind reading. It becomes difficult to differentiate between empathy and mind-reading. This type of thinking pattern is common among children than older adults. For the difference between empathy and mind-reading, one should consider all the events rather than just one or two, which confirms the suspicion of any kind.

Mental filtering

Filtering is associated with neglecting all the positives and focus solely on the negatives. The habit of this type of thinking leads a person towards hopelessness. The extremity of this type can lead a person towards suicide. Also, it worsens the depression and anxiety of the affected person.

Discounting the positive

This thinking pattern is similar to that of mental filtering, but the person acknowledges the positive as mere luck and by the chance occurrence of the event. They do not consider the positives to be due to their skill, determination, or accurate choices. They think of it as an accidental event. This results in a lack of motivation.

"Should" statements

A cognitive distortion is thought to be on its way when a person thinks of the "ought" and "should" statements. It makes it difficult for the individual to be satisfied with what has been done. People with this type of thought pattern tend to perceive everything in their life with negativity. This pattern mostly generates from greater family expectations or due to cultural expectations. They greatly impact self-esteem and increase anxiety levels.

Emotional reasoning

It means that how a person perceives any situation is true and reality on the basis of how it felt by that individual without any validation. However, it is important to analyze the emotion before perceiving it the reality. This is commonly used by any person irrespective of anxiety or depression.

Labeling

Labeling is associated with entitling other individuals or themselves based upon certain things. The labeling is usually associated with negative things. For instance, if a person could not do well in exams, he would be labeled as a failure. One other example is labeling someone as drunk. This is based on the occurrence of the events just one or two times.

5.6 Repetition Can Impact Your Life

Whatever goes in the subconscious mind is extremely important. Repetition of thoughts and words get settled in the subconscious mind and are reflected in their behavior and actions.

The data stored in the subconscious mind is seen through dialogues and expressions. The subconscious mind works effectively to make the stored things a reality. It means that if you repeatedly say that it's impossible for you to earn enough money, then there will be lots and lots of obstacles in your way. This can work oppositely as well. If you tell yourself that you are rich, your mind will automatically look for such advantages. So basically, the thoughts are what make a person's life.

However, this is also a fact that thoughts are mostly dependent upon the circumstances which are faced by a person, and these thoughts are what shape the subconscious part of your mind. But that is also in your control whether you want to give the control to the outside environment or are you going to think the things thoroughly.

Be mindful of what you tell yourself about anything or any experience that you encounter in day-to-day life. The positive things that you should practice in your daily life are known as affirmations. They are so powerful that you will not even believe yourself that what you can get from such positivity-inspired affirmations.

These affirmations must be repeated most frequently throughout the day so that they can be settled in your subconscious mind. You have to do it with intention and attention.

These affirmations must not be in negative sentences. For example:

Instead of saying that I do not feel weak anymore, say I am powerful and strong.

As you see, both have the same meanings, but words are different and later have a greater positive impact than that of the first one. The first sentence is centered on negative words and does not highlight any positivity through words.

5.7 Repetition Of Affirmations In A Specific Way

Only repeating the words to change your life is not enough. You have to work more than that. You must pay attention to each and every word you are saying, along with persistence, faith, and a strong desire to change. It is also important to opt for the accurate affirmation that is needed. You must also be comfortable with the words or affirmations you choose. Creative visualization can also help support the effectiveness of affirmations. They both work in correspondence with each other. You should be aware of the words that you let in your mind and thought process.

Powerful Affirmations Examples

Affirmations that work well for people are powerful. Few of them are

1. With the passage of time, I am more contented and happy.

2. With each breath, I feel like taking in the happiness.

3. My life is filled with affection.

4. There is money flowing in life.

5. I am in charge of myself that makes me confident and in control.

6. I am calmer and at peace with myself and my surroundings.

5.8 Cognitive Restructuring Steps

Making It Conscious

The first and foremost step of cognitive reshaping is to be aware of what you think about. For that purpose, you will have to be more aware of the thought pattern that you are practicing. You will just identify the distortion type without any correction or judgment. Just monitor your thoughts for one week then only you will be able to do something regarding your problem.

Evaluate It

After being conscious about the thoughts you have, the next is to evaluate them on the basis of their rationality and irrationality. You have to give a reality check to certain thoughts and then prepare yourself to change them.

For instance, if you say something to yourself like "I will never be able to get a job", then you have to alter it because you can predict the future, and clearly, it's negative and unproductive in its kind.

So the thought worth changing is identified in this process.

Get Rational

After identification of the thought for its category, you should ask yourself that why it is problematic in the first place. Does it have any actuality to it, or is it just a random negative thought? After reasoning the problematic thought, you will move to the next step.

Replace It

In the end, you have to create or think of something positive that is the negative's alternate. Negative thoughts are usually automatic, and the person becomes habitual of them. For replacement, you do not have to stop the thought but realize it when you catch yourself in doing so. Then you can replace it with something positive at that point.

For instance, if you find yourself thinking that your friend hates you, remind yourself that you are mind-reading. SO the purpose is to replace such distortions with something rational. But this step requires a lot of effort and self-awareness. You can do it all by yourself or even get help from a professional.

5.9 Cognitive Restructuring Effectiveness

There is scientific evidence that cognitive restructuring is functional if applied properly. It is more effective than any other relaxing technique to minimize stress and anxiety.

The purpose of this restructuring is to help people be mindful of their automatic thoughts. It is due to the reason that thoughts result in feelings, and feelings are the thing which has a drastic impact on the overall health.

Chapter 6: CBT - Cognitive Behavioral Therapy

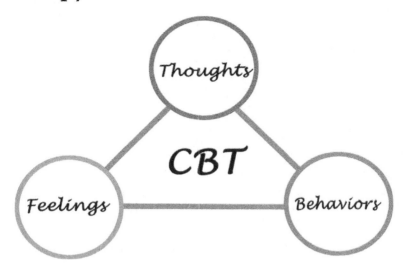

Cognitive therapy for behavior or CBT is a type of psychological treatment that has proved to be constructive in treating a variety of issues like depression, alcohol problems, drug problems, marital issues, anxiety disorders, drug use issues, and extreme mental illness. Quality of life and functioning is significantly improved by CBT, according to research. In several studies, CBT has shown more or at least as much effect as any other type of psychological therapy or medications.

The improvements in CBT have been made possible with both clinical practice and research. There is a lot of evidence that supports the fact that CBT actually impacts the lives of individuals in a positive manner. This way, CBT stands apart from different types of therapies.

6.1 Core Principles Of CBT

Psychological issues, in part, are based on unhelpful or faulty ways of thinking.

Psychological issues, in part, are based on learned unhelpful behavior patterns.

Better ways of coping can be learned by individuals suffering from such issues, thereby becoming relatively effective in their environment by relieving the symptoms.

This treatment usually entails efforts to alter thinking patterns. These efforts might include:

- Learning to acknowledge one's distortions regarding thinking which is a source of the problem, and then to evaluate them again in light of truth.
- Acquiring a better understanding of regarding motivation and behavior of others.
- Utilizing problem-solving methods to comprehend situations that are difficult.
- Gaining insight into developing a better sense of confidence in one ability of oneself.

Efforts to alter patterns of behavior are also made in this treatment method. These interventions might include:

- In order to prepare for interactions that may be problematic with others, the use of role-playing is done.
- Facing one's angst instead of running away from them.
- Learning to ease one's body and calm the mind.

All of these interventions are not utilized by all CBT. The patient and psychologist instead work together to form a comprehension of the problem in

a synergic fashion in order to achieve a treatment strategy.

CBT focuses on providing individuals with tools that enable them to treat themselves. Through "homework" tasks outside the clinic and during sessions involving exercises, CBT helps the patients to form coping skills. This enables the individuals to alter their thinking patterns, problematic behaviors, and emotions.

CBT therapists focus on the current life of the person instead of the patterns that have led them to this situation. The information regarding history is still required, but the emphasis is basically to form effective ways in moving forward and taking control of life.

6.2 Cognitive Distortions

Unhelpful styles of thinking or cognitive distortions are methods that make our thoughts biased. We are always explicating the environment around us as conscious beings, attempting to understand what is going around us. Our brains use " short cuts" in some cases and form inaccurate results. Distortions in our way of thinking or different types of bias are formed by various cognitive shortcuts. We might criticize ourselves for acts that are not our doing; in other instances, we might assume worst-case scenarios due to cognitive shortcuts. These distortions are an automatic process- we don't think inaccurately consciously- but unless we make efforts to notice them and find a solution, they can affect our lives and moods in an invisible manner. Aron Beck was the first person to notice these distortions in his research with patients who were depressed. The core part of a cognitive theory by Beck was formed by this research. This theory later became CBT.

6.3 Mental Filter

Selective abstraction is the term used by Beck to give cognitive distortion's example, which is referred to these days as a "mental filter". It explains how we emphasize one thing and blow it out of proportion and overlook other relatively important details of an event. For instance, a person delivered a lecture and got a standing ovation at his workplace and a lot of positive reviews regarding his performance. While going through the feedback forms, he observed a form with a poor rating and critical comments. He could not get over that one negative feedback. He criticized himself, saying, "I am such an ineffective lecturer". He felt awful as a result. His process of thinking was distorted since he had managed to overlook all the feedbacks that were positive and fixate on one negative feedback. He did this without even realizing what he had done.

Cognitive distortions are normal and common and not our culpability. Humans cannot be rational and logical 100 percent of the time. But when we see such thinking styles which are unhelpful in our daily lives exceed to the point where they are hindering our daily activities, they are related to poor mental health. Research shows that individuals with anxiety and depression think in characteristically unhelpful and biased ways. Recognizing the unhelpful thinking patterns and then overcoming them is a vital aspect of depression and anxiety treatment using CBT.

6.4 Thinking in A Healthy Way

Cognitive therapy's core component is to help patients think in a more healthy fashion. Practitioners may have to move patients via a number of steps in order to aid them to overcome their habitual and unhelpful cognitive biases effectively.

Understand The Automatic Thoughts

The therapist needs to make the clients understand that automatic images and thoughts are experienced by everybody. Essential information to convey is that these thoughts and images are involuntary cognitions. External stimuli from the environment around us trigger these thoughts. These thoughts can also be triggered by our emotions which are internal stimuli. Memories, thoughts, urges, images, and body sensations also fall in the category of internal stimuli that can trigger these thoughts. These thoughts are mostly believable to a large extent, and if you let them pass unchallenged and believe them, your emotional state can be heavily impacted by them in a detrimental way.

6.5 Train The Patients To Use Thought Records In Order To Catch These Thoughts

The cognitive content is of interest for traditional therapy. This implies that the patients need to understand what images and thoughts are running inside their minds if they seek to balance the thinking patterns. Automatic thoughts can be cached using thought records. Whenever a significant change is noticed in patient's feelings, they are encouraged to conclude thought records. This provides a significant hint that they have undergone an automatic thought. Thought records, in the simplest way, include a form with an area to record the situation's information in which the thought occurred, the image or the thought itself, and the way they felt about it. Patients are encouraged to make a record of their images and thoughts as close as practicable to the time of their occurrence. This way, the information recorded is more likely to be thorough.

6.6 Notice These Biases And Understand Them

Understanding these thinking patterns can be highly de-stigmatizing and normalizing. You can also see handouts regarding cognitive biases. Patients can be asked whether they recognize themselves in any of the biases. Usually, they will identify with a lot of these biases or even all of them. A dysfunctional record of thought can be used to help patients recognize unhelpful thinking patterns in their lives. There are columns to record standard information regarding situations, emotions, and thoughts, but also include ways to aid patients in practice observing the biases in their thoughts.

6.7 Cognitive Restructuring

Challenging the material of negative thoughts or cognitive restructuring is the focus of CBT. There are a wide variety of techniques that can be used to challenge negative thoughts.

Traditional disputation

This cognitive restructuring method involves the examination of evidence, both in favor of and against the thought. It is easy for people to believe why a certain thought is correct, but initial assistance is required for people to think that thought might not be true 100 percent of the time. Once you generate evidence both against and in favor of evidence, people are made to write a thought which is balanced and takes all the evidence into account.

Court-trial style disputation

The use of the court trial metaphor can be helpful for some people to see the process of dispute. The thought places "in the dock". The defense lawyer's job is to insist that this is an accurate thought, while the prosecution's job is to insist that the thought is false. The evidence is weighed by the jury, and the judge presents a verdict which is a considered alternative. This takes all the evidence into account.

Compassionate cognitive restructuring

A compassionate framework can be used to complete the cognitive restructuring by viewing the thought that is negative via a compassionate lens, utilizing the system of self-other compassion by contemplating a scenario where a friend was in a similar situation and what you would have advised him or her. By thinking what another compassionate person would have told you, you can activate this system of compassion.

Turn the restructured thinking into a habit.

Intervening with lesser techniques but making sure that clients get the maximum benefit is the preferred approach of many practitioners. Over learning the usage of this technique to identify automatic thoughts and reconstruct this pattern can be helpful. Once an individual has undergone the process of pencil and paper thought records multiple times, they can be encouraged to undergo the practice of disputation in their minds. Most people report that noticing automatic thoughts becomes easier for them, and they ask themselves, " Is there any evidence to back the authenticity of this thought?"

Once you have remitted the symptoms (at least momentarily), turn the focus on assumptions.

Assumptions underpin every cognitive distortion which is specific to the distortion. For instance, catastrophizing is reinforced by the beliefs " you are likely to face the worst" and "always think of worst case scenario", and the assumption "understanding of event's chain right now that steered to an outcome which is bad implies that the incident was anticipated at the time" underpins the hindsight bias. If you hold onto assumptions that are dysfunctional like these, you are more likely to think in a manner that is distorted. The goal of therapy is to unveil these assumptions and alter them to equip you with methods to show resilience against these thoughts. There are a variety of methods that can effectively counter assumptions, including:

6.8 Taking Action To Counter The Assumption

Listing disadvantages and advantages of the assumption
Examining the utility of assumption in the short term vs. the long term

Modification of cognitive bias

This approach is a recent intervention with only early supporting evidence. But it is still an effective way to deal with patterns of thinking which are unhelpful. Processing of selective information drives the vulnerability to anxiety. This is the theory behind the modification of cognitive bias. For instance, anxious individuals, during cognitive testing, reliably show intentional favoritism towards information that is negative and are more probable to decipher them with meanings that are negative when bestowed with vague stimuli. Whereas cognitive restructuring traditionally deals with thoughts that are distorted once they have come to light, bias modification is "shaped to alter the processes of cognition that give birth to such type of thinking". This is done through repeated tasks that are computer-based which work to record how a person elucidates vague stimuli. Trait anxiety and anxiety sensitivity in analog populations can be reduced with interpretive modification of bias, according to some research.

6.9 Exposure: Facing Fears

Reducing anxiety by avoiding things is a normal thing. But this is only for the short term. For instance, if you are afraid of enclosed, small places like the elevators, you will prefer to take stairs which will reduce your anxiety. But when you avoid things, it hinders your learning ability. You won't realize that the things which make you fearful are not as dangerous like you think. And, in this example, avoiding the elevator and taking the stairs prevents you from learning the fact that when you do choose the elevator, it won't harm you in any way.

The procedure of facing fears is termed exposure in CBT. The role of this process is very important in learning the effective management of anxiety. Exposure involves repeated and gradual facing of fears until you are no longer as much afraid of the situation as you were before. You begin with things that are less anxious for you, and step by step, you move onto things that cause you an intense amount of anxiety.

You make a list of things, places, and situations that are fearful for you in the first step. For instance, if spiders make you fearful and you want to enjoy camping with your group by overcoming this fear, you may include looking at spiders' pictures, observing an aquarium having spiders, standing across the room from a person carrying a spider, and watching videos of it in your list. Order the list from least to the scariest situation once you have made it.

Begin with the situation or object that leads to the least amount of anxiety and repeatedly face the situation or take part in that particular activity until you feel a lot less anxious while doing it. When you no longer feel as much anxiety while facing a particular situation, you can move onto the next thing on your list.

6.10 Preventing a relapse

In order to manage a problem effectively, you have to exercise certain things which keep you in shape and help you to perform efficiently in daily life. But it is normal for people to lose track of their growth and return to old habits. This is called a relapse and leads to loss of improvements. The complete return to your old methods of behaving and thinking before you grasped new strategies for controlling your problem is termed as a relapse. People can go through a brief period of relapse during times of fatigue or low mood and stress. But it is not necessary for a relapse to take place during such times. You can use the following methods and tips to prevent relapses or lapses:

PREPARE A SCHEDULE OF SKILLS THAT YOU ARE GOING TO WORK ON WEEKLY. Recognize the instances in which you are more prone to relapse, for instance, during periods of change or stress. Identifying these periods will enable you to combat the relapse. You can also list down signs that act as a warning for you. For example, frequent arguments with people and anxious thoughts might be signs of your increasing anxious thoughts. Once you realize the red flags or warning signs, you can then come up with a plan to cope with these feelings. You can practice some CBT techniques for this purpose, like challenging the negative thoughts or calm breathing.

This is a journey of growth like for everyone else on this planet. You should keep working on new challenges to prevent lapses in the future. If you are consistently making efforts to work on different and unique methods of overcoming anxiety, you are less likely to return to old habits which hindered your growth.

Try to figure out the situation which led to a lapse if you have one. This will assist you in the future in handling difficult situations by giving you a plan in advance. Keep in mind that having lapses is a normal thing, and there is a great deal of learning in each one of them.

Your later behavior is heavily impacted by the way you think regarding a lapse. You are more likely to give up if you believe that you are a flop and have wasted all of your work, and end up relapsing. You should instead keep in mind that unlearning all the tricks and going back to square one is impossible, which in this case is not recognizing how to manage anxiety while having it. This is because you actually know how to handle anxiety. You can make a comeback once you have a lapse. It is similar to riding a motorcycle: you don't forget riding a motorcycle once you have learned it.

Keep in mind that it is normal to have a lapse, and you can overcome them. Don't call yourself a loser or an idiot because this won't make things better. Understand that we all make mistakes occasionally and treat ourselves kindly.

Reward yourself for putting up all the effort and hard work to change your life. You can buy yourself something nice or go out for a fancy meal to treat yourself. It is not always easy and fun to manage anxiety, so treating yourself is a good way of motivating yourself for further work.

Chapter 7: Social Psychology

When people are in very long-term relationships, sadly, the charm gets lost. People tend to live a mainstream life, and the adrenalin rush at the beginning of a relationship disappears. It is sad but true. Many types of research justify this bitter reality. According to a study, "The unfortunate reality is that when they get to know each other more, the passionate desire that engulfed them when they first courted fades. It then turns into an ember. A lot of the time, it's ash." This statement clearly shows that passion dies. But this chapter will tell you about the psychology behind successful relationships and how to keep that passion alive.

7.1 The Psychology Behind Success Of Relationships

There is not even a single couple who do not fight. Couples disagree with each other at some point and usually lose their temper. But studies suggest that when there is some disagreement or fight between two people, never lose your calm; otherwise, things might go way out of control and lead to a breakup. You should always keep in mind that this relationship is worth more than this petty issue you are fighting over. If you want to live in a healthy relationship, you should always be willing to sort everything out calmly and not make the situation worse.

People should be able to discuss even major fights calmly and with no aggression because once you start making an effort to remain calm just at the beginning of a heated conversation, you will be able to keep things under control, and ultimately, no one will get hurt.

Separations

When you and your partner are going on your way in the morning for work, make sure you ask them what they have planned for the day and any notice-worthy thing they plan to do. If you are in a long-distance relationship, you guys can do this over the phone. And when you guys come back to each other, always ask them about how their day went. When you are listening to them, always listen to them generously and make them feel that at that instant, only they matter and nothing else.

Boost the Love Map

When you are in a relationship, you should always take an interest in their likes and dislikes. You should know little details about their life to understand them better, and you two can get along better. They should feel that they are your priority and their interests and opinions matter to you. For instance, you can simply start by asking them questions about their lives.

- Who is their new best friend?
- Do they have a favorite album or television show?
- What is the most pressing issue they are now dealing with?
- What are their ambitions in life?
- Which of their family members do they adore or despise the most?
- What is their good or bad memory from childhood?

- What is the vacation spot they have always dreamt about?

When you ask them such questions and take an interest in their lives, they will figure out that you are willing to make efforts to get to know them better out of all the people.

7.2 Hearing Good News or Bad News

Psychology tells us how we should react to good news or bad news. We should always be there to give a shoulder to our partner to cry on. According to a study, "The interesting result is that the most connected, loving, and trustworthy partnerships tend to be defined not by how couples react to each other's disappointments and setbacks, but by how they react to positive news (2013)." For instance, if your partner had a good day or has achieved something, you should always be there to capitalize them, which means you should always listen to them generously. Never consider it as a competition that your partner is succeeding in something and you are not. You should always appreciate them and ask them the details and tell them how proud you are.

The same goes for the bad news. When your partner had a rough day, you should always be there to have their back and providing them a shoulder to cry on. When your partner tells you about their bad day, or any sad news, always be empathetic towards them without judging them. So if you genuinely want to get close to someone, always cherish their victories and never give any negative or jealous remarks. In this way, you will always be the first person they will come to after having either a good day or a bad day.

Change it up with kindness

Studies have shown that being kind to your partner helps to build up a strong relationship. It has always been advised to do small acts of kindness for improvements. But always spice things up a little bit. Please do not repeat the same act for longer periods because it will lose its charm. For example, if you make breakfast for your partner every morning, this will increase the love they have for you, but chances are they might get bored of it soon, so you have to come up with another act of kindness to keep things fresh between you and your partner. There should always be an element of surprise between you two.

Physical Contact

Physical touch is important to take your relationship to the next level. We are not talking about sexual intimacy but small gestures like holding hands, a quick warm hug, holding the arms, a pat on the head, etc. People do not even notice such gestures, but our brains perceive them and release cuddling hormones that ultimately lead to an increase in love, care, and intimacy.

A Message for Everybody

We know that nobody is perfect. We all have flaws. Your partner must have too. Maybe his flaws are that he keeps a wet towel on the floor or that he watches weird movies, but that's okay. Until and unless he is not abusive or disrespects you, do not let your partner go. This goes the other way around as well. If your girl is moody or clingy but not disloyal, do not let her go. Do not give up. Make efforts to keep your relationship healthy. There are very small things that can bring your relationship to extraordinary levels, like asking about their day, taking an interest in their interest, showing concern when they have a bad day, appreciating them, making them feel good about themselves, etc. All these tiny efforts are extremely important to maintain a healthy relationship.

7.3 Importance Of Reciprocity In Relationships

In most relationships, we do not consider reciprocity. We agree that it is important but do not act upon it. Also, if we think that two people can reciprocate in the same way, it is not possible because whatever one person can do, the other person might not do so. People reciprocate according to their weaknesses and strengths.

An Overview of Reciprocity

There are many types of research on reciprocity in relationships and its importance. People have also studied the effects of reciprocities on human behavior. These studies have helped people in toxic relationships, especially women who are being abused by their partners. Various factors help to develop reciprocity in any relationship. For instance, if two people are willing to cooperate and love each other, they will most likely develop this and help their relationship grow. But when one of the two partners is arrogant and controlling, reciprocity is impossible in such scenarios. In this case, only one partner would be doing all the efforts while the other person would do nothing about it. People who think that they are superior to their partners can never be successful in maintaining a healthy relationship because no one likes to take orders and be involved in a one-sided relationship. Reciprocity requires freedom and cooperation and willingness to spend a good life.

When two people are equally willing to love each other and make efforts for each other, the sense of fulfillment is unmatchable. Most of the time, people effortlessly reciprocate each other's feelings only because they are so in love. When two people invest in the relationship, their relationship grows, and they live a very healthy and peaceful life. Commitment, love, and passion are the essential points for any relationship to work. When people reciprocate feelings, it shows how important their relationship is for them and how badly they want to maintain it. Partners invest even emotionally in such cases.

Reciprocity Building

Reciprocity develops between two mature people. By maturity, we mean that two people are mature enough to take responsibility for everything. Reciprocity does not mean that one person puts the entire blame on the other person if things do not go smoothly. People have to be emotionally mature enough to accept the responsibilities. And achieving this level of maturity requires a lot of hard work and time.

When two people are ready to be in an interdependent, reciprocated relationship, the next step would be communication. People should talk about their concerns regarding the relationship. They should talk about what they expect from their life partner and how they want to do everything. And while talking about it, partners should listen and understand each other and should be willing to compromise if needed. People should talk to each other about how they want to be loved and respected.

One thing that people should reciprocate is respect. In any relationship, people should feel respected. If someone is not feeling that he/she is getting enough respect, they should talk about it. By reciprocating respect, we mean that people should respect each other's professions, dreams, intelligence, and personal growth. People should be honest about their opinions as well as respect their partner's stance on everything. If there is no respect in a relationship, it gets really hard to maintain it no matter how much love both partners have for each other.

Before starting any relationship, it is better that you openly discuss the areas where you want reciprocity. For instance, you should talk about the division of labor among the partners and reciprocity in emotional or sexual intimacy. There is no harm in talking about all of these things beforehand. You can save a lot of effort and time by this.

When one partner gives out some negative energy and reciprocates the same negativity, it harms the relationship. There should not be reciprocating of negativity at any cost. When one partner feels that there is some negativity in the relationship, he or she should talk to the other partner. Proper communication saves a lot of damage. And if things still do not seem to be under control, you can always go for couple counselling.

7.4 Developing Relationships And Reciprocity

For any relationship to last longer and healthy, reciprocity is very important. This kind of reciprocity is way different than all other sorts of reciprocities in other relationships. Before committing to anyone, you should have an open discussion about what kind of love they expect from their partners and how they are planning to make this relationship healthy and growing.

When people are first attracted to each other, there is an adrenalin rush, and people think that they are ready to get into a relationship. But the truth is this attraction fades away really quickly, and people are left with their capabilities to build a happy relationship. When choosing a partner, you should see if they are willing to build a healthy relationship or not. You should see if the other person is compromising enough or not or whether they want the same thing from life or not. When you have such an intimate discussion with anyone before getting into a relationship, this helps people from a lot of toxicity.

Relationships Based On Commitments

Human beings are generally in a relationship with everyone around them. These relationships could be with their families or friends or life partners. They stay in those relationships because they love each other. Love holds them together. But few things play an important role in maintaining these healthy relationships apart from love. Commitments and passion towards each other make any relationship so much better. We will discuss what a commitment is and why it is important for healthy relationships. We will also figure out when to end a commitment when it gets toxic and things get out of your hands.

Commitment Meaning

Commitment simply means when two people are willing to live with each other, and they both agree to that. In all of the relationships, either with family or with your friends, commitment is important to some extent, but your relationship with life partners needs a very serious commitment. In other words, when we label our relationships, we are committing calling each other friends or married means there is a commitment in that relationship. And when people get into relationships, there is an unspoken contract of rules that both the partners expect from each other without even telling them.

When two people are in a commitment, they feel safe and protected. They start to believe that they can overcome any obstacle and deal with anything coming their way. For instance, it is easy to raise a child when two people are there to take care of that child instead of a single parent. It is important for everyone to feel safe and secure in this world where you have to face so many challenges every day, and being with a person who is there to deal with everything together makes these same challenges so easy to deal with.

Commitments And Relationships Nowadays

Relationships today are like when two people are loyal to each other, they will go out of their ways to make that relationship work, but when there is infidelity, no one tolerates that. Also, it is very easy for people nowadays to break up whenever they want and consider themselves never committed to each other.

Being Committed Is The Right Thing To Do Or Not

If we talk about relationships of this era, we will notice that most people are in toxic relationships. Their point of view related to commitments and relationships are very different. They like to control their life partners. They want their life partners to act upon their orders. People also want their partners to fulfill all of their expectations without even communicating. People expect their life partners to be perfect in everything, and hence commitments do more harm than good. Following are the two points that will tell you how relationships become toxic in no time.

An Untold Contract Between Partners

When you get into a relationship, you start by making up your mind that your partner will fulfill your expectations without saying anything. You think that your partner is flawless and will do everything perfectly. And this leads to disappointments and fights and ultimately ruining the relationship. But if you just change the criteria and simply do one thing, communicate. Tell your partner what you want in a life partner and what you expect from them; this will make your relationship better in so many ways.

Control Over One Another

If you to keep things smooth between you and your partner, you need to stop depending on them for everything, including your happiness. You should not burden your partner with responsibilities. Otherwise, your partner will feel suffocated and want to leave. The other thing you should do is to stop controlling your partner. They should be free to make their own decisions and live life independently without being answerable to you for all the things. If you give orders and try to control your partner, this will harm your relationship badly. We cannot set up our own rules and ask the other person to follow them; rather, there should be a mutual agreement. When you commit with someone, you must make compromises to make it work. But you should not go to extremes for this to work out. You should not bear any torture. You are allowed to leave if you are not satisfied. There are some ways which make things easy between two partners, and they can live a happy life. Communicating what you need, expecting less, and letting your partner know that he is free and you do not own him make your relationship last way longer than they already do. But there is no point in dragging a relationship in which you are not happy.

Making A List Of Rules And Expectations

When you get into a relationship or if you feel like the already existing relationship is in danger, and you have to make it better, there is one thing you can do that is to make a list of expectations. But keep in mind that the expectations have to be reasonable. You can talk to each other about it, and you can make your relationship far better and long-lasting. By doing this, the other person would know what you are expecting from them, and in this way, there will be fewer disappointments and fewer fights. Following are some basic things which we can expect and things we should not expect from your partner.

Unreasonable: Problem With Emotional Responses

People respond differently to different scenarios emotionally. You cannot control their response. Some could be very emotional, while others find it hard to cry. You cannot expect a person to respond to certain occasions, according to you. For instance, if you find some movie scene very emotional, that does not mean they find it too. And it is irrational if you expect them to respond according to you. It is not unreasonable if you ask your partners to control their anger and not be aggressive. But in general, you have to accept your partners just the way they are.

Reasonable: Wanting Affection

While there are things we cannot expect from our partners, wanting affection from them is always fair. Your partner should be affectionate towards you, and they should never shy away from expressing their love and affection for you. The way people show affection might vary from one person to another. Some people prefer physical touch while others are comfortable with their words. It is okay if you tell them how you want them to be. You should communicate about it so that the other person knows exactly how you want to be loved. There is nothing unreasonable about it.

Unreasonable: Expecting A Perfect Partner

Nobody is perfect in this world. We are all humans, and we all make mistakes. So if you expect your partner to be perfect at everything, to never fail at anything, then it is quite unreasonable. You cannot expect your partner never to make a mistake, never hurt you, or always fulfill your expectations. Your partner will have flaws, and you have to accept that. If you expect them to be a perfectionist, it is going to disappoint you a lot.

Reasonable: Having A Respectful Relationship

Everyone deserves a respectful relationship, even if not a perfect one. There are some things you should never compromise, and respect is one of them, and respect means that the other person should always be considerate towards you. Suppose you expect your partner to understand you, make efforts to keep you happy, listen to you, be willing to make the relationship work, not harm you in any way, and fulfill the promises. In that case, you are not unreasonable at all.

Unreasonable: Making Your Partner The Only Source Of Your Happiness

Healthy relationships indeed help you stay happy. If you are in an abusive kind of a relationship, you can never spend a happy life. So it is understandable to want to have a life partner that keeps you happy, but at the same time, it is very unreasonable if you make them your only source of happiness. Your happiness should not entirely depend on how your relationship is going. You should be able to make yourself happy. You should control your happiness irrespective of how your job is going, if your relationship is working out for you or what kind of family you have. Your happiness should not get affected if things do not go smoothly between you and your partner.

It is fair if you think that a good relationship helps you spend a happy life, but it is unfair to rely on your partner for it completely. It is not fair if you put the whole burden of your well-being on the other person. You should value a good partner, but you should not burden them. You should be able to keep yourself happy. Be easy on each other and do not make the other person regret their choice.

Reasonable: Making Time For Each Other

When you are in a relationship, you need to make time to let the other person know that they are your priority. You should make time to see each other or to call just to keep a check on them. It is not unreasonable at all if you ask for your partner's time. You can expect your partner to make time for you so that you guys can spend time together. Giving each other time is essential for every relationship to work. It is not even unreasonable to ask your partner to give you more time if you think you are not getting enough of their time. You have all the right to ask them that. But you should always communicate it in a good way.

You should always be willing to compromise if you guys are facing difficulty in giving each other time. You should always understand why they are not giving you enough time. It is only fair to compromise in this case and not give up. Never let the other person think that this relationship is not your priority.

Unreasonable: Expecting The Other Person To Want The Same Things

Some people think it is fair to expect their partner to have the same ideas or opinions just like them. They believe that both partners should agree on everything; otherwise, they cannot get along. But these expectations are only reasonable if you expect the other person to have the same thoughts on marrying, having children, moving to someplace together, etc. It is very unreasonable if you want them to agree with you every single time on every little thing. You should not force them to have the same thoughts or opinions on politics or religion or any other concept of this sort. You should be willing to compromise, and you should be okay with these differences. If you both are not agreeing on something that does not mean you guys do not love each other. When you start respecting each other's opinions, your relationship will get far better.

Reasonable: Challenges Faced By Partners In A Relationship

One way of taking your relationship to the next level is all about facing challenges and how exactly you face them. And it is fair to assume that both partners will face challenges, but these challenges will only help them grow. These challenges could be of any sort. They could be a difference of opinion in certain aspects like religion or politics, or these challenges might be related to parenting, losing a child, or some serious life-changing accidents. But all of these obstacles should only help in strengthening their bond and love. When partners face these challenges together as a unit, they do not struggle at all. These challenges start to seem easy to them. The key to overcoming these obstacles is communication, and this way, their bond, and love will get stronger and stronger.

When you are in a relationship, it is very reasonable to expect some things from the other person. But these expectations have to be reasonable. These expectations will not harm the relationship only if there is good communication between the two people and they know how to convey their feelings or expectations to the other person, and the other person should be willing to understand them. In this way, they can easily make their relationship work for longer periods.

Chapter 8: Psychology Of Success

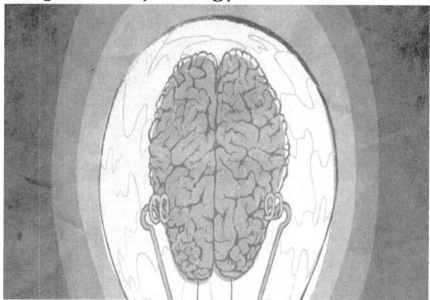

What comes to your mind when you think of a leader who is perfect?

You might think of a person who keeps his temper in control at all times, no matter what the circumstances are. A person who always listens to his or her team has the full trust of the staff, makes informed and careful decisions, and is easy to communicate with can also be thought of as a perfect leader. You can see these qualities in an individual with emotional intelligence of a higher degree.

8.1 Clarity Of Purpose

"The definiteness of purpose is a quality that should be possessed by a person to win, the knowledge regarding one's wants and a never ending desire to achieve it" - Napoleon Hill.

In order to achieve success in life, it is vital to get clarity of your purpose. You need this sense in your life to make your dreams come true by working towards a specific goal. For this, you need to make your goal specific, and it needs clarity for that. While daydreaming about being successful and rich is fun, you need to understand and define what your values are clear.

Every type of success requires this clarity. Whether you are trying to lose weight, traveling abroad, or getting a brand new car. How can you get something if you do not truly realize what you want?

Once the purpose becomes clear, you can take steps towards your goal. You start focusing on your goal after realizing the purpose without wasting energy or time. This clarity is equivalent to focusing a light source on your goal, which makes it clear.

8.2 Achieving the clarity

- Understand what it is that you want.
- Ask yourself that why this goal holds value for you and what is the benefit of achieving this.
- Make up your mind about really achieving this goal.
- Learn and read regarding your goal.
- Visualize this goal clearly.
- Ponder over all the details inside your mind.
- Declutter your life.
- Learn how to focus the mind on this goal.
- Display perseverance and self-discipline in life.
- Be specific about the details of your goal.

8.3 How Do You Explain Emotional Intelligence?

EI or emotional intelligence is the capability to manage and understand your emotions as well as those around you. People who have a higher degree of EI understand their feelings, the meaning of their emotions, and the effect their emotions can have on other people.

EI is essential for the success of leaders. Because at the end of the day, what type of leader is more likely to successfully manage his or her team – one who shouts under stress at his team, or the one who remains in control and assesses the situation calmly?

Emotional intelligence has 5 key components, according to an American psychologist, Daniel Goleman, who had a role in the popularity of EI:

- Motivation
- Self-regulation
- Empathy
- Self-awareness
- Social skills

Your emotional intelligence is measured according to your ability to manage every one of these areas as a leader.

8.4 Why Is Emotional Intelligence Necessary For Success?

When emotional intelligence was first introduced to people, it played the role of a missing link in a strange finding: Individuals with IQ levels that are average outperform individuals with the most IQs in many cases. This irregularity gave individuals a huge jolt as IQ was considered the sole factor required for success.

Emotional intelligence is considered the critical component which distinct the best performers from other people after decades of studies.

The "something" in every one of us which is bodiless is called emotional intelligence. It impacts our management of behavior, making personal decisions for positive results, and navigation of social complexities. 4 core skills make up emotional intelligence, and these can be paired into 2 primary competencies: social competence and personal competence.

8.5 Emotional Intelligence, Personality, And IQ Are Different

The fundamental component of behavior is tapped into by emotional intelligence, which is different from your intellect. There is no connection between emotional intelligence and IQ that is known to science. You cannot predict someone's emotional intelligence based on their smartness. The ability to learn is called intelligence, and it is similar at the age of 15 and 50. Contrary to that, emotional intelligence is an ever-growing set of skills. This growth is done by practice. Even though some individuals have more EI naturally as compared to others, this can still be developed if you are not born with it.

The final part of the puzzle is personality. Personality is the solid "style" that explains all the individuals. Hard-wired preferences shape the personality, like leaning towards extroversion or introversion. However, you cannot use personality to predict EI, just like you cannot use IQ to determine EI. Personality, like IQ, is stable throughout life and does not change. IQ, personality, and EI each surround specific ground and aid in explaining what compels an individual to tick.

Emotional Intelligence Anticipates Performance

What is the impact of emotional intelligence on your success professionally? The simple answer is plenty of impact! It is a powerful way of focusing your energy at one point and having tremendous results. Talent Smart evaluated EI alongside thirty-three other vital workplace skills. They found that EI is the best predictor of efficiency, describing a full 58 percent success rate in all sorts of jobs.

The foundation of a number of critical skills is based on your EI. It impacts almost everything you say and do every day. Most of the top performers have a higher degree of emotional intelligence. In comparison, the amount of bottom performers with high emotional intelligence is very less. It is less likely to be a top performer with less emotional intelligence. Research also shows that people with higher emotional intelligence earn more. The relationship between earnings and emotional intelligence is so immediate that 1300 dollars are added to salary annually with a one-point increase in EI. This is true for people all over the world working in all sorts of fields at all levels.

Increasing Emotional Intelligence Is Possible!

The link between your rational and emotional "brains" is the source of EI physically. The pathway for EI begins at the spinal cord in the brain. The primary senses go in from here, and in order for your brain to think regarding the experience rationally, the senses must reach the front of the brain. However, the sense travels via the limbic system, which is the area responsible for the generation of emotions. Therefore, we react to the events emotionally before being able to engage our rational minds. An effective link between emotional and rational centers of the brain is required for emotional intelligence.

The ability of the brain to change is called plasticity. As you practice and discover new skills of emotional intelligence, small arms are branched off by billions of neurons. These neurons line the road between emotional and rational centers of the brain like a tree. 15000 connections can be formed by a single cell with its neighbors. In order to adopt a new behavior in the future, this link of cells plays an important role. The training of the brain repeatedly by practicing new behaviors which are emotionally intelligent leads to the formation of pathways required to turn them into habits. You soon start responding with emotional intelligence towards your surroundings without any effort. And while you reinforce these new behaviors, the pathways supporting destructive and old behaviors will diminish.

8.6 Leadership And Emotional Intelligence

Self-awareness

Self-aware persons know about their feelings at all times, and they realize the effect of their actions and emotions on people around them. When you are in a position of leadership, being self-aware also implies that you have a clear picture regarding your weaknesses and strengths, and it includes having humility.

How can you work on increasing your self-awareness?

Slow down

When you experience strong emotions like anger, slow down and examine the situation. Keep in mind that no matter how bad the situation is, you can always react wisely to it.

Keep a journal

You can work on your self-awareness by keeping a journal. Spending some time writing your thoughts on a paper every day can improve your self-awareness.

Self-regulation

People who control themselves constructively hardly attack others verbally, make emotional or rushed decisions, give up on their values, or stereotype people. These people become successful leaders. Having control of yourself is the core of self-regulation.

As per Goleman, the component of EI also includes a leader's commitment and flexibility to personal accountability.

Hence, what are the ways to work on self-regulation?

Realize your values

Are you sure about the areas where you will not compromise at any cost? Do you realize the most important values for yourself? If yes, then you will not have to think again when facing an ethical or moral decision– you will make the correct choice.

Hold yourself responsible

Stop blaming others when something goes sideways. Commit to admitting your shortcomings and facing whatever consequences are there. This will earn you the respect of the people around you. This will not tarnish your image in any way and open doors for positive growth.

Work on being calm

Observe your actions next time during a challenging situation. Does shouting at someone make things better? Practice exercises like deep breathing to calm your mind and body. Also, keep in mind to write all the negative stuff that runs through your mind in this situation and rip the paper. This way of expressing emotions is a lot better as compared to shouting them at your team. In addition, it aids you in countering your emotions to make sure that they are fair.

Motivation

Leaders who are self-motivated work towards their goals consistently. They also set high standards for their work's quality.

What are the ways to work on your motivation?

Re-Examine The Reason For Doing What You Are Doing

You can easily forget about the things you love regarding your career. So ponder over the question that why you took this job. If you are struggling to realize this and feeling unhappy regarding your role, try the technique of 5 Whys to find the core of the issue. Beginning at the core is often helpful to analyze the issue from a new perspective. Keep in mind to make your goal statements energizing and fresh.

Realize Your Position

Find out about your motivation in relation to the role of leading.

Stay Hopeful And Look For Something Good.

Optimism is the quality of many motivated leaders, no matter the issues that they face. You need to practice this mindset in order to master it. The effort is worth the reward in the end. Try to find something good about the situation even when you fail or face an obstacle. It can be a tiny thing as well as a long-term thing like a vital lesson absorbed. You can almost always find a good thing about any situation.

Empathy

Empathy is an important quality for leaders. It is necessary to manage an organization or a team successfully. This quality will enable you to put yourself in other people's shoes and see things from their perspective. This quality enables them to aid the growth of individuals in their team. They give effective feedback to others, challenge people who act unfairly, and listen to their team members.

If your goal is to earn the loyalty and respect of people in your team, you need to develop this ability.

So, what are the ways that can help you with the development of empathy?

Place Yourself In Other People's Positions

It is easy to see things from your perspective. But you need to look after everyone else. This requires that you see things from the perspective of others. Imagine yourself in situations that are difficult and how challenging it would be for you to come up with solutions. This way, you will be able to empathize with others while gaining their confidence. This will boost their morals and their motivation to find the solution of things which will benefit the whole team in the end.

Keep Your Body Language In Check

When you are talking to someone, you might hold your arms together in front of your body, bite your lips, or move your feet. These movements can give the other person a clue about your feeling of the situation, and the information transmitted is not positive! Learning this art of reading body language can be really beneficial for leaders as it allows you to understand other people's feelings. Therefore, you can respond to others appropriately.

Pay Attention To Feelings

When you tell your assistant that there will be extra work today and he might get late again, even though he agrees, there is disappointment that you can hear in his voice. So try to address the feelings of your assistant and respond accordingly. Express your appreciation of him for working the extra hours and admit that it's frustrating to work late. This will enable you to understand the feelings of other people. If possible, try to minimize the issue of working late in the future (for instance, by allowing him to take the next morning off).

Social Skills

A leader with great social skills in light of emotional intelligence is the best communicators. They can listen to both good and bad news as efficiently, and they are a pro at getting the support of their team for a new project or mission. They can easily get their team excited for a task and motivate them to give their all. Such leaders can effectively solve conflicts and manage any change on the way to the goal. They are never satisfied by leaving things halfway, but they never expect that everyone else works while they just sit and give orders. They lead others as an example through their behavior.

What are the ways to improve your social skills?

Learn The Art Of Conflict Resolution

The responsibility to resolve the conflicts among the members of the team, vendors, or customers is of leaders. This is a vital skill on the road to becoming an effective leader.

Praise Others Often

If you praise your team members, you can easily gain their loyalty and inspire them to work even better. This is an art that is worth the effort required to develop.

Chapter 9: Using Psychology To Re-Program Your Habits

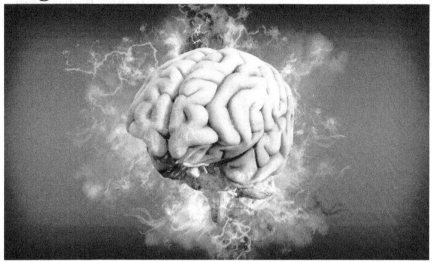

Procrastinators delay the work of the day before yesterday to the day after tomorrow.

We all delay work, which seems tedious or unpleasant every now and then. Taking the trash out, making phone calls, cleaning the car, or cleaning the house is not a fun way for anyone to spend their time. But where many of us do this once in a while, procrastinators practice this for most of their time which is a big problem.

9.1 Effects Of Procrastination

Procrastination leads to stress

Procrastination is stress-causing behavior as it makes wishes and plans fail at the point of what should have been a fulfillment point. Vacation packages and theatre tickets sell out before a person who is a procrastinator gets around to calling. Deadlines pass, planes take off, other applicants get the job while they are still thinking.

Procrastination has bad effects

The research group on procrastination at Carleton University performed an online survey. 2700 responses were received to the question, "What is the negative impact of procrastination on your happiness?"

Almost every second person (46 percent) said "very much" or "quite a bit," and approximately one out of five persons said "highly negative effect."

Procrastination is a threat to happiness

Even though people downplay procrastination most of the time, people who procrastinate suffer when they fail to fulfill their potential or when their job crashes.

Procrastination in the bigger picture or the long term can turn into a bigger threat than just the personal health, productivity, or happiness of individuals: it can spread that threat into our communities and companies.

Traits of people who procrastinate

What are the ways to identify a chronic procrastinator?

Procrastinators try to hide information regarding their abilities, their focus is on the past, and they don't work on their aim, they make bad estimates of time, they may also take up service-related jobs.

These attributes are related to low self-esteem, non-competitiveness, perfectionism, self-control, anxiety, depression, self-confidence, self-deception, and perfectionism.

There are no simple answers

You cannot find a simple answer to the problems of a procrastinator. As said by Joseph Ferrari, a psychology professor at DePaul University: "the problem with chronic procrastinators is not just about management of time. To tell such a person 'just get it done' is similar to telling a person to cheer up who is clinically depressed." You need to observe the type of procrastination practiced by individuals to understand why they do it and seek the right cure.

What is the reason for procrastination?

Make a guess! Ferrari observed that a few procrastinators had fathers that were authoritarian. He looks at this habit as an ongoing revolt against those requirements.

Others put the blame on parents who do not give their children space to form initiative.

A worker at York University, Clary Lay, maker of the procrastination scale, gives a different opinion regarding the thinking of procrastinators and says that they act and think in terms of "dreams and wishes" while individuals who do not develop this barrier move on with "obligations and oughts." He also says that the thinking of procrastinators is neurotically disorganized, which makes them forgetful and rarely likely to plan well.

How do individuals procrastinate?

Research regarding procrastination is a new area of study, but researchers are beginning to describe various types of this problem. Two common types of procrastination are decisional and behavioral procrastination.

9.2 Behavioral Procrastination

This is a self-sabotage approach which people use to transfer blame and avoid work; for instance, a student may perform badly in a test and utilize procrastination as an escape. Such people create the notion that instead of ability, they lacked effort. Therefore, they can use time as an excuse for their failure. Procrastinators also suffer from self-doubt and low esteem and worry about the way people view their abilities.

They view their self-worth on the basis of their ability. So as per their logic, you can never determine their ability if they never complete the task.

A cycle of behavior that is self-defeating is formed from failing to perform sufficiently and prolonged procrastination. This results in self-esteem's downward spiral. The embarrassment of this sort and self-inflicted humiliation mostly leads to mental health issues and stress in the future.

9.3 Decisional Procrastination

The strategy to put off forming a decision while dealing with choices or conflicts is called decisional procrastination. Individuals who practice decisional procrastination of high level are often afraid of mistakes and are perfectionists mostly. Such individuals look for more and more knowledge regarding alternatives before trying to make a choice if they make a choice at all.

Decisional practitioners who are over-informed run the risk of running into an additional self-sabotage scheme termed optional paralysis: they form so many scenarios for themselves that it becomes impossible to choose, or they fear choosing an option that is somewhat short of perfection.

9.4 Initial Steps To Alter The Behavior

The first stride towards change is insight. The next step is understanding. Then a course of therapy for behavior modification may help, particularly if procrastination is leading to serious issues in relation to relationships and work.

Even though procrastination does not have any Band-Aid solution, any step that aids procrastinators to take positive strides has a prolonged effect on rebuilding self-esteem and a fine level of attainment. These strides help procrastinators feel good about themselves.

9.5 Psychological Approaches To Beat Procrastination

9.6 How to defeat procrastination

It is possible to get the better of procrastination like many other negative habits. Following are some of the ways you can prevent and deal with procrastination:

Understand That You Are Procrastinating

In order to re-prioritize your amount of work, you might be delaying a task. If you are delaying a task briefly for a really good cause, then you are not necessarily procrastinating. But if you are putting things off forever or you are shifting focus in order to avoid doing a task, then you are probably procrastinating.

Other signs of procrastination are:

Prioritize tasks that are of low priority throughout the day

Leave something in your list of To-Do for ages, even though it is important.

Start a task of high priority and then leave to prepare coffee.

Read emails plenty of times and still not make a decision regarding action.

Spend time doing tasks for other people while ignoring your own important tasks.

Work On The Reason For Procrastinating

You need to find out the reason why you are struggling with this issue before you can look for answers to solve it. For example, do you have a habit of ignoring a specific task because you think it is unpleasant or boring? If yes, try to complete this task as soon as possible so you can move on to the tasks that you feel are enjoyable.

Procrastination can also be due to poor procrastination. People who use To-Do lists that are prioritized overcome procrastination easily and create schedules that are effective. Therefore, organized individuals overcome this problem easily. Such tools enable you to arrange tasks by deadline and priority.

You can get swamped by a task even if you are organized. Maybe you are tensed about failing and have doubts regarding your ability. To avoid this tension, you put off the task and look for comport by working on things that you believe you can complete.

Some people are afraid of success just as much as they are afraid of failure. They fear that once they complete a task, they will be overloaded with requests to complete more tasks. Surprisingly, most people who are procrastinators are also perfectionists. Most of the time, they avoid doing something at all that they believe they cannot do perfectly.

Poor decision-making also leads to procrastination. If you cannot make up your mind regarding what to do, you will most likely avoid taking any action in fear of making the wrong decision.

Adopt Strategies Of Anti-Procrastination

Procrastination is a deeply implanted behavior pattern. This is a habit that cannot be broken down in one night. You can only overcome habits once you stop the practice of doing them, so practice the strategies given below in order to give yourself a fighting chance.

Make a commitment towards the task. Focus on working and not on avoiding the task. Take a paper and write the important tasks that need to be completed. Specify the amount of time in which you are supposed to complete the task. This will enable you to tackle your work proactively.

Do not curse yourself for the amount of time wasted. According to research, self-forgiveness is a great way of feeling good about yourself. This will reduce the chances of avoiding the tasks in the future.

Reward yourself. Give yourself a treat once you complete an important task. Go for dinner at a fine restaurant or have a slice of cheesecake. Make sure to put an emphasis on the feeling of completing a difficult task.

When you get an important task, try to get on with it as soon as possible instead of letting it build up for one more day.

Peer pressure can help with overcoming procrastination. So, ask someone to keep checking up on you. The principle which underlines the self-help groups is peer pressure. If you do not have someone to ask, you can use a tool like procrastor, where you can monitor yourself online.

Rephrase the dialogs within yourself. The phrases "have to" and "need to," for instance, suggest that you have no other choice. This leads to a sense of disempowerment and may even cause self-sabotage. Instead, you can use the dialog, "I choose to," which implies that you are in control of the situation.

Try to remove distractions from your life. Turn off social media and your email. Do not sit near a TV while you sit down to work!

Try to "eat an elephant beetle" every day, first thing! Research shows that getting those tasks out of your way that you do not find pleasant as soon as possible works like magic in battling procrastination. You can work on the tasks that you like for the rest of the day. This way, you will feel good and get the difficult work done as well. Try focusing on the "long game" if you are procrastinating due to an unpleasant task.

Studies show that people who are impulsive are more prone to procrastinate as they are looking at a short-term gain. Identify and focus on the long-term benefits of completing this task. This will help you to overcome procrastination. For example, could it have an impact on your bonus at the end of the year or on your performance review at the end of the year?

You can also focus on the consequences of delaying a task that may be unpleasant in the future. This can make your difficult task relatively bearable. For example, what will be the consequences if you do not complete the task? What will be its impact on your team, organization, or personal growth? You can also reframe the work by looking at its relevance and meaning. You will hold a greater value for this task, and your work will be made worthwhile. Also, observe that the unpleasantness of the work can be overestimated at times as well. So keep in mind and give the task a try. You may not find it as bad as you thought.

If you procrastinate as a result of being disorganized, the following strategies can assist you in getting organized:

Make a list of things to do. You can prevent yourself from "conveniently" forgetting about those overwhelming and unpleasant tasks.

9.7 Prioritize The To-Do List With The Help Of
Eisenhower's Urgent Principle

This principle will help you to shift your focus on the important work while ignoring things that are not of as much importance.

Become a pro at project planning and scheduling. If you have multiple projects or one big project going on and you do not understand where to begin, the following ways can help you in organizing and carrying out the tasks.

Tackle the most difficult tasks when you are full of energy. Do you work more effectively in the afternoon or in the morning? Recognize the time of day when you work at your best and carry out the most difficult tasks in that time.

Give yourself a time target. In order to achieve your goals on time, setting a deadline for yourself will help you to a great extent. Divide the work into very small time targets. For instance, if you are supposed to write 10 thousand words in 5 days, give yourself a target of writing 2 thousand words each day. Divide the day into further parts and try to write 500 words in one hour. Give yourself a tiny treat after every one hour and get on with the next hour of work.

Use apps for managing tasks and time. Apps like Toggl and Trello can help you with the management of time and tasks. Take the previous example of diving words in hours and set that target using an app. This will keep you even more focused.

Professionals suggest 15 minutes activity bursts for tackling tasks. You will gain a sense of achievement from these tiny tasks, and as a result, you will feel less overwhelmed and more positive regarding your approach to a bigger project.

9.8 Creative Visualization

The process of forming extreme mental imagery for the purpose of affecting positive psychological changes is called visualization. You can think of it as a rehearsal that goes on in mind. By visualizing bright sceneries of your goal's accomplishment, you condition the subconscious to work on the goal. The reason behind this technique is that your subconscious cannot differentiate between an imaginary experience and a real-life experience, as per scientific research.

The subconscious begins to believe the imagined thoughts after constant repetition. When this occurs, beliefs, mindsets, behaviors, and habits are altered accordingly. Every action and thought is aimed towards the completion of the goal as a result. Furthermore, the mindsets, mental strength, and beliefs required for accomplishing your goals are formed within you. These modifications will allow you to keep working towards your goal even when you are faced with challenges.

Your neural pathways can also benefit from visualization at the same time. By visualizing certain actions continuously, the action will feel relatively known once you actually perform it. The reason behind this fact is that the same neural pathways are activated in great part by visualization and real-life action. To add to the list of surprises, research says that some athletes gained almost similar strength from only visualizing a specific exercise, just like a person who gained strength from that exercise in real life.

9.9 Why Does Visualization Work?

Scientific research has shown plenty of times the way visualization works, but it still has not found a way of explaining the reason why it exactly works. Yes, it is understood by scientists that visualization affects neurological networks and impacts the subconscious mind, but the reason why it impacts a person's life in such a strong way is still not known. Explaining the fact that visualization of physical exercise results in gains in strength which are almost similar to gains as practically doing this exercise is a struggle for scientists.

One way that this mystery can be answered is by looking at the enormous power of thoughts. Particular mental laws are applied through visualization, which controls the creative potential of thoughts. Energy constitutes the thoughts, and by applying an intense focus on a particular idea, we nurture it using emotional energy and attention. This process can impact internal variations that are seen in the environment around us. Therefore, we can change our world by merely changing the way we think. The reason for this working is debatable, but it works.

9.10 How To Perform Visualization?

It is a very simple process. It takes anywhere between 5 to 10 minutes. But in order to get results, it requires regular practice and dedication. The reason why many people struggle with visualization is due to a lack of dedication. They perform this activity for around 3 days and give up as they have not become millionaires. Practice patience and keep doing it; only then will you be able to see results.

At the start, it is vital to seek something that you require. Preferably, it's a realistic and meaningful goal. The visualization can start once you have found what you desire.

Imagine yourself in a comfortable place. Make sure that you sit in a quiet environment that has no distractions.

After shutting your eyes, begin imagining in intense detail the way you reach your goal. See yourself experiencing or having whatever it is you wish. Repeat this step within your mind again and again.

Keep these instructions in mind:

Make it look like it is real. Intensive imagination of the way success feels or having what you desire is the principle of visualization. Creating mental images only is not enough to achieve success in visualization. Even though the formation of mental imagery is the description of visualization, it doesn't include only forming visual images. Feel as being successful instead of just visualizing it. Feel the joy, happiness, and excitement. Feel the beats of your heart and the way adrenaline runs through your body. Smell, hear and feel how it looks like to have ultimately accomplished what you have wanted for so long. The goal of this strategy is to form such an extreme mental image that it feels as it were true.

Participate and do not just watch. Most individuals make the error of seeing their actions from the perspective of a third person during visualization. They do not see themselves reaching their goals from the perspective of the first person. It is just like they are watching a film without being involved in it. You should always bear in mind that visualizing from the perspective of the first person is critically important in this process. Otherwise, it is similar to watching a person achieving all these goals that you are dreaming of. Due to this factor, you must engage and participate in the process of visualization. Be the principal point of focus in the entire film and not just an observer.

Be specific. It is suggested to visualize distinct goals in general. Visualizing a promotion at the job might not give quick results. Try to imagine how exactly you are going to get this promotion instead. Visualize all the steps that you are going to take on the way to a dream career.

Practice regularly. Becoming a pro at visualization takes a lot of effort and time. Many starters struggle with forming and maintaining the imagery inside the mind. Therefore, you need to be focused while performing visualization. Also, keep in mind that practice is required to get results. Visualizing a task only once or twice, which is difficult to complete, will most probably not work.

9.11 Easy Techniques For Visualization

There are plenty of powerful techniques for visualization that you can use. Following are a few techniques that you can utilize to make things more interesting. Use these proven and powerful techniques for visualization to get what you want in your life.

Treasure mapping

As the name suggests, this powerful method forms a treasure map that exhibits the reality you look to create. It is a huge physical picture that shows how you envisage your future in intense detail. You can create the map by drawing it. You can use Photoshop as well or even magazine pictures. Your mind will picture the dreams again and again while you spend time forming the map. Once you are done with the map, it can be used to maintain an elevated level of motivation just by reminding yourself regularly of your ambitions and dreams.

Modified Memory Visualization

This method specializes in aiding you to cope with the past in a better way instead of emphasizing a craved state in the coming life. This technique helps you to modify memories of the past. Therefore, you can form a relatively positive echo of what took place in the past. The aim of this technique is not to undone things or change the past. It is also not aimed at suppressing your memories. The goal is instead to assist you in resolving the negative memories. It will allow you to unhand the resentment and pain you link with the memory. You can create a better future if you manage to alter the way you think regarding the past.

Visualizing During Meditation

If you understand meditation, you can utilize it by starting to visualize after you are meditating for some time. Once you have achieved an intense relaxation level, it will aid you in starting the visualization. You will get a much better connection as well, which assists **you to** emphasize more deeply on the visualization.

Conclusion

Human behavior is one of the most complicated things in this world. A lot of things play a vital role in the formation of human behavior, and it keeps evolving at all stages of human life. These behaviors shape our whole life and personality. Therefore, it is really important to understand the science of psychology in order to understand the actions of others as well as yourself. This will enable you to adapt better to your surroundings and excel in life. This knowledge will always keep you a step ahead of others around you. You can identify the negative thoughts and behaviors that hold you down in life. This will enable you to eliminate these behaviors from your life and provide you with a more stable mindset that is required for success in both work and in relationships in your life.

Book 2: How to Analyze People with Dark Psychology

A Speed Guide to Reading Human Personality Types by Analyzing Body Language. Understand Their Psychology, Their Intentions and Recognize Manipulators in Day to Day Life

Introduction

Reading and analyzing people and their behavior has been an interesting topic for decades. This book will give you insights on how you can read yourself and others; why do you behave the way you do? Or how some people always get want they want? For years & years, detectives, investigators know who is lying and who is telling the truth. All of this can be known without speaking any words; yes, you read that right. But, communication is more than just speaking. The way a person meets your eyes, talks, or uses their hands, their tone and pitch of voice convey more than they know. Facial expressions, micro-expressions can tell about your actual inner state of emotions. As per research, 65 to 93 percent of communication is done by gestures, expressions, postures without words. It means the way you speak, behave tells a lot about you, other than words.

Body language matters a lot, from day-to-day life to being interviewed for a job. Yes, you can get your dream job just by using positive body language. Furthermore, if you learn to read and analyze people, it will make your life easier; you will know who is trying to manipulate you, who is sincere, and who just wants something from you. Even if someone is saying one thing, and your instinct says otherwise, observe their body language; their body language will always tell the truth. With the correct body language, you can convince the other person what you want without using words. You can communicate your needs, wants and develop emotional awareness. Why you feel a certain way, or how can you protect yourself against people who just want to manipulate you.

After reading this book, you will benefit by reading and analyzing people, and you will know what their intentions are. You will learn to train yourself to get an advantage in any situation. Law enforcement, police officers, and detectives can read people's body language, expressions, and postures. Hence, they can resolve difficult situations and save innocent people, thanks to analyzing and reading people. You can also possess such abilities after reading this book.

Chapter 1: Analyzing Yourself & Others

Communication with words is straightforward. You can always tell people with words what you want. But, this can also be done without words, without speaking with gestures, stance, postures, and body language. Many experts and law enforcement officers can easily read people and analyze them with body language and behaviors. Such as, you must have experienced this before; if a person stomps their foot and rolls eyes, you would know what they are trying to convey. Although this kind of body language is obvious and much easier to read, unintentional expressions and body language are difficult to decipher.

1.1 Analyzing Other People's Behavior

The ability to understand and share the emotions of others is called empathy. One single word cannot describe the concept and understanding of empathy, as it is a vast brain network of multiple mechanisms. But we can try and sum this concept in three ways.

- The first is Affective empathy, and it is the capability to understand and share others' emotions. Many individuals who have a higher score on affective empathy will show an extreme reaction to watching a horror movie because they will feel fearful and can also feel others' emotions within themselves strongly. You might be one of those people who share other people's emotions rather than just feeling them.
- The other part is cognitive empathy, and it is the capability to understand other people's emotions in a better way, rather than feeling it in themselves. A good example is a psychologist who understands other people's emotions and guides them rather than living them.
- The last is emotional regulation. It is the ability to control and regulate your emotions according to the situation. Such as, doctors will regulate and control their emotions if they are dealing with a person who is about to die soon.

Every one of us feels the need to understand others and analyze other people's behavior. If we do not do that, we would never understand what the other person conveys. Relationships, partnerships will fall apart. Non-verbal communication plays an essential role in analyzing and understanding others with different levels of empathy. Different people may convey the same thing with different body language, but most of it is universal. Many people will tell you that psychologists do not have empathy, but this is not the case as you may know by now they possess cognitive empathy rather than affective empathy. On the other hand, psychopaths lack sympathy; they know they are the reason to make another suffering, they do not care about it.

But why do we feel the need to analyze others and ourselves?

If you are curious by nature, it will make you question other people's behavior and why they do and behave in a certain way, we all have been there questioning other people's motives. You may be one of those people who just cannot accept what you see; you know there is deeper reasoning to it all. But this does not mean questioning others will always get you an answer. You may end up with more questions than answers.

On the other hand, if you are not a curious person. You might not think too much about other people's behavior and only see what they show you and accept it for what it is.

If you are interested in human psychology, it is a greater possibility that your intentions are pure. For example, you do not want to hurt others by learning what makes them tick, or your intention is not to manipulate others after learning why they do the way they do things.

Many people, especially in the business environment, may be looking at people's psychology to get the upper hand to make them do what they want by manipulating. They may look at human psychology to control others and get what they want.

As you are reading this book, I would like to think you fall under the first category to explore further in this realm and get the answers to everyday questions.

Many of us have gotten hurt in our lives, either by partners, parents, friends, or family, and we question what they did a certain thing? To regulate our inner pain it is our right to ask questions and find answers to those difficult questions. If you cannot question that person straight away, the curiosity might come back harder than before. What this means, each one of us is curious to understand other people's intentions and behaviors.

The curiosity to analyze others can come from just experiencing an emotional reaction; it does not mean if you experienced a reaction and affected you greatly, you just do not understand what has caused these emotions in you. Such as in relationships and dating, you might feel obsessed with the other person, and you want to know what is it about them that is special to you? Or, after breakups, why is it so difficult for one person to move on and for another person is so difficult. In a way or another, we have asked these questions ourselves.

After breaking up, if someone cannot seem to move on, it can be because they avoid their emotions or are too caught up in another person's progress rather than theirs. It is possible, a person who feels stuck does not understand what is happening. This interest in another person's life will make them lose interest in their lives and avoid the pain they need to face to move on, and they are unintentionally keeping the pain at bay. Deep down, they do not want to face deep, sad emotions that will eventually set them free.

For understanding and analyzing others, it is essential to get out of your own mind and let go of the need to analyze others, and you must understand yourself and know why you are feeling a certain way or what you need. You need to analyze yourself. It will give you a deep understanding of who you are what you want? Many of us often forget to question ourselves. If you can understand yourself, there is a greater chance you will be able to understand another person's behavior and get the answers you need. Better communication always means a better connection, which is true when it comes to connecting with others.

For example, if one loses someone and cannot get over the loss, analyzing the situation arises. It means the person is not ready to let them go emotionally, keeping them stuck in analyzing themselves.

On the other hand, analyzing and understanding others is important to improve the quality of an ongoing relationship, to make it better. Understand what the other person is trying to convey and what their needs are without them speaking words. When you know your needs and emotions, you will be able to convey emotions in a simpler and better way.

Understanding and analyzing people are also important. It enables you to connect with your superiors better and get that promotion you have always wanted after understanding what is expected of you without speaking. When you finally master the art of reading and analyzing people, you will be able to instantly read other people's intentions and save yourself from harm's way.

If your partner finds it difficult to communicate, you must understand their emotional needs and find the right way to connect with them. The motives to analyze and understand others do not end here; the opportunities and situations are endless when reading and analyzing other people.

1.2 Why Analyze Others' Body Language?

In communication, it is important to understand the non-verbal part of the communication: body language. It is made up of gestures, postures, movements, and facial expressions. How you move your body and interact with others gives others a lot more information about yourself than the speaking part of the communication.

You must have heard the saying that actions speak louder than words. The way you move your body, the placement of your hands, eye movement tells a lot about you or vice versa. Even if someone does not want to talk about being vulnerable, their actions will clearly tell you. Different actions of body language, such as a genuine smile when you see someone after a long time, even without words, will let you know that they are happy to see you.

While talking to someone, a subtle tilt of the head, curious eyes, and certain hand gestures will let you know that they are interested in what you are saying. Or if someone is standing with closed arms and broad shoulders, downturned lips will let you know that they do not like what they hear. These are some obvious signs, but you can read others' body language even when they show nothing. You will be aware of their intentions, actions, and further actions towards you. You will correspond accordingly to their body language with your gestures, postures, and expressions to make you seem more approachable or closed off depending upon the situation.

1.3 The Importance of Body Language

In everyday life, job interviews, and careers, body language plays a huge role in conveying your actual and inner state of emotions and feelings. You can manipulate a situation for your good, such as in interviews, to convey confidence even if you do not feel that way. According to research, only 7% of the message is conveyed with words, and 93% is conveyed with nonverbal communication. This communication model is known as the Mehrabian Model, and it further states that body language is more crucial than the words and in which tone they are being said. This model of communication conveys attitudes and feelings.

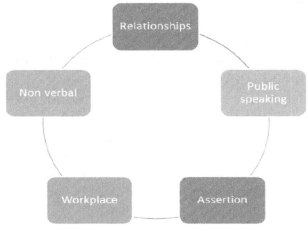

Workplace Accomplishment

In the corporate environment and workplace, body language, when used right, conveys a positive message. Positive body language helps people associate with their team leaders, making them feel comfortable and boost their energy and will to work. Even if you are on the other side of the team, being a member and displaying positive body language will earn you the respect and support of your colleagues. You will understand how to convey respect for your superiors, and conflict resolution will be easier if any. Assigning responsibilities will be more manageable, and connecting with others will be a breeze. When you are in a meeting, you can show reception, joy, interest with positive body language. You just have to make eye contact, lean forward, open your palms while talking and keep a gentle smile on your face. This will support your argument, build rapport with other team members, and build a friendly yet professional environment.

Successful Relationships

If used negatively, even unintentionally, negative body language can convey misunderstanding and wrong emotions than you are actually feeling. For example, in the first meeting, having a closed-off posture and showing little to no interest with body language can give an opposite message to the one you are trying to portray. Such as, if you want to tell others how you feel, you need to be in tune with yourself and know what you are portraying and conveying without words.

For instance, when you are in a good mood, your spouse teasing and joking with you is a good thing, but if he or she cannot read your body language when you are tired or not in a good mood, the same jokes, teasing can put a strain on the relationships and cause damage, so you need to know how to convey what you are actually feeling.

Public Speaking

Body language is the most important aspect of speaking, giving presentations, or public speaking. If you are giving a lecture or holding a seminar, your body language is defensive, closed off, or limited. It is possible, that the audience might not be able to connect with you or listen to you attentively. According to research, if such is a case, the audience will only understand 35 percent of the communication and miss the 65 percent due to lack of interest. Now you know why some teachers seemed more interesting in school than others. Thus, it is important to give the audience the correct gestures, postures, and facial expressions while conveying your message to connect with them as part of the group rather than just a speaker.

If you think body language is not important and words can make up for it, you will need a lot more talent to cover bad or negative body language. Negative or bad body language includes hiding behind the chair/desk, moving too much and too little while being on stage, turning away from the audience. Such gestures can negatively influence your office or school environment. Playing with fingers, biting nails, and being too aggressive are bad examples. If you are a good speaker, positive body language will only improve your bit. You will be able to connect more with the audience. You can convince people to buy something or to invest, or go on a date with you. It is important to pay attention to others and your body language for a powerful impact.

Body language is a form of communication that conveys what you do not wish to speak. It can tell without words. Such as if your friend is telling a great story, instead of cutting them mid-sentence and telling them to keep going, it is not a positive response. Instead, you can nod your head and lean forward a little to show interest and encourage them to keep going. Thus, it is necessary to learn to read body language to pick up on cues about what others wish to say. One more example is thanks; this word, when reading here, gives a positive response, but what if someone says thanks and rolls their eyes or says thanks in a harsh tone. What will you pick up from that experience? You would be more likely to believe that person was not happy with you even if they spoke the word thanks to showing positivity. You can see how powerful body language is and how it can impact and change the meaning of the conversation.

Although some parts of body language may vary from culture to culture, some beliefs will remain universal. Expressions of happiness, sadness, disgust, and surprise are universal gestures that do not need any words to show emotions. In this way, body language helps break the barriers, show uniformity, and build connections with people around you without verbal communication.

1.4 How to Analyze Others?

Here are some body language signals you should pay attention to when conversing with others or observing body language. What are you trying to tell others subconsciously with your body language?

- If you cross your arms, it says that you are feeling closed off, defensive and self-protective.
- If you are standing with hands on your hips, it will convey that you are in control or a sign of aggressiveness in certain situations.
- If you have clasped your hands behind the back, it tells that you are bored, angry, or anxious.
- Drumming fingers can also be a sign of boredom, even frustration or impatience.
- If you want to convey that you are not interested in talking or interacting, cross the legs. It will display you need privacy, but if you want to show that anyone can approach you or feel friendly, keep an open posture. Exposing the trunk of the body to

others will get a signal of willingness and openness. If you have a closed posture by hunching forward, with legs and arms closed. It indicates unfriendliness or hostility in some situations.

Some emotions can be seen and indicted via facial expressions such as (emotions & feelings):

- Happiness
- Fear
- Sadness
- Excitement
- Contempt
- Anger
- Surprise
- Disgust
- Desire
- Confusion

These emotions make us trustworthy and others to us; if you keep a neutral face rather than a slight smile on your face, chances are you are not inviting friends or people but pushing them away.

1.5 Importance of Analyzing People

When one cannot read or ask the other person directly what they are thinking, you can learn a lot about themselves with their body language or vice versa. Body language will tell you more truth about them than the words they will speak, even when their words do not match their actions.

You will meet many people in different situations in the world, and you cannot instantly ask every person what their intentions are with you. Analyzing people's behavior will come in handy. When you know others are analyzing or trying to read you, you can make a good first impression, as "the first impression is the last impression." Sitting behind your desk also conveys some vital information about your attitude towards the job/work. If you want to come across as a strong, confident individual, try to look people in the eye while talking, but do not forget to blink, and remember staring is rude. Shifty eyes, looking everywhere but not the eyes, will tell the other person you feel nervous or not confident.

Personal place plays an important role in body language, and personal space may vary between introverts and extroverts. It is necessary to respects others' personal space while talking and interacting with them.

Although there is a popular belief system that from our childhood, our body language is fixed. Keep in mind, we can always learn new things and copy others around us who are successful in a certain area of life. Again, it is not necessary we correctly perceive what others are trying to convey with body language. So, in important circumstances, one should keep their body language in mind what they are indicating with their body language, such as job interviews, important presentations, first dates & much more.

Do you come across as a confident and take charge person, but in reality, you are submissive? Or the opposite is true, and you should definitely take notice of your body language the next time interacting with people. Get to know yourself. Do you know if a certain situation presented itself, how would you react? What do you show when you are out with a group or how you behave alone?

Stand proud & tall

You must have heard the saying, stand tall, and the world will stand with you, but if you slouch, you slouch alone. Confidence is the key no matter the circumstances, and even if you are a shy person, you can fake it till you make it. Standing tall indicates you are open and confident. People who stand tall will more likely look interested in life, and people will often gravitate towards them. Seems like they are ready for the world. I am sure your parents or teachers must have told you to keep your head held high, there are some facts behind this statement. A high head shows confidence, good self-esteem, and interest in people around and the conversations.

Who are you more likely to approach a person who seems friendly, confident approachable, or someone who is slouching, seems angry, and disinterested? Yes, your answer is the first person, so if you want to seem approachable by your colleagues, employees try portraying positive body language.

Handshaking is yet another important part of body language, when done confidently and firmly, tells both sides are equally interested. You are more likely to shake hands with the other person before saying anything. Make sure it is firm and confident, with dry hands, especially in a professional setting. Master the art of good, firm handshakes. Make sure it seems natural rather than forced and awkward. Another person's handshake also tells about their confidence, trust, and interest in the meeting, professional or otherwise. Many people you will meet talk with their hands; you might be one of them even without releasing. This is widely accepted and mutual among many cultures and societies, or even universal. People tell stories with their hands, and you need to know what they are saying.

If their palm is open and upwards, it shows they accept other people and their ideas. Especially if you lead a team or group of sorts, you must show you accept every one of them. This gesture also shows honesty, being approachable, and openness. On the other hand, crossing your arms while dealing with a crowd shows skepticism, uninterest, and negativity.

How would you feel if you are talking with someone and they seem uninterested? The same goes for you, always keep this in mind and make an effort to participate more, and seem active and interested if the other person or the meeting is important to you. One trick is to say the other person's name while conversing with them to show interest. Such as you can tell your friend, "It must have been a difficult decision to make, Brittany; how are you doing now?" Ask more questions, nod your head, lean forward to show interest, and keep these gestures in mind. If the other person uses them on you, you will know they are interested in you or interested in the topic. Again, not everyone interested in you will be doing this, and the opposite is also true; learn to differentiate between manipulation and genuine interest. In a business meeting, you can say the other person's name and ask more questions but know when to stop talking. Let the body language talk for you and show confidence and commitment.

You can totally change your body language as per your environment, if you want to dominate the environment, or if you want to look unapproachable or approachable or friendly, or you just want to be the most interesting person in the room. All can be conveyed with body language.

Beware of unconscious body language. If you are unintentionally drumming your fingers during an important meeting, yawning, or slouching, chances are your boss might not take it too well and will not choose you for promotion. Improving your body language will make your chances of success higher than the rest. This not only suits professional language, but even in informal meetings, you can improve your body language and create positive changes. The importance of body language is not only limited to formal communication. Change your stance from slouching to bring confidence and better your self-esteem. As your partner, employees and friends will react positively to you and your attitudes. Your confidence will increase, and your motivation will also improve.

Gaining this knowledge will not go in vain, after speaking your words or even not speaking. Your gestures, handshakes, eye movement, closed, open body postures, the position of legs, feet will tell you a lot about yourself. If you are interacting with someone, and that person's feet are positioning towards you, there is a greater chance of interest in you and what you have to say. This tip is excellent for when you go on a first date, and you might be able to tell about their level of interest.

Hence, it is important to understand yourself and others if you are part of public speaking, or a teacher, or a person who works in a corporate environment. It is necessary to know your intentions and other people's intentions when interacting with each other. It is crucial to analyze yourself and others. You can instantly recognize another person's personality. You can manage and recognize difficult situations and plan your behavior and reaction accordingly. By gaining this information, you will be able to know other person's emotions. You can change a room's environment by being charismatic and confident. You can persuade people to your advantage, but do not forget to be ethical.

Chapter 2: Personality Types & Your Identity

If you want to read and analyze people, it is better to start with their nature and psychology and know what makes them unique, including you.

2.1 What Is Personality In Psychology?

The word Personality comes from persona, a Latin word, which means a theatrical mask that performers wear to show different roles or hide their identity. Our personalities work the same way, and we can show what we want and hide what we do not like.

In the simplest terms, personality is the blend of behaviors, feelings, and patterns of thoughts that a person projects or shows to the world that makes them unique. It is a fair belief that a person develops a personality. This personality sticks with them for the rest of your life, but do not forget if you find something about your personality that you do not like and know you can change it anytime in any way. A personality is the amalgamation of patterns, traits of emotions, thoughts, behaviors, and motivations. This mixture tells you to behave in a certain way, think, behave and feel. Thus, making you a completely different person than the rest. With time these patterns and traits impact your values, attitudes, expectations, and perception of the world and others.

The study of an individual's personality is known as Personality psychology and how it is different in different people and populations. This is not a new study; people have been doing it for more than 2000 years and have developed different theories for personality and traits. However, personality psychology has taken roots as people started questioning their and others' behaviors. As per research, in 2007, many researchers identified the questioned that gave birth to this discipline. Out of many questions, 20 questions were deemed more important than the rest, some of them are:

Who am I?

Who are you? How are we different?

Can I improve myself? How?

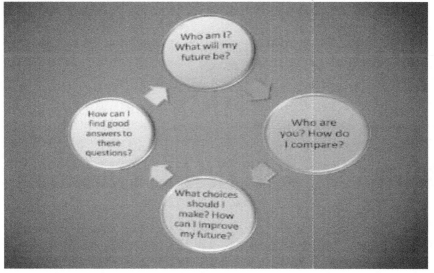

Many theorists, such as Jung, Alder, Horney, and Erikson, tried to expand Freud's theories, but they researched culture's effects on personality and social environment. The biological side of this discovery focused on genetics role and how it affects the brain's thinking. The other side of this discipline dealt with evolutionary theories, how each and every personality is different, and it all comes from natural selection.

Now you must be wondering what all of this has to do with your identity; when groups of personality are divided into categories, it makes up your identity. Your emotions, thought patterns, and traits play an essential role in discovering your personality. As well as some of the characteristics help decided about your personality.

Being consistent: the way you behave, there is a regulation and order to your habits and behaviors. If a situation presents itself, there is a higher chance you will behave in the same manner every time and only change your reaction to it when you intentionally do so.

Physiological & Psychological: it is believed that your personality is a product of your psychology, but research has put forward that your personality is subjected to biological needs and processes.

Actions & behaviors: your personality decides how you behave and how you react to the environment; certain behaviors are also influenced by your personality.

Various expressions: we cannot say that personality only influences our behaviors, but our relationships, interactions with others, feelings, and thoughts are also a product of our personality.

Different authentic personality tests help one to understand and process their unique preferences, strengths, and weakness. Some tests developed by many psychologists can even tell about your personality type. Whether one is extrovert, introvert, or a mixture and balance of both (ambivert). Many different valuations can tell you about your personality change over time, their responses to a particular situation. These tests can tell about what kind of job will suit you the most, or you may have had to take a personality test to see if you would fit in the corporate environment. Or, what kind of behavior does the company needs, and do you possess it? and much helpful stuff.

2.2 Jung's Theory of Personality

Carl Gustav Jung, a renowned psychiatrist, developed the Jung Typology and Jungian Psychology. It is, to this day, the most well-respected and well-established behavior and personality model. Carl Jung wrote a book, in 1921, on Psychological Types. He first introduced the personality theory in this book. With rational functions such as thinking (T) & feeling (F) and irrational function such as sensing (S) & intuition (N) that helped categorize individuals into 16 types of personality. He developed tests that, upon taking, will give you a type that is suitable for personal development, team building, assessment centers, coaching, and much more.

Jung divided people into 4 straightforward types, feeling (F), intuition (N), thinking (T), and sensing (S). Jung decided on these terms as they were already accepted and explored and easier to understand. According to him, as people understood these terms, there was a greater chance to further explore these terms in reality and see their effects. These terms were further divided into 2 major categories or fundamentals of life attitudes, introverts and extroverts. These categories were further divided when paired with extroverts (Se, Te, Ne, & Fe) and introverts (Fi, Si, Ti, & Ni).

According to his theory, each individual has a primary function and a prevailing life attitude. Based on that, he divided our personalities into 4 more straightforward psychological functions

- Judging contrasted with perceiving

- Sensation contrasted with intuition
- Extraversion contrasted with introversion
- Thinking contrasted with feeling

Different functions and life attitudes will be opposite to each other, to cause a distinction in different personalities.

As we discussed, someone who spends their energy outward or outside of themselves is extraverted. On the other hand, an introverted is someone who spends the energy inward, more towards the world inside. The type of thinking is based on practical thinking. Feelings, on the other hand, are based on what is in one's heart.

The intuitive type is based on indescribable internal feelings, and the sensation type is based on the outside's sensory stimulus. Your lifestyle and personality will be dominated by how you behave and how you perceive the world around you.

You will be delighted to know this theory of Carl Jung led to the idea of the Myers-Briggs Type personality indicator. As per Jung's theory, each of us is inclined to lead in either Introversion or Extraversion. Depending on how we would like to spend our energy, inward or outward, in extraversion, to the extremal world or towards our minds. This all beings with deciding on our essential type E (Extraversion) or I (Introversion). This will be your primary attitude type, and this one thing will influence your whole life and your attitude towards others and yourself.

2.3 Jung's 8 Personality Types

Carl Jung further developed 8 personality types, and these types will become the basis of Myer Briggs's different 16 personalities. Carl Jung 8 personalities are

- The type of Extraverted Thinking
- The type of Extraverted Feeling
- The type of Extraverted Sensing

- The type of Extraverted Intuition
- The type of Introverted Sensing
- The type of Introverted Thinking
- The type of Introverted Feeling
- The type of Introverted Intuition

This basic life attitude influences the development of functional types intuiting, thinking, sensing, and feeling. Furthermore, your personality has a dominant primary function, secondary functions, and lesser-known other functions and behaviors.

To understand this better, let us look at this example if we categorize someone as the type of introverted thinking. Their dominant attribute toward life is an introvert. Hence their foremost function be thinking, the secondary functions will be intuition and sensation, and the lowest function be feeling, which will be the less developed one, as thinking comes opposite to feel.

Now let us discuss the Carl Jung personality types in detail.

The type of thinking introvert will be a person who has pronounced intellectual activity, but at the same time, has difficulty connecting and interacting with others. When it comes to achieving their goals, they can be persistent and stubborn. These people see the world in a creative a subjective way. Their analysis comes from their internal knowledge. They also work in science fields. They are interesting, some see them as misfits, but they cause no harm.

The type of sentimental introvert is a person; who resembles private individuals who have difficulty interacting and creating social relationships with others. They can be emotional individuals, and melancholic These people like to remain silent and do not draw any attention towards themselves at all. Despite all this, they love to take care of others' needs, or at least quite aware of others' needs. They are always finding a hidden or a deep meaning to anything. They do not believe something is without any reason, and their internal feelings decide these reflections. They work well in the art fields

The type of feeling introvert is a person who is a musician or an artist. These people love to experience sensory experiences. They love to give meaning to texture, value, shapes, or color. These people work in the art field and base their feelings and beliefs on emotional feelings. They rely on internal experiences for inspiration.

The type of intuitive introvert person is the one who is extremely sensitive to any stimulus. These are the people who can predict what others are feeling, thinking, or what it is they want to do. They love to idealize, love to dream, and being imaginative in their own bubble. They find it difficult not to live in their imaginative world. These people based their findings on inner desire. They feel good about subjective ideas, and they make good religious figures or artists.

The type of thinking extrovert is the one who is like brainy people and acts based on their reasoning of things and circumstances. These people will only accept a fact when enough proof or evidence backs it up. They see the world in solid ideas and complex thinking, although these complex ideas do not come from them. You will find these people working in the science and mathematics field. They can be manipulative in certain situations, not so sensitive, and even be dictatorial.

The type of sentimental extrovert is the one who can establish social relationships and can understand others well. Although they are good at communicating their needs and wants, they find it difficult to separate from others and suffer when ignored. These people interpret the world and reality, keep an eye on current events, what and where it is happening, and other's opinions do not influence them. They work well as proofreaders or taste testers.

The type of feeling extrovert is the one, who assigns different magical qualities to things, has a weakness for objects, and unconsciously attributes qualities to objects. They would not like to be passionate about ideas. Instead, they are interested in how an idea took shape or came into being. These people based their findings on known and factual information. Their beliefs and social values on assessments. They are often politicians or work in the business field. Their pleasure comes above all things.

The type of intuitive extrovert is the one who is like an adventurer. They are much active and quite restless. These people need stimulus at all times. They are determined to archive their goals and quickly move to the next goal after achieving the first goal and forgetting about the last one. They have one flaw that they do not care much about others around them. These people support the meanings of things on factual things rather than feelings. They do not like to get in touch with their feelings, and which makes them an inventor.

2.4 Myers Briggs Personality Types

We all are familiar with Myers-Briggs Personality Types and may have taken a test or two being curious, which group we belong to. This theory of personality types is an advanced version of Carl Gustav Jung's psychological types of personalities. Jung thought of them as stereotypes, which serve as a reference to comprehend one's unique personality. In most basic terms, Myers Briggs deals with 4 main preferences. Potential & possibility as (N or intuition), or reality & facts as (S or sensing). One's lifestyle that goes with the flow as (P or perception), or a lifestyle that is well thought out and structured (J or judgment). Relationships & values as (F or feeling) or truth & logic as (T or thinking). Ideas & information as (I or introversion), or things & people as (E or extroversion).

This theory came into being by the daughter-mother duo of Isabel & Katharine Briggs Myers. If you have not taken the Myer Briggs test, you should take it and figure out which category you fall into.

Every type from 16 Myer Briggs personality type is listed by 4 letter code

- ISTJ - feels like The Inspector
- ISFJ - feels like The Protector
- ENFP - The Champion
- INFJ - feels like The Advocate
- ENTJ - The Commander
- ISTP - feels like The Crafter
- INFP - feels like The Mediator
- INTJ - feels like The Architect
- ENTP - The Debater
- ISFP - feels like The Artist
- INTP - feels like The Thinker

- ESFP - feels like The Performer
- ESTP - feels like The Persuader
- ESTJ - feels like The Director
- ESFJ - feels like The Caregiver
- ENFJ - The Giver

In this theory, for every pair, the preferred style dominates over the other. The middle group, which allows for the balance of 2 were allowed in Jung's theory. You will associate the letters as per your preference to get the Myers Briggs personality type. For instance, if you prefer I, N, F, and P, it will give you the personality of INFP. However, you can decide, then you will get 8 styles, in the very same manner that 70-95% people in the world are right-handed, yet they use both hands for the job.

Introversion & Extraversion: this pair deals with the direction and style of energy one spends. Such as if you prefer more of the outside world than the inside one, you like to deal with situations, people, and things you prefer extraversion. On the contrary, if you prefer to deal with beliefs, ideas, and information in the inner world, it will give you the personality of introversion.

Intuition & sensing: this side deals with your preference of things and information. If you like to deal with clarity, facts, tell people what you saw, or know some information, your preference will be sensing. On the other hand, if you prefer to deal with anticipation, look for what is not apparent, bring new possibilities, look for what is hidden, then your preference will be intuition. As you saw, the letter "I" has been reserved for introversion, so the letter "N" has been given to intuition.

Feeling & thinking: this side deals with your decision-making abilities. If you like to go for a detached approach with all facts and figures based on objective logic, your personality will be the thinking type. On the contrary, if you like to make decisions based on your values, such as who and what is important, your preference will be feeling.

Perception & judgment: this side deals with the lifestyle type you would like to live or currently to live. If you like a life that is well thought out, and you know what your next step is going to be, or your life is structured. Your type will be judging, which is different from judgmental. On the other hand, if you like to go with the flow, be flexible, and deal with things as they come, rather than planning for them, you are the perception type.

Now that you have known all about how personality comes in psychology, you can choose for yourself and see what category you fall into. But, remember, nothing is set in stone if you like to take your life in a particular direction by making some changes. You can always start today or tomorrow.

Chapter 3: Communication Styles & Their Importance

Verbal

- Use a strong, confident speaking voice.
- Use active listening.
- Avoid filler words.
- Avoid industry jargon when appropriate.

Nonverbal

Notice how your emotions feel physically.
Be intentional about your nonverbal communications.
Mimic nonverbal communications you find effective.

Visual

- Ask others before including visuals.
- Consider your audience.
- Only use visuals if they add value.
- Make them clear and easy-to-understand.

Written

- Strive for simplicity.
- Don't rely on tone.
- Take time to review your written communications.
- Keep a file of writing you find effective or enjoyable.

As we all communicate every day, we can see how important it is to understand all communication aspects. Another step in reading and analyzing people is understanding your and other person's communication style and the meaning behind their non-verbal communication. In general, communication can be classified into three groups.

- Verbal communication
- Non-verbal communication
- Paraverbal communication

3.1 Verbal Communication

When you use words to share information or talk with others, it is known as verbal communication. All written and spoken communication comes under this type. But, many people disagree and only include spoken communication in this type. This type of communication is all about what words are spoken and how the other person decides to decipher them. If your verbal skill is not good, it is a possibility that the other person will not be able to understand clearly, and consequently, the response would not be satisfying. This is not the only problem with verbal communication; when it comes to listening, it is also possible the listeners could not listen to spoken words clearly, or intercept them differently than spoken.

The success of verbal communication depends upon the speed, tone, pitch, clarity of words, quality of words, and body language. The response of verbal communication is instant since another person's brain receptor receives the message on the spot. The one who is speaking needs to make his tone high and audible, so everyone who is listening is getting the message instantly, the audience type, their clarity level should also be in the speaker's mind. Since verbal communication is more susceptible to error, it is necessary to express it in such a way that is clear and does not have a double meaning to it. No matter the situation, whether formal or informal, verbal communication applies to all and everyone.

Importance of verbal communication

To maintain any kind of relationship, let it be personal, business great verbal communication is required. It increases productivity, makes goals clear, removes errors, and lets the business or operation or relationship run smoothly.

Even if you are not a leader or a worker, your communication with your superior and colleagues matter a lot; your first impression or last makes or breaks the deal. Effective verbal communication is necessary when presenting your idea, project, or organization's motive, as well as employees' communication, should be good with each other. Good verbal communication is necessary for building an excellent relationship with suppliers, organizations, and customers.

Assertive and clear verbal communication is necessary for an environment of diverse backgrounds. It lowers the barriers, increases productivity, and lets people feel at ease with language and cultural differences. Many successful companies arrange verbal training programs to boost morale and increase productivity that proves beneficial for a long time.

For achieving a satisfactory level in relationships, it is necessary to make your verbal communication skill clear and adaptive. People feel secure when they can understand someone and can be understood. It increases the sharing of ideas, exchanging concepts, and thoughts. No matter what you plan to do with your life, let it be business, arts, finance, or writing. Your verbal communication skills need to be perfect or at least close to perfect, and you can always learn today how to make your verbal communication better.

Improving Your Verbal Communication skill

It will help to improve your verbal communication skills by lessening the chances of misunderstanding and enhancing clarity. You can try these techniques or tips to be better at verbal communication.

Before starting with verbal communication, be prepared: first and foremost, ask yourself what information is necessary to convey? What is the least ambiguous way to say it? Then think of the receiver; will they best understand it over the phone or face-to-face? Or which means of communication is available to you? Are they sufficient to convey clarity? Decide on what you would like to say; if there is a cultural or language difference, choose words or speech that is easily understandable. Otherwise, the message will be lost and your efforts. Use the correct vocabulary for the occasion.

Speak clearly, be mindful of your speech and your volume. Speaking much softly will make it difficult for the other person to understand you. Speaking too loudly will not convey the whole thing; try to find the right balance according to your audience, and that will not make them uncomfortable or put them to sleep.

Use a tone that will indicate your true attitude and feeling towards the situation and the people. Such as, your tone will convey anger, happiness, sadness, shock, or surprise, but do not try to scare your audience off if you are in anger; try to control your anger and be balanced instead.

Try to make eye contact; the other person or the audience will be more likely to understand you better when making polite eye contact while speaking.

Pause and look at your listener occasionally to get opinion or feedback; please ensure the person is listening and understanding what you are trying to communicate. Observe their facial expressions and body language; a simple nod from the listener would suffice.

Try to avoid distractions; if you are at a place with noise, if noise cannot be removed, make sure your listener understands you clearly. If something personal is to be said, try to find a quiet place. If you are talking on the phone, make sure the other person is not distracted and is willing to listen and communicate well.

These tips will help you to make your verbal communication better, if not perfect.

3.2 Non-Verbal Communication

This type of communication is the exchange of knowledge and information through your body language, including gestures, postures, facial expressions, body postures, and much more. Such as meeting someone for any formal or informal occasion, a polite smile on your face will convey openness, friendliness, and acceptance. This type of communication majorly depends on the distance between the people talking to each other and their body language. Whether someone realizes it or not, everyone is communicating non-verbally without even knowing. This form of communication depends on physical movements, analyzing and seeing the other person or vice versa.

According to research, a major portion of communication is non-verbal. Each and every day, we respond to non-verbal communication with eye gaze, facial expressions, voice tone, and postures. The way you shake another person's hand, style your hair tells a lot about you and how you interact with others. When paired with verbal communication, these cues and body language give additional information about the speaker's situation. According to research. 70-80% is nonverbal communication.

Researchers have grouped 7 dimensions of non-verbal communication, which is more than verbal communication.

- Body movements or kinesics include eye contact and facial expression.
- Vocals include timber, volume, rate of speech, and pitch.
- Your appearance
- The environment around us, physical objects, and artifacts that make the environment.
- Personal space to one another
- Haptics or language of touch

- Time

Types of Nonverbal Communication

Non-verbal communication can be divided into these types, and these types have further subtypes.

- Facial expressions
- Para-linguistic
- Gestures
- Body Language
- Eye contact
- Silence
- Space & Distance
- Visual Communication
- Personal Appearance
- Proximity
- Humor
- Posture & body orientation
- Touch
- Symbol

Here are some tips that will help you to convey your emotions and feeling non-verbally.

- Do not slouch; sit with a straight back on a chair or try leaning forward to show you are interested.
- When a serious conversation is happening, try not to smile or laugh. Keep your expressions neutral.
- Speak to convey your emotions in a balanced manner; this is crucial to punctuate the key point and show excitement, happiness, etc.
- A nod to let the speaker know you are listening and understanding.
- Observe other's body language to your talking.
- During the formal presentation, try to talk with your hands to show interest or develop an interest

in your audience. Keep a balance between verbal communication and gesturing with hands.

- In a meeting or interview, do not be engaged on your mobile or spend time drinking, eating, or anything that can distract you, and you will come across as unprofessional.
- Do not touch your hair and face with your hands.
- When the other person is speaking, do not disturb, let them finish talking, then you present your point.
- Keep your arms open, and closed body posture shows defensiveness.
- Do not drum your fingers; avoid shaking limbs or fidgeting much.
- Make polite eye contact, nod your head, do not do it too frequently.
- Your focus should be on the conversion.
- If you are being interviewed by a group, make sure to look all of them in the eye politely.
- Read and analyze people with nonverbal signals. If they seem confused, ask them a question and provide clarification, know when they have heard enough.
- Do not force a laugh to a joke or humor.
- Start with a firm handshake and polite smile to show you are interested, and your palms should be dry.
- Do not look at your mobile or clock; it shows you are disinterested.
- Always respect the other person's personal space while communicating.
- Try to stay calm in nervous situations, such as interviews, presentations. Do not deliver the lecture or your points in a monotone

Importance of non-verbal communication

Nonverbal communication can tell a lot about another person without using words. I am sure you have experienced this multiple times in your life that if someone nods their head yes, it means they understand what is being said to them. Or when you ask someone a question, instead of replying, they just shrug shoulders to let you they are as much as in the dark as you are.

Facial expressions play an important role in non-verbal communication, along with your body language, voice tone, pitch, lets people know how you feel at this moment without speaking a word. You must have asked your friend are you doing okay? You do not look alright. Even without their telling, their body language and facial expressions conveyed the message.

Nonverbal communication strengthens your relationship with others. People who are interested in each other will mirror each other's body language. This is one big clue you can use on the first date; if you want to know your partner is interested, you can look at how their body behaves. If they hold hands like you, smile at the same time. Turning to you completely while talking to you. These small gestures tell a lot about them, and it means they feel connected to you.

Nodding and smiling tell the other person you are interested and listening and vice versa. Hand gestures and movements will show they wish to contribute to the conversation. These indirect signs tell a lot about the other person or yourself.

With many signals, you can keep the flow of the conversation going. Nodding, smiling, closing of lips firmly to show remorse. Looking other people in the eyes to show you understand or you care, all without words.

Nonverbal communication eliminates the need to speak repeatedly to let the person know you are still interested in the conversation. It can even convey that you are done with the conversation or would like to move to another topic or if you want to ask questions. Or if the other person is telling the truth or lying.

Nonverbal communication helps when you do not have words if your employee has performed well instead of praising them with words. You can give them a pat on the back. Or a pat on the back from your superior will give you confidence.

Nonverbal communication with verbal communication will enhance the meaning of your words. Smiling while telling someone you loved their gift will be a source of confirmation for the other person.

3.3 Para Verbal Communication

Para verbal communication is a part of verbal communication that conveys our emotions and how we present ourselves if we are sad, confident, happy, frustrated, or confused. As per research, approximately 30 to 38% of communication is para verbal communication. Using para verbal communication with non-verbal communication and verbal will give the message a new tone, a different meaning, and different influence. If you emphasize a word, pitch, tone, or at speed one delivered the message. These different aspects highlight the use of Para verbal communication. Such as if you say, "I didn't say you eat my leftovers." If you emphasize each word, it will give a new meaning to the line you have just spoken.

"I didn't SAY you were stupid."

"I didn't say YOU were stupid."

"I didn't say you were STUPID."

Generally, three components of Para verbal communication are important. For make sure you include them in your conversation. Here are three components.

Pitch

This is the hearing quality of sound that varies from high to low. It is the key on which you will deliver your message. High pitch noises or messages are linked with distress or anxiety, and low pitch is associated with the authority and seriousness of the message or speaker. In some cases, a high pitch can also show happiness or friendliness. It indicates you have raised your voice many octaves to show excitement. A high pitch also shows one is terrified or scared. At the same time, a lower pitch will also show carelessness or peacefulness. Listeners are more likely to respond to your pitch of voice; they will assume either you feel a certain way if you speak in a certain pitch. It tells about your feeling, character, and attitude towards the discussion, meeting, conversation, or topic at hand.

Your pitch of voice will keep the other person engaged or vice versa. You are more likely to be engaged in a conversation where the speaker's pitch suits your ears or the mood you are in; the pitch also increases the other person's interest in the conversation. Using low pitch and high pitch with varying one another can make the message more interesting to deliver or to listen to.

Tone

The mixture of different pitches results in the tone of the message. Tone delivers and develops the mood and tells the other person where they should emphasize while listening. It is recommended to use more variations in voice to keep the listeners interested rather than delivering a message in a monotone. If you would not emphasize the important parts of the conversation, the other person might not understand the conversation or even try to understand. Your voice's tone will also decide the mood of the speech or discussion. As you transfer from one tone to another, it keeps the other person interesting in listening to you; what are you saying. Try to keep a balance between talking gently and raising your voice, according to the discussion environment.

Pace or Speed

The pace or speed of your voice will tell how fast or slow you are talking in the speech you are delivering or in a conversation. Your speed will set the mood, keep the other person interested or make them frustrated. We all know, if someone is talking at a rate where you cannot understand them, you are more likely to be pissed or frustrated than someone who is talking at a uniform or reasonable speed. Although, speaking at a low speed will not keep the other person interested in what you have to say. They will get bored and will try to distract themselves.

Speaking too fast will tell the audience or the other person that you are nervous or excited, depending upon your situation. The content (sad, happy, frustrated, or other) and tone will also affect your speech's speed. If you give an important presentation, speaking too fast will show anxiousness or nervousness. You need to practice more in those cases where you feel nervous; you involuntary will try to speak fast.

Use pauses will show you are saying things from experience rather than memory, and it will give your listener the time to process your speech. Speaking at a moderate pace will show you are confident in what you are saying and support the argument.

But in cases, one delivers a message with all forms of communication. Nonverbal communication is more to be believed than any other form of communication. Such as, if someone with angry eyes, clenched fists, high pitch voice tells you that they are fine, what would you believe as the truth?

No matter the conversation type, verbal, nonverbal, and Para verbal communication work together to deliver the intended message in all cases. If the message is not delivered properly, the listener will not understand the context of the situation. Inconsistency in messages or delivering style paired with wrong nonverbal communication can deliver the opposite message than intended and sabotage a relationship, whether professional or non-professional.

Chapter 4: Understanding & Reading Body Language

Non-verbal communication includes gestures, body language, paralanguage (tone, pitch & speed), visual activity, the study of eye movement (oculesics), the study of personal space (proxemics), the study of time with communication (chronemics), and communication with touch (haptics).

Reading and analyzing people with body language develops emotional and social development. According to research, even kids in early childhood need a kind touch to develop their feelings, like humans and animals. Body language speaks a lot, even when the person is not saying a word. As you know, 60% of communication happens non-verbally with body language. So, learning how to read body language is a treasured skill. From corporate environment to personal relationship, you can pick up cues on body language and steer the relationship in the needed direction. From eye movement to feet placement, everyone tells a story that only skilled people can read. With this information, you can change the situation to your advantage and know what the other person is thinking.

Body language has been divided into four dimensions, so make it easier to understand.

4.1 Kinesics Communication

In nonverbal communication, kinesics holds the most important position. It is concerned with nonverbal cues and their interpretation, linked with eye movement/ contact, gestures, body movement, facial expressions, and postures. This type is mainly referred to as body language.

The scientific study of body language is kinesics. Hence kinesics communication means communicating with body language, as it a form of nonverbal communication. However, all body language and non-verbal communication cannot be summed up with just kinesics communication. Body movements are made up of head, hand's movement, whole-body movement, postures, and gestures. These movements can highlight what a person is not saying, how they feel, their attitude, and their emotions.

In some cases, there is a possibility that body movement may not align with what a person is feeling or thinking. An expert observer will be able to tell such inconsistencies within feeling and body language and can probably detect the correct answer about the other person. Kinesics communication is the most well-known form of non-verbal communication. That gives a lot of information about one's thoughts, feelings, and personality.

Body movement includes many different subtypes, but some important ones are discussed here.

Gestures

It is communication through arms and body movement. The movements of the face, hands, arms, and other body parts can convey messages mixed with verbal communication or alone. Scolding someone with a pointy finger or just smiling to convey friendliness to strangers or others, all these things come under the gestures category.

Friesen and Ekman (the researchers) divided gestures into 5 categories:

Emblems, Illustrators, adaptors, regulators & body movement.

A brief introduction is here.

Emblems

Gestures, when used to replace a word's command, are called emblems. It is the direct substitute for words. Such as the gestures for comer here, okay, and the movement with hands to show you need a ride. Although some emblems are universal but keep in mind some may have entirely changed meaning in different cultures depending on different situations.

Illustrators

Gestures, when used to send a message paired with verbal communication, are known as illustrators. It helps in shaping what a person is saying. Such as if you do them repeatedly with your hand while speaking the term or saying "over there" while nodding your head and pointing with your hand.

Regulators

During the conversation, when one uses gestures to give opinion or feedback are known as regulators. Sounds as mmm, hmmm, uh-huh, or head-nodding to show interest or boredom are called regulators. It helps in changing the flow of conversation. These regulators let you or the other person show if they are interested or not interested in the conversation. These also help the other person to change their conversation or to keep the same flow as before. If regulators will not be present, it is difficult to decipher whether the other person is interested or you should change the topic or style of the presentation. Again, cultural differences can be present in these terms.

Adaptors

These are some non-verbal behaviors that fulfill the psychological need for emotions with physical gestures. It is the form of tension relievers and others. Some examples of adaptors are adjusting specs (in uncomfortable situations), scratching, biting nails (if nervous), which will represent a psychological need. Adaptors can be subconsciously happening, but you can control them in business situations or public places. Even if you start to do them in private and would like to quit, avoid doing them in private also. Adaptors often indicate the feeling of hostility or anxiety.

Body Posture & Movement

This is the movement of all body parts such as shoulders, legs, feet, and hands, voluntary or involuntary, that can even emphasize what is being said or contradicts it.

Your postures tell a lot about you, whether you want to or not. How you slouch, stand, and sit gives information about your self-image, status, gender, emotional state, feelings, and attitude. Such as, if someone is sitting with their head in their hands will show you are not feeling well, or something has upset you. Sitting with the feet on the desk will show one is feeling superior to others. If a person holds their body in a certain way, it tells a story about them. Open body postures can indicate domination and be at ease with yourself, and closed body postures can indicate that the person feels inferior to others or is uninterested. While copying another person's movement and postures shows liking and trust.

Facial signals

In all communications, unless on phones, you will look at other persons' faces, and a majority of the signals are sent with 90 muscles in the face. Facial expressions facilitate nonverbal communication with facial muscles that shows behavior, thoughts, and emotions. This is the primary way to let the other person know what is going on or show feedback on something the other person has said. Facial expressions depict your internal state of emotions. Tilting the head is a conversation for people who like to analyze and read people. The mouth conveys a lot when it is turned into a smile or pursed or turned downward.

Eye contact

Eye speaks a lot when communicating, and this is the first feature one sees when they look at you. Eyes break and rebuild connections many times. Forehead and eyebrows also help the facial expressions such as anger, fear, and surprise. One tool is eye contact to make sure the effective communication. Eye contact means you are inviting the other person to talk to you. Eye contact also means interest, attention, emotions, power. It influences other person's emotions, attitudes, and chances of interaction. Conveys your emotions and state of being and vice versa.

4.2 Oculesics Communication

It is a form of nonverbal communication that deals with eye behavior and its meaning. This comes under the category of kinesics, as it deciphers eye behavior, eye movement, gaze, and everything your eyes can convey. Oculesics is the study of pupil dilation and eye contact as communicating non-verbally. Making eye contact tells about your openness, interest, excitement. In some case, harsh or impolite eye contact or staring means the person is mad, hostile, or maybe even harm us. Lack of eye contact also gives information about being bored, not interested, or not paying attention. Cultural differences play a huge role in studying eye contact; Asian cultures might not support too much eye contact as it is considered rude. Instead, American culture asks you to make as much eye contact as to convey your message.

In general, these four factors are under consideration when studying eyes or eye gestures.

Eye Movement

You will notice, people often shield their eyes when they see something that makes them repulsed or when they feel scared. Shielding eyes is discomfort or signaling towards being uncomfortable. According to research, this is such a primal experience that blind children still shield their eyes if they eye something bad or loud. Another form of eye shielding is excessive blinking and eye rubbing. Eyelids that are lowered will suggest you are hurt or sad. Squinting shows you are suspicious of someone. If you raise your eyebrows, it means you want to show the likeness. If someone can't look you in the eyes, it means you intimidate them, or they feel insecure; darting eyes show they are looking for an escape from this conversation.

Intensity

Your iris (the colored part of the eye) controls your pupil size as well as the amount of light that can enter your eye. As per research, when a person looks at something they like, the light enters more into the eye to give yourself a better look at someone or something you like. This phenomenon is known as pupil dilation, and in the scientific term, you can call it "mydriasis." Pupil dilation is a sign of curiosity and interest, so the next time you are on a date, politely try to notice another person's pupil dilation, if you can. But do not make them uncomfortable. On the other hand, when you look at something you do not like, your pupil will constrict to block the entry of light somewhat, known as pupil restriction.

Direction

If you are conversing with someone and look directly in your eye, you should take it as a good sign. All of us have been there, where we like to show interest by making eye contact. Sometimes, people look away to process something or think of something.

Looking up shows thinking, but looking down is not a good sign as it can show disinterest or someone is guilty of something. If someone keeps looking down constantly, it shows they are submissive. Looking at the right side in the upper direction shows the individual is trying to think of something from their recent events. Looking on the left lateral side shows someone is trying to recall a song from their memory. If you want to know if a person is talking to themselves, they are more likely to look at their lower left as to where the devil is.

If someone is lying, they are more likely to look toward the right upper corner of their eyes, and this gesture could also indicate they are trying to make a visual image in their brain. One interesting fact you can try, when you close your eyes unconsciously, your eyeballs will move toward the lower part. You can try it right now. As more than 90% of our conversation is non-verbal, the practice of reading and analyzing is interesting and tells a lot about others' personalities and current emotions.

4.3 Haptics Communication

The word haptics is derived from the Greek word "haptikos" it emphasizes technological, biological, and medical applications of touching. This form of nonverbal communication is associated with proxemics communication that involves territory and space. This form of communication has a different meaning because of cultural differences.

Haptics communication is divided into 5 types

- Social or Polite
- Sexual or Arousal

- Friendship or Warmth
- Functional or Professional
- Love or Intimacy

Co-workers and managers need to understand the importance and effectiveness of touch. An encouraging pat on the back or a firm handshake. But also, Co-workers and managers need to be very cautious in situations where the touch would not be inappropriate or even misinterpreted. Hand on the shoulder may encourage one employee but can be taken out of context for others who are strict about their personal space or do not like to be touched. Handshake also shows an open way to show trust.

These rules change due to cultural differences, relationship status, and the context of the situation. Haptic communication is a form of nonverbal communication that delivers the message instantly. Some forms of haptics communication include tickle, handshake, embrace, slap, hit, pat, kick, kiss, hug, and massage, etc. Every form of touch conveys a message such as love, fear, pain, disgust, gratitude, encouragement, violence, anger, and sympathy. Furthermore, haptics communication is based on interpretations and environment as to who is on the other side of these haptics communications, the circumstances, when and why. This kind of communication has a purpose that differs from the environment, such as seeking, punishment, arousal, professionalism, greeting, guide, attention, sympathy, and friendship.

We all communicate through touch, no matter where we belong, and it enhances the development of social needs. Haptics communication can happen subconsciously or consciously, and it can give rise to negative or favorable conditions. Touching is essential, effective, and direct and can help babies and kids to feel safer; in the same manner, a fetus senses the world around. Haptics communication can carry the intensity and direction of your emotions and can vary from good to bad. This form of communication influences other people's psychological stimuli.

Voluntarily and Involuntarily, animals and humans show their curiosity and interaction with the environment via touch, and sometimes it's a survival instinct. Haptics communication gives your emotions and feelings a physical way to express themselves, creating bonds, comfort, rapport, intimacy, and peace.

Although haptics communication is a form of nonverbal communication, it is not always understood clearly. Haptics communication is often linked with eye movement. The benefits of nonverbal communication are endless. It can replace words, attraction, compliments and can help illiterate or physically challenged people. There are significantly fewer disadvantages except for cultural differences, misinterpreting, multi-channel, or missing information.

Touch is one of the sixth senses in humans; hence, no communication is happening, or touch is also lost, humans will feel depressed and feel abandoned. Haptics communication senses like emotional attachment, ritual contact, and arousal. But all these meanings depend upon the environment, others understanding of touch, and tolerance of strategic touch communication

Applications of Haptic Communications

Haptic communication is an advanced way to nurture and handle children intimately. Any verbal communication when paired with haptics will enhance its meaning, as it influences others' psychological needs. Haptics communication comes easily to physically or mentally challenged people and is an excellent way to communicate for people who can't speak properly.

In the field of artificial intelligence and robotics, haptics communication helps a lot. This kind of haptics communication has helped in medical procedures and sensors and has changed the gaming world.

4.4 Proxemics Communication

Proxemics communication is a part of non-verbal communication. It refers to attaining goals of communication with the use of personal space and others. Edward Hall discovered this concept of space and territory, and he presented this theory that animals mark their territory with physical posture and urination. As per research, based on Edward Hall's theory, the same way humans use material objects and personal space to define their territory.

Proxemics can be divided into four main dimensions

Body Territory: it is your personal bubble or personal space; this is space you need to maintain to feel comfortable.

Primary Territory: it is your home, living space, or the vehicle you travel in.

Secondary Territory: it is an organized space where some specific people can enter, and some defined rules are followed, such as a church, school, or office.

Public Territory: it is an open space; this is the place where everyone can come and go as they please, like shopping malls, parks, etc.

In some situations, territories can intersect. Such as, you can arrange a book club meeting at your house. The house is your primary space, but for other members, this is their secondary space. These territories are marked and work as a protection for you, your comfort, your possessions, and your interest from other people.

Proxemics & psychology

If you or another person comes across a proxemics behavior that is different from their own, it can trigger some form of anxiety, or it can activate your fight or flight reactions. According to research, if an animal feels threatened as someone invades their personal space, they either will attack the intruder or run away. This situation will repeat itself if someone tries to invade your personal space. Exceptions are always present, in such cases, where you willingly give up your personal space, such as in a crowded elevator or room full or part people. According to research, humans can set aside their discomfort for personal space when it comes to achieving goals in daily life, and one example would be going to your office, sacrificing your personal space in the process without being hostile for others. You ask why the change? According to research, it is because of making no eye contact when sacrificing personal space.

If you do not make eye contact with strangers while in close physical contact, it will cause you less anxiety. All of it comes down to eye contact in proxemics communications.

Culture Differences

In order to understand how different cultures communicate with each other nonverbally. Scientists have divided culture into 2 main categories: non-contact & contact. In a culture where contact is common, establishing interpersonal relations, psychical touch is allowed or even necessities such as in Turkey, French, Latin America, or Italy. In cultures with non-contact, touch is reserved for intimate associates only, such as Southeast Asia, Japan, Norway, etc.

Later on, Richard Lewis, a British linguist, advanced the idea of non-verbal communication style with cultural background into 3 styles. This classification of cultural styles is known as "The Lewis Model." You can also take a test to see which cultural communication style you prefer or are more inclined to. They are as following:

Linear active is a non-contact style, with decisiveness, logic, and coolness. The speakers with talk in facts will be direct or sometimes impatient. Examples can be given of Northern European cultures and The U.S.

The multi-active style is contact-based and is impulsive and warm. The speaker will make more likely to tell personal stories rather than facts. They will speak devotedly and express emotions. These people will show impatience and can interrupt conversations. Such as Greece, Mexico, and Brazil.

Reactive style is also based on non-contact style or non-confrontational or accommodating. The speaker will prefer diplomacy, decorum over emotion and facts. These people will be patient listeners, and their expressions and body language will be reserved, such as in China, Japan, and Vietnam.

Measuring Proxemics

Research has considered many factors when deciding and studying proxemics. The research's factors include environmental noise, physical distance, gender, measured posture, social status, conversation topic, body angle, eye contact, age, available space, and touch. These factors helped in deciding for types of distances humans create with one another.

These factors come into play in many, if not all, situations. Such as, if two women are talking quietly in a corner, is it because? Are they good friends? Or coworkers who are planning a birthday party for their colleague? Or, if a loud siren goes, are they strangers who want to walk away together from the siren towards safety? Hence, many variables play a great role when researching and looking for factors that are an integral part of communication styles. This kind of research decided which factors to include and others to exclude. With many researching seniors, research happens based on observation, and they plan the setting in natural or laboratory settings. In this observation, the distance at which one subject keeps from another is measured according to their condition. The instance of touching, their eye contact, and its duration is also observed. In some research, a method 'projection' is used. In this case, the proxemics behavior is stimulated, and dolls or other objects are used on a surface, according to the situation presented. Scientists then measure the distance according to the defined scale.

The Approaches to Theory of Proxemics

According to research, proxemics has developed 2 theories for proxemics on why humans use space while communicating.

One theory is Equilibrium Theory: According to this, Proxemics helps people in keeping the affairs as they are. As per research, factors of proxemics during communication will be adjusted by people to keep the relations at a reliable level of intimacy.

Another theory is Expectancy Violation Model: according to this, Proxemics helps humans to get what they desire. People who disrupt the three-dimensional space expectation of other people are more likely to get their communication goals. As per research disrupting gives you a better outcome than maintaining the affairs.

To make this easier for you, let us discuss proxemics in clear-cut distance terms. In the U.S, there are 4 types of distance that people use to have a face-to-face conversation.

These 4 types are:

The intimate distance ranges from 0 to 2 feet.
Personal distance ranges from 2 to 4 feet.
Social distance from 4 to 12 feet.
Public distance is more than 12 feet.
Let us discuss each category.

Intimate distance

This is the distance that is used for many private and intimate conversations. Science has given it a range of 0-2 feet in space for 2 individuals. An example of intimate distance communication will be 2 individuals hugging, standing with each other, holding hands. These two people have a certain level of closeness and comfort when it comes to one another. If someone approaches your intimate distance with whom you do not have a close relationship, it will cause you the anxiety of flight or fight response.

Personal distance

This is the distance that is used for conversing with friends and family.

However, the distance between individuals increases in personal distance, but still, it is pretty close in terms of intimacy; sometimes, this distance allows touching. This distance ranges from 2-4 feet. Likewise, with intimate distance, if someone you do not know comes in, your personal distance, uninvited, will make you discomfort or cause awkwardness.

Social distance

Social distance is the distance used in meeting new people, networking with groups of individuals, and business transactions. This distance ranges from 4-12 feet; it gives a wide distance, depending upon the situation. This circle of distance is used for acquaintances, students, or colleagues. These people in the social distance from each other do not interact with each other in physical contact. Different people will prefer a different range of distance in social distance. Some need more space for themselves with strangers than others. I am sure you have experienced many situations, as someone you do not know comes into your social space. If you are uncomfortable, you are more likely to go back and give yourself the space you need.

Public distance

Public distance is the distance that is more than 12 feet between 2 people. Such as, if someone is sitting on a bench in a park, you are more likely to sit as far as possible or far enough to make you both feel comfortable.

4.5 Reading Body Language & Signals

No matter your place, whether it be in the office or having fun with friends. Your and others' body language tells a lot about a person. According to research, body language makes up 60% of communication. As you are interested in reading and analyzing people, this is such a treasured talent. The way anyone moves their eyes to how they place their feet tells a lot about their personality. Let us discuss some important signals that will help you analyze and read people.

4.5.1 Facial Expressions

In most cases, if not all, your facial expressions always tell your true emotions and how you are feeling. As someone says, they feel fine, but their face will tell a different story.

Your face can show many emotions, from happiness, sadness, anger to disgust and contempt. As you meet someone, the expressions on their face let you know whether you can trust them or not, or what they are saying is true or a lie. According to research, if you want to know how to tell the difference, the most reliable and truthful facial expressions are a slight polite smile with a slight lift of the eyebrow. These expressions, when combined, show openness, confidence, and friendliness. According to scientists, these expressions are universal facial expressions and sadness, joy, fear, anger, and surprise.

Research also suggests we like to judge other people's intelligence on the facts of their expressions and faces. One study proved that people with prominent noses, narrow faces are more likely to be observed as intelligent than others. Individuals with joyful expressions, smiling faces were also observed as intelligent than people with angry emotions.

Blinking

Individuals are more likely to rapidly blink if they are under stress. Although there is an assumption, rapid blinking shows dishonesty, but this is not the case in most scenarios.

There are many interpretations of when someone is blinking fast, and they may be

- Not feeling comfortable
- Worried/afraid about something
- Working on a difficult problem

Pupil dilation

As we discussed before, the pupils will dilate when looking at something or someone positive or interesting; this can be because of romantic attraction, but not always. As per research, pupil dilation also happens in response to the arousal of the nervous system or if someone is afraid or angry. Likewise, if you look at something you do not like, the pupils will get smaller or contract.

Gaze direction

Someone's eyes will follow the person or a thing they are interested in. So, you can always look at someone's gaze to get information about their interest or current mood. I am sure it would have happened to you; when you are at a restaurant and the person you are talking to keeps looking at the buffet table, it is safe to say they are interested in that buffet more than this conversation at that moment. Such as, if you keep looking at the exit, you subconsciously may want to leave.

People also move their gaze to one side or look down when:

- Thinking of something problematic
- Remembering memories or try to recall information
- Working on a problem

Eye blocking

Eye blocking can manifest in different ways, such as

- Shielding eyes with hands
- Closing eyes to do a long blink
- Squinting
- Rubbing the eyes

It is in most cases, happens unconsciously, but it shows how you or the person performing them is feeling. It also means they feel distressed, irritated, or dealing with something they do not want to deal with. It also tells about reluctance and disagreement. Such as if your spouse suggests tomorrow is a chore day for you, your hands will go to the eyes, even before you realize it.

4.5.2 Lips

Smiles

Smiling is one of the expressions that does not need any decoding. But different smiles mean different things.

- When your or someone's mouth corner turns up, eyes narrow, wrinkles appear the corner of the eyes it is a genuine and true smile.
- When someone's eyes are not involved in smiling, it is an insincere smile and can happen because of discomfort.
- A partial smile or smirk, followed by a microexpression of contempt or displeasure, can mean dislike, uncertainty, or disdain.
- When one smiles and is followed by prolonged eye contact, head tilt, and a long glance, it can mean they are attracted to you.
- Narrowed and compressed lips can mean unease.
- Pursed lips mean disagreement or anger.
- Quivering lips mean sadness or fear
- Parted, slightly open lips, someone feels at ease, or they are relaxed.

4.5.3 The Legs, Feet & Arms

Legs and arms play an important role in conveying what you are feeling. When looking for analyzing and reading people, these postures of arms and legs are important.

- If you cross your arms, it means you are defensive.
- If someone crosses their legs away from you, it means they do not like you or do not feel comfortable with you.
- If someone expands their arms widely, they are trying to seem larger or commanding to others. On the other hand, crossing your arms shows you are trying not to get noticed or minimizing yourself.
- If someone is standing with their hands on hips, it shows they are in control or ready for the situation, or in some cases, it can be a sign of aggression.
- Hands behind the back show you are feeling bored, or you are angry, or you are anxious.
- Crossed legs can show you are closed off or need personal space or time.

People cross their arms when they are feeling

- Anxious
- Vulnerable
- Unconcerned or thinking of another perspective
- Crossing your arms also shows confidence, depending on the situation, if you cross your arms while leaning back and smiling. It shows you are comfortable or at ease; you feel in control of the situation and not vulnerable.

People use their arms to get a sense of protection. If someone does these behaviors:

- Putting their arm to make distance
- Holds something against their chest
- Uses one arm to hold the other behind their back
- Brings their arms to rest on a table or a chair

As these actions happen subconsciously, it means these people do not feel completely comfortable in the present situation and would like to protect or steady themselves in one way or another.

- The legs and feet show restlessness and nervousness by these gestures
- Jiggling leg
- Shifting from one foot to another
- Tapping with feet

Feet are the body part where one's personality leaks and tells what they are interested in. Feet are so obvious to read because people often try to school their facial expressions and control their upper body movement, so they do not pay much attention to their feet. You are in on this feet secret from now on, and you can read them easily or control the situation. These foot gestures can be applied to group situations or between two people who are talking.

If someone is sitting or standing, look at their feet' direction; what direction is that? This is where they would like to go.

Crossing your legs also suggests you are not willing to listen to what others say when crossed legs are paired with crossed arms.

If you are conversing with someone, notice the feet and their direction as they reveal a lot of information about a person.

If their feet are towards you, it means they like talking to you and hope to keep conversing with you. On the other hand, if their feet are pointing away from you, it means they are more likely to leave the conversation and do not want to engage in this conversation, regardless of how upper-body gesture points in your direction.

4.5.4 Hands

You would have seen most people while speaking will use their hands. This technique has some great advantages. According to research, you are more likely to answer someone quickly if they gesture with their hands while speaking. True, isn't it?

Look at people's hands either they are in pockets, or they are on head. This will tell you either they are nervous or being deceptive.

If someone unconsciously points towards someone, it tells a lot about their interest. For example, if your superior unconsciously points towards you in a meeting, it is a good sign as they may have an affinity towards you.

If someone is resting their head in hand and the elbow is on the table, it shows that they are listening well and want to focus.

Your **level of excitement** will depend on the other person's usage of hands while talking. When people feel close to you, they will gesture towards you without even realizing it.

When observing people, you should pay attention to these signs.

Outstretched hands with open palms unconscious show that the person is open.

If someone has their **fists clenched,** it tells they are frustrated or angry, especially if they are trying to suppress these emotions. With neutral expressions and clenched fists, you might want to stay away from this person.

Unconsciously touching their cheek, if someone does this, it is a sign that they think what you said is important or interesting. Such a good sign to look for when presenting a business idea or some important discussion with colleagues.

4.5.5 Body position

Someone's posture or the way they hold themselves is not easy to regulate, making it hard to read them. But, posture gives us important information about themselves.

If someone's posture is different from usual, it a tell-tale sign that something is not right.

These are some important gestures to look for

If someone is leaning back on the wall or supporting themselves means disinterest or boredom.

If you are talking with someone and they lean into the conversation or towards you, it suggests excitement or interest.

If someone is standing straight or stands with hands-on-hips, it shows confidence, excitement, or eagerness.

If someone is standing with their hand at their sides, it shows they are at ease and would listen and communicate and willingness to engage.

If you are resting your head in one hand, it shows interest; on the other hand, resting your head in both hands shows fatigue or boredom.

If someone tilts their body or head to one side, it shows they are focused and interested, and it can also show attraction when paired with other body language gestures.

If you have an open posture that is exposed or the trunk of your body is open, it shows you are willing, friendly, and open towards others.

If your body posture is closed, that means your arms, legs are crossed, or you are hunched forwards; it tells others, you are anxious, unwilling, or unfriendly.

4.5.6 Distance

As you are conversing with someone, their feeling for you or their mood can be guessed by how much distance they put between you and them. But bear in mind more people, in general, puts a lot of space between themselves and others, until or unless you know them and their habit of personal space, do not get to this conclusion instantly that they do not like you. Likewise, some people need less space to function and interact. They would like to sit close to you or stand close to you because that is how they are.

Keeping this information in mind, you can also look for these gestures and their meaning to analyze them further

If someone always sits close to you and stands close, it means they like your company.

If you go to stand near someone and take a step back, it means they would like to maintain distance, either emotional or physical, from you.

If someone sits close enough to you to touch or leans into you, it shows they are physically attracted towards you especially paired with the fact they have briefly touched you.

If someone puts up their arm or hand and takes a step back, it shows they would like a physical block or distance.

4.5.7 Mirroring

In an important conversation, you should look if the other person is mirroring you. It involves moving their body how you move yours, and this happens subconsciously.

Such as if you are discussing something with someone and place your one elbow on the table, wait ten seconds. If the other person also subconsciously places their elbow on the table, it means they are in tune with you. But, do not make it obvious as the mirror effect will go away.

You can also take a sip of your drink if anyone also drinks right after you while talking to sitting with you. There is a good chance as that person is trying to build a rapport with you.

4.5.8 Head movement

As you are speaking and the listener is nodding their head, at what speed they are nodding indicates their patience or otherwise. If the nodding is slow, it shows they want you to keep talking and is interested in what you have to say. If they are nodding fast, it means they would like you to stop talking so they can have their turn for talking instead of listening.

If someone tilts their head to one side during conversing or listening, it shows they are interested in what you have to say.

If you are tilting your head backward, it means either you are uncertain or suspicious of something. People points with their face or head towards people they are interested in or have an affinity for them.

You must have observed in a meeting, and you can see who is more powerful based on their body language who just wants to shy away and do not want to draw attention to themselves.

4.6 Body Language & Attraction

Body language can make a lot about your interest, attraction, or otherwise.

4.6.1 Women's body language & attraction

You can clearly tell when a woman is attracted to another person with their body language. As per research, the majority of the women are interested in men who show masculinity and dominance with their body language, as it triggers their fertility and submissiveness responses. You need to pay a little more attention, as you can easily miss these signals.

These are the signs where female shows interest and attraction through body language

Showing Fertility

Body language is related to sexual attraction, which in some ways is linked with fertility, even if your mind cannot comprehend these signals. If she is attracted to a man, she may keep her hair down, flip her hair to release pheromones, keep her wrist and hands visible to show she has soft skin.

Purse Behavior

The way a woman keeps and holds the purse tells a lot about her interest in a partner or if she is interested or attracted to that partner. How well she is willing to engage. If she is holding her purse against her body or clutching it in her lap, it means she is not interested in the partner she is talking to or feels uncomfortable. On the contrary, if she feels attracted or sees some potential in the other person, she will keep her purse away to interact better with that person; she may keep it on a different chair, table, or floor.

Do not forget your circumstances or the environment; if space is limited or security is limited, she may keep her purse with her for safety, but do not base your entire experience with someone of this gesture.

Lips Licking

A woman will often lick her lips if she is attracted to the person she is talking to. Often times it is a subconscious result of what she is feeling and may not be aware of doing it, but sometimes it can be intentional to show interest. Or she could just part her lips slightly and sweep the tongue over the lips to show interest, unintentionally. Or it can be a quick run of the tongue over her lips that if you are not paying attention, you might just miss this. Pair this gesture with eye contact, and it is a good sign that she is interested in you and sees potential with you.

Hip Thrust & lifted shoulder

If you want to know, a woman is interested in you or not, look for her posture if she is standing with one hip thrust out or with a lifted shoulder. There is a chance that she is interested in you. This, unintentionally, is an invitation for dating, love, or willingness to engage with you. Subconsciously hip-thrusting shows fertility and brings attention to her lower body. Lifted shoulders can show her chest. These gestures can be done consciously or subconsciously.

4.6.2 Men Body Language & Attraction

Men also show their attraction to women with body language. Men are more likely to show off in basic terms with their strength and masculinity if they are interested.

His body language and his intentions indicate a man's attraction. What he hopes to happen with you or a potential partner. Such as if he wants to remove space between you two or form an intimate relationship. To know his attraction for you, you can look for these signs and gestures.

Showing Fertility

Just like women, he will also show his fertility if he is attracted to a woman. You can notice his attraction in his posture. He will square his shoulders, stand up straight and plant his feet at more distance from each other. This is subconsciously his effort to show his masculinity and confidence. He will also show his palm and open his hands to show a willingness to engage with you. You do not have to be an expert in reading and analyzing people, and you can easily tell if a man is interested in you with his body language.

Raised Eyebrows

Men often raise their brows, and it has to mean something, right? Often men do this gesture when they are attracted to women or someone they are interested in romantically. It is a subconscious invitation from them to further engage with you. This eyebrow gesture happens quite quickly. The eyebrow goes up and down in a flash or a slow rise to the eyebrow. Men can do this intentionally or unintentionally, depending upon their intention and interest.

Parted Lips

Most men will not lick their lips or use the help of makeup to make them seem interesting or with smooth skin, but one thing you can look for is slightly parted lips when making eye contact with the opposite sex. When this happens, it means he is attracted to the opposite sex or the person he is looking at. This gesture can be brief or prolonged when paired with other gestures of attraction.

Flared Nostrils

If a man flares his nostrils, it is an open gesture and a true sign that man is extremely interested and attracted to the person he is engaging with. Open expressions and flared nostrils can tell he is ready for what the other person will discuss, or he is open to what is happening between him and the other person. This is also a sign of sexual or physical attraction. This gesture happens subconsciously and cannot be turned into a manipulation technique that they want to show something different from what they are feeling.

Hands-On Hips

If you are talking to a man, you being the opposite sex, and he places his hands at his hips, there is a great chance that he is attracted to you. This gesture can happen subconsciously or consciously, as he presents an open view to you, an invitation of sorts, and he wants to focus on you as he finds you interesting and attractive. He may thrust his hip or pelvis as showing his sense of fertility or pheromones. One more sign you can see in his posture is he will sit with an open leg posture. Like he is at ease with himself in your company and interested in you.

4.6.3 Gender Neutral Body Language with Attraction

If you do not identify your gender as male or female, no need to worry. Some attraction gestures can be seen in body language that is very common, regardless of who you are.

If you are out and about with someone you are interested in and see them exhibiting these signs. You can make sure they are interested in you, or they are enjoying your company.

Being available

Being available is a gesture that everyone can relate to, no matter if man or woman. If someone is interested in you, they will make sure that you know they are available and want to get to know you better. This can be in their body language, such as with open arms and uncrossed legs. They will look at your face rather than down or your feet, or their phone or down at the table. In short, they will pay attention to you, in what you have to say, or they will mirror your body language even for brief seconds.

Smiling

People smile because they think of you as an attractive or interesting person. This is also a great way to show your availability and show interest. Subconsciously we feel we look great when smiling; this is true and wants to convey that we are attracted to another person we are feeling attracted to. Some people smile forcefully, I am sure you will spot that, but genuine smiles are obvious (we have covered genuine smiles in facial expressions). A genuine smile is a smile that their eyes will seem like smiling also. If a person is genuinely smiling at you, you are sure to return the smile. It means they are interested in you.

Leaning In

If you are talking with someone and they lean into you, it is a strong sign of attraction. Leaning in is a good sign in a group situation if you are talking to someone and they lean towards you specifically. It means they are attracted to you and want to pay more attention to you than others. The degree to which they lean towards you tells exactly how much they are attracted to you.

Tilting the Head

If someone tilts their head while talking with you, this is a sure sign of interest. Tilting the head means they are paying attention to what you are saying, and they are willing to listen to you and are open to engaging with you. In most cases, women do the head tilting gesture more than others, but you can observe in others also.

Blushing or flushed

I am sure you have encountered this before, either in yourself or others. You will blush when you meet someone attractive or someone you are interested in. If the attraction is growing, blood will rush towards the face, feeling like you are flushed or seeing it on the other person's face. This cannot be faked or controlled by another person, as it happens naturally, so it is one of the true signs of someone's attraction towards you. Lips become redder, and eyes become bright and white.

Increased heart rate

Increased heart rate is one of the responses that cannot be faked, and it is an unconscious reaction to the surroundings or one's mental state of being. It naturally happens if someone is attracted to you, their heart rate will increase. I am sure you will not measure someone's pulse on a date or while conversing, but warm hands and quick breaths are a sign of attraction with increased heart rate.

Feet's direction

In the human body, you can manipulate certain body parts to tell others how you are feeling. As we have discussed before, if someone is interested in you, they will unconsciously point their feet towards you. Although it may not tell if that person is attracted towards you, it is a sure sign of interest, or at least you are holding their attention at this very moment.

Eye Contact

If you are in a group or one-on-one conversation, if a person is making eye contact with you, it means they are interested in you. It means they are paying you attention, or you have successfully held their interest. Extended eye contact means they are attracted to you. But on the contrary, if someone does not look you in the eye or keeps looking everywhere else while talking. You might want to invest your time in someone else, as they are showing no interest.

Facing Forward

As the case with feet, the same happens with the rest of the body. If someone is interested in you and talking with you, and their full-body is facing you. It means they are interested in you. To make themselves at ease, they may tilt slightly to one side, but their body will be facing you most, as they will be deep in the conversation with you or willing to engage.

Pace or speed

If you want to know about someone's mood, at what speed they shift, the body tells a lot about them. If someone is moving purposely and slowly, it means they are showing confidence and attraction towards you. If their shifting is jerky and fast, it shows they are nervous and are not confident in the present scenario.

4.7 Differences in Body Language

According to research, our brain places non-verbal communication above verbal communication. As we discussed before if you give someone mixed signals or they give you mixed signals, such as they say they care about you and do not give you any attention. While conversing with them, your brain will believe they do not care about you. Your brain prefers nonverbal cues.

But, if you tend to travel or not, you should keep in mind that many nonverbal cues or somebody's language gestures are not universal. Every part of the world interrupts some gestures differently than others.

Cultural differences

Cultural differences play an important part in influencing body language and how to read it.

Eye contact duration's length

For how long you can look into the other person's eyes has culturally different meanings. Different cultures accept different duration, or some prefer no eye contact at all. Such as in Western cultures, if you are talking with someone and looking them in the eye simultaneously, it shows honesty and trustworthiness. In the middle eastern community, eye contact symbolizes strong interest. In African cultures, to show humbleness, you should lower your eyes. In Japan, prolonged eye contact is thought of as being rude, threatening, or even disrespectful, and the same is the case in China; extended eye contact comes across as being rude.

But if you belong to the western culture, you might be thinking, how long is too much? As per research, the comfortable time is three seconds for comfortable eye contact, and it will take 3.3 seconds to make the other person uncomfortable.

Nodding your head can have different meanings depending upon the culture. Nodding means agreeing to what the other person is saying. Or, nodding also means just listening.

Eye contact can have different meanings depending upon the culture. Many cultures, such as eastern cultures, do not allow extended eye contact as they lower their eyes to show respect; in western cultures, eye contact means socializing, interest and openness.

Developmental differences

Neurodiverse and neurotypical people (individuals on the spectrum or else) understand body language differently from others. Such as, one fidget when they feel bored or cannot focus on a thing. Instead, neurotypical people will fidget to self-soothe, increase their focusing ability, to calm their nerves.

In some cases, mentally challenged people may not be able to understand a gesture and do it differently. Such as autistic people may not be able to understand your body language or recognize your facial expressions.

Psychological differences

Mental health may interfere with someone's ability to understand or impact their body language. If someone has social anxiety, they will find it difficult to look you in the eye, although they may be interested in you. There are people, who do not wish to touch others or vice versa, so they may not hug you or shake hands. You should be aware of the other person's boundaries before making assumptions about them.

Chapter 5: Unmasking The Lies

Lying, we all do it from time to time. Some do it more than others and with reasons to manipulate than harmful lying. According to research, on average, a person tells 1 or 2 lies each day. Good news for you, as per research, you can spot the signs of lying. Common human behaviors include harmless lying and some form of deception.

In 2004, a survey was conducted on how much people actually lie, and according to research, as a result of that survey, 96 percent of people confessed to lying at least once each day.

According to a body language expert, to look for signs of lying in people, you need to know their regular behavior in day-to-day life. But, what if you do not know them? In that case, look at how they respond to a basic question such as where did you grow up? How is their voice while answering this harmless question, the movement of their eyes?

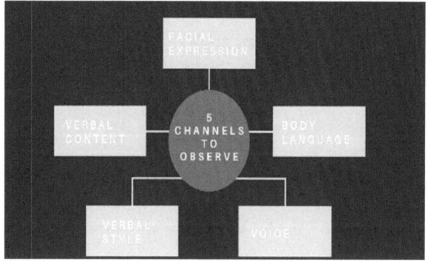

In 2009, One study surveyed and published the result of thousands of adults who participated. 60 percent of them said they do not lie at all. But researchers found only 5 percent of the subjects told half of the lies. According to this research, it was suggested, although even not a majority tell lies, there is a small number of people present who lie constantly.

Yes, I know; you must be thinking the number was higher before. All of the lies people tell are often white lies, harmless lies. These lies are told to make someone feel good or protect their feeling, such as you do not look fat, or you are rocking that shirt. In other cases, some people lie black lies, such as they lie when investigated about a crime involving or lying on their resume to get the job or lying to make someone feel bad about themselves.

According to one study conducted in a controlled lab environment, 54 percent of the people detected lies accurately, but this number is not good enough as the outside environment as 50 percent is a chance those people detected correctly. Behavioral differences are present between lying and telling the truth, but people still find it difficult to detect the lies. But this does not mean you can never tell when someone is lying; research has progressed so much that they have shared some secrets on how you can tell when someone is lying. Although not everything can be just as simple as when someone lies, their nose goes bigger, but there are some helpful pointers to tell about detecting lies. Like in most cases, the one thing that will help detect if someone is lying is to trust your gut instinct. It may not give you a 100 percent result, but you will learn to trust yourself. With time you will become better at it and can also help others. This way is more accessible for people you already know, and you can detect their behavioral and vocal changes if they tell something differently or behaving in a different manner while talking to you.

Here are some red flags to notice if someone is lying to you. According to research, these are things or behavioral changes people will go through if they are deceptive. If people are being

- Offer fewer details or being vague, not telling the whole thing
- Repeat your questions before answering
- Do not speak the whole sentences; rather, speak in fragments
- Play with their hair while talking
- Press their fingers to lips
- Start fidgeting too much or start averting eyes
- When their story is questioned, they fail to go small details
- Do not look you in the eye
- Much obvious is they start to sweat

5.1 Types of Lying

Science has divided liars into four categories
- Delusional Liars
- Deceitful liars
- Demoralized liars
- Duplicitous liars

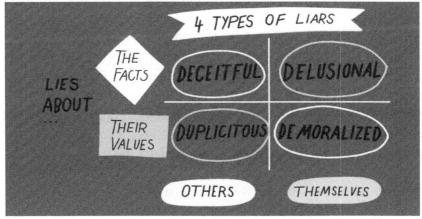

5.1.1 Deceitful Liars

These are the people who lie to other people about facts. This is prototypical lying, that is, lying about facts. We have done it one time or another. According to research, children learn to lie from age 3, and it is believed to be healthy development of the brain.

If someone wants to lie, they need to look at things from other people's perspectives. According to psychologists, it is called the theory of the mind. It means if someone has to tell a lie, and they will have to understand the other person's perspective, get in their head, give them what they want to listen to. If lying about facts and these lies are not white lies or harmless, they can cause severe damage to relationships and be for personal gain, and if they keep lying like this, it is possible society will just shut them out and start excluding them. People label habitual liars as undependable and untrustworthy and will give them a bad reputation that does not easily go away, especially in this age and time. Opinions about one person like this spread like wildfire, and they can go out of business or in total loss.

5.1.2 Duplicitous Liars

These are people who lie to other people about their values. Often people lie about their values just like the facts. When someone says they are dedicated to doing something or being someone a certain way, their actions do not match their values. The word duplicitous is derived from a Latin word that means double or twofold. Hence these types of people are known as two-faced. This type of lying is more harmful to lying than lying about specific facts. When one presents themselves as faithful or loving or has no emotional baggage, they tell the other person they are ready and faithful in love. So, they start counting on you, but if you do not perform like that, it means they lied about who they are.

5.1.3 Delusional Liars

These are the people who lie to themselves about facts. This lying not only involves one is lying to others but when one lies to themselves. If you have talked to someone, rudely you might convince yourself that it was not rude. Or, you did not take more than others or more than your fair share, or you worked hard than everyone else.

Many of us do this all the time; as per science, healthy psychological working requires some sort of self-deception. Although, all levels of self-deception are not equal and have different impacts. There is a clear difference between lying that does not harm others or yourself or some self-deception that can cause manic depression or can be because of schizophrenia-like mental illness. Different categories of lying wear down different levels of our integrity.

5.1.4 Demoralized Liars

These are liars who lie to themselves about their values. People lie to themselves about values for some of the same reasons as to why they lie to themselves about facts. These people would like to think of themselves as more trustworthy, diligent, or honest than they actually are. They will tell you they keep promises, always tell the truth, work hard, but their actions will not match their words.

This kind of lying is similar to lying about facts, but in the meantime, these people are lying to themselves and do not confront themselves, sacrificing their integrity.

Here are some other forms of lying that law enforcement describes after inductive interviewing some people, as an interview is a form of communication but with purpose.

- In this case, where the liars completely deny any allegation or claims, it is called a lie of denial. Now, how to differentiate if they are actually telling the truth and minimization, eliminating factors, asking them about small details can give you the actual truth.
- In this case, where the liars make up a story to tell a lie, it is known as a lie of fabrication.
- In this case, no lie is told, but important details are often left out purposefully, and you need to watch

out for non-verbal cues of lying to catch them. This type of lying is called a lie of omission.

- In this case, significant detail is told in a way to minimize it and its impact or significance on the situation to evade the implications; this type of lying is known as the lie of minimization
- In this case, the liars overstate the details as the liar sees best to achieve his purpose; this type of lying is known as the lie of embellishment
- In this case, the liars do not tell the truth. Instead, he makes up another lie to cover up the past lies, which is known as the lie of reference
- In this case, the liar deceives the other person in a way to get them distracted so they will not ask relevant questions, known as the lie of evasion
- In this case, the liar changes the definition of a term to defend his actions, which is known as a lie of the definition
- In this case, the liar will tell double, triple, or many negatives to cause ambiguity in the details, known as the lie of double negative
- In this case, the liars very precisely tell a true technical statement to mislead the other person, but it hides the truth, which is known as a lie of distortion

5.2 White Lies & Black Lies

Universally, black lies for personal gain or otherwise are thought of as being atrocious. On the other hand, white lies are told as everyday communication to please your spouse and are seen as innocent. But can white lies have no bad parts or adverse consequences? This question often comes to mind.

Every day people tell a lot of lies, black and white. In both types of deception, one person or a group of people is deceived. But as we know, there is much difference in both kinds of deception. Black lies or deception is done to get something after deceiving someone for personal gain.

In simple terms, the deceivers take advantage of someone's habits, lifestyle, job, or more to get personal gain. One example would be when you buy a car, the budget is limited, and you need a car. The car dealer will take advantage of your need and limited budget. He might lie about an inferior car or tell the price wrong to take more money or sell something cheap that will cause you more problems down the road. But, when it comes to white lies, the scenario is different. This kind of lying has nothing to do with someone's personal gain. Such as if your spouse has gotten a new shirt, and they asked how does it look? You can see they like this shirt, and you say yes, it looks good. Although deep down you do not like this shirt, you do not want to make them upset by telling the truth.

The deception in both cases described above has different needs and motives; that is why black lies are equal to deception. But at the same time, sometimes white lies can also have some motive or cause some harm. People may use white lies to manipulate relationships or cause different relations. Although the person has nothing to gain from such interactions. But in the case of public questionnaires, health surveys and eyewitness investigation can cause more harm than necessary by damaging the effectiveness of someone's hard work

5.2.1 Why Is Deception So Common?

The act of deception is common and prevalent not only in humans but only in animals. According to research, apes take food from weaker apes, and sometimes they use deception to gain that food.

One experiment was performed; apes were given 2 tunnels to reach food, one opaque and the other see-through to get to the food. Apes often used the opaque tunnel to get to the food, so other apes would not notice any movement from them. Such a scenario is known as exploitative deception because the ape deliberately misleads other apes to get food for himself. But why did they do it? Or, why people deceive others to get a personal benefit?

As per research, one important aspect of deceiving others is to think they will get caught or not? If chances of getting caught are low, they are more likely to deceive others, such as tax paying. This behavior is known as rational because if chances of being detected increase, the gain will also reduce. For example, in the previous example, if the car dealers told the truth about the care being not fully functional, you will not pay the extremely high price, and his chances of getting personal gain will go down. Most people believe that it will be more beneficial if they deceive the other person for higher gain than lower gain. But, according to psychological research, this is not the case. People will deceive others no matter how high or low the gain is.

People still find it charming to deceive for higher gain than for lower gains, but this whole thing also costs the deceiver their psychological health. Yes, you read that right. People who deceive will have internal discomfort, and they feel they are going against their will or beliefs or value, which is true in most cases, if not all. The guilt is present, but people push it away, and it depends on the extent of the lie.

But this psychological cost that one experiences while deceiving is related to what that person thinks of themselves. If someone thinks highly of themselves and thinks they are an honest person. They find it difficult to deceive others and tell big lies. But, if they tell someone more minor lies that are just tweaked enough, this lie will go with their image in mind. According to one study, making a reasonable justification for one's lie is an essential part of deceiving others. If the deceiver cannot come up with a reasonable justification, it increases their chances of not deceiving.

5.3 Body Cues of Lying

According to a body language expert & behavioral analyst, the first step to observe someone lying is first to observe their normal behavior, such as it is normal for them to over-share or make up characters for themselves. Also, bear in mind some people can be so skilled at lying that they can get away with lying even if you are a body language expert. So, do not feel bad about yourself if you could not tell if someone is lying; their other body language behavior will tell you to stay away from them. It is not one factor or one body part that can tell if someone is lying; it is a combination of different gestures, postures, and micro-expressions.

With these facts in mind, let us go through some signs that suggest that the other person is lying

- Individuals who are lying will shift their head quickly

Such as if you are conversing with someone and ask them a question that you think they will lie about. They will make a sudden head movement it suggests that they are lying. It can be in the form of a head jerk, or retraced back, tilted suddenly, or cocked the head. In most cases, you can expect this movement right before they are about to lie.

- According to an expert on investigating and deception investigating trainers, if someone is lying, they will talk with their hands after telling a lie, not when they speak or before the conversation.

The psychology behind this move is that their mind is busy making a story, replacing facts, omitting truths, or thinking if their story adds up piece by piece, so they will not use much of their hands. So, if this person was telling the truth, their gestures could be during the conversation or after. If lying, they use their hands afterward.

According to a study, the Michigan University in 2015 observed 120 clips of court cases to recognize when someone was lying and when someone was telling the truth to get a better understanding of these two common situations. As a result of that study, they concluded people who were lying gesture with both hands compared to those telling the truth. 40 percent of the lying clips had people who gestured with 2 of their hands when only 25 percent of the clips which were telling the truth gestured with both hands.

They concluded that when someone is lying, they will face the palms of their hands away from the other person. It is a nonverbal unconscious sign that tells they are not giving the full truth, or hiding emotions, or telling lies. Some examples would be putting their hands under the table or putting them in their pockets.

- People who lie often start fidgeting or itching.

According to a body language expert & psychologist, if someone is lying, they will start shuffling their feet, rock their body back and forth, tilt or move their head to the side; these are the signs of deception. Science backs these signs up by explaining how the ANS (autonomic nervous system) regulates bodily functions. As people lie or become nervous, ANS can make people tingle or itch as a result of lying or being nervous, which leads to fidgeting of the body. One psychology professor from UCLA reached a conclusion when people are lying, and they will show grooming behaviors like playing with hair, fidget, etc. This shuffling feet behavior is when our brain tells us to run, but if we are lying, we can be trapped in a situation where we do not want to tell the truth, so we lie instead.

5.4 Facial Cues of Lying

You can notice these signs of lying on someone's face.

The eyes

It is strongly believed; eyes are the window to the soul, and this path may lead you straight to truth or lies. According to one study in 58 countries came to this conclusion as people were lying, they averted their gaze. If you can see more white in someone's eyes, that means they are afraid of giving an honest answer to your questions. They start darting their eyes to other points.

In some cases, habitual liars will not avert their eyes, but still, you can track their movement of pupils if they constrict, or expands or slightly avert from the point as they were at the beginning of the conversation and slightly avert when asked that sensitive question, indicate deception or lying.

According to another research, when someone is lying, their eyes will behave in 2 manners: they will look away at important detail or stare at one point elsewhere, or move their eyes like they are thinking about something. Another research at UCLA backed this fact up when someone is lying, and they may briefly look away. One study at the Michigan University in 2015 found people who lie are more likely to stare than those who tell the truth, such as 70 percent of the people in the video clips, who were lying, stared directly at the other person. One study in 2012 found people who lie often look or stare at one specific point or in one direction. Although you might not be able to tell someone is lying right away, but with practice, you can get better at it.

Some people, when lying, also tend to blink really slow or very fast, depending upon the deviation from their usual behavior. When asked if they are cheating in a relationship, or when asked about something wrong in the office place, gaze aversion, pupil movement tells a lot about deception.

The mouth

According to a researcher, when people hide their lips in their mouth to the point where you cannot even see them or disappear completely can be a sign that this person is hiding emotions, facts, or telling a lie. So, watch out for that. In UCLA, one study conducted that lying people will purse their lips when asked the question. It could be a reflex reaction, or it means they do not wish to engage in this conversation, as they are being asked questions, so instead, they lie.

According to a researcher, trained behavior analyst, most of these signs should be observed in non-confrontational talking and eliminate the triggers and stressors that can cause interference with your observation. If you observe your close friends, spouse, or kids, you need to form a baseline behavior with them and observe naturally without any triggers. You can easily catch people in lies when you know how they normally act; like with some people, they will always look you in the eye, others will never try to look you in the eye, so eliminate normal behavior. Deviation from baseline would only help you recognize out of the ordinary, and then you can differentiate if this reaction is because of lying or some other stress.

Other clues

Their complexion will change. You might have noticed that sometimes someone goes 'white as a ghost' when telling saying something. According to an expert, this can be a sign of lying, that the blood rushes out of their face.

They might be sweating. According to research, as the nervous system triggers in response to lying, it can cause sweating face, especially around the mouth, upper lip, chin, and forehead. Or have completely dry eyes or mouth. They can be blinking excessively, swallow hard, bite their lips or lick too much their lips.

People who work really hard to be the good guy are the ones you should be aware of as they can easily deceive you or manipulate you to get what they want.

According to an expert, if someone you asked a question has waited more than 5 seconds to reply. It is a good chance that they are lying.

According to research, as people lie and purse their lips, their smiles can seem forced or tense. On the other hand, when someone tells the truth, their eyes will shine when they smile, and crow's feet will occur.

- Either they will fidget or stand very still
- Liars tend to repeat phrases or words
- Liars will cover their mouth or touch their mouth while telling lies.

5.5 Tone of Voice

Their voice will become high-pitched. According to research, when people are lying or nervous, the vocal cord's muscles tighten up (this is a reflexive action to stress). Hence these people sound like high-pitch. Their voice may break or creak in one's voice. Throat clearing happens to open their muscles, which sometimes means being deceptive or dishonest. Their voice volume can change suddenly. According to science, if someone is lying and they want to defend their fact in a loud voice, it can be a sign of lying. But, again, you need to remember some people may talk loud in normal life, so do not forget to look for signs that deviate from baseline behavior.

On the other hand, a convincing, softer tone implies this person is not telling the whole story, instead of holding some important information.

5.6 Content of Speech

According to an expert, if someone is lying, they may try to convince you of their lie a little too much, some phrases such as 'I will tell you the truth' or 'I want to be straightforward with you.' They are trying a little too much.

They will use other words, such as um, like, uh, or more, in their speech. According to one piece of research, when people start talking with more vocal fill, it is a sign of deception. Liars use these words to get themselves more time to think about what they would like to say next in order to make a foolproof story.

Some phrases such as "I do not remember," 'I think so,' "I cannot say with certainty." These are the phrases used by someone who is lying.

Many people are not liars from birth. So, although some become habitual liars, they still sometimes slip the truths. Such as when someone starts telling a story then changes the details, it means one of them is the truth. For example, when someone says I was late because I went to dinner, wait, I was working late that night. As details do not match up, you may be interacting with a liar.

Matching Words & Body Language

In some cultures, if not all, shaking your head from side to side means no; shaking your head up and down means yes. According to one expert, if someone shakes their head, yes, but tells that they did not do it, it means their head is subconsciously moving and telling the truth. Head movement, nonverbal movement are more reliable than words.

During the research, they watched many clips of high-status investigation cases, and these criminals were lying while shaking their heads yes. You can also search for some of these examples on the internet.

5.7 Micro-Expressions & Facial Action Coding System (FACS)

Dr. Ekman is a psychologist and professor at the UC (University of California), encouraged the development of FACS (Facial Action Coding System). This was the only tool to look for facial movement accurately. In 1978, Dr. Ekman and W. Friesen developed this tool, and a third author J. Hagar revised this tool in 2003.

Dr. Ekman used to work with patients in clinical cases who lied about their emotional state. He further advanced his research on patients who said they were not depressed, but later, these patients committed suicide due to depression. When he studied those tapes of patients again and again, and in slow motion, he stumbled upon micro-expressions of the face, which showed the patient's negative feelings, those feeling they hid from the rest of the world, but for few seconds, the truth slipped out.

Micro-facial expressions occur within a second or even less than a second. These genuine emotions that slip out for a brief second tell about a person's actual emotional state. According to other research, it proved that no matter how well a person is hiding their emotions, their face will crack for a brief second leaking their true feelings.

In research, some people were asked to lie in the coming interview; later, when reviewing those clips, their true emotions leaked out on their faces, from $1/5^{th}$ to $1/25^{th}$ of a second. As per research, our faces have an extremely complex muscular structure compared to the rest of the body. Many of these muscles you can control, but some are not in your control, and these muscles only activate or show your true emotion; you cannot manipulate them, no matter how hard you try.

Some **macro expressions** are normal or obvious expressions on the face.

They last for half a second to four seconds. They match what is being said and the content of the discussion.

Micro-expressions can be missed altogether or often not judges correctly. These expressions only last for half a second. These expressions show the hidden true emotions.

When someone is lying, their face has 2 messages one is what they want to show, and the other is what they want to hide, as these hidden emotions can be seen as micro facials for half a second.

Micro-expressions are the most important indications of what someone is hiding, but Dr. Ekman also said not to take them out of context as these micro-expressions should be paired with the rest of the body language. Here are some micro expressions you can read on someone's face that give away their true emotions.

Fear Micro expression

- Eyebrows will be drawn together and raised, such as in a flat line
- Wrinkles will appear in the middle of brows, not across the forehead
- The lower eyelid is drawn up, and the upper eyelid will be elevated
- Eyes will be showing the upper white part rather than the lower white part
- The mouth will be open, lips slightly tensed or drawn back or stretched

If someone is lying according to FACS, you can look for these micro-expressions on their face for half a second, be very careful and alert to spot these micro-expressions.

Anger Micro expression

- Eyebrows will be drawn together and lowered
- Lines (vertical) will appear in between the brows
- The lower eyelid will be tense
- Nostrils will be dilated
- The lower jaw will project out
- Eyes will be bulging or in a hard stare
- Lips will be pushed together firmly; corners of lips will be down. If that person is shouting, then the mouth will be in square shape

When expressing anger, all 3 areas of the body will be involved.

Benefits of reading Micro Expressions

As you learn to read micro-expressions, it will increase your emotional awareness. These micro-facial expressions are universal, unlike gestures or other non-verbal communication. These emotions depict someone's actual state of emotions in a moment.

Someone's face is the best option to look for their genuine emotions, and you do not have to put yourself in a difficult position to look somewhere else. No matter what personal background, culture, or language they use, the facial expressions will be the same everywhere you go.

All you need is practice, do not be discouraged if you find looking for these clues difficult. Microexpressions help to detect deception. No matter how hard someone tried, true emotions will escape on their face. Although for a brief second but it will be there.

5.8 Trust Your Instincts

Sometimes even when all the signs point in the right direction, but your gut says otherwise, you should listen to it or at least investigate the manner more. Your gut might be accurate than any lie-detecting you are trying to do. According to one research, 72 people participated and were asked to watch the videos of mock suspects. Although some of the suspects stole 100 dollars from a place and others did not, but all suspects were asked to tell they had not stolen the money. The watchers were asked to choose the people based on their gut instincts who had taken the money. 48 percent of the truth-tellers were recognized by people based on their gut reaction.

You should always give priority to your gut. If, though, it will make the wrong decision one or two times, but eventually, you will start trusting your gut more.

Chapter 6: Dark psychology & Analyzing Others

Dark psychology is somewhat prevalent in our everyday life; some use it without even knowing, or others use it to manipulate others. As you learn about dark psychology, you will know if someone is trying to use it on you or if you are unintentionally using it on others. You can use it within ethical limits to change the circumstances in your favor.

6.1 What Is Dark Psychology?

Dark psychology is the science and art of mind control and manipulates others. In dark psychology, people use coercion, motivation, manipulation, and persuasion to get what they want from others. Dark psychology is based on The Dark Triad. Based on the dark triad, criminologists and psychologists recognize the criminal behavior in others but also problematic partnerships.

These traits make up the dark triad

- Narcissism: this has the traits of egotism, grandiosity, and lacks empathy.
- Machiavellianism: people who suffer from Machiavellianism manipulate, exploit and deceive others with no sense of remorse.

- Psychopathy: although these people are charming and friendly, but they lack any remorse, have no empathy for others, and use selfishness

Dark psychology is mainly used to manipulate others, and any dark psychologist can either be an abuser, trickster, criminal, or manipulator, or all of these charterers. Dark psychology can have many motives, from personal defense to personal gain to get revenger from others.

Although no one wants to manipulate others, I am sure you would not want to be manipulated. But often, manipulation or dark psychology happens either from your side or the other person's side.

You can look for dark psychology in your office, advertisement, sales techniques, internet ads, or other people's behavior. People who have children, I am sure they have experienced manipulation and dark persuasion many times. This is also true; this coercion and manipulation often come from an individual you love and trust. Here are some of the techniques used by people in dark psychology.

- Lying: people will tell you untrue events, exaggerate stories, tell half-truths, and outright lie.
- LOVE FLOODING: it can manifest as Complimenting you unnecessarily, affection, or buttering you up to ask you for a favor
- Withdrawal: the other person can give you the silent treatment or avoid you completely to make you do something for their gain
- Love denial: they will withhold affection or attention from you
- REVERSE PSYCHOLOGY: telling you one thing or doing something with the purpose to make you do the exact opposite of what you want

- Choice controlling: they will give you some options to choose from, portraying themselves as the good guy, in reality distracting you from the actual choice you want to make
- Semantic Manipulation: this one is tricky when someone uses words or phrases that have an ordinary meaning, but the manipulator later will tell you that meant something else when they said those words

6.2 Who Uses Dark Psychology?

These people often use dark psychology for their personal gain.

Narcissists

Individuals who are clinically narcissist (diagnosed) often think of themselves as superior to others. They also need others to agree with them or with their sense of superiority. They like to be adored even when wrong. They use manipulation, persuasion to an extreme extent to get what they want.

Politicians

Some officials will use dark persuasion or coercion to get people's vote and not do anything later; they want to win and get it in the limelight.

Sociopaths

Individuals who are diagnosed as sociopaths are impulsive, charming, and often intelligent. They lack the ability to feel remorse and have no emotionality. They use dark psychology to make shallow relationships to get benefits from them and take advantage of others.

Lawyers

Some lawyers just want to win their case rather than doing the morally right thing. They will use dark persuasion to manipulate others and get the result they want.

Salesperson

Many individuals become so fixated on getting their number high in sales that they forget to keep moral values in mind. Instead, they use manipulation, dark tactics to persuade people to buy things that are low quality.

Speakers & selfish people

Some public speakers use manipulation to amplify listeners' emotions, get themselves a following, and sell more of their products while pretending sales numbers do not affect them.

Anyone who has a personal gain to achieve can go to any limit and exploit anyone and get their goals at other people's expense. They do not care who they have hurt in the process.

6.3 Why People Use Dark Psychology?

Now that you have gotten a brief introduction to dark psychology and who uses it. But the next question is, why would someone use dark psychology?

Some instances of someone using dark psychology because of these reasons.

To get power over others: When someone feels powerless, they want others to give them what they want. They portray themselves as someone who had nothing, and others will feel guilty and pity them; thus, they can get what they have asked for.

To manipulate the conversation: when someone wants to manipulate a meeting, get some advantage from taking the meeting in a certain direction, they use dark tactics to persuade people

Social climber: when someone exaggerates their efforts to make them look like they did so much than what they did and get more credit than others. Such as someone in a group project who does nothing but manipulate others and get the credit.

Selfishness: when a woman tells other women to be strong and not give in so easily, then does the opposite of this and makes things easier for herself.

Here are few scenarios of dark psychology you can find in your daily life:

6.3.1 Dark Psychology in Relationships

People use dark psychology in relationships to get more power and control over their partners. Although there is less struggle in relationships than dating, sometimes less is more when people want to control their partner's behavior. If someone controls the other partner, they are more likely to live their life as before with added benefits by using dark tactics.

When one partner is insecure or does not feel good about themselves, they use dark tactics, manipulation, coercion, and more to control others. Sometimes these tactics include abuse, jealous controlling, and shaming them for their physical and psychological needs. So, they will think of themselves as not good enough; hence, becoming insecure will not seek validation elsewhere as they have no confidence in themselves.

Some obvious signs of dark psychology in relationships are

- Creating drama to make highs and lows of emotions
- Devaluation
- Silent treatment
- Conditioning with love, punishment, and reward
- Instilling fear of abandonment to make them depend only on you, rather than themselves

If someone is dating a dark psychologist, they date without regard to other person's boundaries; their mental and psychical wellbeing does not matter to them.

The Male Dark Psychologist

If you are dealing with a dark male psychologist, they will show these signs:

Will string the other person along without the relationship; he will lie about his true intentions, saying he is a committed person, but will provide commitment later, just not now.

He often cheats as he does not regard your emotional needs.

He manipulates her into thinking he is what, she wants and portrays himself as the man she likes rather than showing who he is, leading to having similar goals and getting to the relationship part quickly.

The Female Dark Psychologist

Not only men but females are also manipulating others to get what they want.

She will portray herself as the ultimate prize, and she will reject the guy, make him chase her, show low to no interest. Despite all these, she wants him to still commit to her and invest in her, serve her.

Many women will manipulate their partner's physical needs and control this aspect of the relationship to get what she wants. By giving the silent treatment, withholding love and affection to get him to do what she likes, she will not give him equal rights but wants to keep him around.

6.3.2 Dark Psychology in Groups

In many groups, dark psychology is used, but how can you tell?

Leaders will gain more power and control, and followers will give up their independence and power, sacrifice their goals to work for the group. One good thing is to research before joining and getting in a group. Check their reputation and ask around. Many toxic groups who use dark psychology will want to strip their followers of their individuality and power. So members will be more dependent on the group leaders and seek their approval.

Here are some of the dark psychological tricks that groups will show, and you can recognize them:

They will make your problems look bigger than they are, so you will think you alone cannot handle these and need much more power as they have to solve them.

They will mock other opinions and make them as they hold no value or are wrong. They will tell you how uninformed others are and manipulate you into thinking; the only solution to your problems is this group, as others do not know anything about these problems.

These groups will encourage you not to listen to other groups as they do not have the whole information, mislead you, or manipulate you. (yes, I know, they might say that).

They will portray others as the big enemy that cannot be fought alone. Hence, people will want to seek help from a more significant entity such as their group.

If someone is holding onto their individuality and their right beliefs. This will not benefit the group, so the group will want you to sacrifice your interest, your beliefs leave your individuality out of the door so they can gain more power as a whole

6.3.3 Dark Psychology in Seduction

You can see dark psychology in seduction, as it is most common. People will bond with you based on leverages, traumatic bonding, and making emotional wounds to make you depend on them, rather than connecting with you with affection or mature love. If you have gone through emotional or physical abuse, the dark psychologist will try to connect with you based on these traumas, known as traumatic bonding. The individual will make you go through fighting and making upcycles, so keep you confused, known as an emotional roller coaster.

The dark psychologist will keep you secretes, blackmail you, get you to do what they want. Meanwhile, give you physical satisfaction and portraying themselves as the good guy while keeping you for their satisfaction.

When they want something from you, they will make you feel special before asking a favor, shower you with gifts, dinners, and endless attention. Then, ask you for something, how you feel in debt to them, and do what they have asked of you. Especially when they know, you would say no. This is psychopaths' preferred method of manipulation.

All of these dark traits one can naturally possess as it is in their psychological built-up. Or, people learn these manipulative techniques from others to get what they want. Or it is a possibility you might have been using these tricks unintentionally. If this is the case, you can always change your approach to a situation and start over.

6.4 Dark Psychological & Emotional Manipulation

Dark psychological manipulation happens with the purpose of gaining power or control or create emotional exploitation, mental falsification, and gain advantages at the expense of others.

Dark manipulation is different from healthy social influence. Healthily, the social influence is a part of the relationship where give and take are equal, and nobody feels exploited. On the other hand, dark emotional manipulation happens when only one person feels in control and all the benefits are at the other person's expense. Who feels exploited? More importantly, they will not know what is happening?

Here are the signs you should look out for if you suspect dark emotional manipulation around you.

When you go to meet someone who you suspect might emotionally manipulate you. They will ask you to meet them at a place where they will feel in control. It can be their car, their office, or their home. So, they will feel more in control and are more familiar with their environment, thus have more control over the situation. But, on the other hand, you will not be prepared at all.

They will let you speak first to look at what you want and how they can manipulate you. This is a classic dark psychological trick for a salesperson. They will let you speak to tell them what you are looking for. They get a general idea of your weakness, your behavior, and your thinking. So, they can exploit your needs by presenting you with something that is out of your budget and more in their pocket but has all you need.

They will manipulate the facts, will lie to you. Make excuses. Blame others for how they behave. Do not tell you the whole truth. Strategically withhold information to exploit you but coming across as someone who wants good for you and will not harm you.

Some people will psychologically manipulate you by telling you they know more than you or are an expert in that field or intellectually bully you. They may exploit you by telling wrong facts, statistics, and other information you know little about. This can happen in meetings, sales, or some other professional discussions or social settings. They do this so that they can have power over you or control over the situation, and you will listen to them more easily and do not question them. Most manipulators might just do get a sense of superiority.

Some manipulators to get a sense of superiority or exploit you will make you busy in procedures, laws, paperwork, roadblocks, and much more to maintain their power and make your life difficult while benefiting from this.

You must have experienced this one; if you argue with someone or discuss, they will raise their voice and manipulate you. The psychology behind is the dark manipulator thinks if they raise their voice, they will come across as authoritative, and you give up your side of the argument and get what they want, or they want you to be afraid of asking your fair share. This voice-raising can be paired with showing negative emotions and strong negative body language.

Some dark manipulators would like to put the other person off balance and get a psychological benefit by negatively surprising the other person.

This can happen in certain situations where the manipulator will cancel last minute, so you will have to do all the work. Or withhold information then deliver at a wrong time so through you off balance but displaying themselves as the guy who did not do anything wrong.

These dark psychological tricks are many, and you need to trust your intuition and other person's behavior to know and keep yourself safe.

Chapter 7: Purpose of Using Dark Psychology

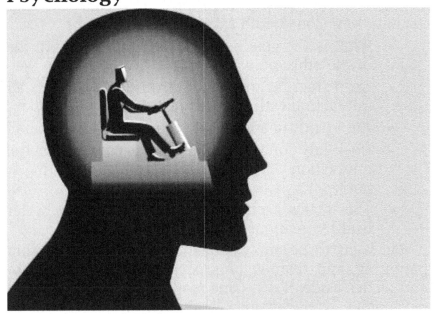

We all can use dark psychology; yes, it is tempting to get what you want and when you want it. But using dark psychology has some severe implications for others; they may not recover from being exploited, used, or manipulated.

What makes someone an easy target of manipulation?

If someone's caretaker were manipulative in childhood or grew up in a dysfunctional family where they had to take care of themselves. Or their parents used them to satisfy their beliefs or needs. Thus, as a child, that person had to hide what they needed in order not to cause drama or receive any abuse. That person will soon become someone who has no sense of confidence in them, or they do not think so highly of themselves. So, any type of attention is good, even if it is terrible.

Unless that person breaks the cycle and recognizes manipulation for what it is, they will be trapped in this cycle of dark manipulation.

So, before you use dark psychology on someone, you must think of your intentions and others' mental state. Whether these tactics are for your gain or their exploitation? You should ask yourself.

- What is the goal here? Am I benefiting from this or the other person?
- Do I feel at peace with myself when I am interacting with this person?
- Am I truthful and honest to myself? And others?
- Does any long-term interaction come from this interaction? Or the other person is benefiting or not?
- The tactics I am using, does it lead to a better, healthy relationship with the other person?

If you want to be successful in your work, leadership, parenting, and relationships, keep the dark persuasion and tactics aside. If someone realizes you are using dark psychology, you can lose credibility, trust, and more. Doing dark psychology wrong can lead to long-term failure, poor relationships, and no trust in you.

7.1 Why Would You Feel The Need To Manipulate Others?

Even if you are a good person, you sometimes feel the need to manipulate others and get what you want. It does not have to be something malicious, but the need is still there.

You may find it hard to communicate your needs directly. Or you grew up in a house where manipulation was the only way to get what you wanted. As per research, many people who use dark manipulation were not taught how to communicate. This need for simple communication will be embedded in dark manipulation.

If someone has a narcissistic personality, they may try to avoid connection by manipulating others and treating them as a means instead of building friendship.

If someone has a fear of abandonment, they may use manipulation out of fear in situations where they feel out of control, such as fighting in relationships or breakup talk.

They believe that if you want to get to your goal, everything else is justified by any means necessary

Many use dark psychologies in defensiveness to show they are still the good guy. As they have low self-esteem, they always want others to see them in good light, and they can go to an extreme extent for this.

In some cases, when people are manipulating others to give themselves and others positive value. Such as to create a peaceful environment in the office, they will be cheerful with others, even if they do not feel like this.

These financial advertising, marketing, or political parties are devoted to manipulating others for their gain. Change people's minds get them to buy things they do not need or want.

Dark Manipulators' Mindset

The most practiced and mindful dark manipulators have this attitude

- In their mind, someone plays you, or you manipulate them. In their mind, this is a dark place where no one is safe, so they have to manipulate others before they can do something
- Nobody wins. According to them, there is no winning. We all lose, some more than others, so no need to even try.
- Equal relationship or balance partnership do not exist, you either are a winner or lose, so you want to win at all cost.

- Nobody can trust anyone here, in their mind. Everyone is out to get anyone, so we cannot trust anyone, and they also do not think of them as trustworthy.
- No matter how hard they try, dark manipulators cannot get out of their heads and look for things as they are.
- According to research, many dark manipulators think affection and attention available to them are going away fast, so they need to manipulate others into giving them.
- They often think they cannot win by regular means, so dark manipulators have to deceive and manipulate others to get what they want.
- Dark manipulators feel they are entitled to whatever they want, by any means. If something is good, they get to have it, no questions about it.

7.2 Negative Purpose of Dark Psychology

Gift giving

If someone happens to be nice to you or gifts you something for no reason. Make sure to check the attached strings. If they manipulate you by buying your affection or making you feel like you owe them something so later, they can use you as they please. These narcissists have a goal. To get to that goal, anyone is a fair game.

Under Pressure

It is integrated into our DNA to make ourselves look good and nice, so this need often overrides our intuition to ask questions when someone pushes us to do something for them, so we over-accommodate. Dark psychologist loves to do this, and they will keep asking and asking until you give in to what they want you to do.

Poor Me

I am sure you have come across someone in terrible circumstances, so you have to help them. They portray themselves as someone who is going through some hard circumstances; if anyone else had at their place, they would go crazy. All these are just dark tactics to manipulate you into giving them something or doing something for them. Then, as the dark manipulator has achieved his goal, you are not needed anymore. You will see many children who will ask their parents to come to rescue them as they are drowning, but it's a ploy. The dark manipulator has not aged more than their childhood and sometimes uses the same ploys. This is misplaced empathy.

Physical Touch

For human wellbeing and survival, physical touch is important. According to one research, those babies who did not get enough physical affection from their parents failed to thrive and had less brain growth than other babies who did. Unfortunately, many people come from a toxic home environment, where a warm hug or heartening pat on the back was missing. All were giving no attention or wrong attention.

As you know, nonverbal communication is more important than verbal, and in the same way, touch is ten times more powerful than emotional or verbal touch. So, when a dark manipulator realizes you are touch starved or have not dealt with healthy touch in your childhood, they might exploit this need by putting an arm around you and ask you to do something for them. At the moment, it will feel nice to be touched so lovingly, but it has a dark purpose behind it.

The touch might so be subtle that you would not recognize it but feel happier and want to do what this person asks of you. As your body is releasing oxytocin (the feel-good hormone), you will do anything at that moment.

Eye gazing

Eyes play an important part in social interactions. If you have a good relationship with your parents, you know mutual eye gaze is necessary and a sign of trust and involvement. This look of love is what shapes our personality and self-worth. Dark manipulators have an advantage as they know how to read others' eyes? (but you also have this advantage now how to read people). If someone feels vulnerable or sad, the dark manipulator can cheer them up and later get what they want.

They will start by warmly looking into your eyes to get your attention. You will feel good as someone is there for you, then after they have made their connection. You are under their spell and will do what is asked of you. But if you are aware of your needs, weaknesses or know how to read and analyze the other person, you can save yourself. Eyes can be the way to manipulation.

Passive-Aggressive Behavior

Dark manipulators know how to make someone guilty, or impart shame in you, to make you do what they want. Dark manipulators will mention how people go above and beyond for them but hinting you are not doing enough. Thus, making you feel guilty that you are not doing enough.

Bit by bit, this kind of behavior will strip your self-worth and make you feel not enough. To prove that you are equally as good as others, you will unintentionally do what is asked of you. You will think about what you can do to get in their good books or get their praise and acceptance. You will want to be their favorite person. Parents often use this trick by telling you how your siblings are so great. How Mrs. Karen's child is scoring high in the test as well as practicing piano? What are you doing instead? Or parents will pit the siblings with each other.

If you are a parent, you unintentionally are doing this thing. Please be careful and stop doing that. It can affect your child's whole future and their self-worth.

In some cases, you will see a dark manipulator using humor to tell you how unworthy you are. They will be smiling but tell you something that shatters your confidence. No one will want the other person to list your insecurity, and they will try anything to get them to stop talking.

Protective Boundaries

The one way to avoid being manipulated is to change yourself; yes, it is that easy. Know your psyche; know yourself. You can always change yourself and know you are the only one in charge and rewire your thinking process. Build your self-worth, and know it is not easy to make it crumble. Listen to positive affirmations so that your subconscious mind will come and save you; it will strengthen your intuition. Make strong boundaries around you; only people who make you feel good, not just timely, people who are always there for you can cross those boundaries and come close to you are not the victim; even if you were once, you are not anymore. When it was easy for others to manipulate you, forgive yourself, but now you know yourself better and avoid all these dark manipulators.

The most important aspect is not letting your common sense be buried when someone loves bombing you, praising you, or flattering you. Even in close relationships such as family and friends, know when someone is draining your energy or using you for their benefit or goals. You do not have to drink your feelings; speak up when someone hurts you.

7.3 Positive Aspects of Dark Psychology

Although dark psychology does not have a good effect on people's mental health, it can be used within ethical limits. Such as, you can make your life easier but do not forget, you do not have to harm others to get what you want from a situation.

You should use Body language to your advantage. It means you can understand others and know their intentions. You can influence them by telling them what they want to listen to. Such as in official meetings, you can see what your boss or superior needs, you can understand their want and perform accordingly and get the raise you always wanted. Or you can also portray with your body language what you want. You can show what you want to convey, genuine concern or show that someone made you happy. You can also show the other person you are in tune with them, by mirroring their body language (but for few seconds, do not freak them out by copying each gesture).

You can change the other person's perspective by tweaking or manipulating a situation. We unknowingly do this every day. Such as if you are selling your car, you tell the other person all the good things about your car first, then tell the one negative part briefly. Then, when the other person is making pros and cons, the pros will outweigh the cons.

Talk about something like you know about it, rather than showing you do not know much. Such as if you want to convince your colleagues to stop printing each and every email because it is bad for the environment. But, If you do not know anything else about it and you can convince your colleagues, less paper means less work. Think outside the box, and not everything has to be straightforward. You can always change other person's perspectives and make them look in a new direction that will benefit you and them.

You can also trick your mind and get the benefits. Such as

If you have a big meeting tomorrow and you are tired, you can trick your mind into thinking you have slept well and are feeling better, and your brain will catch on.

One more effect is smart people undervalue themselves, but ignorant people think they are geniuses.

Observe people and their psychological needs, and use them to steer the relationship. Their need can be included, or accepted, or left alone. If you provide them with the exact circumstances of what they need, their weakness will become your strength. It does not have to be malicious. You just need to figure out how to use this information while being ethical.

As you keep observing others, you will know their psychological tendencies and needs, how they think, what makes them tick, etc. You can influence their thoughts or provide them an environment in which they can flourish. You can use this information to your advantage while being within limits.

According to one Psychologist, J. Sniechowski tells about how you can distinguish between emotional leverage and manipulation. He gives 3 guidelines to follow so you do not cross any unethical boundaries.

You want to provide them an environment in which they can reach their full potential, discover their vision. So that they discover, it is the right decision for them to move in your chosen direction without being exploited.

If they crave some sort of environment of any need, they are attached to some emotional base, no matter how much they deny it. So be very careful.

You can merge your benefit with their benefits and work together towards your mutual goal.

Time and opportunity are 2 great aspects of success. You should know when to ask your boss for a promotion. Or when to ask your spouse to do something for you, read the room and their body language.

You should know when to make your move. Most people do not need to be taught when to ask for something, even from childhood. You know when to ask for cake from your mom when she is in a happy mood. But in most cases, ask for favors when they are preoccupied and tired. People are more likely to say yes when they are tired and busy to get you off their heads. Do not force people, instead wait for them to come to you. You may have to wait for weeks, but the fruit will be much sweeter. Half of the battle is won when the other person is in the right mood.

The possibilities with dark psychology are infinite. This is something worth putting in your time and effort. You can always understand dark psychology and look at things from your or the person's perspectives. Paired with analyzing and reading people, you will be skilled at getting what you want in the most ethical way possible. You can always save yourself from being manipulated also.

7.4 Who Falls Prey To Dark Psychology?

Anyone can fall prey to dark psychology, but these people are more susceptible to being manipulated than others.

People who can't see bad or lies: good people also think everyone else is just as good or does not manipulate people. We all have been there. People lie when they absolutely have to or tell small insignificant lies, but they also think others do not lie. Naïve people believe there is less evil in this world. According to research, people who tell the truth are more likely to believe everyone else is just like them.

People who are too careful if something bad happens to this person. They think it is their fault, or they were needy or did not investigate it enough. Do not be that person, as anyone can be manipulated.

Who cannot say yes or no, so they cannot save themselves from situations where they can be manipulated.

People who seek other people's approval are more likely to do what is told even if they have to break their boundaries.

People who love to justify others' actions, if someone manipulated them, then they must be going through something in their life. We all need to understand that sometimes a bad person does something bad because they do not care.

People who are overly submissive or financially dependent on the manipulator or are emotional. Their emotions cloud their judgment.

If you were manipulated in the past or could not read people's bad intentions, then you are not at fault. We all have faced this issue in a way or another. You can now be aware of others' emotions and intentions but saying you will never get hurt by the other person's manipulation is difficult. However, you can practice some strategies to ensure firm boundaries around you.

Always keep your communication direct and clear. This way, it is easier for others to understand what your intentions are and what you hope to happen in a certain situation; it will be easier for you to identify dark tactics; actions may not be clear or specific.

If you suspect someone to use dark tactics or manipulation on you, you can tell them what you will tolerate and what not. This way, you would know who is having a bad day or is trying to manipulate you.

It may be difficult for you to differentiate between manipulation, dark tactics or reading someone wrong. However, you can always ask a trusted person's opinion if the situation is like how you perceive it or be mistaken. Above all, do not forget your gut instinct.

In all this, do not be afraid to open up or to trust people. Do not let opportunities pass you by; welcome them and be aware of yourself and others' intentions. If you are presented with an opportunity, it is necessary to know half the battle is your attitude towards the opportunity.

You cannot always save yourself from something bad happening to you, but you can learn from it. As you know how the manipulator thinks, you can save yourself from his dark tactics and persuasion, so the first step is to know yourself better, change your attitude where you have to, keep firm boundaries around you. Surround yourself with people who are good for your emotional and physical health.

Conclusion

Dark psychology is way more than manipulation, but you can still benefit from analyzing and reading people. Changing situations to your benefit within ethical conduct. Using dark psychology can help you in many situations; as you have learned what manipulation and dark psychology are, you can save yourself from being manipulated and read people and their intentions like books. Some people are more manipulative than the rest, as they use dark psychology, but also some people have more ethics and values; you can always change yourself if you have been manipulating others without knowing or vice versa.

Now, you know what dark psychology is and what is not. When paired with body language secrets, you can read people and analyze them without being so obvious. If someone is lying to you, you will know. You can know what people are trying to convey with their behavior, facial micro-expression, gestures, postures, and without speaking. Dark psychology can also be seen in sales techniques, ads, the internet, and many influential people use it. Your kids may manipulate you to get what they want, or you can manipulate them to do good in their lives and make wiser choices. Dark psychology can be used for good by getting the job you want, succeed where you want, whether it be business or personal life. Sales use dark psychology's persuasion and manipulation to make you buy more than you need in many marketing programs. Many businesses and people believe what they are doing is right. But we know the truth; the next time you interact with someone that raises your hackles, you can trust your instinct, differentiate between your anxiety and see right through other people's manipulation. Analyzing and reading people does not only give you an upper hand, but you can use these techniques to save yourself. If you happen to fall under manipulation, you can always change yourself, recognize alarming situations and protect yourself and others from harm's way.

Book 3: Manipulation And Dark Psychology

A Guide on How to Detect and Identify Psychological and Emotional Manipulation and How to Defend Oneself Against the Manipulators

Introduction

Manipulation is an all-too-common occurrence. People with poor personalities often find themselves in a situation where they are being exploited by their substantial other or even a kid. They are the innocent targets of persons who are struggling with emotional or mental problems that enable them to manipulate others.

As they battle to maintain ties with loved ones or colleagues, the sufferers, particularly the manipulators, may endure greatly from this manipulation. Manipulators can alienate themselves in their attempts to dominate a circumstance and gratify their desire for power to create themselves up. Because these isolated individuals may find it tough to shake the behavior, the cycle may continue to feed itself.

Individuals may eventually realize the deceit and end things. A manipulator may also fool oneself into thinking that their actions are necessary for their own or the person they are manipulating's well-being.

Manipulators have several fundamental goals that may startle those who are taken advantage of.

They are as follows:

- In order to achieve their purpose and personal gain, they must sacrifice others.
- They're power-hungry, and they need to feel dominant in their relations.
- They're control freaks who need to be reminded all the time that they're the dominant partner in a relationship.
- They have poor self and need power over others to enhance their perspective of themselves.
- They regard manipulation as a pastime because they have a psychopathic inclination.

If you encounter somebody like that, be aware of both their and your own behaviors. Continue reading to understand how to spot a manipulator's signs and how to deal with them.

This book is for everyone who has been deceived or believes they have been. The book's purpose is to provide tools and psychological support to help him regain his self-esteem and "shatter" some of the variables that have brought him psychological and emotional harm.

After reading this book, the reader will be able to recognize the psychological profile and behavioral characteristics of those who wield power over others, gaining comprehensive knowledge and eventually comprehending how to resist oneself.

Chapter 1: Manipulation

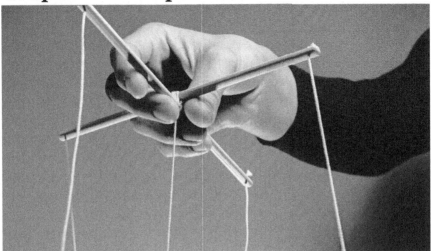

For the purposes of this book, it is critical to define a clear definition of manipulation. It will be impossible to distinguish between instances of manipulation and other forms of persuasion without a clear knowledge of what defines manipulation.

While you may have your own definition of manipulation, it is critical that you use the book's definition in order to understand the practical guidance in the following chapters.

1.1 What Is Manipulation?

Manipulation is a type of mind control that can be used in a variety of ways to influence how a person thinks. Manipulation will be used to refer to psychological manipulation throughout this book. This is a sort of social interaction that aims to alter other people's behavior or perceptions. This is accomplished by the use of harsh, deceitful, and underhanded methods. This type of mind control is employed to advance the manipulator's objectives to the detriment of others. The techniques utilized are frequently described as deceitful, cunning, abusive, and exploitative. Many people are aware of when they are being controlled or when those around them are being manipulated, but they are unaware that this is a sort of mind control. Because the manipulation frequently occurs between the person and someone they know well, this can be a tough form of mind control to avoid. Manipulation gives the impression that the person has no say in the situation. They'll have been told blatant lies or half-truths and won't comprehend the entire scope of the situation until it's too late. The agent will be able to blackmail and utilize the subject to get to the end aim if they are aware of the circumstance ahead of time. The subject is effectively trapped since the agent has planned everything in a way that they will not get into difficulty, the subject will be able to bear the blame or be wounded if necessary, and the agent will achieve their ultimate aim. The most problematic aspect of this is that the agent is unable to sense the needs of their subject or any other person; they will not care if the subject suffers mental or bodily injury as a result of the process. While the subject will be emotionally immersed in the scenario, the agent will be able to walk away from it without feeling remorse or regret (as long as they achieve their end goal). This can be a hazardous sort of mind control because the agent will be an expert at it, capable of blackmailing, threatening, and doing whatever else is required; at times, they may even be able to manipulate the subject into believing they are going insane.

Manipulation is a type of deliberate influence defined by a person or party (the manipulator) attempting to modify the behavior of another person or party (the target), usually with the purpose of accomplishing a goal in the manipulator's best interests.

There is no indication of anything malicious, and it is not stated whether the manipulator is acting in the target's best interests, against the target's best interests, or with no regard for the target's best interests. Everything is conceivable. This results in a definition of manipulation that is not restricted by ethical principles that are subjective. However, this does not imply that you should renounce your values as well!

Because it is objective and straightforward, this definition is useful. It's also useful because you'll learn manipulation tactics in this book that will assist you in reaching your objectives. It would be a mistake to ignore persuasion in this regard, as it can play a significant part in manipulation and is inextricably linked to the suggestions in this book.

However, there are still two issues. The first is about "intentional influence." The intent is difficult to define because it entails accountability.

In reality, everyone, especially children, manipulate others around them all of the time. It would be incorrect to label a child's temper tantrum as manipulation simply because they aren't old enough to rationalize their actions. For that matter, adult temper tantrums are the same. As a result, intent does not always indicate conscious activity; it can sometimes be instinctive. This also allows for the very real occurrence of people who are "naturally manipulative."

The second issue is the frustratingly ambiguous conclusion: "usually to attain a goal in the manipulator's interests." Not only is it difficult to define "the manipulator's interests," but the presence of "usually" creates uncertainty. This section merely serves to normalize the concept of manipulation for the purposes of this book, and it would be unsuitable for a more broad definition. After all, how can someone know their own interests perfectly? Of course, it is conceivable to skillfully manipulate someone and still end up killing oneself.

The latter issue is addressed throughout the book at various moments where it is pertinent. Despite its shortcomings, this definition of manipulation is enough for the book's practical sections.

1.2 Examples of Manipulation

With the definition in place, it's time to look at some examples of manipulation. Some are prevalent in regular life, while others are associated with one-of-a-kind or exceptional events. While this book focuses on personal manipulation, there is a little conceptual distinction between manipulation on a small scale and large-scale manipulation. The same concepts usually always apply, but the practicality of manipulation tactics such as deception, between, for example, warring states, can be more complicated.

When I was younger, I had a habit of being sick when I didn't want to go to school. Whenever this happened, my folks would fawn over me at first. My mother suspected my shenanigans after two emergency trips to the clinic. I wasn't taken to the clinic for the next several visits but instead was allowed to stay at home. My pals called me enthusiastically during one of my stomach problems to tell me that a local actor was coming to the school for a visit. I begged my mother to take me back to school, oblivious to the fact that I was suffering from "an awful gut ache." My mother advised me to stay put since she didn't want to take any risk. There was no amount of weeping or pleading that could persuade her to change her mind. Even after I admitted to faking my stomach pains, hardly one believed me. When I came to school the next day, my friends showed me all the great stuff mister actor had brought for them, and I was green with envy. To put it mildly, I never pretended to be sick to get out of school.

When it comes to the things humans do to control a situation, this anecdote is only one of many. Many adults I know still make up a cold to obtain a day off work. Isn't that altogether bad? We've all been duped into making decisions that aren't in our best interests. When a buddy presents you with a great pair of running shoes and a one-month membership to a local gym, you know they want you to improve your fitness. Have you ever gone out to lunch with a friend only to be interrupted by a potential date and a pressing emergency (for your friend, of course)? I've been there before. Surprisingly, when we are threatened, manipulation is one of the tactics we use to get out of a bad situation if brute force is not an option.

That is to say; the ability to manipulate others is inherent in our species. When it concerns psychological manipulation, though, things turn a lot darker and evil. In this case, underhanded tactics that are either aggressive, dishonest, or both are used to influence a person's behaviors or ideas. In this case, the person being manipulated is not given the option of accepting or rejecting the manipulator's will. They are merely compelled to comply.

Manipulators are motivated by a variety of factors. It can be anything as simple as gaining financial benefit, like in the case of the fictional soldier who defrauded my neighbor of her entire life savings. These people are determined to advance their own personal agenda in the workplace, even if it means slamming a few heads against each other. Their guiding idea is simple: if you want something, you must reach out and take it. It's mainly about gaining power and maintaining control in relationships. Their need to be in command drives everything they do, and they will go to great lengths to obtain it.

Then there are those that enjoy manipulating people for their own amusement. They are simply bored and resort to deceptive activities to pass the time. It's obscene and violent, but that's how they think.

Lying is one of the most popular tricks used by manipulators. The art of deception is mastered by a master manipulator.

They have a knack for concocting great tales that have nothing to do with the truth. Alternatively, they can use deception and lie by omission. Some people are so skilled at lying that you almost never notice until it's too late. Manipulators also use guilt-tripping and shaming as a strategy. When asked about something they've done wrong, they'll immediately deny it, then flip around and make you feel awful for questioning them in the first place.

They demonize their victim in order to deepen their grip on them, effectively turning the victim into the abuser. This type of manipulative method is commonly used in domestic situations, where the abuser claims that the victim's character, words, or actions inspired their own behavior in the first place.

The use of elusive, non-committal responses to queries is another subtle tactic utilized in manipulation.

If caught, they rationalize their acts and manipulate reality to fit their narrative. Some manipulators use sex and seduction to achieve their nefarious goals. Anger and projection of blame are rapidly employed to manipulate the situation to their advantage when they are discovered with their hands in the cookie jar.

Manipulators, on the other hand, do not always choose their victims at random. They are drawn to particular characteristics in their victims, and certain vulnerabilities make it simpler for the manipulator to carry out their crimes. It's simpler to control lonely persons with low self-esteem and a desire to please than it is to handle assertive social types. However, there are persons that exhibit comparable tendencies to the latter and are controlled as well. Manipulators research these people's personality defects and weaknesses before utilizing them against them. Appearances can deceive even the most impressive people. Brash people who make compulsive decisions are more prone to be duped into making hasty decisions with long-term consequences. People who are materialistic and greedy are more likely to be conned.

1.3 Requirements to Successfully Manipulate

A good manipulator must have strategies at their disposal that will allow them to use people to achieve their own end goal. While there are many views about what constitutes a good manipulator, we'll focus on the three distinguishing points laid down by George K. Simon, a successful psychologist. The manipulator, according to Simon, must be able to disguise their hostile behaviors and intents from the subject.

To establish which methods will be most effective in achieving their objective, they must be able to determine the weaknesses of their targeted subjector victims.

One should also have some ruthlessness on hand so that they don't have to deal with any concerns about harming the subjects if necessary. This harm might take the form of either bodily or emotional harm.

To successfully control their subjects, the manipulator must first conceal their hostile behaviors and intents. No one will stay around long enough to be manipulated if the manipulator goes about telling everyone their plans or is continually rude to others. Rather, the manipulator must be able to keep their thoughts hidden from others while acting as if everything is normal. Those who are being controlled are frequently unaware of it, at least at first. The manipulator will be pleasant, act like their closest friend, and possibly assist them with a problem. By the time the subject realizes the problem, the manipulator has gathered enough information about them to force them to continue.

Following that, the manipulator must be capable of determining the vulnerabilities of their chosen victim or victims. This can assist them in determining which methods should be used to achieve the ultimate aim. The manipulator may be able to complete this step with just a little observation, but other times they will need to engage in some form of interaction with the subject before developing the comprehensive strategy.

The manipulator must also be vicious, according to the third condition. It will not go well if the manipulator puts in all of their efforts and then becomes concerned about how the subject will fare in the end. If they were truly concerned about the issue, they would not have gone ahead with this proposal. The manipulator is unconcerned about the subject and is unconcerned if the subject suffers any bodily or mental harm as long as the main goal is achieved. The fact that the subject often does not recognize they are being manipulated until later in the process is one of the reasons manipulators are so successful. They may believe that everything is OK; they may believe that they have made a new friend in the manipulator.

The subject is hooked by the time they discover they are being used or no longer want to be a part of the process. To get their way in the end, the manipulator will be able to utilize a variety of strategies, including emotional blackmail.

1.4 Manipulation Techniques

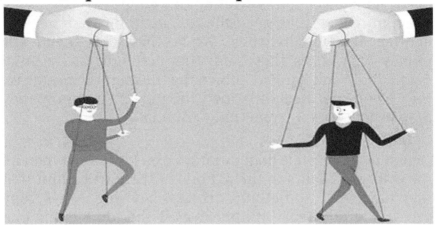

Simon has also devised a list of strategies that manipulators must employ in order to maintain influence over their targets. Some of these are identical to Braiker's list but with greater information.

These would include the following:

Lying

Manipulators are extremely skilled at deceiving their victims. It is often impossible for the subjects to tell when they are being lied to at the moment. When the subject becomes aware of the seeming falsehood, it is usually too late to intervene. The only method for the subject to ensure that they are less likely to be lied to is to keep an eye out for different personality types who are specialists in cheating and lying. The manipulator will lie about anything to get their way, and most of their victims will be completely unaware of what is going on until it is too late to intervene.

Omission Lying

With a few minor differences, omission lying is identical to the techniques outlined above. Omission lying is more nuanced since the manipulator will give certain truths while withholding essential information that should have been revealed. This could be considered propaganda in some situations. The manipulator may claim that they need money to get gas so they can go grocery shopping when in reality, they need the money to buy narcotics or another illegal substance. While they did spend the money on gas, as they said, they left out an essential detail. If the subject had known the finish of the narrative, they would not have provided the money, and now they may be involved in something criminal.

Denial

Denial is a skill that manipulators excel at. Even when all the evidence points to them, none of them will admit that they have done something wrong. They will always deny everything and make it appear as if the topic is the one that is at fault. Rationalization: When a manipulator makes up a reason to make themselves look good, this is called rationalization. They may claim that they merely conducted the act in order to assist the person. This strategy is closely linked to the spinning technique.

Minimization

Minimization is a hybrid of reasoning and denial strategies. The manipulator will assure everyone that their actions are not as reckless or damaging as the subject believes. When the manipulator argues that an insult or taunt they delivered was only a joke and that the subject shouldn't take it seriously, this is an example of this.

Selective attention or inattention

Selective attention, or inattention, is a method in which the manipulator tries to avoid paying attention to anything that can divert their attention away from their ultimate purpose. They will belittle it and make it appear unimportant to them, which it is not. When the manipulator says, "I don't want to hear that," this is an example.

Diversion

Manipulators are masters at not only lying to their subjects but also at avoiding giving straight answers to inquiries that are posed to them. If they are asked a question they don't like, or if they are asked openly if they are lying, the manipulator will try to steer the conversation in a different way. Frequently, the manipulator will give a terse answer to the question before shifting the conversation to another subject.

Evasion

With a few exceptions, this approach is extremely similar to diversion. The manipulator will respond to inquiries using weasel words, imprecise comments, rambling, and irrelevant responses to the question in this method. When they're finished, they'll leave the topic with more questions than answers.

Intimidation

The manipulator will strive to keep the victim on the defensive throughout the process in order to keep them on the same team. This is frequently accomplished by threatening the subject with veiled, implied, indirect, or subtle threats.

Guilt Trip

Manipulators frequently employ the guilt trip as a kind of intimidation to persuade their targets to do what they want. The manipulator will attempt to make the subject feel guilty in some way, such as by implying that the subject has it too easy, is too self-centered, or just does not care enough about the manipulator. As a result, the victim will begin to feel sorry for the manipulator. The manipulator will then keep the subject in a submissive, fearful, or self-doubting stance, making it simpler for them to be used.

Shaming

The manipulator's main purpose is to make the subject feel awful or sympathetic toward them so that they will continue to follow the plan. One approach for the manipulator to do this is to embarrass the subject with insults and sarcasm. The subject will feel unworthy as a result of this strategy. The majority of the shaming tactics will be subtle, such as subtle sarcasm, rhetorical comments, an unpleasant tone of voice, or a harsh look.

Victimization

Playing the victim: No matter what, the manipulator wants to appear as the victim, despite the fact that they are the one in charge. When the manipulator acts as if they are a victim of their circumstances or someone else's actions, compassion, sympathy, and pity will be elicited. The majority of people will be unable to watch as someone suffers, and the manipulator will find it simple to enlist the help of these same individuals.

Vilifying the subject

This is one of the most effective methods since it puts the victim on the defensive almost immediately while also concealing the manipulator's aggressive intentions. The manipulator will attempt to turn the situation around so that the subject appears to be the villain and the source of all the problems. The subject will then try to modify his or her mind and return to the manipulator's side, making it easier to manipulate. Manipulators frequently disguise their own goals by making it appear as if the job they are doing is for a good cause. They merely made a snide remark about your dress because the principal wants to start cleaning up the school's appearance, and they wanted to assist. This category also includes the phrase "just doing my job."

Seduction

Manipulators can use seduction to obtain the things they desire. Intense encouragement, flattery, adulation, and charm are examples of tactics that fall under this category. This is done in order for the subject's defenses to be lowered. After some time, the subject will begin to trust and devote their devotion to the manipulator, who will utilize it as they see fit.

Projecting the blame

Placing blame on others: The manipulator will spend a lot of time criticizing others for their issues. It's often difficult to notice when this is happening, so no one can call them out on it.

Feigning innocence

If the manipulator is caught in the act of achieving their own goals, they will try to convince you that any harm done was wholly inadvert. They may even deny ever having done anything in the first place. When confronted, the manipulator will show surprise or indignation on their faces. The purpose of this tool is to make the victim question their own sanity and judgment because they appear to have made a mistake.

Feigning confusion

Another thing that could happen if the manipulator is caught is that they would act confused. If the manipulator tries to act as if they have no understanding of what the topic is talking about, this will happen. When a significant matter is brought up to them, they may also appear perplexed.

Brandishing anger

When a manipulator utilizes rage, it tries to make the subject feel regretful or sympathetic towards them. The manipulator will be able to shock their subject back into submission if done correctly. The manipulator is frequently not truly upset; they are simply putting on a show to obtain what they want.

As can be seen, the manipulator has a wide range of tools at their disposal in order to achieve their objectives.

Often, these techniques are utilized in such a way that the subject is unaware of what is going on at first, and it takes time for them to realize what is going on. After that, the manipulator will be able to use some of the tactics mentioned in the following section to keep the subject moving in the appropriate direction. The manipulator is competent at using these skills to accomplish what they want, and it makes no difference to them how much the other person suffers in the process.

Chapter 2: Identity kit of the Manipulator

2.1 Warning Signs

You've probably picked up this book because you believe you've previously been emotionally manipulated or because you want to know if you are an emotional manipulator. You can be a manipulator without even realizing it, believe it or not. You might think what you're doing is for the betterment of your relationship, but it's not.

If you're an emotional manipulator or attempting to figure out if you're with one, here are some telltale indications. It's worth noting that many of these will be employed in tandem, but the manipulator's ultimate purpose is to achieve their objectives at any cost to their victims. As a result, they will measure their victim and then select the best choice or combination of alternatives to fulfill their objectives with that particular victim. The following are some of the possibilities available to a manipulator.

2.1.1 Positive Reinforcement

If you're dealing with a manipulator, positive reinforcement will be used to persuade you to do what they want. For example, when something bad happens to you, they'll show you superficial sympathy and employ superficial charm. Excessive apologies To acquire what they want, they utilize money, presents, and approval. To generate a good response, they utilize a faked smile or laugh.

All of these techniques are part of the manipulator's overall strategy for obtaining their desired outcome at the price of their victim's emotional, financial, or physical well-being. After all, the carrots they use for positive reinforcement are just that: carrots. The following option may appear to be a carrot, but it frequently ends in a stick.

2.1.2 Negative Reinforcement

Negative reinforcement is when you take someone out of a bad circumstance in order to get them to do what you want. For example, your significant other might suggest, "If you fix the sink, you won't have to do the laundry." To achieve their purpose, the manipulator offers a reward or a way out of the unfavorable position. However, by giving the manipulator what they want, the person being influenced may find themselves in another unpleasant scenario before they realize it.

2.1.3 Intermittent Reinforcement

This is when you only obtain what you want on rare occasions. It's analogous to a game of chance. You know that doing the dishes may bring you a lot of positive feedback, so you do them all the time. However, you don't always get compliments for it, so it's a bit like playing the lottery. You can get a lot of positive reinforcement for cleaning the dishes one night and then receive the cold shoulder the next. Nonetheless, that small taste of truly wonderful positive reinforcement makes you want more, so you keep trying.

The manipulator takes advantage of your need for approval as well as your efforts to maintain control over the situation. They'll keep you guessing while still receiving what they want from you, whether it's in the form of deeds, emotional fulfillment, or financial assistance. This form of reinforcement also works in a carrot-and-stick manner. The second one, on the other hand, is employing the stick to achieve the manipulator's objectives.

2.1.4 Punishment

If you don't seem to respond well to the aforementioned methods, people who are attempting to emotionally manipulate you will utilize punishment. The following are examples of possible punishments:

- Yelling
- Silent treatment
- Nagging
- Intimidation
- Emotional blackmail
- Threats
- Swearing
- Sulking
- Crying
- Playing the victim
- Using guilt trips

The manipulator is well aware that this form of emotional blackmail will eventually force you to give in. As a result, they're using a stick to get people to comply with their goals and demands. It's all designed to appeal to their victims' emotions or psychological well-being, leading them to give in to the manipulator without recognizing the harm they're doing to themselves by doing so.

2.1.5 Traumatic One-Trial Learning

You just have one chance to make this individual happy, or you'll be punished severely. These instances are designed to educate you that you are not the dominant person in the relationship, and you are supposed to be schooled to avoid any future circumstances that may upset them. This allows them to employ more subtle tactics that you aren't aware of at this stage.

Many manipulators use this approach in combination with punishment to establish who is the boss early in the relationship. The trauma can prevent the victim from examining other aspects of the relationship that are not beneficial to them. The victim will also stick to their prescribed role, lowering their own self-worth and value in the process. As a result, they assist the manipulator by gradually becoming easier prey.

2.1.6 Lying

It's difficult to catch someone lying in the act, but if you do, don't ignore it. In a relationship, lying is extremely risky and indicates that something is wrong. Understanding that psychopaths exist is one of the strategies to reduce your chance of being deceived. They lie on a regular basis.

They'll do whatever it takes to keep you on the hook if you catch them in a lie. While you should not continue to trust them, a manipulator will do all possible to keep their power. As a result, they will try to persuade you that the lie was minor or that it was a simple misunderstanding. The manipulator may make it appear as if it was their victim's fault, therefore exploiting guilt to achieve their goal of staying close to their victim.

Furthermore, keep in mind that lying by omission is also lying. It's subtle, but don't underestimate its influence. Lying by omission is the practice of withholding crucial facts in order to elicit diverse responses. As a result, a manipulator might keep their victim in a position where they are unable to make educated decisions by withholding facts.

2.1.7 Denial

You'll never hear a manipulator acknowledging they made a mistake. It will always be someone else's fault for whatever has occurred. They've mastered the art of assigning blame.

As a result, denial frequently goes hand in hand with lying. A manipulator will frequently feel compelled to fill their denial with lies about other people's behavior. Nonetheless, the manipulator's true goal is to keep their victim in line. They don't want their victims to have any doubts about their motives or deeds. If a victim does, more flaws in the relationship may appear, something a manipulator does not want to happen.

2.1.8 Rationalization

This is a ruse used to justify inappropriate action. Don't underestimate manipulators' ability to rationalize. They have the ability to reason their way out of nearly any issue. After all, Ted Bundy was able to argue his way out of jail twice.

When it comes to justification, the victim is usually the one who is to blame. The manipulator's acts somehow become the fault of their victim or situations that the manipulator ostensibly has no control over. From a psychological standpoint, the combination of denial and justification can be employed to work on the victim. Everything a manipulator does is aimed at keeping their grip on the victim, but they are also continually asserting their authority in order to fulfill their goals.

2.1.9 Minimization

Manipulators will make everything look like a joke or that the situation isn't as severe as it appears. For example, a manipulator may do something heinous to a coworker and then claim that it was all a joke. They were actually trying to harm that person.

This strategy also treats the victim's sentiments as second-class, making them feel unimportant. They heighten the victim's vulnerability to other sorts of manipulation by acting on them from a psychological aspect.

2.1.10   Diversion and Evasion

Diversionary methods are used by manipulators, such as avoiding delivering a direct answer or redirecting the conversation to a different topic. During a conversation, they will evade by being meandering, ambiguous, or unimportant.

However, their ultimate goal is to perplex the victim and make them doubt the truth. The manipulator takes advantage of the victim's perplexity. Because the manipulator will make them doubt what they think and believe is true, the victim may find it difficult to tell what is real and what is not overtime.

2.1.11   Guilt Trips

Their main weapon is guilt. With an emotional manipulator, you can never accomplish anything right because they are always looking for a way to make you feel guilty. Your guilt earns them compassion, which means they'll finally get what they want. Even when you catch them in a lie or see some of these other tactics, the guilt makes you doubt yourself.

For example, your significant other or a friend informs you that they had an argument with their mother about how they don't want to go to a particular college, and now she won't pay for them to attend. In actuality, there was no fight about college, and there was no conflict at all. An emotional manipulator will make you feel obligated to be the hero, and you may find up giving them money for tuition when the money is actually for something else.

Be wary of individuals who refuse to fight their own fights and look after themselves. Instead, they'll enlist the help of their victims. As a result, the victims bear the brunt of any consequences, whether financial, emotional, or psychological.

2.1.12 Playing the Victim

Have you ever met someone who constantly seems to be dealing with a situation that is worse than yours? Whenever you try to tell them something, they either already know or are experiencing something worse than you are. They have a knack for derailing the subject and refocusing it on themselves.

You tell someone you have a headache, for example. They claim to have a migraine and to be really ill. Worse, they'll tell you about a time when they had such a severe headache that they mistook themselves for having a brain tumor. This is emotional blackmail, designed to make you feel sorry for them rather than for yourself.

If you confront them about their behavior, they will accuse you of being selfish and constantly wanting to be the center of attention. As a result, the manipulator gets the victim to focus less on themselves and more on the manipulator and their needs.

As the victim falls under the manipulator's spell, they will gradually find themselves devoting time and sympathy to the manipulator, who will profit from it.

2.1.13 Seduction

The seduction trap is one of the simplest to fall into. In order to earn loyalty and trust, a manipulator will utilize flattery, charisma, charm, and the backing of others. They will give assistance only to gain access to a person's circle so that they can employ more subtle approaches.

The seduction technique can be particularly effective for a victim who has issues with their self-esteem, physical image, or personal sense of themselves. It allows the manipulator to get close to their victim by becoming a source of enjoyment for them before using other strategies to expand their control by exploiting their victim's self-doubt.

2.1.14   Projecting Blame

Manipulators will make it appear as if the victim, rather than them, is at fault. They'll tell a lie so that they can speak a more convincing falsehood in the future. They will say that the victim is the one who is abusing them, rather than the other way around, and they will even say that the victim is insane.

Keep in mind that the ultimate goal is to gain control over their victims. As a result, whatever blame they throw on their victims is intended to aid them in gaining control and getting whatever else they want from them. The victim, on the other hand, may begin to doubt their own sanity as a result of the manipulator's actions. Regardless of the exact circumstances of the case, the victim will begin to believe that it is their fault. As a result, even if they catch the manipulator in a lie or other manipulation technique, the victim is more likely to doubt themself before questioning the manipulator. This strategy ensures that the manipulator maintains control over the victim's connection.

2.1.15   Feigning Confusion

When they are accused of something, they will try to appear dumb. Furthermore, when something important is brought to their attention, such as a lie they told, the manipulator would act perplexed. The manipulator will then perplex the victim, causing them to mistrust their own perception. The victim eventually comes to believe whatever the manipulator is telling them. Another strategy to turn the victim into the bad guy is to use this technique.

As you can see, several of these strategies put the victim in a situation where they believe they are to blame or the cause of the situation. As a result, the manipulator gains the upper hand while simultaneously eroding the victim's sense of self and instilling self-doubt.

However, the manipulator's long-term success depends on his or her ability to overcome self-doubt. No matter what, the manipulator's capacity to keep control is contingent on the victim's refusal to doubt or challenge him.

2.1.16   Brandishing Anger

The manipulator isn't genuinely angry; they're just using fury to obtain what they want. They'll have rage fits and sob uncontrollably, only to be threatened with things like reporting abuse to the police. All of this is done to put the victim in their proper place as a submissive.

A victim who is readily manipulated is referred to as a docile victim. All of a manipulator's efforts are geared at attaining that aim for as long as it takes to gain what they want from their victim. When they utilize rage, their outbursts leave them feeling guilty and as if the victim is to blame for the problem. The victim believes that if they work hard to improve themselves or make other changes, the manipulator will not be offended.

The truth is that this kind of behavior helps the manipulator by making the victim even more manageable.

This type of strategy, in combination with punishment and other strategies, works to push the victim to a point where they are so psychologically damaged that they will do anything the manipulator wants.

2.1.17   They Hate Your Honesty

Someone attempting to manipulate you will not appreciate your candor, and it will not assist you in this case. They're not in it for the sake of being a couple. It's all about them and their interests in this relationship, not yours. As a result, the more you try to bring out the true facts of a situation or express your sentiments, the more likely the manipulator will resort to one of the previously stated strategies to force you into submission once more.

Your significant other, for example, have forgotten your birthday. You try to be open and honest with them, telling them how much this has affected you, but instead of apologizing, an emotional manipulator will tell you a falsehood to make you feel awful. "I was having a really difficult time at work today since Kathy lost her husband," your substantial other might say. I had to calm her because she was crying uncontrollably, and you want me to remember to drive to the store and get you a gift? However, you are correct in that I should have acknowledged your birthday. I apologize."

You may or may not recognize at this time that they aren't truly apologetic. They may even use real tears to persuade you that you are overreacting by failing to consider their feelings. However, because the tale you just told was a lie, you'll have to soothe this individual rather than forcing them to admit they conveniently missed your birthday. As a result, the manipulator achieves their objectives since they have transferred the responsibility away from themselves while also having you apologizing to them for their own thoughtlessness.

You're dealing with a manipulator if you notice any of these characteristics in your significant other or a friend. All of these techniques will be used by a true manipulator, sometimes in groups. No matter what the scenarios or assertions of the situation are, the goal is to make you feel as if your needs, wants, and desires are second fiddle to theirs. Furthermore, these techniques can diminish your strong sense of self, making you more vulnerable to manipulation.

After a while, they'll have taken such command of the relationship that you'll be apologizing for catching them lying or hurting their feelings. As a result, they've turned you into a psychological wreck.

Be aware of their tactics and, if necessary, seek advice from friends, family, and a psychologist. One of the most important aspects of manipulation to remember is that you have made yourself a target in some way. To avoid becoming a victim, you will need to work on various aspects of your personality or other factors. This includes boosting your own self-esteem and forcing others to demonstrate how crucial the relationship is to them through their own actions.

2.2 Types of Manipulators

Manipulation is a sort of deception that many of us are aware of. Manipulators are persons who employ deceitful techniques to get what they want, regardless of the consequences to those around them, especially to those who are the victims of their tactics.

Manipulators aren't concerned with how their actions affect you personally or the psychological harm they do; all they worry about is attaining the desired results. These outcomes could range from being able to choose the restaurant to having access to the finances or gifts required to maintain a certain social status.

Knowing the warning signs is a good start, but understanding the type of emotional manipulator you're up against can also help you fight yourself against their deceitful tactics. So let us discuss the numerous types of manipulators that exist in the world so that we can obtain a better knowledge of how they work to achieve their goals.

2.2.1 Indifferent manipulator

The first is the indifferent manipulator, who acts as if they don't give a damn. These manipulators typically appear unconcerned about what you're doing or saying. This apathy is not limited to your acts but extends to all aspects of your life, including troubles and even joys.

These people have attracted your attention by acting uninterested. You devote time and effort to achieving that breakthrough in order to attract their attention and establish a deeper connection. However, because they have previously singled you out for some reason, they will supply just enough intrigue to keep you hooked without breaking the cycle of indifference.

Because you actually care, the more indifferent they act, the more inquiries you will ask. When you start asking questions, however, the manipulation becomes more serious because the manipulator can now utilize the knowledge gained from those interactions to dig their hooks in even deeper. They have begun to tug on your heartstrings without having to do or say anything explicitly, attaining the purpose of your personal emotional commitment in their life.

As the victim, you are now in a position where they can use your sympathy to "help them feel better," but in reality, the manipulator is only getting started with their sting to get anything they want from their victims, from the emotional to the material. When the victim is left with nothing, the manipulator moves on to the next victim, usually without remorse.

You are still a goose to be fleeced at this time, so the apathetic manipulator may take advantage of another sort of manipulator, the one who is always in sorrow or poor me.

2.2.2 Poor Me or the sympathetic manipulator

This type of manipulator may be the quickest to recognize, but when combined with other characteristics, they are easy to fall for again and again. So, how do the POOR ME manipulators cope with their victims so effectively? The poor me manipulators rely on sympathy and guilt to persuade their victims to try to aid another human being in need or to aid someone out of charity or faith. One continuous way that a manipulator will try to get into someone's head is by appealing to their victim's better nature. A manipulator can often use their victim's goodness against them.

It is simply part of our human nature to sympathize with those who are going through difficult times or who are confronting obstacles that are not the same as ours. We respond by doing everything we can to assist them, so we tend to give in to their requests without understanding we are being duped.

The demands may appear acceptable at first, but they will only become more complex over time. These requests quickly devolve into commands, which are notoriously time-consuming. As a result, your entire universe becomes entirely focused on the manipulator. As a result, isolation might set in, making it more difficult for you or your loved ones to see and point out the manipulation.

2.2.3 Critic manipulator

This manipulator, like other manipulators, is a little more hostile than the first two. They'll pay close attention to their victim's behaviors and emotional indicators. Following the discovery of areas of vulnerability or fragility, the manipulator will actually focus on them, initially subtly, then more boldly over time.

While it may be obvious what a manipulator is doing, many of us who fall prey to them are powerless to resist it unless we focus on changing our mentality. Anti-manipulation strategies are another strategy to prevent being a victim or to get out of a manipulative scenario.

Because the victim is attempting to please, the critic utilizes criticism to obtain what they want. However, the critical manipulator will set a bar for their standards that the victim will find impossible to fulfill. Constant criticism of their victim contributes to their victim's feeling that they are not and will never be good enough. The critic manipulates you into believing that you are worthless and that they are superior to you.

As a result, in order to gain a greater feeling of self-worth, the victim will try to be more like the critic or do things exactly the way the critic prefers. Personality changes may emerge as a result of the victim's desire to obtain the critic's affection and approval. The victim, on the other hand, is unaware that this desire is just unattainable. The critic can employ a carrot vs. stick method to keep their victim within their grip and readily swayed using the strategies we described before.

Even as nasty as these kinds of manipulators can be, there is one that is considerably worse. What is the reason for this? Because they are willing to go to great lengths to attain their objectives, including resorting to fear and violence.

2.2.4 Intimidators or the dictator manipulator

When this manipulator is at work, the victim may find themselves in a very perilous situation. The worst of the bad, these manipulators are much more aggressive than the reviewer. In fact, the intimidator is not only harsh but he or she also uses hate and paranoia to make their victims cower.

These manipulators are more accustomed to employing a stick than a carrot-like method. These manipulators may simply get their requests met once their prey is terrified. The method of exploiting anger, as well as the need to punish, is frequently used in violent relationships with intimidators. Both of these strategies play into the intimidator's fear factor.

Let's face it: when we are terrified of someone, we tend to give in far more quickly than when we are in a position of authority or defense. The goal of these manipulators is to take away any sensation of being able to defend yourself, whether physically or psychologically.

Nobody dares to speak up to someone who manipulates them with terror because they are physically scared of what that person might do. The manipulator completes their hold on the victim by using violence or the fear of harm. This style of intimidating manipulation with a mix of violence is all too common in abusive spouse situations.

Now that we've gained a better grasp of manipulators, their sorts, and strategies, it's time to learn more about the victim. If you identified a loved one in the preceding information, you might also identify some of the features in the following chapter. However, it's possible that you're the one who exhibits those characteristics. Let's look at how those characteristics play into the hands of a manipulator, and then we'll look at strategies to guard against manipulators or make the appropriate actions to get out from under their control.

So, what about your personality or the way you carry yourself raises red lights for a manipulator to notice?

2.2.5 Seductive manipulator

A seductive manipulator is one that uses flattery, charm, and sexual power to manipulate its victim. They are aware of their charisma and attractiveness and uses these traits to their best in order to gain benefits. They are confident and hence are considered the danger of all the manipulators as they play with the emotional feelings of their victims.

2.2.6 Selfless manipulator

Most of the time, manipulators seem to be selfless and kind towards their prey and hence are not easily detectable by others. They do not always intentionally manipulate their victims, but their kindness and selflessness appear to be of a kind that let others drive through the road of manipulation.

2.2.7 Skillful manipulator

A skillful manipulator is one that uses words in such a way that you can't hold them accountable for their actions. And they observe your reactions and twist them in such a way that it seems that you have wronged them.

2.2.8 Parental manipulators

Yes, it's correct. Our parents also manipulate us. We can never understand this, but our parents manipulate us in order to imply their own desires, opinions, thinking, and thoughts on their children and hence try to control their life.

2.2.9 Partner's paternal manipulators

Every parent wants their kids to be happy, and some are far too obsessed to make their kids happy that they interfere a lot in their marital life and end us ruining

happy marriages. They continuously nag their child's spouse and thus lead to broken homes.

2.2.10   Shy manipulator

Sometimes a manipulator doesn't actively and openly manipulate you but does so in a very dominant and shy manner. These are the shy manipulators. They will act innocent and sky and act in a certain way that even though you identify their manipulation, you will not find yourself in a position to confront them because of their extremely shy persona. Hence, they and their manipulation will go unnoticed by others.

Chapter 3: When And Why Manipulation Is Used?

3.1 Manipulating consciously or unconsciously?

It has happened to everyone, at least once in their lives, to be manipulated but also to manipulate.

Saying one sentence too many to achieve our desires, our needs, making the other do something that they would not want to do in order to get what we want.

Sometimes these are harmless behaviors that still go to respect the other; sometimes, they unleash very strong feelings of guilt.

Is It Possible That Manipulation Can Have Both Positive and Negative Consequences?

When you hear the word "manipulation," the first thought that comes to a head is the bad implications that come with it. Manipulation is a term that refers to deception. Manipulation is defined as the use of unethical and deceptive methods to take benefit of another person Manipulation entails deception and plain lies. Manipulation is against the law.

Over the years, the term has gotten a bad rap, and even the terms used to describe game manipulation conjure up images of something unsightly or nasty. "She has him wound around her little finger," "I said just what my boss wanted to hear," "He has a record for being a heartbreaker," and "I persuaded my pal to do what I wanted." These classic examples of manipulation do not paint a favorable picture of the scenario for both parties involved. It portrays the manipulator as selfish, self-serving, deceptive, and careless about exploiting others for their own gain while portraying the victim as naive, naïve, and potentially even weak in spirit for "letting" themselves be duped so easily.

Manipulation has long been thought of as a brutal, devious, and cunning act in which one person is used or taken leverage of. When the cunning individual has heartlessly neglected the feelings of another, putting their own selfish wants above everyone else, manipulation is regarded even more severely. Even worse, the manipulator has taken advantage of the other by posing as a friend and then exploiting confidential knowledge against them.

There is one fact that never changes, whether it is in our personal and professional lives. Nobody enjoys the feeling of being duped. Nobody. With so much hostility connected with this issue, it's almost inconceivable to think that manipulation might be used for good or that it may conceivably bring about positive change.

Manipulation, as shocking as it may seem, isn't all terrible. Manipulation is everywhere, and proof of it can often be found without looking very hard. Take, for example, the incessant messaging from marketers and advertising encouraging us to purchase this, purchase that, quit doing this, and quit doing that. They're all attempting to influence our judgments in some way. Which sorts of manipulation, on the other hand, are actually attempting to persuade us to alter for the better

Advertisements encouraging us to quit smoking and eat healthier are attempting to influence our decisions, but in this case, they are attempting to effect good change. It is in your best interests to stop smoking. So it's all about eating well. Isn't it a beneficial sort of manipulation if it's for your own benefit? Governments all around the world use their citizens to influence them. Religion has a similar effect. Yet, because it comes from a more "authoritative" source, we may opt to dismiss it. Businesses regularly influence their customers by inventing products to enhance sales and then informing buyers that they "can't live without it."

Manipulation, whether for "good" or "evil," is still manipulation at the end of the day. Do any of us have the right to impose our will on another's choice or behaviors, even if we believe it is in their best interests? What makes the concept of manipulation so unsettling is that we don't enjoy the idea of someone else telling us what to do or pressuring us into doing stuff we wouldn't otherwise do.

Managers at work are constantly attempting to manipulate their employees, though effective leaders do so in order to keep their employees motivated and performing at their best. Effective managers have perfected the art of positive manipulation and turned it into a powerful weapon for managing employee performance and motivating people to achieve their objectives.

The distinction between what is classified as manipulation and what is referred to as persuasion is this distinguishing element. Persuasion is still a sort of manipulation, but three factors distinguish it from the bad stigma associated with manipulation:

- It was your intention.
- Your sincerity.
- What will be the benefit or positive impact for the individual you're attempting to persuade.

We are not always aware of this; in fact, manipulation can be conscious or unconscious.

Unconscious or unintentional manipulation:- When we as victims are not aware of us being manipulated and let the perpetrators manipulate us, that is called unconscious manipulation. In this type of manipulation, our mind accepts manipulation unconsciously as it considers manipulation as normal and justifiable. Our mind never regards the manipulation as so and hence gets manipulated at the hands of the manipulator.

Also, sometimes things happen that manipulators, not knowing that such behavior is manipulating, continue to do so. This also amounts to unconscious manipulation in terms of the manipulator.

Conscious or intentional manipulation:-When we as victims knowingly lets the individuals manipulate us, that is called conscious manipulation. Sometimes in a relationship is of such a manner like father0son, master-slave, husband-wife that we are aware of the manipulation lets the perpetrator manipulate us.

Also, some people may manipulate others intuitively, without realizing it, while others may actively try to improve their manipulation techniques. Manipulation can be identified by the following signs:

- Implicit threats
- Withholding information
- Gaslighting
- Use of sex to achieve goals
- Passive-aggressive behavior
- Dishonesty
- Isolating a person from loved ones
- Verbal abuse

Because the motivations for manipulation might range from unconscious to intentional, it's critical to determine the conditions of the manipulation. While dropping stuff off in circumstances of abuse may be necessary, a therapist can assist others in learning to deal with or face manipulative behavior from others.

3.2 When Our Unconscious Mind Accepts Manipulation Or Why We Let Ourselves Be Manipulated?

The use of undue influence (emotional, interpersonal, domestic, sensual, economic, technical, etc.) for the aim of enriching the manipulator to the detriment of their victims are known as psychological manipulation.

Willful psychological manipulation where one willfully lets the other manipulate oneself differs from healthy social influence, which involves a typically fair exchange of information between people. One person uses another for selfish and dishonest advantage in a psychologically manipulative relationship.

- History of the family-Was the person in question influenced in his or her life by manipulative family members? Was there a struggle for social or economic survival in the family dynamic? Was there a struggle for power, control, affection, relational position and acceptance, prestige and advantage, financial and physical resources, or other real or perceived "advantages"? "What are your thoughts on this? Were there any power battles, either inside the family or with "outsiders," "for more power and influence?"
- During the individual's formative years, did she or he have any social flaws or disadvantages? Did she feel "excluded" in any manner (socially, economically, culturally, or professionally) and wished to fit into the accepted norm?
- Were there any cultural, professional, or institutional standards that favored cunning, plotting, negotiating,

bargaining, manipulating human flaws, designing Machiavellian ruthlessness, or other types of indirect power and influence? Some professions, for example, are far better at influencing others than others. In economic and social relations, some societies legitimize aggressive bargaining, while others do not. Certain linked groups have made it clear that their goal is to persuade others to see things their way. If a person has been heavily influenced by any of these factors, he or she may have internalized some manipulative strategies into behavioral norms.

Chronic manipulation is most often (but not always) the result of highly competitive surroundings in which opposing groups (friends and relatives, schoolmates, co-workers, friendship organizations, societal affiliations, and financial interests) grunt for power, effect, assets, and leverage, and one feels a lack of real and plentiful strength over a situation. When faced with a sense of scarcity, inadequacy, and inferiority, or a desire for more authority, influence, and advantage, the manipulator turns to cun and deviousness to get what he or she wants. This kind of conduct can become persistent and repetitive over time, with unavoidable negative effects.

In short, a manipulation is a psychiatric act of exploiting and, in the worst situations, abuse that begins as preservation of competitive impulse for self-preservation.

Personality, sincerity, honesty, creative problem-solving abilities, and good communication and relationship skills are all strong alternatives to manipulativeness.

In case of manipulation, you should never sit back and sob on your weakness, but you should be bold enough to practice the following:

- Express yourself; if there are topics you disapprove of, say so and explain how you feel.

- Express your ideas and feelings as clearly as possible so that he can understand that he cannot influence your judgment from criticism.
- Speak in the first person
- Only take responsibility for yourself

These points mentioned above are just some of the very important solutions that the "manipulated" can adopt to interrupt the process of manipulation; in front of these communicative responses, the manipulator will find himself displaced.

3.3 Why Do People Manipulate Others?

Manipulation may be an unintentional approach for certain people to deal with a cutthroat society where revealing sentiments is often prohibited. Manipulation is a common occurrence in everyday life, and most people use manipulative ways from time to time. People who use manipulation as their primary mode of engagement, on the other hand, tend to share several characteristics. These include:-

3.3.1 Poor communication skills

The direct conversation may make some people uneasy. Others may have grown up in homes where deception was the norm. So they think manipulation is normal and justifiable.

3.3.2 A desire to avoid connection

Some people use manipulation to dominate others by treating them as a means to an end. This can be a sign of a personality disorder like narcissism.

3.3.3 Fear

People may manipulate others out of fear, particularly fear of abandonment. This is common during breakups or arguments in relationships.

3.3.4 Defensiveness

Manipulation might be used to avoid taking responsibility. While some people avoid taking responsibility in order to dominate or harm other people, others do it because they are afraid of being judged, have low self-esteem, or find it difficult to face their own flaws.

3.3.5 Social norms

Manipulation is common, and in some cases, even advantageous. For example, numerous people learn that in order to grow professionally, it is necessary to be sociable and happy around coworkers, and hence they embrace manipulation.

3.3.6 Marketing, advertising, and other financial or political incentives

Enormous enterprises are dedicated to influencing people's emotions in order to persuade them to alter their thoughts, buy things, or vote in a certain way, and we being the general public acknowledge this manipulation easily.

3.3.7 Others

Other reasons apart from the above one that states why people manipulate are as under:-

- A need for control or power over others
- Fear of abandonment
- A need to raise their own self-esteem
- A willingness to prioritize their own feelings and desires over the needs and well-being of others
- Feelings of helplessness, worthlessness, or hopelessness

Chapter 4: Characteristics of Manipulated People

4.1 Behavioral Traits Of Victims Preferred By Manipulators

Six billion people are around the globe, and not everyone is the victim of a manipulator; why? Because not everyone has the specific behavioral traits that are manipulators see in their victims. The following stated are some of the behavioral traits of victims preferred by manipulators:

4.1.1 Personal responsibility ignored

Those people who ignore their personal responsibility easily fall prey to manipulators as they are irresponsible and always need someone to provide them support and also need someone to take their responsibility. Hence they easily get influenced by people who are givers and those manipulators who give take a lot from these victims in exchange.

4.1.2 Can't stay alone

Those people who cannot stay alone and are scared of loneliness and abandonment always fall prey to manipulators. They are always in need of someone so that they can depend and rely on that person. This dependency makes them easily attacked by the manipulators.

4.1.3 Sense of helplessness and fear of abandonment

This is also one of the behavioral traits of victims of manipulation; if one fears abandonment in a relationship and experiences a sense of helplessness while cutting yourself off from others, then one can be an easy target of manipulation.

4.1.4 Intolerance of criticism

A strong mind is not easy to fall for manipulation, and it's one of the traits of a strong mind to accept constructive criticism. One who is intolerant towards criticism is a week mind and is an easy subject of manipulation.

4.1.5 Trouble in taking decisions

The one who can't make decisions about himself and others in day-to-day life can fall for manipulation.

4.1.6 Pessimism and a lack of trust in oneself

Again, a strong mind that is immune to manipulation is optimistic and sees the bright side of life and the situations surrounding him. But those who are a pessimist and are filled with negativity towards oneself and others are easily deceived by manipulators. It is obvious for you to trust your actions and your instincts; if you fail to do so, you fall into the pit dug by manipulators.

4.1.7 Insecure or emotionally fragile

Sometimes being emotional is not a negative trait but being emotional all the time and feeling highly insecure is a negative behavioral trait that can land you in the land of manipulators.

4.1.8 Idolizing others easily

Those who idolize others easily become the prey of the manipulators. One should not be quick in idolizing individuals around them.

4.1.9 Afraid disappointing others

Those who are always putting efforts to please everyone are the easy victims of manipulators. These people are easily manipulated as they are givers and can easily give what the manipulator asks as they don't want to disappoint the manipulator by saying no to them. This trait of being generous for no reason can result in them being manipulated by others. These people should learn to say no.

4.1.10   High capacity for empathy

Being empathetic and sympathetic is a good virtue, but being highly empathetic can be a huge drawback as people with a high capacity for empathy can be easily exploited by the manipulators. The manipulators may seek their help, and these foolish empaths will show empathy towards their prey and let them manipulate their own selves.

4.2 How Manipulators Select Their Victims?

These points below are certain characteristics that manipulators look for in their prey or the victims.

- The tendency to please the other
- Addiction to seeking the other's approval and acceptance
- Fear of expressing negative emotions, including anger, frustration, and disapproval
- Lack of assertiveness and a fragile ability to say "no."

- Poorly defined personal identity and dependent on the confirmation of others
- Lack of confidence in one's own abilities
- External attribution of the reason for their choices
- Naiveté: victims do not accept the idea that some people are devious, treacherous, and ruthless
- Victims often give manipulators a second chance, imagining that they can change
- Questioning of their own positions and a low level of assertiveness
- Difficulty understanding the reasons why a manipulator might hurt them
- The more dependent a victim is, the higher the risk of being manipulated. Emotional dependence underlies the presence of a submissive personality in need of validation.

This could be manipulation if you've ever felt weird in a close relation or casual encounter—like you're being coerced, controlled, or even doubting yourself more than normal.

"Manipulation is an emotionally destructive psychological tactic employed by people who are incapable of directly asking for what they want and need," explains Sharie Stines, a therapist in California who specializes in assault and dysfunctional relationships. "Those who strive to control others are attempting to manipulate them."

Manipulation can take many forms, from a forceful sales associate to an emotionally abusive partner, and some actions are more obvious than others.

4.3 Signs That Show That You Are A Subject Of Manipulation

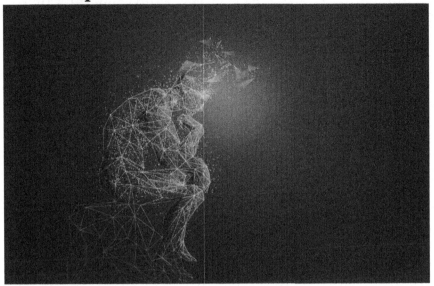

Here, experts explain the telltale signs that you could be the subject of manipulation.

4.3.1 You feel fear, obligation, and guilt

Fear, obligation, and guilt, according to Stines, are three variables that characterize manipulative behavior. She emphasizes that when someone tries to manipulate you, you are indeed psychologically coerced into doing things you don't want to do. It's possible that you're terrified to do it, that you're forced to do it, or that you're guilty of not doing it.

She separates two categories of manipulators: "the aggressor" and "the sufferer." A bully, she claims, makes you feel terrified and may dominate you with fury, threats, and coercion. The victim makes their intended target feel guilty. Stine explains, "The victim typically seems to be in pain." However, she says, manipulators are the ones who have generated the problem despite the fact that they typically play the victim.

Those who are pursued by manipulators who play the victim, according to Stines, usually try to help the manipulator in order to feel less guilty. Victims of this kind of deception frequently feel obligated to help the victim by doing anything they can to make their pain go away.

4.3.2 You're questioning yourself

"Gaslighting" is the act of persuading someone to doubt oneself, their actuality, emotions, or ideas. A manipulative person, according to Stines, may distort what you say to make it about themselves, control the discussion, or make you feel like you've made an error when you haven't.

If you're gaslighted, you might feel a false sense of guilt or ambivalence, as if you've failed completely or must have done something wrong when this isn't the case, according to Stines.

Manipulators, she believes, are to blame. "They refuse to take responsibility for their actions."

4.3.3 There are strings attached

"It isn't 'for fun and free' if a courtesy isn't done for you just because," Stines explains. "If there are strings attached, manipulation is taking place."Stines coined the moniker "Mr. Nice Guy" to describe one type of manipulator. This individual has the potential to be really kind and do a lot of services for others. She explains, "It's pretty baffling since you don't notice anything is wrong."

"On the other side, every good conduct is accompanied by an expectation." According to Stines, if you don't meet the manipulator's demands, you'll be labeled ungrateful.

Abusing the norms and ideals of reciprocity, according to Jay Olson, a postdoctoral scholar at McGill University who researches manipulation, is among the most typical forms of manipulation.

For example, a salesperson may make it appear as if you should buy something since he or she got you a decent bargain. In a relationship, a spouse could buy you flowers and then demand something in exchange. "These strategies work because they exploit cultural standards," Olson explains. "It's natural to want to repay favors, but we often feel we forced to respond and collaborate even when someone is acting insincerely."

The 'foot-in-the-door and 'door-in-the-face' strategies are certainly familiar to you.

Manipulators, according to Olson, generally use one of two tactics. The first is the foot-in-the-door method, in which a small and legitimate request—for example, do you have time?—leads to a larger request—for example, I need $eight for a taxi. "In street scams, this is a frequent tactic," adds Olson.

The door-in-the-face technique, according to Olson, is getting a massive request, having it refused, and then making a smaller demand.

Anyone conducting contract work, for example, may request a large amount of money upfront, then request a smaller figure after you deny, he says. According to Olson, this works because, following the larger request, the smaller plea appears reasonable compared.

4.4 What To Do If You Think You're Being Manipulated?

You should have a fair idea of what manipulation is and how it works after reading this far. You should also be more aware of the warning signals of a manipulator, as well as how they select their victims. Learning to harden your resistance to manipulation is a fantastic approach to avoid becoming a victim in the future, but it won't necessarily help you in your current predicament.

If you're reading this book, there's a good probability you're dealing with a manipulator. Perhaps you've had enough of being walked all over and are looking for a solution to shift the present relationship's behaviors.

You're ready to stand up for yourself and reclaim control of your life, but you don't know how to do it since you don't have a road map for successfully evicting a long-term manipulator. Learning to resist manipulation is a fantastic start, but you also need to understand how to defend yourself from manipulators, especially if you're currently in a relationship.

If you're ready to understand how to protect yourself against manipulators in your life, which you must be if you've read this far, there are a few actions you can take to secure your success, not just in the short term but also in the long run. Remember that your safety comes first, so if you're dealing with a manipulator who's prone to violence, take precautions to keep yourself and any youngsters safe while you're changing or terminating your connection with the manipulator.

4.4.1 Step One: Be Aware

You must first be aware of what you are looking at before you can take any action, regardless of the scenario. To put it another way, if you want to defend yourself against manipulators, you must be able to recognize and identify the people who are attempting to manipulate you.

Look for any indications of the strategies we've already outlined. These might assist you in identifying the manipulator in your life as well as the most toxic connection. One of the most difficult aspects of identifying manipulators is their subtlety. After all, they wouldn't be successful if they admitted to manipulating others.

We discussed the warning indications of manipulators earlier in this book, as well as what manipulators search for in a target.

Start spotting the manipulators in your life using what you've learned. Once you've figured out who they are, you may begin defending yourself using the following steps. However, you must keep in mind that in order to truly change the manipulators in your life, you must be willing to take action. No one else will be able to help you with it.

4.4.2 Step Two: Realize it's Not Personal

This remark isn't fully accurate, but how accurate it depends on the manipulator. Most manipulators, on the other hand, aren't out to harm you personally; they're only interested in getting what they want and will go to any length to obtain it.

In most circumstances, you are simply in the way of the manipulator, so they will do anything they can to persuade you to give them what they want, even if it involves making you feel awful or causing you pain. You must realize that it is their choice how they conduct as a person; you have no control over their decisions or behaviors.

As a result, you must place the manipulator in charge of their activities and overall behavior. Stop blaming them for their decisions or making it your fault in some way. After all, they're already attempting to accomplish this in order to reach their end aim. You don't have to assist them by establishing an internal discussion that supports their long-term objectives.

4.4.3 Step Three: Give Yourself Some Space

Giving yourself some space from manipulators is one of the best things you can do. To put it another way, do everything you can to avoid them. When it comes to creating space, it can be as simple as refusing to travel to places where they congregate or not returning phone calls or text messages. In today's social media-driven environment, you may need to disown or delete these people from your contacts.

To be honest, this is sometimes easier said than done, particularly if the manipulator is someone close to you, such as a family member or perhaps a spouse. When your significant other is the manipulator in your life, there may be more people involved than just you, such as youngsters and extended family. With the support of a counselor or other professional, you may be able to make changes or carve out space for yourself, depending on how your spouse manipulates you.

Other concerns with marriage may necessitate sticking to your guns in order to effect change while accepting the fact that you may not be able to separate or divorce. Others may find that the mental and emotional anguish caused by the manipulation is too big to overcome without a physical divorce. Working with a professional is thus an important first step in determining where you might want to go in terms of establishing space and distance between yourself and the manipulator.

If you aren't ready or able to let go of the manipulator, you will simply have to learn how to cope with them efficiently. The following steps can help you maintain your sane while working and living with a manipulator.

4.4.4 Step Four: Work on Improving Your Mind

Now, no one can genuinely devote all of their time and attention to avoiding deceptive people, no matter how much they want to. And, while it's better to avoid them, the problem is that you attracted them at one point, so you'll continue to be a magnet for them unless you change some things about yourself.

For a brief while, disposing of a manipulator will provide relief, but without modifications to your own attitude and personality, another will emerge to take its place. Throughout this book, we've covered the characteristics and other elements that influence how a manipulator selects a victim. We've also considered how we may improve in certain areas. If it seems overwhelming, get expert help. They will be able to assist you through the measures taken to eliminate the target from your back that attracts manipulators.

To truly defend yourself against manipulators, you must improve your attitude as well as change other behaviors, such as your internal conversation. Telling yourself good things that promote a fair sense of self-worth will make the world's manipulators less likely to target you. After all, their targets are those who can be swayed due to their own self-worth issues and reliance on others for affirmation.

4.4.5 Step Five: Learn Anti-Manipulation Techniques

You won't need this step once you've developed a strong attitude, but until then, you'll want to learn and practice various anti-manipulation strategies, which may be found later in this chapter.

Anti-manipulation tactics are a collection of skills that can be utilized to defend your mental health. Remember that you are a target for the manipulator, and they will see their wants before they will recognize any damage they may have caused you.

As a result, it's critical to realize that in a relationship with a manipulator, the strongest protection you have is yourself. Although they will try to convince you otherwise, using strategies to defend yourself from their tactics is not selfish.

You'll want to rehearse the tactics before you start utilizing them, and we recommend doing so with someone you trust. Role-playing is a fun approach to master new skills and cement them in your mind. As a result, when the situations arise, you will answer naturally and without appearing forced. When it appears forced, the manipulator detects a possible weak area and launches an attack. Don't expose a weak place for them to try to exploit!

The more you practice these approaches, the better you'll be able to respond when you're confronted with an issue in your everyday life. But you should be subtle when using the techniques or when dealing with a manipulator.

4.4.6 Step Six: Be Direct

Manipulators act the way they do to acquire what they want, as we've studied throughout this book. Their primary focus will always be themselves, but if they are interacting with people who do not prioritize the manipulator, they may become confused.

Although the games are subtle, you are not required to participate. By asking what they want right away, you can show the manipulator that you aren't going to play the game.

If someone is trying to persuade you to do anything or give up money or other valuables, don't play their game; instead, come out and ask them what they want. If you pursue this path, make sure you pay attention to what they have to say and don't pass judgment.

In some circumstances, lending a sympathetic ear can demonstrate to a manipulator that there is an alternative strategy or approach to obtaining the items they desire.

While this may not change their conduct, it will give you a sense of independence because you will no longer be under their control.

4.4.7 Step Seven: Be Consistent

Now that you've begun to defend yourself against manipulators, you must continue to do so. This necessitates consistency, even if there are occasions when you doubt your own ability to do so.

You'll wind up sending mixed signals if you're not consistent. These mixed signals will offer manipulators a green light, encouraging them to continue acting in this manner. Whether it's an anti-manipulation strategy or being direct, choose an approach that you think will perform best and that you feel comfortable doing.

Then keep practicing it, especially when interacting with the manipulator using your favorite manner. They'll eventually realize that their tactics of manipulation aren't working, so they'll move on to another target.

However, be prepared for a strong onslaught from the manipulator in the beginning, as they will try harder when you first begin to stand up to them. This is because they want to shatter your willpower and restore the connection to its previous state.

When you're under duress, it's sometimes the greatest option to put some distance between yourself and the manipulator. This brings us to the next level, which is movement-based.

4.4.8 Step Eight: Leave

People will attempt to manipulate you no matter how hard you try or how consistent you are. If this is the case, the best thing you can do is end the connection and walk away from that individual.

As previously said, ending a relationship with a spouse entails more than simply walking away. You'll need to set aside time to consult with a specialist so that you can limit the harm to yourself and your children.

It may be difficult to make this decision, but you must prioritize yourself. Accepting manipulative behavior will wreak havoc on your mental and emotional well-being. From an emotional, economical, and psychological aspect, the harm can be assessed. There is no relationship worth risking the consequences of sticking it out with someone who simply wants to interact with you from a manipulator's perspective.

At the same time, keep in mind that the whole goal is to improve your situation. Since you've established that this is a poisonous relationship, treat it as such and do everything you can to get it out of your life.

4.5 Tips for Adopting an Anti-Manipulation Mindset

Nobody can control you if you don't let them. This is one of the most crucial things you'll ever learn about manipulation. Allowing someone to manipulate you implies that you have given them control over you, whether knowingly or unconsciously. Because so much of what makes you easier to manipulate is based on how you perceive yourself and others, it's critical to spend time getting to know yourself.

Most of the overdone ways of interacting with people that worked against you were discussed during our examination of the features that attract a manipulator. Consider that for a moment. Those who are constantly seeking outside approval, those who desire to please others, and those who are narcissistic all prefer to delegate their authority to others. As a result, a manipulator can quickly elevate oneself to the position of the most important person in their life.

Isn't it easy to see how it can devolve into unwitting acquiescence to the manipulator?

Personal characteristics might expose you to a lot of danger.

Anti-manipulation techniques are a fantastic way to defend yourself against individuals who are attempting to manipulate you, but they will be ineffective if you are not in the correct frame of mind. Your current mental state is obviously not healthy, as it is allowing others to manipulate you. What you need to do is change your mindset, adopt new beliefs, and adopt a new attitude. As we've seen, a variety of defensive strategies are predicated on a shift in how you interpret your connection with the manipulator.

So, how do you alter your thinking?

Here are a few pointers that you might find useful.

4.5.1 Take Responsibility for Your Feelings

You are the only one who develops your sentiments; what other people do or say has no bearing on your emotions or thought patterns. However, other people's activities might serve as triggers for various emotions and thought patterns. If you observe particular triggers that bring up consistent feelings, it may be necessary to investigate the trigger as well as the sentiments to determine the underlying basis of the problem. You can settle it and so eliminate the source of those emotions if you can find it.Your feelings are influenced by your mental state, as well as your attitude and beliefs in light of the circumstances. Taking responsibility for your feelings improves your thinking because you are regaining control and not handing it over to people who are attempting to manipulate you. The more you practice, the better you'll get at deciding how you want to feel and how you want to react to those feelings. After all, you have no control over what occurs to you, but you do have control over how you respond.

4.5.2 Ignore Guilt

You can only be accountable for your own emotions; you can't control how other people feel. They are created in the same way that you make your own feelings. Manipulators frequently utilize guilt to acquire what they want from the people they have chosen to be their victims. You must learn to dismiss any guilt trips that are thrown your way. It is their problem and obligation to deal with, not yours if they are sad, mad, or whatever they say they will feel. In the same way, you cannot be accountable for what others do; you can only be responsible for your own acts. After all, you don't have the power to compel someone to behave in a certain way.

When you reach maturity, you have the freedom to choose how you will act. No one else is capable of doing so.

4.5.3 Don't Feel Fear

This one is similar to guilt in several ways. Manipulators utilize it to acquire influence over you, and they frequently try to profit from your worries. What you need to do is learn how to confront and overcome your worries. We've talked about how vital it is to seek help when dealing with your anxieties and worries several times in this book. There are numerous professionals who can provide you with the necessary tools to deal with them. After all, if you aren't terrified of something, like losing your job, the manipulator won't be able to use that fear to force you to do what they want. We now know that overcoming your fear is not as simple as it appears. You'll have to take it one day at a time, but you must accept your fear and go on each time it arises; this will gradually help you come to grips with it. Again, don't be afraid to seek help if you're having trouble dealing with a phobia, but also take the time to write down exactly what you're frightened of. It may not be as frightening once it is reduced to black and white.

4.5.4 Let go of the pain

Old hurt is a manipulator's gold mine, and we all seem to have some buried deep within us. If you have any old hurt buried deep within you, the one thing you try to avoid thinking about at all times, you must let it go. You can always seek the aid and guidance of a licensed therapist if you can't do it on your own. Forgiveness, which is essentially about letting go of your resentment in order to find peace for yourself, maybe a part of letting go of the suffering. After all, the resentment and hurt are troubling you as the one who is carrying it around, not the initial cause of the damage. This kind of burden is almost unbearable.

Who wouldn't want to relieve themselves of that burden?

4.5.5 Love yourself

We all know that persons with poor self-esteem are easy prey for predators of all kinds, including manipulators. These people take advantage of everything you don't like about yourself in order to acquire what they want. This is a tactic that the manipulator can use again and time again to get consistent results from their victims who have poor self-esteem and self-worth. What you need to do is learn to accept yourself for who you are, accept the good with the bad, and let things go. This is often easier said than done, but it is doable if you work on it consistently. Nobody can use anything against you if you are content with who you are. You can utilize a variety of self-improvement tactics to help you boost your self-confidence and self-esteem. However, none of this will work unless you are prepared to put in the effort and modify your internal conversation.

4.5.6 Detach yourself

You can't claim to belong to anyone or anything. You are not, for example, your work or job. When you believe you are your job, you will naturally be afraid of losing it, which manipulators can take advantage of. You must separate yourself from the things with which you identify. You must realize that you are simply yourself; you cannot be anything else. Things don't make you who you are; you make yourself who you are. If you identify yourself by what you own or what you do, you may find yourself struggling in difficult times. At the same time, your sense of self as a result of your attachment to objects might make you a target for a manipulator.

4.6 Anti-Manipulation Techniques You Can Use

You're ready to start practicing anti-manipulation tactics once you've gotten yourself in the correct frame of mind. The beauty of these strategies is that they may be used whenever you need to defend yourself against manipulation, regardless of when or how it occurs. However, in order for them to work correctly, you must be in the appropriate state of mind, so gather your thoughts before beginning. Then practice them until they become second nature.

As a result, you're developing natural barriers to deal with manipulators as well as others who seek to take advantage of you.

4.6.1 Translator

This anti-manipulation strategy is not only the simplest to learn and use, but it is also the most successful. This method is quite straightforward: you simply switch stuff around on your manipulator. When you're being manipulated by someone, summarise everything they're asking for in a single, concise sentence.

Then simply inquire as to whether or not this is what they desire. This strategy is quite straightforward and lays out all of the cards on the table.

This is the most effective way for fully understanding what the other person is experiencing or thinking. People today have difficulty in that they aren't very direct; they don't state what they want or need, and they feel obligated to do things in an indirect way. You can discover more about the other person and what they want out of the relationship by employing this strategy. This is a method that may be used in any relationship to show that you are actually listening and regard the other person as an individual. Because you'll be able to define where each of you is coming from and get difficulties or worries out in the open, the translator approach is ideal for resolving a number of situations.

4.6.2 Literal

This method, like the translator approach, works with the subtext of a discussion but in a somewhat different way.

The literal method ignores the subtext, whereas the translation technique relies on putting things out in the open. If someone is avoiding you and you are picking up on their indications, simply ignore them and go on. When you're aware that someone is attempting to manipulate you, this strategy is ideal. It's also useful when dealing with people with whom you have a relationship, although these bonds may not be as strong with you as they are with others.

One of the best aspects of this strategy is that it is really rational. It is founded on the idea that people should ask for what they desire. If they don't bother to ask, they shouldn't expect to get anything by having people guess what they really need or desire. It's all about being honest in this strategy. If you don't say something, the problem, desire, or request doesn't exist. Just bear in mind that this strategy necessitates dealing with a lot of pressure, so be prepared. After all, as you continue to reject the pressure, it will become more noticeable and more difficult to deal with.

4.6.3 Subtext Exaggeration

This strategy is similar to the literal way, except that instead of ignoring the subtext, you react to it solely. You pay little attention to what is being said and simply react to the subtext. You must, however, do more than simply react to it; you must go above and above. When responding to the subtext, you must accentuate your actions. If someone is attempting to persuade you to go somewhere, react with what you assume they would say based on the subtext you believe is currently there.

If they've intimated that you're a bad person for turning down their request and breaking their heart, say so. Keep in mind that no matter what you say, no action is required. After all, you're not going where they want to go or doing what they want, so ignore that portion as well. Simply admitting the subtext does not bind you to anything, but it does inform the other person that you are aware of their strategy.

When you are absolutely certain that someone is attempting to manipulate you, the subtext exaggeration strategy is one of the greatest to apply. This strategy allows you to make it crystal plain to that person that you know what they're up to and that no matter what they try to accomplish their aim, it's not going to work. You must be able to swiftly read the subtext in order for this strategy to be effective since you must respond to it swiftly. You'll be sending a message to your manipulator that will throw them off and make them think twice before trying again.

4.6.4 Time Delay

When you know without a doubt that you are being controlled, but you don't know how they are manipulating you, the time delay is the greatest option. This is frequently employed when you can't interpret a person's subtle communications or when you're not sure what they're asking. If you're not sure about anything or feel pressed to make a decision, put it off. This will give you time to consider the situation and determine whether you understand what they want and are willing to comply with their request.

What's key with a time delay is that you tell them you'll let them know as soon as you make up your decision. This puts you in command, not them. Not to mention that handling any request in this manner will make it impossible for them to continue bugging you on the initial subject. While they may try to push the matter the first time, warn them that doing so simply makes you less likely to comply with their request. After all, they are the ones that are looking for something from you, not the other way around. You must remember that you are the one holding the cards in your favorite, and you must reply appropriately.

They will almost certainly bring it up again since they are manipulators, but stick to your beliefs and assure them that you will let them know what you decide after you have made up your decision. This is a very useful method for people who are dealing with a weak state of mind or who feel like they are going to give in to someone's demands. It can also be used as a last resort while you focus on improving your mental health.

Now that you know what features a manipulator searches for in a possible target, you have some weapons to use to combat a manipulative personality, and you know where you can develop to avoid being a target, let's talk about how you can tell whether your relationship is manipulative and has negative consequences for you and your family. Let's have a look at the steps to evaluating your relationships and creating an action plan to assist you in enhancing your interpersonal interactions.

Chapter 5: Emotional Manipulation

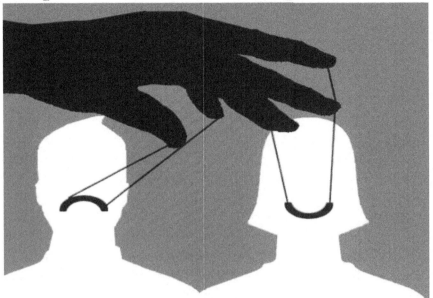

Those in psychology's "dark triad" are the most skilled and dangerous manipulators. Psychopathic, narcissistic, and Machiavellian characters lack compassion and manipulate others for their own selfish benefit, regardless of the cost to others. They are cruel, inconsiderate, arrogant, and opportunist people who take advantage of others and act out against them in order to further their own goals. A member of the evil triad might easily be your lover, friend, neighbor, relative, coworker, or boss. They try to hide who they are by putting on a fairly regular, and often charming and pleasant, persona, but their malevolent intent is still present beneath the mask. Individuals like them are harmful to the mental health of everybody who comes into contact with them.

People without major psychiatric illnesses use manipulation to acquire what they want, sometimes without even realizing it, and occasionally with malevolent intent. It's been suggested that we're all guilty of manipulating others rather than articulating our needs and desires directly. There is a considerable distinction between a compulsive manipulator and someone who uses persuasion on occasion to accomplish what they want. Malignant manipulators have no other method of relating to others and have nothing substantial to offer in terms of love and connection in a relationship. There's nothing you can do about it.

Manipulation erodes your ability to make conscious judgments and take activities that are in your best interests and consistent with your personal beliefs and limits. To put it another way, influence gets you to do things you wouldn't normally do.

Emotional manipulation, at its worst, systematically erodes your self-worth and self-confidence, as well as your belief in your own judgments. It has the potential to cause you to unintentionally sacrifice yourself to the extent where you lose your self-respect and create a distorted perception of reality. You are even more susceptible to additional manipulation with your defenses compromised or fully disarmed in this way.

An experienced, emotional manipulator might persuade you to trust him or her with your feeling of self-worth and psychological well-being.

They whittle away at your personality and unleash hell on your mental health once you've been duped into making that catastrophic error.

A deliberate and malevolent manipulator must know your weaknesses, conceal their violent motives and conduct, and be callous enough not to care how much pain their manipulation causes you in order to be successful. All that matters is gaining power and achieving what they desire.

You can detect hidden aggression by becoming aware of the strategies used by manipulators. However, manipulators rely on your trust, skepticism, and powerful emotions — guilt, terror, love, and humiliation - to keep you from thinking clearly and recognizing the manipulation. In many cases, they purposefully create these emotions for that reason. That is how manipulators are able to get away with their actions. As a result, it's critical to notice when you doubt your own senses or instincts or when you're feeling a feeling that makes you subject to manipulation.

The described manipulation techniques are just that: manipulation techniques. Many of the techniques used by manipulative friends, relatives, coworkers, superiors, neighbors, and even children are similar to those used by manipulative mates, families, work colleagues, supervisors, neighbors, and even kids.

5.1 Emotional Manipulation in the Relationship

Emotional manipulation can be so subtle and covert that it can keep you under its influence for a long time before you realize what's going on if you ever do. Some manipulators are masters of their craft. They're regarded as puppeteers, and if you don't recognize the symptoms, you can end up as a puppet.

You perform exactly what the puppeteer wants you to do as your threads are pushed in various directions. You believe you are behaving of your own volition, but you are not.

If you've been the victim of manipulation, you're undoubtedly aware that something isn't quite right, but you're not sure what it is. You may even suspect that you are being manipulated, but you have no way of knowing for sure if you are or how it is being done. One thing you do know is that you want to know whether or not you're being manipulated. How do you know?

It's much simpler and more evident than you might assume.

Manipulation is harmful and has significant negative consequences for us, even if we are unaware of it. Those unfavorable consequences are the evidence left behind after a manipulation crime has been committed.

There's a good chance you're being manipulated if you detect any of the following indications while in a relationship:

1. Your happiness at finding love has transformed into apprehension at the prospect of losing it. Your emotions have shifted from joy and pleasure to anxiety, sadness, and even hopelessness.

2. You're unhappy and unsure about the relationship most of the time, yet you're scared of losing it because you're happy and content every now and again.

3. Your relationship appears to be quite complicated, despite the fact that you have no idea why. When discussing it with others, you may find yourself stating, "It's difficult to describe." It's just that it's extremely difficult."

4. You talk about it to anyone who will listen all the time. It serves no purpose.

5. You constantly inquire if something is amiss with your lover. Something doesn't feel quite right, but you're not sure what it is.

6. Your partner has often pointed out to you that you appear to have developed a problem with trust, jealousy, insecurity, wrath, or overreacting.

7. Your mood is entirely determined by the health of your connection, and you're going through extraordinary highs and lows.

8. You have a sneaking suspicion that you are to blame for the best thing that has ever happened to you, but you're not sure how.

9. You worry over the relationship all the time, studying every detail in a pathetic effort to "figure it out."

10.You're never sure where you stand with your partner, leaving you in a constant state of worry and anxiety.

11.You're always on the defensive. You have a strong need to explain and defend yourself because you believe you have been misunderstood.

12.You've earned the title of detective. You scan the internet for information about your spouse, monitor his or her social media accounts, and feel compelled to check their web search history, texts, or emails. When they aren't at home, you want to know where they are because you are concerned about their safety.

13.You try to keep bad ideas and emotions to yourself since expressing them feels constrained or even forbidden. You're frustrated because you can't talk about the things that annoy you.

14.You're always worried that you're not living up to your partner's expectations. You're self-conscious.

15.You hold yourself responsible for your partner's withdrawal. You're baffled as to why you keep damaging your relationship.

16.You can explode like an emotional volcano at times, exploding with rage, irritation, and even animosity. You've never done anything like this before and swear you'll never do it again, yet it keeps happening no matter how hard you try.

17.You have the impression that you have no idea how to make your lover happy. You put in a lot of effort, yet nothing appears to succeed, at least not for a long time. You used to make them quite happy, and you're not sure why.

18.You don't like yourself as much as you did before the relationship. You are less confident, secure, intelligent, sane, trustworthy, attractive, or in any other manner "less than" who you were previously.

19. You're constantly feeling guilty and making a lot of excuses. You're constantly attempting to fix the harm you believe you've made.
20. To keep your lover from withdrawing their affection again, you carefully control your words, actions, and feelings around him or her.
21. To render your partner happy and keep things intact, you do things you aren't really happy with or that goes against your principles, restrictions, or boundaries.

You should have received your response by now.

There is one condition, however. If you've experienced a pattern of insecurity, mistrust, or fear of abandonment in previous relationships, you may have a psychiatric problem that requires expert help.

You may be perplexed as to how you or anybody else could stay in a relationship that produces fear, anxiety, despair, self-doubt, bewilderment, and frustration.

Aren't you aware that something is seriously wrong?

Why would you want to stick around?

To begin with, manipulative relationships do not begin this way. In fact, most of these relationships get off to a great start. He or she appears to be your ideal lover — perhaps even your soul mate — and the honeymoon period is blissful. You have no notion what is truly going on when things start to go wrong. Naturally, you want to resolve the situation and reclaim what was previously so promising and great. You hold on and try to repair the harm you believe you created and restore your partner's affection after being duped into condemning oneself for the troubles. Your perseverance appears to have paid off, and you and your companion are once again supportive and loving... at least for the time being. It turns into a cycle that you aren't entirely aware of.

Second, manipulation starts slowly and insidiously and builds up over time. According to Harriet B. Braiker, Ph.D., author of "Who's Pulling Your Strings," "manipulation is a dynamic process over time." According to Braiker, victims are manipulated through a series of promised rewards and threatened losses, which are carried out surreptitiously through a range of manipulation techniques. In other words, the abuser steadily increases the level of manipulation by shifting back and forth between giving you what you want and intimidating to take it away.

"In the end, it doesn't matter how you got into that connection; what matters is the knowledge that it is one-sided, exploitative, and toxic," says Joe Navarro, M.A., a 25-year FBI veteran and author of the book Dangerous Personalities.

The questions that must be asked are straightforward.

'Do they use their charms or actions to manipulate you or others for their own gain?

Are they attempting to manipulate you?

Are they causing you harm or putting you in danger?

Do you believe this is a one-sided relationship? Is this connection causing you any pain?'

If you answered yes to any of these questions, it's time to detangle yourself from the toxic ties that bind you so you may reclaim your life. Take note: you are under no social duty to be victimized at any time."

Emotional abuse is emotional manipulation. A person who uses covert manipulation to manipulate your sentiments and conduct does not value or appreciate you or care about your health. If at all possible, end the relationship and seek professional help if necessary. Working with a talented manipulator can cause substantial and long-term psychological damage.

However, you can decide whether a relationship is useful and worth saving or whether it is harmful to you and should be ended.

One of your primary defenses against covert manipulation is awareness.

Emotional manipulation has the potential to destabilize intimate relations and leaving the manipulation target powerless, befuddled, and dissatisfied. Nonetheless, everyone manipulates others from time to time—often unintentionally. And other definitions of emotional manipulation are so wide that they can encompass any act, even something as simple as a baby wailing for food.

5.2 Indicators Of Ongoing Emotional Manipulation

Below are some important "alarm bells" that act as indicators and give you a signal that you are being manipulated.

5.2.1 Recurring nightmares or disturbing dreams

When someone plays with your emotions, your subconscious mind gets disturbed, and it is natural for you to have a disturbed sleep cycle or repetitive scary nightmares.

5.2.2 Low confidence in one's sense of reality

When you are continuously manipulated, you never feel confident about your own self.

5.2.3 Frequent feelings of bewilderment or confusion

You never are sure about your decisions and never feel confident to take major steps in your life.

5.2.4 Inability to remember details of discussions with the manipulator

Your subconscious mind never accepts the manipulator and their manipulation as a defense mechanism, and hence you find it difficult to remember the details of the discussion you had with a manipulator.

5.2.5 Anxiety symptoms

It is quite general for you to experience anxiety when you are constantly manipulated emotionally. You may experience either stomach upset, rapid heart rate, tightness in the chest, or panic attacks.

5.2.6 Frustration

You always feel frustrated when you think about the statements said by the manipulator, which affects the way you normally live your life.

5.2.7 Fear or agitation in the presence of the manipulator

Whenever you feel agitated or scared in front of a person, then that person definitely is your manipulator. So be cautious.

5.2.8 False-positive affirmations

You go out of your way to tell yourself and your friends that your relationship with the manipulator is perfectly fine. You want to never accept the fact that you are unhappy and emotionally drained.

5.2.9 Anger

There is a huge ball of anger inside you whenever you think of the person who manipulated you. You need to control yourself and preserve your energy so that you can distance yourself from them. Reacting in a certain way will be your own loss.

5.2.10 Sadness, even to the point of depression

You are no longer able to experience joy and satisfaction in your life while being manipulated and even get depressed due to it. Your trusted friends and relatives express concern and disappointment with your relationship with the manipulator. You continuously feel your integrity and dignity are compromised while being in any kind of relationship with the manipulator.

5.3 Common Emotional Manipulation Tactics

People can manipulate others using hundreds of tactics. Some of the most common include:

5.3.1 Using a strong emotional bond to exert influence over another person's actions

In a love relationship, for example, an abusive individual may try to manipulate an individual by moving too quickly. To reduce their victim's defenses or make them feel obliged, they may bombard them with love actions.

5.3.2 Taking advantage of a person's insecurities

Advertisers use this strategy all the time, such example, when a cosmetic firm makes a person feel miserable or "aged." It's also effective in personal connections. Someone may, for example, persuade their romantic partner that no one else could ever love them.

5.3.3 Lying and the refusal to admit something

Manipulators may assault their victims with several falsehoods. When they are detected, they may try to refute the lie or to cover it up with another deception.

5.3.4 Generalization and hyperbole

It's difficult to reply to claims that you've "never" been loving or "never" worked hard. Specific facts can be disputed, but broad allegations are sometimes more difficult to refute.

5.3.5 Changing the focus

In a disagreement over someone's actions, the person may try to redirect attention away from themself by criticizing their critic. "How about [X]?" the deflection frequently takes the form of. When one partner raises concerns about their partner's drug usage, the other spouse may criticize their partner's parenting abilities.

5.3.6 Moving the goalposts

When a manipulative individual adjusts the criteria that must be met in order to satisfy them, this occurs. A bully, for example, might use a coworker's clothing as a pretext to harass them. If the person changes their clothes, the bully may imply that they don't "deserve" level of respect unless they change their hairdo, accent, or some other characteristic.

5.3.7 Using fear to exert control over someone else

A person may, for example, make acts of harm or use physically demeaning body language.

5.3.8 Using societal disparities to exert influence over someone else

A neurotypical individual, for example, can try to discount another person's experiences by blaming them on a cognitive handicap.

5.3.9 Passive-aggression

This is a broad category of conduct that encompasses a variety of tactics, including guilt-tripping, backhanded compliments, and others. Passive hostility is a means of expressing dissatisfaction or anger without expressing it directly.

5.3.10   The silent treatment

It's perfectly OK to request time to think about a disagreement or to inform someone who has profoundly upset you, and you no longer wish to speak with them. However, ignoring someone in order to punish or terrorize them is a manipulative strategy.

5.3.11   Gaslighting

Gaslighting includes persuading the victim of manipulation to distrust their own perception of reality. For example, an abusive individual may deny that the abuse occurred, claiming that the victim's memory is faulty.

5.3.12   Enlisting the assistance of others to assist in the manipulation

An abusive parent, for example, would beg family members to remind a youngster of how much the parent has given up on the child. The child may be persuaded to cease complaining about abusive behavior due to peer pressure.

Depending on the situation, a manipulative individual may use a combination of these strategies or alternate between them.

5.4 Protecting yourself from emotional manipulation

Know that you are not to blame if you have fallen prey to manipulative tactics in the past. Almost everyone has been duped at some point. It's impossible to avoid all manipulation.

A number of tactics, on the other hand, can help you lessen the impact of emotional manipulation and establish clear limits. Hereunder are some of them:

5.4.1 Communicating in a straightforward, clear, and detailed manner

Direct contact models the conduct you want to see in your relations and can help you spot manipulation more easily.

5.4.2 Knowing when manipulation is acceptable and when it is not

Most people make passive-aggressive or deceptive remarks on occasion. When manipulation is part of a comprehensive attempt to control or damage another person, it becomes more troublesome and may even be abusive.

5.4.3 Defining explicit limits for manipulation

When someone tries to manipulate you, tell them how you want to be treated and then stick to your own rules. "Mom, I understand you made a lot of sacrifices for me, but that doesn't give you the right to dismiss me," for example. I won't be able to talk to you about it until you agree to quit shifting the subject."

5.4.4 Enlisting the help of reliable third parties

This can be dangerous because deceptive persons are known to recruit strangers. However, if you have a partner, friend, acquaintance, or close relative you can trust to remain objective, they may be able to provide you with useful information.

5.4.5 Therapy may provide relief to victims of long-term manipulation and emotional abuse

A therapist can help you recognize manipulation, live away from an abusive situation, and lower your chances of falling into one again. In therapy, you'll learn how to set appropriate boundaries and overcome any hesitation to enforce them.

Families and individuals who are victims of manipulation may benefit from treatment. A therapist can help all sides know why clear interaction is difficult for them, develop healthy patterns of communication, and find more effective ways to communicate their needs.

Chapter 6: Advanced Techniques Of Mental Manipulation

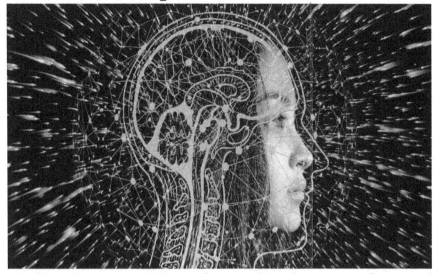

In this chapter, certain advanced techniques of mental manipulation are discussed. They are:-

6.1 Love Bombing

"Love bombing" is a unique type of flattery that deserves to be classified as such. To entangle a target, manipulators use love bombing. It's a full-fledged flattery campaign that "bombs" the target with nonstop positive reinforcement, including compliments, praise, and admiration; statements of once-in-a-lifetime affection; spending as much time with them as possible; frequent calls, texts, and email messages; goodies; fantastic lovemaking; and participating in a variety of fun and romantic activities. It can (and frequently does) happen only online.

What flattery could be greater than someone believing you're the most lovely person they've ever met, someone who actually values you and believes you're deserving of their attention, focus, energy, and heart?

The victim is swept off their feet and thrown into a relationship that will prove to be the worst experience of their lives. The manipulator's quick pace is a sign that you're being manipulated using love bombing. It takes away your ability to catch your breath and think clearly and carefully about who this person is and what motivates them. When someone expresses their undying love for you before getting to know you, it's likely that their sentiments are fleeting and that they'll lose interest in you just as fast. That doesn't mean they'll go; it just means they'll stay long enough to slowly and deliberately depreciate you over months or years, causing you to depreciate yourself in the process.Slowing down the speed of any relationship that begins with such idealization and passion is your best defense.

When you believe you've met your soul mate, it's easier said than done! Regardless, keep it in mind. Remember that getting to know someone's actual character takes time. Some people are not who they appear to be at first glance. We all think we're good character judges, but in reality, we're not. There is no quick fix; it requires patience and observation. Take lots of time to observe a potential mate in a variety of scenarios — at least a year, preferably more. Never judge someone based on their words, but rather on their actions. Goals, boundaries, activities, interests, and relationships should all be maintained. If someone truly loves you, they will not abandon you.

6.2 Learning process

The learning process is also a tactic that influences the mind of learners and hence is an advanced technique of mental manipulation.

The victim is a learner who never tries to question his teacher because he is in the stage of learning and hence gets manipulated at the hands of what he is being taught.

The learning process is a trivial but most common technique of manipulation that is used by politicians and other authorities as a way of manipulating young minds and learners of their country into respecting them and accepting what they do for the country.

Not just that, but the religious learning process is also a manipulation technique the influences the mind of the one who tries to learn the religious teachings.

Learning is what one does from the cradle to the grave, and in the process of learning new things, individuals get influenced and manipulated.

6.3 Groupthink

Individual members of small cohesive groups are more likely to accept a position or result that represents a perceived group consensus, regardless of whether the group members believe it is legitimate, correct, or ideal. Within such organizations, groupthink diminishes the efficiency of collaborative issue solving.

Groupthink has the potential to devalue a group's labor and, in the worst-case scenario, cost people their lives.

Groupthink, according to Janis, occurs when there is a strong, compelling group leader or a high degree of group cohesion or outside pressure to make a good decision is intense.

In reality, it is now commonly acknowledged that Groupthink-like behavior may be found in a wide range of contexts and in all sorts of groups and teams. As a result, it's critical to keep an eye out for the essential signs and symptoms.

Groupthink's Signs and Symptoms
- Rationalization
- Peer Influence
- Indulgence
- High Moral Ground
- Prejudice

- Censorship
- Illusion of Unanimity

To avoid Groupthink, it's critical to have a system in place for verifying the fundamental assumptions that underpin significant judgments, validating the decision-making process, and assessing the risks. Make sure your team follows these steps in their decision-making process when making major decisions:

- Examines the goals.
- Considers several options.
- Encourage people to challenge one other's viewpoints without fear of retaliation.
- Examine the dangers of choosing the desired option.
- Put assumptions to the test.
- Go back and re-examine any initial choices that were rejected if necessary.
- Obtain pertinent data from outside sources.
- This information is to be objectively processed.
- Has at least one backup plan

6.4 Financial obligations

The financial obligation may sound absurd as a technique of mental manipulation, but it the universal and most common of mental manipulation.

The decisions and resolutions of the individuals that shape their lives are influenced by their finances. The financial obligations play a major role in decision making and hence is one among an advanced technique of mental manipulation.

6.5 Social Control

What happens when a social rule is broken?

If a driver is caught speeding, he or she may be handed a speeding ticket. A child who texts in class will receive a warning from their lecturer. Adults who have a habit of belching loudly should be ignored.

All civilizations practice social control, control, and norm application. An organized effort aiming at altering people's behavior is a broad definition of social control.

One of the more advanced techniques or tactics of mind manipulation is social control.

The manipulator manipulates an individual using this approach in the name of societal control and norms and regulations. The heads of corporations, preachers, parents, and government officials all play a role in the social control maze.

They generate fear or dread in the minds of individuals, implying that if a certain norm or set rule is not followed, they will face repercussions and so influence them to achieve their own goals.

6.6 Labeling

Labeling also influences people and leads to manipulation.

When in a society a certain act and certain individual is labeled as so and so, then the masses accept the label of that act or the individual. The label creates a significant image which the act or the individual failed to create.

Most of the time, when a manipulator desires to manipulate a situation as per his requirements, he finds it easy to label things and then make his prey fall for that label and manipulates the prey in that sense.

The human mind is fragile and dynamic and changes as per its likings. The labels attract the minds the most, leading a path for the manipulators to use this fact in order to accomplish their desired goals.

6.7 Hidden Deception

With this in perspective, it's easy to see how deception and manipulation are linked. To deceive someone is to persuade them to believe something they don't. Of fact, this can be a very effective manipulative instrument. Consider yourself as the manager of our automobile dealership once more. She would be fooling her staff if she threatened to dismiss them for refusal to negotiate late but didn't have the ability to carry out the menace or if she held a persuasive but false pistol to their heads. She'd be persuading them to act in a deceptive manner.

Rather than modifying or restricting her team members' options (i.e., coaxing or trying to coerce them), she would predispose them to act in the way she desired by diminishing their capacity to comprehend their choices. Here's an instance of deception used to manipulate someone. The team members are aware that their supervisor is affecting them, but they are misled about how she is doing it. They are fed incorrect information about their options, leading them to make decisions they would not make if they knew all the facts.

As a result, a deception is an essential tool in the manipulator's arsenal, but it is far from the only one. While teaching misconceptions is a crude method of influencing another person's decision-making, there are more clever ways of influencing someone's beliefs. Human reasoning is "circumscribed" in significant ways, according to social scientists. People utilize a range of faulty tricks and techniques when interpreting information, which psychologists refer to as "cognitive biases." Individuals are often swayed by useless data (so-called "anchoring effects") and give more weight to the material they can easily recall (the "availability heuristic," as Daniel Kahneman and Amos Tversky famously established). People come to various judgments based on how information is communicated ("framing effects"), and so on. Manipulators can simply treat these cognitive biases as a weakness to attack because they are common and foreseeable. Manipulators can recall victims of insignificant information so that they place a considerable burden on them.

They can point out how certain things are believed by their targets' friends in the hopes that they will believe them as well. They have the ability to frame facts in deceptive ways. Manipulation does not have to entail explicit lying; the facts can also be utilized to influence our decisions.

In reality, manipulators don't even need to sway people's opinions. There are various "psychological levers" a deceiver can "tune" to use Noggle's analogy. The use of emotions and desires is one of the most common forms of manipulation. You can quietly reveal the cause of guilt in discussion to break down your partner's resolve if you and your partner are having a fight and you know they are still feeling bad over something unconnected from the week before. Rather than creating clear advertising in which items take center stage, marketers aim to relate their items to our imaginations and goals by paying stars to pose with them or having them appear on television and in films in an unobtrusive manner.

Although people like to think of themselves as trustworthy and self-sufficient decision-makers, they actually have a number of flaws that can be exploited. Beliefs, want, and emotions are formed as a result of a multitude of circumstances, many of which operate from outside conscious awareness. A manipulator just needs to intervene in a way that goes under the metaphorical radar if they wish to affect someone without their knowledge. Deception is a type of manipulation that takes advantage of one type of vulnerability: a lack of perfect knowledge. Exploiting flaws in how people generate and regulate desires and emotions, on the other hand, is manipulative.

Chapter 7: Powerful Emotional Manipulation Techniques

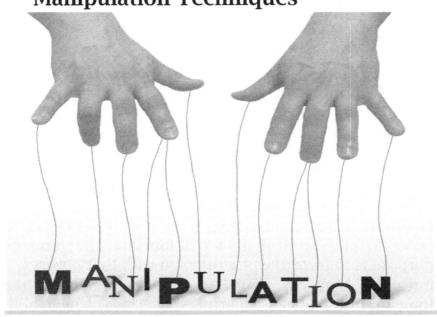

7.1 How To Tell If You Are Emotionally Manipulated?

A relation with a manipulator might last years, particularly if the manipulator is a member of your own family. It's much easier to cut links with manipulators who aren't related to you, but what if the manipulators are your own relatives or brother and sister? Or buddies with whom you've spent your entire life and who you've grown up with? Remembering your fundamental rights is the first step toward understanding how to cope with these people. You have the legal right to:

- Express emotions
- Express desires
- Be respected
- Express opinions
- Establish priorities
- Get what you paid for

- Protection against physical harm
- Do what is in line with your happiness
- Say no without guilt
- Take actions to safeguard and defend yourself from any moral, mental or physical harm

These are fundamental rights that we all have, and no one has the authority to dismiss or violate them. Remembering these rights when interacting with manipulators helps strengthen your will to fight back against their attacks. Realize that you are in charge of your own life and happiness, and you should never put those two things in the hands of somebody else, notably if that person is a manipulator.

Emotional manipulators frequently play mind games in order to gain control in a relationship. The ultimate purpose is to force the other person with that power.

Integrity, empathy, and mutual respect are the foundations of a healthy partnership. This is true in both personal and professional interactions.

People will sometimes try to take advantage of these aspects of a bond to be able to profit themselves in a certain way.

Emotional manipulation can show up in a variety of ways. They're often difficult to spot, especially when they happen to you.

That doesn't make it your fault; no one ought to be taken advantage of.

You can learn to spot manipulation and put a stop to it. You can also educate to safeguard your sanity and self-esteem.

Hereunder are the most prevalent types of emotional manipulation and how to spot them.

7.1.1 They are able to keep their "home-court edge."

Being in your comfort zone, whether it's your own home or a favorite coffee shop, can give you a sense of strength.

If the other people insist on interacting in their domain, they may be attempting to establish a power imbalance.

They take that space as their own, putting you at a deficit.

"When you have a chance, come over to my office," for example. I'm way too busy to make the trip over to see you."

"You're aware of how far it is for me. Tonight, come over here."

7.1.2 They make people uncomfortable for expressing their worries.

If you ask a question or offer a recommendation, emotionally manipulative people will almost certainly respond aggressively or try to engage you in a debate.

This method allows them to exert control over your actions and choices.

They might even try to make you feel guilty for voicing your worries in the first place.

"I don't see why you don't just believe me," for example.

"I'm just a nervous person, you know. I can't help myself; I have a strong want to understand where you are at all moments."

7.1.3 They are constantly criticizing you.

Emotional manipulators may disregard or disparage you without using sarcasm or irony. Their remarks are intended to erode your self-esteem.

They're designed to make fun of you and push you to the margins. The manipulator frequently projects its own vulnerabilities.

"Don't you think that outfit is a touch too exposing for a customer meeting?" for example. That's one method to get the account, I suppose."

"You do nothing except eat."

7.1.4 They gave you the opportunity to speak first.

This is a common strategy in some corporate partnerships, but it can also occur in personal ones.

When someone wants to take charge, they may seek clarification to get you to express your opinions and worries early on.

They can then utilize your answers to sway your decisions if they have a hidden objective in mind.

Consider the following scenario:

"I've never heard anything nice about their company."
"How did your experience go?"

"Well, you'll simply have to explain why you're furious at me once more."

7.1.5 They get too close, too fast.

The usual get-to-know-you phase may be skipped by emotional manipulators. They "share" their most vulnerable and terrible secrets.

What they're really attempting to do is make you feel unique, so you'll tell them your secrets. They may subsequently exploit your sensitivity against you.

Consider the following scenario:

"It feels like we're connecting on a very deep level," she says. This is the first time it's happened to me."

"You're the first person I've ever had share their ideas with me. We were destined to be in this around each other."

7.1.6 They're aggressively passive.

A person who is passive-aggressive may avoid confrontation. Instead, they connect with you through people in your immediate vicinity, such as friends.

They might also discuss you behind your back with coworkers.

Consider the following scenario:

"I'd chat to you about it, but I know you're busy."

"Because we're so close, I thought it would be best if you heard it from someone else rather than me."

7.1.7 They take advantage of your emotions.

Someone who is manipulative try to make you feel guilty about your sentiments if you are upset.

They can criticize you for being rude or not investing enough.

"If you truly loved me, you'd never question me," for example.

"I wouldn't be able to take that job." I wouldn't want to be so far away from my children."

7.1.8 They downplay your issues while exaggerating their own.

When you're having a difficult day, emotionally manipulative people may use it to bring up their own problems.

The idea is to discredit what you're going through so that you're compelled to concentrate on them and put all of your emotional energy towards solving their difficulties.

"Do you think that's bad?" for example. You won't have to cope with such a coworker who is constantly on the phone."

"Thank your lucky stars; you have a sibling. "I've always felt alone."

7.1.9 They bully people with their minds.

When you ask a question, someone may use statistics, language, or facts to overwhelm you. This is an example of emotional manipulation.

Some con artists masquerade as experts and try to impose their "knowledge" on you. This is especially prevalent in financial and commercial circumstances.

For example, "I wouldn't expect you to comprehend because you're new to this."

"I realize these are a lot of items for you, so please bear with me as I go over this again slowly."

7.1.10 They act as if they are a martyr.

Someone who manipulates people's emotions may excitedly agree to assist with something, just to turn around and dither or look for ways to get out of it.

They may act as if it's become a tremendous weight, and they'll try to manipulate your emotions to get through it.

"I understand you need something from me," for example. This is a lot, and I'm already feeling drained."

"This is more difficult than it appears. When you asked me, I don't think you knew that."

7.1.11 They distort the truth.

Emotional manipulators are experts at distorting reality through lies, fabrications, or mischaracterizations in order to perplex you.

They may embellish events in order to appear more vulnerable.

In an attempt to attract compassion, they may downplay their part in a quarrel.

For example, "I enquired about the project, and she screamed at me about how I never helped her, but you knew I do, right?"

"I wept all night and didn't get a wink of sleep."

7.1.12 They do not accept responsibility.

Emotional manipulative people will never admit fault for their mistakes.

They will, nevertheless, attempt to make you think responsible for everything. from a brawl to a botched project

Even if they're the one who's at fault, you can find yourself apologizing.

For instance, "I only committed it because I adore you."

"You could have completed this assignment the right way if you hadn't gone to your kid's awards program."

7.1.13 They bully people in the bureaucracy.

In the workplace, emotionally manipulative people may try to stifle you with documentation, red tape, processes, or anything else that can slow you down.

This is especially true if you express disapproval or make suggestions that call attention to their flaws or limitations.

"This will be far too difficult for you," for example. I'd simply stop right now, and you'll save trouble."

"You have no clue how much of a headache you're giving yourself."

7.1.14 Whenever they say anything unpleasant or hurtful, they always insist it's "only joking."

Critical comments can be veiled as sarcasm or humor. They may act as though they're making a joke when what they're really attempting to do is sow seeds of mistrust.

"Wow, you seem exhausted!" for example.

"Well, if you got up and walked around a little more, you wouldn't get out of breathing as quickly."

7.1.15 They are constantly one step ahead of you.

They find a way to pull the focus away from you while you're happy. This can also occur in a bad way.

Emotionally manipulative people may try to make their difficulties appear bigger or more serious after you've had a catastrophe or setback.

"Your wage raise is excellent, but did you see somebody else get a complete promotion?" for example.

"I'm sad to hear of your grandfather's death. At least it's not as horrible as losing both of my grandparents in three weeks."

7.1.16 They take advantage of your insecurities.

They can utilize your weak places to injure you if they know about them. They may make remarks or act in ways that are intended to make you feel vulnerable and upset.

"You mentioned you didn't want your children to grow up in a shattered house," for example. Take a look at what you're doing to them right now."

"This is a difficult crowd." If I were you, I'd be nervous."

7.1.17 They employ guilt trips and ultimatums to get people to do things they don't want to do.

A manipulative person will make theatrical claims during a disagreement or conflict in order to put you in a tough situation.

They'll use incendiary words to attack emotional flaws in order to force an apology.

"If you abandon me, I don't deserve to live," for example.

"I think it demonstrates your degree of commitment to our office if you can't be here this weekend."

7.1.18 They regard you in a hushed manner.

They don't answer your phone calls, emails, messaging, or other forms of communication.

They utilize silence to exert control over you and make you feel accountable for their actions.

7.1.19 They say or do something, then deny it afterward.

This method is designed to make you doubt your memories of past events.

They can place the situation on you when you're no longer sure what happened, making you feel guilty for the misunderstanding.

Consider the following scenario:

"I never said anything like that." "You imagine things once more."

"I'm not sure I'd commit to it." I'm sure you're aware that I'm way too preoccupied."

7.1.20 They're constantly "too cool,", especially in stressful situations.

Manipulative people frequently have the opposite reaction to the person they're manipulating.

This is notably true in circumstances that are emotionally sensitive. This is so they can manipulate your reaction to make you feel hypersensitive.

You then assess your response in light of theirs and determine that you were out of line.

"You noticed that everyone else seemed to be in a good mood." You simply became too agitated."

"I didn't want to say anything, but you appeared to be a little out of it."

7.1.21 They make you doubt your own sanity.

Gaslighting is a deception technique in which people try to convince you that you can't trust your own intuition or expertise.

They persuade you that events that actually occur were merely a fiction of your imagination. You lose touch with reality.

"Everyone knows that's not how this works," for example.

"I wasn't running late." You simply forgot when I said I'd arrive."

7.2 Emotional Manipulation Tactics

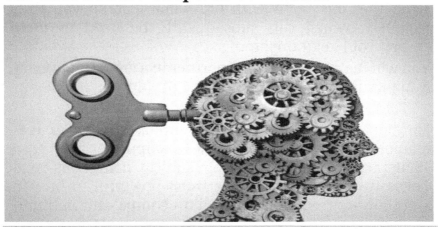

7.2.1 Triangulation

A manipulator's armory includes the clever and efficient method of triangulation. A triangle is formed between you, him, and a third person beyond your relationship by the manipulator. It's meant to make you feel apprehensive about your connection, making you want to satisfy the manipulator in order to maintain him or her around.

Sometimes in a way, the manipulator will introduce another man or woman into the relationship (figuratively or physically). They might casually — and often — discuss an old flame, a colleague, or someone they see on their daily coffee run. Alternatively, they may be openly flirting with someone in front of you. Their attraction to the other person makes them feel insecure. It's made much worse if they create subtle unflattering parallels among you and the other person, which they're prone to do.

If you approach them, they will deny any involvement in the other person and claim that your uncertainty or low self-esteem is the underlying issue. Where did you first hear that?

It's not unusual for the manipulator to be nurturing the other person as his or her next prey while also devaluing and manipulating you. For instance, the manipulator may engage with another lady in front of you in order to strengthen his bond with her while leading you to act jealously, which can subsequently be used to justify ending your relationship.

You will feel safe with your partner in a good relationship. A manipulator maintains a sense of unpredictability.

7.2.2 Emotional Blackmail

Emotional blackmail is another similar strategy that the manipulator may employ. The manipulator will try to elicit pity or guilt from their subject using this tactic. These two emotions are the most powerful in humans, and they are frequently enough to compel the victim to take the steps that the manipulator desires. The manipulator will take advantage of this feature to accomplish what they want; they will utilize the pity or guilt that they instill in the subject to compel them into participating or helping them. The level of empathy or remorse will frequently be exaggerated, increasing the likelihood that the individual will assist in the situation. The goal of this sort of blackmail is to toy on the subject's emotions more. In traditional blackmail, the target faces a threat, usually in the form of bodily damage to themselves or someone they care about. The manipulator will use emotional blackmail to elicit strong feelings in the subject that will cause them to act. While the subject may believe they are assisting of their own free choice, the manipulator has labored to guarantee that the subject is assisting and will bring up the emotions again when needed.

7.2.3 Insinuating Comments or Compliments

The manipulator "accidentally" says something that is actually a well-constructed insinuation meant to elicit an unpleasant emotional response. He'll tell you that's not what he meant when you take offense. The phrase is sometimes camouflaged as a "compliment," but it isn't really complimentary. However, it is well disguised enough for you to assume you have misinterpreted.The manipulator is well aware of what will irritate you, and he or she will relish the opportunity to drop a bomb like this and watch the consequences.

Their remark is intended to have multiple interpretations, many of which may cause hurt sentiments and doubt. Because there are so many alternative interpretations, you may be perplexed and unable to respond meaningfully when you first hear them.

Your companion, for example, smiles and adds, "You know what? After you've had sex with him, tell him, "You could make millions as a prostitute!" If you ask him about it, he'll tell you he meant it as a compliment. But you'll be left wondering what he truly meant for a long time.

You could wonder why your boyfriend was thinking about prostitutes in bed with you; why he knows so much about prostitution in the first place; what he actually thinks of you; and how much you should put on the bill you're inclined to send him. You'll also question if he was simply complimenting you on what a terrific lover you are, as he said.

Comments like this will have a negative impact on you, causing resentment, future disagreements, and relationship uneasiness. It's simple for the manipulator to make it appear as if you misunderstood, but there's a clue: the manipulator claims that he or she meant it as an innocent compliment that you mistook. Of course, you did; praise isn't supposed to damage your feelings or leave you scratching your head for years about its true meaning.

7.2.4 Minimizing

This strategy is used by the manipulator to persuade you that whatever she did wrong wasn't as horrible as you think. When you question her about her misbehavior, she will tell you that you're making a big deal out of nothing or that you're exaggerating or overreacting.

If a manipulator employs this strategy, you can be certain that they will repeat the same harmful behavior in the future.

7.2.5 The Silent Treatment

The manipulator declines to interact with you and punishes you with emotional or physical withdrawal, ostensibly because of something you did. This is also known as withholding, obstructionism, or quiet treatment.

According to Steve Becker, LCSW, it displays contempt and implies that you are not worth the manipulator's awareness of your existence, let alone his or her time, affection, care, or respect. "The silencer's goal is, above all, to suppress communication," he writes. More specifically, it seeks to make the other invisible, instilling feelings of impotence and guilt in the process."

According to Becker, the silent treatment is an "abuse method." This may sound exaggerated, but humans require (at the very least) acknowledgment of their presence. Withholding this acknowledgment, especially if it is done for a long time, can have soul-warping effects on a person's personality."

A manipulator can use the silent treatment to get you to behave in a way he or she wants you to.

7.2.6 Lying

The progenitor of all manipulation techniques is lying. Purposeful manipulators often lie and without remorse, and they have a variety of lying tactics from which to choose. Others may feel regret, but they will lie to obtain what they want nonetheless.

Manipulators will say anything to achieve their objectives. Many are skilled liars who can deceive others by lying convincingly, regularly, and with tolerance.

A lie is a false assertion that is purposefully portrayed as the truth. However, lying can be done in a variety of ways that go far beyond simply delivering a false statement. However, those assertions frequently work because we can't believe someone we admire would look us in the eyes and tell us such a bold, bald-faced falsehood.

One of the more sophisticated types of lying is lying by omission. The liar withholds the truth rather than making a misleading assertion. For example, if the manipulator believes that telling you he is married will prevent you from becoming involved with him, he may not tell you. He didn't say he wasn't married; he simply didn't say that he was.

Another fundamental precept of deception is ambiguity. When you approach a manipulator about something, they usually respond, but their response is vague. They rely on you not to interrogate them more.

Lying in the wake of a recitation of truths is a particularly effective tactic.

Liars lie to escape taking responsibility or to persuade you to accept what they want you to assume so that they can achieve what they want.

7.2.7 Invalidation

Invalidation is when someone's sentiments are dismissed, minimized, ignored, judged, or mocked. Invalidation is a sort of emotional manipulation that is extremely harmful. Unfortunately, it occurs far too frequently, and it appears to be a societal epidemic.

People negate others for a number of reasons, both intentionally and unintentionally. An aggressor will use invalidation as a weapon and a tactic of manipulation. Others who invalidate are likely to be lacking in compassion. Some people may be uncomfortable with your pain, or they may feel powerless to help you. Others are merely envious.

Invalidating statements made in reaction to you expressing your thoughts or discussing a difficult situation include the following:
- You should be embarrassed by yourself for having such negative feelings.
- It could get a lot worse.
- That is not how you should be feeling.
- Don't be concerned about it.
- Get it out of your system.
- Don't take anything so seriously.

- Don't be so serious.
- That isn't how things work.
- You've got to be kidding.
- It can't possibly be that horrible.
- You're simply exhausted.
- It's not worth getting worked up over.
- Just let it go.
- It's best if you just forget about it.
- I'm certain she didn't mean it that way.
- You shouldn't be bothered by it.
- All wounds heal with time.
- There is a silver lining to every cloud.
- You have the option of being pleased.

It's aggravating not to be understood and not to receive the help and support you seek. Invalidation makes you worry whether there's something amiss with you because you're experiencing these feelings. It produces self-doubt, which erodes self-confidence. As a result, self-esteem suffers.

7.2.8 Charm

Skilled manipulators are masters at concealing their actual nature and projecting a lovely and enticing image. If you think you'd never fall for something like this, think again.

In a new relationship, we all turn on the charms and put our best foot forward, but manipulators use charisma to further a concealed objective. Charm is a technique used by manipulators to disarm you and win your trust. They make you feel unique, likable, important and cherished. Socially intelligent con artists, skilled manipulators are proficient at displaying interest in you and your well-being, as well as opening up to you and seeming vulnerable.

What distinguishes benign charm from malignant charm? Dr. George Simon advises paying attention to your gut instincts. He argues on his site, manipulative-people.com, that "In their interpersonal interactions, psychopaths and other damaged character types... tend to radiate sociopathic tendencies or glibness. It often goes unrecognized as the gigantic red sign that it is... but if you know what to look for, you can spot it. The smoothness or social ability that these people exhibit is rarely matched by coherent and concurrent emotion. They may have a natural 'way with words,' but their smooth discourse is rarely followed by true emotion that corresponds to what they're saying or can be felt and experienced by others. Still, it's easy to doubt your gut impulses (assuming they're genuine) and permit yourself to be misled unnecessarily." You're basically defenseless once a wicked charmer has disarmed your gut instincts.

7.2.9 Intentional Forgetting

The manipulator claims to have forgotten something crucial to you, such as an accord, a promise, or a pledge, or even ingredients you need for dinner that night that he promised to pick up on his way over. The manipulator will look you in the eyes and maintain a straight face as they apologize for forgetting your request or not remembering making that commitment. When a manipulator "neglects" something vital to you, they are attempting to absolve themselves of responsibility by blaming circumstances beyond their control.

Furthermore, the manipulator is saying that whatever they forgot wasn't significant sufficient for them to recall, and neither is it essential enough for you to remember.

7.2.10   Brandishing Anger, or "Traumatic One-Trial Learning"

The manipulator will put on an outward display of rage in order to frighten you into surrender. This is known as "traumatic one-trial learning" since it teaches you to avoid addressing, offending, or opposing the manipulator fast.

7.2.11 Scapegoating

A scapegoat is a person or creature who bears the burden of others' transgressions. They are unfairly held responsible for the troubles of others. A scapegoat is sometimes known as a "whipping boy" or a "flinging lad."Scapegoating is the practice of single-outing a victim and holding them accountable for difficulties when they are not the ones to blame. A person can be used as a scapegoat for a relation, a household, or even an entire work.

Skilled manipulators frequently scapegoat someone else on purpose, while others unintentionally "project" their negative ideas and sentiments onto someone else to make them accept accountability for their own faults or failures, relieving the scapegoat of guilt, blame, and guilt.

Victim blaming is present in many of the manipulation techniques outlined above, but scapegoating goes further than that.

People who are made scapegoats experience deep and lasting humiliation, and they adopt a persecution complex.

7.2.12 Belittling

The manipulator will use eye-rolls, laughs, arrogant smiles, cynicism, or a sarcastic tone of voice to devalue and ridicule the victim's beliefs and views, either orally or non-verbally.

This tactic instills feelings of guilt and embarrassment, lowers your self-esteem, and makes you less likely to express your thoughts and opinions in the future.

When a victim's personality is low, it's easier for a manipulator to gain control.

7.2.13 Putting You On the Defensive

Many of the secretive techniques listed here will put you on the combative, making you feel compelled to defend who you are, what you think, or what the reality is verbal. If you're attempting to figure out if you've been duped, this is a crucial clue to look for.Manipulators seek to put you on the defensive for a reason. Surreptitious manipulation strategies elicit emotional responses rather than intellectual responses, which is precisely what the manipulator intends. Conversations that are calm and sensible do not always go in their favor. Furthermore, as you've seen in countless other strategies, they can use your emotional response against you if they want to.

7.2.14 Creating Fear

Most of these manipulation techniques have one thing in common: they make the victim fearful of having lost the manipulator and the connection. We don't want to abandon them, so we act as they want us to in order to prevent losing them.

Because the person who caused our anxiety is the only one who can alleviate it in this case, we unknowingly probably just give them complete control over the relation. Fear is a great tool for gaining control. Politicians are notorious for doing it. They invent or dramatize a potentially deadly condition and then vowed to protect you if you vote for them.

7.2.15 The Pity Play

The manipulator will use this strategy to elicit sympathy from you by portraying themselves as a victim of abuse or an unjust person or organization. This draws your compassion - and your support - because you can't take seeing someone else endure as a person with consciousness. Manipulators are skilled at exploiting our emotions!

The manipulator will use the pity play technique to give you a tragic story that will yank at your emotions. They may claim they were wrongfully fired from their work and need resources to pay their bills, or that their insane landlord has thrown them and they need a place to stay until they can find a new residence. Oh, and the landlord retained their down payment, which means they'll have to save for another one won't be able to assist you with living costs.

The pity game can be a lot more nuanced than you might think. If you discover that your new beau is wedded but hasn't told you, he or she will tell you a devastating narrative about their spouse's psychological abuse and the horrible loneliness they've experienced as a result.

They'll claim that the only reason they lasted in the marriage was that they never anticipated meeting someone else, especially somebody as lovely as you.

7.2.16   Rationalization

This is sometimes referred to as justifying or making excuses. To make their behaviors more intelligible, acceptable, or suitable, the manipulator invents logical and sensible reasons for their undesirable behavior. They do this to get you off their head so they can do whatever it is they want.

"It's not just me; every man watches porn!"

"What I did was also not criminal; if it had been, a law would have been passed, right?"

"Please accept my apologies for hitting you. Because you pressed so many of my knobs, I went insane for a moment."

You try to comprehend someone's actions when you trust them and wish to believe the best of them. Manipulators will gladly assist you in this endeavor.

7.2.17 Flattery

Because you are so brilliant, I'm confident you'll figure out how to spot flattery as a deception tactic.Flattery is the use of excess or false praises and remarks in order to placate yourself with a manipulator in order to further your own goal.

Flattery is used by manipulators because it succeeds. We prefer those who make us feel good about ourselves because we want to feel good about ourselves. It can have a significant effect on us when we believe someone recognizes and acknowledges our positive characteristics.

Flattery has the power to make you feel special, clever, respected, loving, attractive, or unique. You might think that fake praise and accolades would be obvious, yet good manipulators may get away with it without you noticing. It's easy to identify flattery when it comes with a clear ulterior intention. However, if a manipulator maintains his underlying motivation secret, it can be simple to believe that he is telling the truth. After all, why would this person be buttering you up if they don't seem to want anything from you — if they aren't selling you something, attempting to get you in bed, hoping for a promotion, or asking for a loan?

A manipulator's purpose, like their flattery, can be kept disguised. There are flattery techniques that are very covert or well veiled.

Being solicited for your opinion is one of the most subtle types of flattery. It implies that the manipulator envies and appreciates your thoughts, expertise, or competence.

Prefacing flattery with a warning, such as "I don't want to offend you, but..." or "I know you won't need me to say this, but..." is another approach to hide flattery.

Another type of deception is for the flatterer to initially argue with your point of view before eventually agreeing with you. This strategy will make you appear intelligent, convincing, and well-informed.

When you're not there, admiring you to people that you know and expecting them to pass the praise on to you is an excellent mask. The flatterer prevents appearing like an apparent suck-up by employing this technique.

When someone praises you on a feature you have that is rarely seen or acknowledged by others, it's a strong trick that makes you believe the manipulator can recognize and cherish your best attributes. That's the kind of person we'd like to have in our life. Manipulators who are good at finding people and determining their emotional needs are in high demand. They're also great at claiming to be able to fulfill them.

7.2.18   Trance and Hypnosis

Hypnosis is nothing more than a hypnotic trance. Trance is an enhanced mental state that humans experience on a regular basis, which is why it's so simple for a competent manipulator to create or manage.

You are exceedingly calm, and your concentration is high on a person or activity when you are in a trance state. You've been in a trance if you've ever been so engrossed in anything that you were entirely ignorant to interruptions and the aging process – this is known as a "state of flow."

Anything with a repeated element of motion, sight, sounds, ideas, or touches might induce a trance.Trance can be induced by flickering lights, dancing, seduction, massages, computer games, long trips, yoga, singing, and the sound of somebody's voice. The subconscious and conscious minds equally like being in a trance.

When our attention is narrowly concentrated on another person whose attention is strictly concentrated on us, we can fall into a trance. Psychos are wired to focus intensively on their victim, just as predators are wired to focus fiercely on their prey.

When they're "engaged" in someone, they're highly "active," and that intense presence — conveyed through persistent eye contact and targeted, enhanced attention — can elicit a comparable reaction in the subject of their attention. This isn't done on purpose; it's merely an outcome of their normal behavior.

Many people claim that the "psychotic look" gives them shivers and makes them feel repulsed. It may be true if a random look at you that way in the supermarket, but it will come across as charming attentions if it comes from someone you're engaged in or drawn to. You will most likely be enthralled.

A psychopath or other adept manipulator may purposely induce hypnosis or trance in order to exploit a victim. They may use music and candles to create a relaxing ambiance, speak in a calm, soothing voice tone, or involve the victim in a trance-inducing activity. Why would a manipulator do something like this?

Trance and hypnosis weaken our mental defenses, making us more susceptible to persuasion. For this reason, hypnotizing someone without their agreement is deemed unethical.

Increased provocativeness makes it more possible for a victim to accept things made by a manipulator while in a trance and for those beliefs to last afterward. They will also have a higher urge to repeat things they enjoyed while in a trance induce to the increased sense of satisfaction they felt. During trance, a person or action appreciated acts as a particularly strong and persistent draw to reconnect to the person and recreate the action.

Chapter 8: Dark Seduction

8.1 What is Dark Seduction?

We all have the potential to lure others and keep them enthralled in our spell. However, not everyone is conscious of this ability, and we tend to think of appearance as an attribute that only a select few are blessed with, and the others will never possess. To reach our full potential, all we have to do is figure out what it is about a person's personality that inherently stimulates them and cultivate these hidden traits inside ourselves.

Prosperous seductions usually start with a bold move or a clever strategy. That is bound to raise suspicions. Successful seductions start with your personality, with your capacity to exude a characteristic that draws others in and provokes their passions in ways they can't even control. Your victims will be hypnotized by your alluring demeanor and will not detect your following manipulations. It will therefore be a piece of cake to deceive and lure them.

The technique of dark seduction as manipulation is old and was used in ancient times too. Dark Seduction is an art where the seducers use charm, flattery, and sexual charge to manipulate the victims.

Seducers are persons who are aware of the immense potential that may be found in such times of submission. They investigate what occurs when individuals fall in love focusing on the cognitive aspects of the process, such as what sparks creativity and casts magic. They have mastered the skill of making individuals fall in love via emotion and practice. It is considerably more successful in building love than lust, as the early seducers realized.

In love, a person is sensitive, flexible, and easily fooled. A person in passion is more difficult to manage and may simply abandon you once satiated. Seducers bide their chances, creating charm and affection so that when sex occurs, the victim is further enslaved, and here the seducer under the veil of providing the other with pleasure seeks benefits. All seductions—sexual, societal, and political—become models for creating love and enchantment. A person who is in love will give up.

Trying to fight against such power, imagining that you are uninterested in it or that it is nasty and ugly, is fruitless. The more you try to reject the allure of sensuality an idea, a form of authority more intrigued you will become. The reason is obvious: many have experienced the power of falling in love with someone. Our acts, movements, and words have a good impact on this individual; we may not fully comprehend what we have done correctly, but the feeling of power is addictive.

8.2 Dark Seduction Techniques

Following are some of the dark seduction techniques:-

8.2.1 The Trojan Horse

This, in my opinion, is the most pernicious. It is also universally applicable to all genders and cultures. If you donate to someone on a regular basis, they will feel obligated to you. In this situation, it is frequently used in an innocent manner. "Let me buy you a drink," and you suddenly feel obligated to engage in conversation. It can sometimes develop a situation where I paid for your lifestyle and own you. This is the type of activity that you may be willing to participate in at first, but it is much better to steer away from.

8.2.2 The Flatterer

Flattery is when someone gets complimented unnecessarily. You don't want to flatter everyone, but if you flatter them in a way that appeals to their vulnerabilities, they will be drawn to you mysteriously. For example, a man who is self-conscious about his masculinity would enjoy hearing how he seems like a "tough guy." You may even act as if you were annoyed by how he intimidates everyone. Most people's bullshit radar won't pick up on that kind of flattery. When it comes to flattery, the trick is to figure out what they are uneasy about and provide them with the reassurance they require. Another example is a female who feels self-conscious about her appearance due to a weight problem. She would be drawn to you if you gave her the pet name "Lil' Mama" and were able to pull it off.

8.2.3 The Mirror

One acts as if they have the same values. They are fascinated by the same things as their victim, including movies, music, and celebrities. To gain confidence and allegiance, the offender reveals false secrets. The object of the game is to offer them what they want to hear and what they require emotionally. After that, take sexually.

8.2.4 The Silent Treatment

The other half is frequently emotional and, at the very least, knocked off their "plan" when one person offers the other half an unexpected and sudden silence treatment. After a while, the victim realizes they've made a mistake and tries to make amends. The offender knows they have the victim tied around their finger when the victim tries to make amends.

8.2.5 The Big Question

The criminal asks for a large sum of money, knowing that it will be refused. Then you decide on what they were thinking all along, which is a minor, more compatible suggestion. For example, suppose someone approaches you and asks if they can move into your home. No, you say. However, after some discussion, you inform them they are welcome to remain for a couple of weeks for whatever reason.

8.2.6 The Demand

One takes a decision before having time to think about it. "Great, I'll pick you up at 9," for example.

8.2.7 The Normal

One pretends that this is the normal thing to do. An example being it is considered normal for husband and wife to compromise for the sake of their families.

8.2.8 The Logical Fallacy

This one appears far too frequently in children's games. It indicates that anything you do (or don't do) is seen as unpleasant by the subject. The following is a good example of this. "You would marry me if you loved me." If a guy or woman falls into this trap, they will marry in order to prove their love.

8.2.9 Shaming & Guilt

Because of what he has done or will do, the aggressor makes the victim feel horrible about himself. If the aggressor's requests are turned down, he or she will shame the victim by revealing details about what makes this person feel so bad. People know exactly how to aggravate us. Shaming someone for their prior over and over is manipulation and is extremely effective.

8.2.10   The Remote Control

When an unfavorable topic arises, one will bring up something of significant interest to the other half that they can't stop talking about. "Honey, I saw the most beautiful house on Oakwood Lane; do you mind if we move in together someday?" That should get you to stop bugging him about his Fb post, for the time being, right ladies?

8.2.11   The Board Game Request

When someone requests something. "Is it REALLY what you want?" says the responder. The subsequent discourse will make it appear as if the request was bizarre. By the end of the conversation, the two will have landed on something very different but yet considered equal.

8.3 Why Are Dark Seducers So Dangerous?

Dark seducers are dangerous manipulators as they use sex, flattery, charm, and charisma to manipulate their victims. They always want to be the dominant one in their relationships and exploit the feelings of others in order to work towards getting their ego satisfied. They are toxic manipulators. Their following characteristics justify this:

8.3.1 They are attractive, and they know it

Almost every dark seducer is gorgeous, not just physically, but they are far more dangerous because they are conscious of their attractiveness. They leverage their attractiveness to make their victims week in the knees, causing the victim to fall for them and then be heavily manipulated. They use their physical attractiveness to the fullest and seek benefits.

8.3.2 They don't get emotional or affected if they are rejected

A dark seducer's capacity to see little as a big problem is a consistent trait. Nothing, positive or negative, can fundamentally influence the mood and emotion of the most experienced dark seducers, who have a Zen-like calm. The best dark seducers can handle anything, whether it's incredibly positive or terribly negative, with a shoulder shrug and a serene demeanor.

8.3.3 Charismatic core confidence

The best seducers have a deep sense of self-assurance that is independent of what is going on in their lives at the time; it is simply who they are. They're just as confident if they have a million dollars in their pocket as if they don't. They look just as good in a pair of sweatpants as they do in a tailored Armani ensemble. Confidence has been proven time and time again to be one of the most important qualities in being attractive. Dark seducers take it to a new level that only a few others have experienced.

8.3.4 Not in need of validation

A dark seducer never feels ashamed or in need of other people's approval or acceptance.

8.3.5 Self-centered

Since a dark seducer loves oneself more than anyone or anything else, the dark seducer is always able to prioritize their own needs. They will never act in a way that puts others' needs ahead of their own. They are incapable of caring truly about anything other than their goals in life. As a result, individuals are able to make decisions and choices that are always in their best interests. They never let their desire for romance or seduction get in the way of their goals in life.

8.3.6 Everything is a game for a dark seducer

A dark seducer does not regard anything as particularly significant. Such a person can perceive seduction, as well as life in general, as a gigantic game. As a result, the black seducer never falls victim to life's pressures since they don't experience any in the first place. Nothing matters to the evil seducer in the end; thus, nothing can have a profound effect on them. The dark seducer can function in an atmosphere and from a position of detached aloofness, whereas typical people become emotionally entangled in various persons and situations.

8.3.7 They don't acknowledge anything as of right or wrong, and everything is categorized as what works or doesn't work for them

What is said and done is unimportant to dark seducers; what counts is the impact it creates.

8.3.8 Pausing, tone, and eye contact

The ferocity of their eyes at a certain given time, the pauses they make between syllables of words-all of these small subtleties add up to have a tremendous effect, and skilled dark seducers are aware of this. As a result, dark seducers are invisible. They are undetectable and stealthy.

8.3.9 Manipulation is dependent on connection or relation

The art form of a dark seducer is to establish a connection with someone to the point where they can obtain their deepest level of trust and closeness.

8.3.10 They are self-sufficient

They don't need anyone else because a dark seducer satisfies all of their core wants, such as esteem, self-worth, and purpose, within themselves. The first major distinction is that many ordinary individuals pursue seduction and relationships in order to satisfy a personal desire. Dark seducers, on the other hand, have already satisfied their own requirements. They don't have to play the game; they opt to enjoy it.

8.3.11   Strong sense of self

Dark seducers are known for having a strong sense of self. They are not determined by the universe around them or by what is popular or fashionable at any given time. They aren't created by anyone else in their lives. Dark seducers are unconcerned about being a boyfriend, girlfriend, spouse, or wife; they recognize that these are just labels. Their interaction with the other sex is merely a function rather than a personality trait.

8.3.12   They use words calculatingly

Dark seducers will never make a compliment or a remark without first considering why they are doing it. That's because dark seducers understand that words are weapons, and they shouldn't be thrown around lightly. Whereas most people praise someone because they wish to communicate nice feelings, a seducer solely praises for selfish purposes, such as placing pressure on their target to behave in a certain way. The seducer's criterion for praise is not "this person has earned a kind comment," but rather "I want that person to behave in that way again, regardless of whether it benefits them." Similarly, many ordinary individuals would criticize or advise someone because they believe they are assisting them. A seducer, on the other hand, is unconcerned. They will do anything they desire, regardless of what is best for the target. A truly dark seducer, for example, will not hesitate to criticize something that they don't like, even if it benefits the target directly.

8.3.13   They treat their prey effectively

Whereas a mainstream romantic thinks about 'the appropriate way to treat someone,' a dark seducer merely thinks about 'the efficacious way to treat someone.' The thinking of a dark seducer has no moral dimension, only a brutally efficient emphasis on impact and outcome.

8.3.14 They have a sense of presence

An effective seducer's ability to cut off their internal monologue and self-talk and focus solely on the situation in front of them is known as presence. Most people are consumed with their own thoughts, doubts, and sentiments, which are continuously running through their heads. This is a type of psychological distraction that makes it difficult to focus in the present. After all, how can you concentrate on the here and now if you're remembering something that happened in the past or daydreaming about something that might or might not happen in the future? One of the ways that presence aids seducers in being extremely effective is by allowing them to focus all of their attention on their conversation with their seduction target at any given time. Given how uncommon it is for someone to be the sole focus of another's the attention when it does happen, it can have a significant impact. A dark seducer's special form of eye contact is an outward manifestation of his or her inner presence. Such eye contact is usually fairly intense, but it does not appear to be staring. It's similar to the stereotypical smoldering model given featured in advertising. It's a powerful but stable manifestation of inner quiet and tranquility.

8.3.15 Temptation, desire, and guilt

A skillful seducer may say things that elicit both want and guilt emotions at the same time. 'I hope you were just not making me desire you so much right now; you are so shameless,' for example. This is a fascinating line for a variety of reasons. For starters, it assigns responsibility for the seduction on the target rather than the seducer. This is likely to elicit in the target feelings of lust, shame, and guilt in equal measure—a formidable combination.

Second, the enticing temptation of the word 'desire you' is mingled with the repulsive shameless.' The conflicting messages provide powerful signals to the target's subconscious mind, amplifying the emotional intensity and meaning of the sexual encounter.

8.4 How To Avoid Dark Seduction?

Follow the following steps in order to avoid dark seduction.

8.4.1 Maintain Trustworthy Relationships

The manipulator's mind manipulation efforts on you will be kept to a minimum if you maintain close contact with family and friends you can trust. Friends and family you can believe will provide you with the support you need and enhance your faith in yourself, leaving no opportunity for the manipulator to sow doubt or shatter your confidence.

8.4.2 Make contact with your friends and family

Another reason to never let the manipulator persuade you to cut ties with the people you care about and trust is that you can always expect them to act in your best interests. Those that truly care about you (in a non-manipulative way) will constantly be concerned about your safety. If you're ever unsure whether you're being manipulated (even if you suspect it), tell them what's going on and observe how they react. Their instant reaction - shock and rage, for example - should serve as a warning that something isn't quite right.

8.4.3 Choosing to Ignore Their Emotions

Manipulators in relationships frequently pout or throw temper tantrums in order to get their way. If you encourage them, the only person who suffers from this type of conduct is you. When they engage in this type of behavior, they choose not to tolerate it by moving away from the situation. Explain why you won't put up with it any longer, and if they fail to accept, it's time to consider whether there's any reason to stay in this relationship for much longer.

8.4.4 They Should Be Ignored

This is the most useful piece of advice you could provide to yourself. Ignore them since they're not worth your time, effort, or feelings. Ignore them whenever they try to give you "advice." Ignore them when they try to tell you what to do and go ahead and do what you want anyhow. Manipulators could never be entrusted, and they'll always try to persuade you to help them with their filthy activities. They will disclaim any responsibility if you try to hold them accountable. They alter their thoughts as frequently as they change their appearance, flip-flopping and going back and forth. Ignore them and whatever they say; it's the best you can do.

8.4.5 Don't Make an Attempt to Correct Them

When you do, you're merely plunging more into their trap. Remember that they're attempting to make you so confused that you can't see what they're doing when you're emotional, and every time you try to "correct" the situation, you're making it too simple for them to wind you around their tiny finger. They frequently set these small traps to watch how you react so they can find out your sensitivities and exploit them. Don't answer, don't engage, and don't try to correct them. It's a game you'll never be able to win.

8.4.6 Don't be afraid to believe in yourself

That is just what the deceiver wants you to do. This is precisely why you should not do it. You know yourself more than anyone else could, and you shouldn't need anyone else's approval to realize that you're good enough just the way you are. The fact that successful people do not rely on their self-worth the judgments of others is what sets them apart from the rest. They trust their own judgment, and it's fine if they make mistakes in life. They learn from their mistakes and rise again. One of your best defenses against a manipulator's onslaught is to believe in yourself.

8.4.7 Stop attempting to blend in with the wrong crowd

If you have to put in too much effort to fit in with a group, it is not the ideal group for you. Manipulators are appealing and well-known enough to make you want to be a part of their group, and they enjoy exerting power over you by making you work hard to achieve their approval. They know that maintaining you in this state helps them to get away with additional "favors" because you'll gladly do everything they ask simply to feel appreciated. Don't allow yourself to be manipulated by them anymore; if they can't accept you for who you are, don't worry, there are plenty of others who will. When you have to try extremely hard to feel accepted, you're working too hard for the wrong people.

8.4.8 Reverse the roles

Manipulators will try to work with you all the time. They'll make friends with your friends before attempting to turn them against you. They'll get you to perform the majority of the work, then take credit for it behind your back. They'll lure you with the same prize and watch as you try to chase it down again and again. They'll recall all of your previous mistakes and never fail to make you feel horrible about them. If the manipulator you're attempting to get rid of keeps trying harder to create your life a living hell, you need to hit back. Find out what's keeping them going, and then undermine it so the manipulator can't stand on it anymore. This assistance could come from their admirers, followers, subordinate, a skill they possess, or a resource they control. Make friends with their supporters and turn them into allies. Make connections with people who have similar abilities so that the manipulator isn't the only one in charge. Turning the tables on them and reducing their grip will put them off balance, causing them to focus less on attempting to dominate your life and more on attempting to restore their place in their own circle.

8.4.9 Don't Make Sacrifices

While dealing with a manipulator, one of the many huge mistakes you might make is sacrificing your own morals and ideals. When you go against all you believe in to do what they want, you're playing right into their hands. It's fine if they make you feel horrible or guilty about it (it's one of their techniques), and you should let them do what they want. What matters is that you don't have to compromise your own pleasure, sentiments, time, or energy any longer in order to accommodate them. Consider this: if the roles were reversed, would they be prepared to do the same for you? Return to the fundamental norms, where you have the right to prioritize your happiness and needs.

8.4.10   Requesting Permission Isn't Necessary

It's difficult to stop the habit of asking for permission. Since we were young, we've been trained to do it by asking our parents for approval before doing anything. We had to get permission from our teachers for anything we needed at school. Before we take action as adults, we seek authorization from our managers or supervisors. Before making a move in a relationship, we ask for our partner's consent. As a result, asking for approval can be a difficult habit to break. When you let the manipulator have control, you'll find yourself continuously seeking approval and permission rather than taking charge and making your own judgments. Isn't it past time to call a halt to this? This is, after all, your life, not theirs. Why should you wait for them to give you permission to do something?

8.4.11   Have a Goal of Your Own

Your goal isn't to do whatever the manipulator wants you to do. Those who work without the need for a sense of hope make it easy for those with a greater will and agenda to control them. That is why manipulators continue to have power to this day, since so many people walk through life without a sense of meaning, leaving themselves vulnerable to being exploited. When you don't have a strong sense of self, you're more likely to believe what you're told and do what you're told. Because you don't have a higher purpose of focusing on and making decisions based on. What you're willing to do and what you're not willing to do is determined by your higher mission. It's simple to notice people who don't seem to have a clear sense of identity. They're the ones who seem to fly through life with no discernible pattern. They're the people that work in meaningless jobs that either inspire or make them happy but have no desire to change the circumstance. They're the ones who waste much too much of their time on pointless gossip and other stuff with no real value. Manipulators are waiting to pounce on this lack of direction, so if you haven't discovered your sense of purpose yet, it's time to think long and hard about what your mission should be. Give yourself something specific to concentrate on, and you'll be less prone to trickery and distraction.

8.4.12   Take on New Challenges

New opportunities are all around you; all you have to do is be willing to take a risk and leap of faith. Manipulators want to keep you in the same pattern by preventing you from taking up fresh opportunities. They want you to stay in the same cycle as you are because it makes it simpler for them to maintain control. That's why they sow seeds of doubt in your mind and try hard to dissuade you from better yourself or taking advantage of fresh chances.

Every time you gain strength and confidence, you are reducing their grip on you, which is exactly what they are trying to prevent. They'll go to great lengths to maintain you in your place, even to the point of making you feel humiliated for considering new options to improve yourself. Don't let them hold you back, and don't allow self-doubt to hold you back. Even accomplished people made mistakes in life to get to where they are now; the only thing they did differently than everyone else had the confidence to take the risk and make a positive adjustment.

8.4.13 Don't be a punching bag

Only if you enable manipulators to use you as a punching bag will they continue to do so. You have enough self-respect to stand up and declare that you don't deserve to be treated this way. Because you don't have any, return to your core rights, which include the right to be recognized. When someone takes benefit of you, they are not showing you respect. You have complete control over whether or not you put up with it. People will try to take leverage of you, abuse you, and use you, but you have the option to refuse all of it. No one has the authority to control you until you give them that power. Stop becoming a punching bag and start taking responsibility for your actions. Remind yourself that there's no reason to feel guilty for standing up to someone who isn't treating you fairly.

Manipulators will do everything they can to undermine your conviction and weakening you so that they can get control of you. They'll act worried about you or as though they just have your best interests at heart. They'll persuade you that they want to "help," while the truth is that the only person they want to help is themselves, and they'll do it even if it means stepping on your toes. They can be difficult to get rid of once you've let them into your life, but you can do it now that your know-how. Finally, never stop working on building your own confidence; the more confident you are, the less power they have over you.

Chapter 9: 10   Mass   Manipulation Strategies

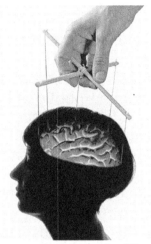

Scientists throughout the last half-century have been capable of accelerating their rate of progress, and as a result, they have caused an increasingly significant gap between the general population's knowledge and that which is employed by those in power. It has, to date, found a way to know the ordinary human better than he knows himself. To put it another way, it indicates that the same person is capable of wielding greater control over himself others than he really does over himself.

An important tenet of modern economics is that there are no airtight compartments inside which economic activity takes place. Many economic policies are implemented in a social framework, which, if controlled appropriately, might result in those same policies resulting in predictable results.

The neo-liberal economic paradigm could not have been widely applied in the West without the employment of the mass media as a tool of "surgical" and "instrumental" usage.

Noam Chomsky, a well-known critic and MIT linguist who has become one among the most prominent vocal advocates of an intellectual dissident in the last ten years, has created notes about the most prevalent and effective tactics used by "hidden" agendas to manipulate the populace via the media.

In the past, the media has shown to be an extremely effective tool for shaping public opinion. Justified wars, social movements, calmed financial crises, sparked on some other intellectual flows, and even provided the incident of media as creators of reality inside the public psyche have all been produced or destroyed thanks to media paraphernalia and propaganda.

But how can we identify the most prevalent approaches to comprehending these psychosocial tools in which we undoubtedly participate? Chomsky was therefore tasked with consolidating and exposing these strategies, some of which are more apparent and subtle than others but all of which tend to be similarly efficient and, in some respects, terrible. Encourage ignorance, shame, diversion, or the creation of artificial challenges and then miraculously solving them are some of these techniques.

9.1 The diversionary tactic

The principal tool to control the society as a whole is the distraction strategy, which uses the tactic of flooding or floods continual distractions and minor information to deflect public attention away from critical concerns and changes dictated by economic and political elites. A diversion technique is also necessary to prevent the interest of the public in critical knowledge in the fields of economics, neurobiology, science, psychology, and cybernetics from waning.

Keeping the public's attention distracted away from genuine social issues and fascinated by trivial topics. Keep the audience occupied, occupied, occupied; there is not any time to think; return to animals and the farm.

9.2 The gradual strategy

For a few years, gradually apply sufficient pressure, bit by bit, to make a bad measure acceptable. During the 1980s and 1990s, new, radical social and economic circumstances (neoliberalism) were imposed in this manner: the minimal state, privatization, instability, fluidity, massive unemployment, salaries that do not ensure secure and efficient incomes, and many other changes that, if implemented all at once, would have triggered a revolution.

9.3 Go to the public as a little child

Most advertising aimed towards the broad public use dialogue, arguments, and characters with particularly juvenile intonation, typically focusing on fragility, as if the viewer were a child or mentally challenged creature. The more you try to deceive the audience, the more infantile your tone becomes. "If one approaches a person as if she were 12 years old or younger, the other person is more likely, due to suggestive quality, to reply or react without much thought like a person 12 years old or younger might."

9.4 Keep the public in ignorance and mediocrity

Making the general people illiterate about the tools and procedures used to control and subjugate them is another tactic. The level of education provided to the lower social classes must be as inadequate and substandard as possible in order for the lower classes to never be able to narrow the gap of ignorance that exists between them and the higher classes.

9.5 Self-blame Strengthen

Make the person believe that he or she is to blame for their own tragedy and cast doubt on their IQ, abilities, or attempts. As a result, rather than fighting against the economic structure, the individual devalues and blames himself, resulting in a melancholy mood that serves to stifle action, and without action, there can be no revolution!

9.6 Invent a problem, then propose a remedy

They construct an issue, a "situation," in order to elicit a response from the audience, and then this becomes the standard for the assessments you would accept. For instance, "let us enhance urban unrest or orchestrate bloody attacks so that the public accepts policies and laws that are harmful to their freedom." Alternatively, make an economic catastrophe in order for the people to accept the deconstruction of public services and the abolition of social rights as a necessary evil.

9.7 The strategy of delaying

The other technique to get public approval for an unpleasant action is to portray it as "difficult and essential" at the time. A future sacrifice is simpler to accept than one that must be made right now. Initially, because the action is not immediately implemented; second, because the general public, the masses, have a natural predisposition to believe that "all will be better the next day" and that the necessary sacrifice can be ignored. This offers the general masses more time to become accustomed to the concept of adjustment and embrace it without reluctance when the actual time arrives.

9.8 More emphasis is placed on the emotional aspect of things rather than the reflective side

Emotional Response is a traditional approach as a result of causing a power surge on logical analysis and, eventually, the individual's critical sense. Furthermore, appealing to emotions allows access to insensibility, making it simpler to implant ideas, wants, anxieties, compulsions, and uncertainties or induce behaviors in accordance with authoritative needs.

9.9 To persuade the public to accept ineptitude as the norm

Make the people believe that being illiterate, vulgar, and ignorant is fashionable while suffocating culture, science, and art that does not fit the stereotypical norms.

9.10 Learning more about the people than they know about themselves

Rapid breakthroughs in science have created a rising gap of knowledge between the general population and the ruling elites during the last 50 years. The "system" possesses a deep grasp of human beings thanks to biology, neuroscience, and applied psychology. The system knows more about the common people than he knows about himself. This suggests that the system has more power over individuals than the folks have over themselves in most circumstances.

Conclusion

Thank you for reading this far; I hope it was educational and provided you with all of the skills you need to reach your objectives, whatever they may be.

In simple terms, manipulating someone is skillfully or unscrupulously controlling or influencing that person. Whether we like it or not, we've all manipulated a person or a situation to achieve the desired result.

Now that you know who the manipulators in your life are (or if you've used these methods yourself), how to spot the signs of being manipulated, and how to cope with them, you can effectively examine the relationships around you and make the educated decisions you need to make in your own life. You can communicate your feelings, thoughts, and wishes without feeling guilty since you have a more objective perspective on things.

You can discover and detect signals of persuasion and manipulation by examining and analyzing the communication clues in your relationships. You will be able to exercise your right to be treated with respect if this is obvious. You reclaim your authority and right to participate in a communicative exchange as equals. You CAN say 'no' without feeling guilty in a relationship where there is an equal balance of power, and you CAN establish your interests according to your own aspirations to create a better life or atmosphere for yourself and the people you care about.

You can avoid getting extorted or unwittingly manipulated if you can read people's mannerisms and see-through deceptive remarks. You are less prone to be affected and driven by the intentions of others, and you are more able to identify opportunities around you. Knowing how to spot these methods, on the other hand, means you may utilize them to your advantage. Always check your moral conscience and remember to treat everyone as an equal individual who deserves to be valued and given the opportunity to make their own decisions.

Glossary

Psychological manipulation- Psychological manipulation is a type of social influence that aims to change the behavior or perception of others through indirect, deceptive, or underhanded tactics.

Emotional Manipulation-Emotional manipulation occurs when a manipulative person seeks power over someone else and employs dishonest or exploitive strategies to gain it.

Fundamental-a central or primary rule or principle on which something is based or forming a necessary base or core; of central importance.

Perpetrator-a person who carries out a harmful, illegal, or immoral act

Aggressor-a person or country that attacks another first.

Psychology-Psychology is the scientific study of the mind and behavior, according to the American Psychological Association. Psychology is a multifaceted discipline and includes many sub-fields of study, such areas as human development, sports, health, clinical, social behavior and cognitive processes.

Instinctive-relating to or prompted by instinct; done without conscious thought

Guilt-Feeling responsible or regretful for a perceived offense, real or imaginary. Can be part of the grief reaction.

Shame-a painful feeling of humiliation or distress caused by the consciousness of wrong or foolish behavior or a regrettable or unfortunate situation or action

Vilify-speak or write about in an abusively disparaging manner.

Omission-something neglected, left out, or left undone, or the act, fact, or state of leaving something out or failing to do something especially that is required by duty, procedure, or law liable for a criminal act or omission.

Brandish-wave or flourish (something, especially a weapon) as a threat or in anger or excitement.

Feign-pretend to be affected by (a feeling, state, or injury).

Sulk-be silent, morose, and bad-tempered out of annoyance or disappointment.

Nag-harass (someone) constantly to do something that they are averse to.

Implicit-suggested though not directly expressed.

Book 4: Dark Psychology Secrets

Learn All the Secrets to Interpreting Body Language and Mind Manipulation Tricks. Become an Expert in Manipulation Tactics in Social Scenarios

Introduction

Dark Psychology supposes that 99.99 percent of the time, this is purposeful and has some goal-oriented motivation behind it. However, the remaining.01 percent seems to be without purpose.

If left unchecked, predators & their acts of robbery, brutality, and abuse may become a worldwide phenomenon & societal epidemic over the next century. Cyber stalkers, cybercriminals, cyberbullies, cyber terrorists, online sexual predators, & also religious/political fanatics actively involved in cyber warfare are all examples of such predators. The concept of predator tends to follow the same framework as Dark Psychology; it includes abuse, assault, & online victimization using Communications Technology & information; whereas, dark psychology analyzes all criminal conduct on a spectrum of severity and purposeful intent.

Monsters & demons were thought to be the sources of aberrant human behavior before scientific advancements. Metaphysical beings seemed to be the only logical explanation for people's barbaric acts. Early civilizations invented tales of demonic creatures rather than fearing the humans.

For over 150 years, this has been quite a research topic. Its origin, however, may be traced back to ancient Greece, roughly 400-500 years BC.

William James, a prominent clinical counselor, developed various approaches & established the functionalist technique.

According to the expert, the brain & the subconscious seem to be two important factors in the general framework of the environment. As a result, we should focus on how a person carries out a specific course of action.

The qualified psychologist also suggested looking into the underlying issues that cause behavioral changes. The emphasis was made on the variables that influence psychology & its implications.

Wilhelm Wundt coined the term structuralism to describe the method he developed.

Edward Titchener, an American psychologist whom Wundt educated, coined the term further. The subject of structuralism centered on both professional introspection and subject matter analysis.

However, it has proven to be ineffective as a platform, for assessing patient well-being over the time. Structuralism is a research method wherein participants respond to their minds' prevailing behavior while performing various tasks.

Since there were numerous differences in the observations and information about the study's subjects, the approach was considered inaccurate.

Wundt did lose in the introspection aspect, but when he launched a lab dedicated to studying the human psyche. It was the beginning of psychology as we know it today.

Since psychology is now a discipline, it aims to investigate the various trigger points of the mind's structural nature using evaluation techniques, examination based on current scientific forecasts, hypotheses and generalizations. Psychologists are well-known for describing & analyzing individuals & their behavior.

Researchers focused on describing the brain's nature and the actual behavior by employing memory & cognitive learning.

Even though modern society considers itself to be advanced in its understanding of the potential for living beings to engage in violent & heinous acts, however how to prevent bizarre & deadly human actions remains elusive.

Thousands of such crimes have been committed throughout history. A few examples include the Holocaust throughout the World War II & ethnic cleansing currently taking place in neighboring countries. History is replete with instances of the damage that Dark Psychology has resulted in.

Dark Psychology, as described above, requires a thorough inspection. As you will learn more about Dark Psychology's foundation, a cognitive structure of understanding will start to emerge.

Chapter: 1 Dark Psychology's Fundamentals

1.1 What is the concept of dark psychology?

A study of the human situation that refers to people's psychological nature to prey upon the other is known as dark psychology.

OR

The science & art of mind manipulation and control is recognized as dark psychology. Dark psychology is indeed a phenomenon in which individuals use dirty tricks of manipulation, coercion, persuasion, & motivation to get what they want, whereas psychology refers to the scientific study of human behavior and concentrates on interactions, actions & thoughts.

1.2 The four personality traits of the Dark Triad

A "Dark Triad" is the term used by psychologists & criminologists to describe a simple method of foreseeing not only criminal behavioral patterns but also broken & controversial relationships.

The following traits make up the Dark Triad:

- Psychopathy
- Machiavellianism

- Narcissism
- Sadism

Psychopathy

Psychopathy is a mental illness characterized by antisocial behavior & atypical emotional reactions.

It refers to the set of personality traits or characteristics that are frequently linked to an absence of emotional sensitivity & empathy, impulsivity, superficial charm, and a lack of sensitivity to harmful consequences. Psychopathy affects about 1 percent of the population, 15-25 percent of the prison inhabitants & it is much more common in males than in females. The neurobiological mechanisms that underpin these traits have been studied using psychophysiological approaches.

Psychopathy has been associated with an absence of emotional reactivity. Skin conductance response (SCR) gets lowered in response to aversive stimuli (Lorber, 2004). Outcomes of the startling concept also facilitate this hypothesis. A loud sound had been used to create a startle response within this paradigm, evaluated as eyes blink (Patrick, 1994). When pleasurable emotional images are seen before the startling audio, the startle reaction is inhibited, particularly in comparison to the neutral response, while unpleasant photographs potentiate the startle response. The startle reaction is inhibited in people with psychopathy when exposed to both emotionally unpleasant & pleasant stimuli.

As a result, psychopathic individuals seem to have a general insensitivity to unpleasant & aversive stimuli and respond to both pleasant & unpleasant stimuli in the same way. Psychopathy is notoriously resistant to psychotherapy, possibly caused by an inadequacy of awareness or emotional sensitivity, both of which are mandated for empathy.

Signs and symptoms of a Psychopath

A Checklist of 20-item Hare Psychopathy is used to diagnose psychopathy, including traits like lack of empathy, compulsive lying, & impulsivity. Each item is rated upon a three-point level depending on whether it doesn't apply (0), applies to a certain extent (1), and fully applies (2) towards the individual. A score of thirty or higher is mandated for clinical psychopathy.

Robert Hare, a Canadian researcher, created the checklist in the 1970s. A mental health expert should conduct the true assessment.

The following characteristics are included in the modified edition of the checklist:

- Aesthetic allure
- A feeling of self-worth that is glorifying
- Boredom proneness/need for stimulation
- Lying that is harmful to your health
- Manipulation/scheming
- Absence of guilt
- Shallow response (such as reduced emotional responses)
- Lack of empathy/callousness
- Parasitic way of life
- Ineffective conduct control
- Sexual immorality
- Early behavioral issues
- Lack of actual long-planned goals
- Impulsivity
- Being irresponsible
- Failure to be responsible for one's acts.
- Juvenile delinquency
- Conditional release is revoked (from prison)
- Criminal versatility (i.e., the ability to commit a variety of crimes)

When does psychopathy start emerging?

Early signs of psychopathy, known as "callous-unemotional traits," can appear early in childhood (before the age of 10) and may lead to a formal diagnosis like conduct disorder. However, exhibiting psychopathic characteristics as a child does not necessarily guarantee that a person would also grow up to be a psychopath.

What makes somebody turn into a psychopath?

Psychopathic traits, like certain other personality traits, are heavily influenced by genetic factors, though research indicates that non-genetic variables play a role as well. Scientists have noticed indications of atypical working of specific brain areas (like the amygdala) in individuals having psychopathic traits. However, there is still a lot to know about the factors that lead to such disparities.

Machiavellianism

In psychology, it refers to a personality trait in which a person becomes so centered within his/her targets that he/she would then exploit, deceive, & manipulate others to accomplish their aims.

Machiavellianism has been one of the characteristics which make up the so-called "Dark Triad," however; the other two are Narcissism & psychopathy.

The term originated from the notorious Niccol Machiavelli, a Renaissance diplomat & philosopher whose best-known work was "The Prince" (Il Principe). This well-known book advocated for strong rulers to be brutal with their enemies & subjects and also that glory & survival justified any measures, even if they were considered immoral & brutal.

"Machiavellianism" became a well-known term to relate to the idea of being deceptive, by the 16th century. However, during the 1970s the two social psychologists, Florence L. Geis & Richard Christie, developed the term "the Machiavellianism Scale.

Such a personality scale has been termed as "the Mach-IV analysis" and is still employed as the major assessment weapon for Machiavellianism.

Machiavellianism has indeed been known to occur more in men. It could, however, happen to anyone – also children.

Machiavellianism's Signs and symptoms

A person with the Machiavellianism trait is likely to have several of the

mentioned characteristics:

- They are only concerned with their interests & ambitions.
- Money and power take precedence over relationships.
- Appear charming and self-assured
- Gain an advantage by exploiting and manipulating others
- When necessary, lie & deceive
- A lot of flattery
- Lacking in values and principles
- Can show up as distant or difficult to get to know
- Cynical about morality and goodness
- Capable of harming people to achieve their objectives
- Low empathy levels
- Avoiding commitment & emotional attachments
- Has the ability to read social situations
- In social interactions, there is a lack of warmth.
- They aren't always informed of the ramifications of their actions
- Because of their calculating nature, they can be patient.
- They seldom reveal their true motives.
- Susceptible to sex encounters

- May find it difficult to recognize their feelings

The Scale of Machiavellianism

A test that contains a set of questions yields a scoring rate of up to hundred on the Machiavellianism scale. Those who rank above 60 are referred to as "high Machs," while those who finish below 60 are referred to as "low Machs."

High Machs are primarily concerned about their well-being. Individuals believe that for succeeding; one must deceive others. They don't believe in human goodness & believe that relying on someone else is naive. They don't truly think that the human species is good by nature, thus they value power over love & affection.

Low Machs tends to empathize with others and are trustworthy on the other side. They care about human goodness & that adhering to good morals will lead to success in life. People who are very low on the list, however, may appear submissive and agreeable.

The 'Kiddie Mach Test' is also available for children.

When Machiavellianism does start emerging

Having such a human in your life can be disturbing & cause significant mental distress & harm. Their ability to manipulate you may leave you questioning your instincts and perhaps experiencing to feel co-dependently 'addicted' to have them in your daily existence.

Narcissism

A mental state in which individuals have an exaggerated opinion of their significance, a profound need for extreme admiration & attention, troubled relationships, & a lack of affection for others — is among many personality disorders. But just behind this confident exterior lies vulnerable self-esteem that is easily shattered by the slightest criticism.

Such a personality disorder can cause issues in various areas of life, including relationships, school, work, and finances. When they aren't offered the special privileges or admiration they deserve, they might become pretty unhappy & disappointed.

They will find their relationships unsatisfying, and most people will not cherish being around them. Talk therapy is used to treat narcissistic personality disorder (psychotherapy).

Signs and Symptoms of Narcissism

The prevalence of narcissistic personality disorder's signs or symptoms varies. The disorder can cause:

- Individuals have an overstated concept of self-importance.
- Have a feeling of entitlement & a need for constant, unrelenting adoration.
- Expect to be regarded as superior, even if you haven't achieved anything to merit.
- Exaggerate their accomplishments and abilities.
- Preoccupied with delusions about success, brilliance, power, beauty, or the ideal mate.
- They think they're superior & can only relate with equally exceptional people.
- Monopolize conversations & dismiss or ridicule people they consider to be inferior.
- Expect particularly unique privileges & unquestioning adherence to their demands.
- Take full advantage of others and get what you want.
- Have quite an unwillingness or inability to identify and respond to others' feelings and needs.
- Be jealous of others & believe that they are envious of you.
- Come across as boastful, conceited & pretentious while behaving arrogantly.

- Emphasize getting the best of just about everything — for example, a best office or car.

Individuals having narcissistic personality, on the other hand, have a hard time dealing with criticism, & they can:

- Often become angry or irritable when they are not given special treatment,
- Have serious interpersonal issues and are easily irritated.
- Respond with fury or contempt, attempting to downplay the other person to appear superior.
- Emotions & behavior are difficult to control.
- Have significant difficulties dealing with stress & adapting to change.
- Feel depressed & irritable because they aren't perfect.
- Feelings of shame, insecurity, vulnerability, & humiliation are concealed.

When Narcissism does start emerging

The reasons for narcissistic personality disorder are unknown. Having a narcissistic personality disorder seems to be complex like it is with psychological development & other mental disorders. The following factors may play a role in narcissistic personality disorder:

Environment — Parent-child relationships are unbalanced, with either too much admiration or criticism.

Genetics — inherited characteristics.

Neurobiology — A study of relationship between the brain, behavior, & thought.

Males are more likely than females to develop a narcissistic personality disorder, usually in adolescence or early adulthood. Bear in mind that while some children exhibit narcissistic characteristics, which may be owing to their age & does not necessarily indicate that they will evolve into a narcissist.

Even though the reason for narcissistic personality disorder is unknown, several researchers believe that overprotective or negligent parenting practices might well have an impact on biologically vulnerable children. In the advancement of narcissistic personality abnormality, genetics & neurobiology may indeed play a role.

Complications

Complications that may occur as a result of it, include:

- Problems in relationships
- Workplace or school issues
- Anxiety & depression
- Problems with physical health
- Misuse of drugs or alcohol
- Suicidal thoughts or actions

Sadism

Sadism is a psychosexual disorder wherein one's sexual desires are satisfied by inflicting pain to another. Richard von Krafft-Ebing, a late-nineteenth-century German psychologist, coined the term, concerning an 18th-century nobleman Marquis de Sade, French, who documented his exclusive practices. Sadism is frequently associated with masochism (q.v.), wherein sexual arousal is induced by pain, & many people react in either role. However, the sadist frequently seeks out victims who aren't masochists because a bit of the sexual excitement stems from the victim's reluctance.

Sadistic violence can range from mild pain to even the most harmless love game to extreme brutality, which can sometimes result in serious injury or demise. The sadist's satisfaction may come from the victim's mental suffering rather than from causing actual physical pain. Although sexual desires may restrict the degree of violence, however, the aggressive impulse takes over & the sadist proceeds to more extreme manifestations of his aggressive tendencies. Sadism could play a role in several violent crimes, such as rape & murder.

Sadism is a term that is sometimes referred outside the sexual framework to describe people who are intentionally cruel or who appear to enjoy humiliating & dominating others within social situations. A few milder styles of sadism, including embarrassing sarcasm like a conversational tool, are quite acceptable in this context.

What is the connection between sadism and the Dark Triad?

Goutaudie, Melioli, Van Leeuwen, Chabrol, and Rodgers (2015) handed questionnaires to about 600 middle school students about the Dark Tetrad to categorize their personality traits. First, the authors discovered that those four traits were correlated, implying that they share some variance. High scores on the sadism questionnaire matched high scores upon the Dark Triad. Second, they discovered four distinct personality clusters in their sample: Those with low scores across all the four categories, those with high scores on sadism & Machiavellianism, those with high scores on psychopathy and Narcissism, & finally those with high scores across all four traits. A sample with high scores across all the four traits was a small minority, accounting for about 15% of the total. These people also had the highest rates of antisocial behavior & suicidal thoughts (without depressive symptoms). According to this study, about

one in ten adolescents within a nonclinical survey are high mostly on Dark Tetrad, and these individuals also well account for most of the antisocial behaviors seen in young people.

Chapter: 2 The Skill of Persuasion

Persuasion, according to Perloff, is "a symbolic method in which communicators attempt to try and convince other individuals to alter their behaviors or attitudes, regarding the issue via the transfer of a message inside a free choice atmosphere."

The following are the vital components of this description of persuasion:

- It requires a dedicated effort to influence people.
- Persons are not forced to make decisions; instead, they are allowed to do so through self-persuasion.
- We can also deliver persuasive messages verbally or nonverbally through the internet, television, radio, or face-to-face interaction.
- Persuasion is a symbolic process involving words, pictures, sounds, and other elements.

2.1 Elements of persuasion

Persuasion has four elements, according to psychologists. We'll go over each one individually below; however, it's important to remember that they're all interconnected, & the success of persuasion is determined by how viable each element is on its own.

Let's examine the components of persuasion.

The source – You

The source, or the communicator, is the first component of persuasion. It's crucial to pay attention to who's conveying the message. One can't really expect clothing lines, for instance, to persuade socially and environmentally conscious customers to buy their clothes; regardless of how good the message is, it will not be credible.

The source must be a credible one. Similarly, an individual with nothing but a Ph.D. in food science is a far more reliable platform of information about the Paleo diet's effectiveness than someone who obtained a certificate from an online course.

Furthermore, charismatic people are far more persuasive than unlikeable individuals. Adolf Hitler persuaded hundreds of individuals to embrace his evil beliefs because, despite being a dark, perverted fascist, he also had the charm that appealed to the massive audience.

The receiver- Customers, partners, employees

The receiver is the second component of persuasion; if we set aside employees & partners, this is one's target audience. And that is why creating a buyer persona is crucial in the very first place. Then, as you go along, collect as much information as possible to comprehend your target market better.

Demographics (age, gender, and race) are important aspects of the puzzle, however, there is a lot more. You should, for example, be aware of their desires, needs, interests and values.

Assume you have a conference today with a prospective client. If you can persuade him to change his mind, it will lay the foundation for your company. So you start telling about how work is your top priority, that you & your teammates work around the clock, and how you even sleep at work occasionally.

The message – (verbal, audio, textual, and visual content)

Major firms, such as Nike or Pepsi, are frequently obliged to apologize for their commercials. Business organizations should be extremely cautious about the message they send out. Nowadays, to be politically correct seems to be the norm, which isn't a bad thing. However, because web users tend to be offended by practically everything, it's not always feasible to avoid poking their emotions.

The channel

Last, the channel by which the message gets delivered rightfully is one of the main components of persuasion. There are hundreds of channels for persuasion – TV, print marketing, radio, social media, online. However, the final choice will be based on whoever you would like to persuade, why you would want to persuade them, and what you would want to persuade them about.

You can't persuade the millennial generation to start working for you if you put an ad in the newspaper. Or you can't expect a particularly written email to convince an investor to grant you money. In this case, personal communication would be the most effective mode of communication.

The most important aspect of the message, irrespective of its format, is its consistent values. It should, above all, speak directly to its intended audience. **(12)**

2.2 Robert Cialdini's Six Persuasion Weapons

Dr. Robert Cialdini published a book on influence & persuasion around 30 years ago. Thus according to studies in the area of psychology, he listed six science-based principles of persuasion.

Even today, 30 years later, marketers use his persuasion techniques to increase conversion rates of potential customers, regardless of industry.

After all, the potential to influence others is extremely valuable, particularly in selling products or services.

What's the best part?

His persuasion techniques could indeed be applied to every aspect of your marketing campaign, from digital marketing to simple brick-&-mortar interactions to boost conversion rates.

The Reciprocity Principle

In several social situations, we repay others for what they have given us.

If you offer anything first, people would feel indebted to you, and they will be more willing to comply with your subsequent requests.

What is the reason for this?

It's because, as humans, we're driven to reciprocate.

There seem to be three factors that would increase the effectiveness of this principle:

- Allow people to look indebted to you -**by giving them something first.**
- Allow people to feel special- **by giving them something unique.**
- Ensure that everyone fully understands it is from you -**by personalizing the offer.**

The Consistency & Commitment Principle

We tend to commit to what we've already decided.

Every day, we come across hundreds of options to choose from. We effectively pick a single choice for the sake of convenience and then stick to it for the rest of our lives.

Using this principle, you can acquire customer loyalty by making them dedicate to something, if it's a stand, a statement, an identity or a political affiliation.

Based on the principle of consistency, they will feel compelled to adhere to the decision they have already made.

It is particularly beneficial for one as a business person since it means you can spend a little less time trying to persuade potential clients to do something & more time linking them with said service or product that best serves their stance.

Use these three strategies to make the most of this principle:

- Request your customers' to begin with small actions - **so that they will be more likely to follow through.**
- Encourage public commitments so- **they are less probable to back out.**
- **Incentivize your customers** for giving the time & effort to your company.

Principle of social proof

We are more likely to trust stuff that seems popular or endorsed by people we trust.

If you have ever started to wonder how social media platforms became so influential?

That's because of the social proof principle. People are quite likely to promote a service or product or to engage in a specific behavior, which has already been endorsed by someone they trust, whether a friend, family member, or an industry expert.

The social influence thus is among the most effective persuasion techniques available today because it's effective.

What is the best way to do it? Use these people's influence - or social proof - to your advantage:

Experts - Validation from reputable experts within the relevant field.

Celebrities - Celebrity approval or endorsement (paid or unpaid).

Users - Approval from current and former users (reviews, testimonials & ratings).

Experts - Approval from credible experts in the relevant field.

Celebrities - Approval from celebrities (unpaid or perhaps paid).

Users - Approval from users (testimonials, ratings & reviews).

'Wisdom of crowds' - Confirmation from sizable groups of people

Peers - Affirmation from friends and acquaintances.

The Liking Principle

When people we like make requests, we are often more willing to comply.

Individuals we like have a higher perceived credibility; unlike people, we don't like for whatever reason. People we like are likely to share our beliefs, interests, & language. As a result, the mind likes to think that an individual we like is credible; otherwise, why else would we admire them in the first place?

People we want could be close friends or complete strangers who stimulate our interests.

This describes why we are convinced with word-of-mouth proposals from our peers and products endorsed by celebrities such as singers, social media influencers, actors, and bloggers. (This is also the reason why influencers are so powerful – we follow them since we like them.)

As you might now assume, liking someone has a big influence on how we make choices. Marketers who realize this have more influence over their intended audience and can persuade them.

Consider the following criteria to make the Liking principle work:

Physical appeal – Optimize your website well-designed, functional, & appropriate for the products you're selling.

Similarity – Act as if you're a friend, not a brand. Please demonstrate that you understand and can relate to them.

Compliments – Have quite a voice; instead of broadcasting, use online platforms to hold intense conversations and build customer relations.

Contact & Collaboration – Fight alongside your customers for the very same causes. Nothing beats old-fashioned teamwork better when it comes to building rapport & closeness.

Conditioning & Association – Associating your brands with almost the same beliefs you would like to communicate & possess is a great way to start.

The Authority Principle

We follow people who appear to realize what they're doing. It is especially true in disciplines where we don't have a lot of experience.

What is the reason for this?

It's much simpler to trust an expert in a field than it would be to conduct your own study on any particular topic.

We can see this in a variety of online marketing, where phrases like **"experts say,"** "scientists say," **"research indicates,"** & **"proven scientifically"** are used as headlines & blog posts.

You can project an air of authority if you take into consideration specific factors:

Clothes – Aesthetic cues that denote authority.

Titles – Positions of experience/power.

Trappings – indirect indicators that facilitate authoritative roles.

The Scarcity Principle

We are almost always attracted to exclusive & difficult-to-find items.

We tend to believe that objects that seem hard to obtain are generally superior to readily available objects.

As a result, the scarcity principle taps into this belief by instilling a sense of immediacy in their promotional language or content.

You can use the following techniques to elicit a sense of urgency in your customers:

Limited-quantity – The item is in a limited supply & will no longer be available once it has run out.

Limited-time offer – The item is only available for a limited period.

It's a one-of-a-kind item special – Occasionally, either of the above strategies is used. And also from the one-off occurrences (for example: collaborations, anniversaries)

Using Competitions – In bids or auctions, we often use our desire to want items more just because other folks want them as well.

These principles are effective because they appeal to subconscious instincts rather than our rational minds. They elicit what Dr. Cialdini refers to as the "click, whirr" automated response in each of us.

However, even though these principles can help raise brand awareness, a great product is the most important factor that eventually impacts customer satisfaction, loyalty, & sales.

As a key element of the marketing strategy, all marketing campaigns would only be successful if they promote a product that provides genuine value to customers.

Chapter: 3 Persuasive Communication

In the corporate world, the potential to persuade does seem to be crucial. It would help if you persuade employees to work forward into company goals or persuade clients or coworkers to consider your suggestions and ideas. You can gain others' support, unite your team, & motivate them to collaborate if you perfect the idea of persuasive communication.

Conger was more concerned in the process of persuasion. He drew some firm conclusions about the qualities required for effective persuasion:

"Effective persuasion evolves into a negotiating & learning process whereby the persuader guides colleagues to a common solution for a problem." It's a time-consuming & difficult process.

3.1 Steps required for effective persuasion

According to Conger's research, effective persuasion consists of the following distinct & necessary steps:

Recognize your target audience

How you craft up your entire message would vary on whether you're going to send a memo to the employees or briefing the entire organization. Persuasive communication takes into account the audience's requirements, values, & desires. Audiences are more receptive to persuasive interaction when they believe the individual speaking to them is similar in some way, whether that similarity is based on age, occupation, and socioeconomic status. If you speak to your audience's concerns, they will look up to you as somebody comparable to them. As a result, they will be more responsive to your message.

Grasp the Attention of the Audience

It would be best if you first capture an audience's attention & demonstrate why is it worthwhile for them to pay attention to your suggestion or idea before you could even persuade them. Begin with an anecdotal story that demonstrates the idea you're attempting to make or with a remarkable fact that explains why what you're saying is significant. For instance, if you're attempting to persuade organization management to implement a no-smoking strategy, start with a statistic of how much sick leave smokers usually take in contrast to an individual who does not.

Establish credibility

You should first prove your credibility and reputation in an attempt to persuade listeners. People are quite receptive to somebody they perceive to be an authoritative figure, whether that individual has direct control over them, including a boss, or an individual who is an authoritative figure within the industry or market. It would be best to try to persuade others about something you can demonstrate or about which you have firsthand experience or knowledge. You should use statistical or anecdotal evidence to back up your assertions.

The credibility of the Source

We can trace source credibility's influence back to Greece (ethos) times. Expertise & trustworthiness are the two significant dimensions in source credibility, according to scientific, social research in persuasion. Although similarity, dynamism, liking & physical attractiveness may also play a role.

The credibility of Sources & Information:

A way to improve expertise: background information, education, formal training, personal experience & subject knowledge.

Legitimacy, talking against one's preferences and endorsement are all ways to increase trustworthiness.

Adapt your message to just the medium

What persuades in written form doesn't always persuade when spoken aloud. For instance, in a written manuscript, you could include stats and figures because readers may take their time evaluating the data. However, if you repeatedly present these figures to your audience during the speech, you risk confusing them & losing their attention. A face-to face conversation is much more impactful at persuading others as you can build a personal interaction with your audience & use eye contact, gestures, & other nonverbal cues to keep their attention.

Communicate the advantages

If you can prove to an audience how your proposal ultimately benefits them, it's fairly easy to persuade them. If you're going to ask the audience to work long hours during a peak period, explain how the additional funds will be used to fund added employee benefits or workplace improvements. If you're persuading your boss to allow you to work part-time from home, then bring up studies showing that employees who are allowed to telecommute are more productive. Describe how applying your idea would enhance the company's image & attract more clients when presenting an idea to the client.

Make use of your body language.

When it comes to verbal communication, your persona is just as important as your words in terms of persuasion. Your audience might well perceive you as angry or hostile person if you would cross your arms. They may perceive you insecure or weak if you fidget. They might assume you're trying to hide something if you seldom make eye contact. Establishing eye contact with your audience will help you sell your message. Standing up straight gives the impression of authority & confidence. Relax your arms & hold them at your sides – if you are using them for gesture – rather than crossing them behind and around the front of you to show your genuineness and openness.

Frame your objectives in a manner that identifies areas of agreement with the people you're trying to persuade

It is a method of establishing even offer in which you must determine the tangible benefits of your goal to the people you are attempting to persuade. If no mutual advantages are readily evident, it is preferable to reconfigure your position till you do. The best persuaders investigate the issues that are important to their peers. They gather vital information through conversations, meetings, & other aspects of dialogue. They are excellent listeners. They put their thoughts to the test with trusted sources & question the people they'll be persuading later.

Chapter: 4 Leadership: How to Influence & Lead Others?

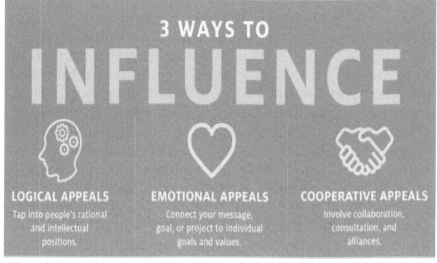

The ability to persuade others is a significant leadership skill. Influence means having an impact on other people's behaviors, attitudes, opinions, & choices. Power and control are not synonymous with influence. It's not about using others to get what you want. It's about observing what motivates work engagement and applying what you've learned for better performance & positive outcomes.

Leadership is about influencing others. It's the most important factor in determining your impact.

So, how would you exercise influence? It all starts with self-improvement, which entails investing in your skills and adaptability, as well as a commitment to continue learning and growing.

A leader's capability to motivate others is built on trust; in actuality, the amount of trust in a relationship rises in proportion to the amount of trust there is. Let's examine how leaders can effectively build trust & influence others

4.1 Great leader's secrets

The seven I's only for influencing others & forming a winning team are listed below.

Identify

Determine the outcomes you desire. No organization or team could create a great plan first without defining the outcomes that must achieve. When scheduling missions within SEAL team members, we will first highlight the main goal, devise a strategy for executing that plan, incorporate contingencies, & then communicate the strategy to the rest of the team. Define the end in mind & work backward from there.

Invest

Make an effort and time to understand the people you would like to influence. Also referred as your team. Constructing deep connections with members of the team is critical in building a high-performing, winning team. Of course, there seems to be a fine line that should not be crossed. Empathy here is a leadership attribute; on the other hand, it goes a long way toward ensuring that team members know you value their contributions & development.

Illustrate

Demonstrate your credibility. We can do it in a variety of ways. To genuinely influence others, a leader must first establish some degree of credibility so that the team seems more inclined to believe what you're saying. Credibility is essential for acquiring success, illustrating consistent performance, the willingness to stay calm and collected a record of making smart decisions, or just plain old-fashioned accountability.

Invite

Inviting people to share their thoughts is a good idea. There could be no leadership without a team. Trust & open internal communication are essential components of any high-performing team's culture. We should always conduct after-action reviews after any training scenario and real-world mission. That would be a time to put rank & emotion aside and talk to one another openly & honestly, should admit faults & plans for improvement should be implemented. To generate a learning culture & continuously improve overall performance, one should hear the team's voice.

Investigate

Look into options that will lead you to the point of agreement. Like the concept mentioned above, good leaders always look for ways to bring their team members together. Successful teams always have unique ideas about accomplishing a mission or attaining a goal as a group. The key is to take the best ideas and put them together into a strategy with the best chance of succeeding.

Intend

Aspire for a result that satisfies everyone's requirements. Leading a high-performance squad entails more than just defining the goals and developing a plan to achieve them. Determining what winning appears to look like is also an essential part of creating a winning team. What does the team's future hold now when they've won? What will be the next step? By assisting the team in visualizing the victory, they will begin planning a roadmap to get there.

Improvise

As needed, improvise. Adaptation is an unavoidable part of the process of achieving any goal. "No strategy survives first enemy contact", one of the favorite lines that relate to both business & combat. Although planning is important, however, preparation & adaptation are so much more important. Success is highly likely if a plan & contingencies are effectively conducted, & the team does have tools & autonomy to create adjustments.

Use these seven I's to help your team achieve a winning record.

4.2 How do you lead people with various personality types?

Every individual has his/her own set of characteristics, & bringing them all together even though as a team is no easy task. As a team leader, however, that is your primary responsibility.

Understanding & trying to manage various personalities at work would be a necessary skill for building a successful team.

However, we all make the mistake of assuming that others communicate and think in the same manner we do, known as false conscious bias. People look up to you to treat people equally; however, the fundamental rule is incorrect.

We must treat people as we would like to be dealt with, which imply that what fits one individual may well not make sense for another, but you must distinguish between the two as a leader.

It appears that good leadership within the workplace is dependent on intrinsic personality concepts. For instance, what drives and inspires one person may not be the same as what motivates and inspires another, but in order to effectively manage a group, you must first understand what causes everyone a click.

You can learn to work efficiently with each person on your team by perfecting how to motivate them, interact with them, & bring them together like a unit to understand their different personalities.

Different personality's types

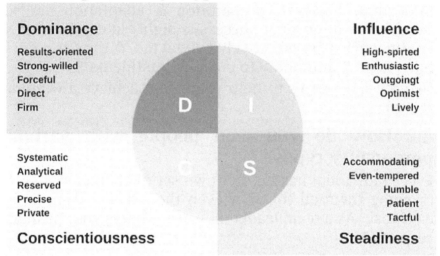

DISC is a widely used personality test that helps people understand their typical behavioral patterns & emotions in a definite way.

The goal of such a psychometric tool has been to provide teams with a common language so that they can better understand & communicate with one another.

DISC will assist you & your teammates in recognizing the characteristics of each personality style, along with your own and help in changing your interaction to meet the needs of others on your team.

Remember that DISC is indeed a guide to assist you in communicating more effectively with your coworkers.

People could be sorted into one of four personality styles, according to DISC:

The "D Style"

The D personality is known as the director's dominant personality. These people tend to be labeled as leaders in the traditional sense. They are individuals who enjoy being in charge & getting things done.

Ds are task-oriented & fast-paced with a strong emphasis on meeting deadlines and seeing results.

Assertive, self-assured, goal-oriented, strategic, competent, & strong-willed are some of their common characteristics.

A professional environment, pressure & direct answers are all good for D people. They necessitate a level of difficulty, control, & decision-making.

A D's suitable working environment includes autonomy, authority, challenging assignments, & advancement opportunities.

The D type of personality is afraid of being exploited, losing control, & being vulnerable. Lack of consideration for others, impatience, & insensitivity are some of their flaws.

Ds inspire others to pursue an inspiring vision by bringing wider picture goals & quantifiable benefits to the team.

A D's abilities also include thinking outside the box & contest the status quo, which renders them great innovators.

Their outgoing personality easily identifies a D. They are self-assured, quick to make decisions, and are not afraid of taking risks.

The "I Style"

Interactive or influential is how the "I" personality has been described. These live by the slogan "have fun while you're doing it" & enjoy spending time with others.Is individuals are energetic, friendly, enthusiastic, & charming because they are fast-paced & people-oriented.

They want to have an exciting experience of life and thrive on praise and approval.

Prestige, the ability to share ideas, the ability to influence others, & friendly relationships are all part of I's appropriate environment.

They are afraid of social rejection, disapproval, & oblivion. The impulsiveness, disorganization, & inadequacy of follow-through limit I's.

That is where your team's cheerleaders come from. With their energy & humor, they inspire & motivate others while also maintaining a positive environment.

They're also innately problem-solvers who enjoy coming up with fresh ideas & solutions.

Talkativeness, animated expressions, & a charming & poised demeanor distinguish an I team member.

The "S Style"

The S personality type is known for its stability and support. They continue living by the song "We're in it together."

The S personality type is similar to I in that it is people-oriented, but it works at a marginally slower pace.

S's are extremely dependable & considerate. They're like an iconic team member who is accommodating, patient, & helpful.

They require a supportive and cooperative environment that involves established routines while remaining relaxed and cordial.

S's react well to affirmation & time to adapt & process information/tasks & they need appreciation, harmony, & teamwork.

Loss of stability, start changing, & offending others are all fears for the S type of personality.

Their limitations involve being too accommodating, resisting change, and also being indecisive.

S's would always wrap up what they start & work to meet the entire team's needs.

The even tempers & soft-outspokenness of an S are easily identifiable characteristics. They can listen & ask too many questions.

When contrasted to Ds & Is, they are more patient & have quite a slower body language.

The "C Style"

The C-type personality is also known as conscientious or cautious, & it is primarily concerned with getting things done correctly, i.e., they are perfectionists.

Cs seem to be methodical and exact. They analyze everything & think logically.

The C personality is reserved, follows protocol quietly, & is skeptical of new ideas before accepting them.

Cs responds well to specific guidelines, a strict system, and time to review their work.

They demand answers, excellence, & attention to detail.

The ideal environment for a C type is structured & orderly, with clearly specified tasks, rules, & procedures, and enough time & resources to finish tasks.

The C type is terrified of being judged, using unstructured methods, &, most likely, being wrong.

Trying to isolate themselves, being extremely critical about themselves & others), & overanalyzing things are some of their limitations.

Cs seems to be task-oriented & slow-paced, so they meticulously complete each project they undertake. They serve as reality checkers for the team & are excellent planners.

A-C can be identified through their careful manner of speech. They are more formal & proper than Is or Ds, with fewer facial expressions & body language.

An effective leader elicits followers' conviction & desire in the goals, rather than coercing them into action. When influence is misused, it can have disastrous consequences. Positive influence, when properly channeled, could bring about significant change in an individual's life.

Actions are in sync with group efforts, resulting in gains that compound exponentially. A leader who, by centered and deliberate action, has a positive impact on others will establish trust & become a genuine driving force for excellence.

4.3 Case studies

- **Niccolò Machiavell**

Machiavelli was a firm believer that the only certification for the power position was the ability to maintain it. Coaches are in charge of monitoring players during games and advising them on how to make better judgments when they are not with the crew. That necessitates an insight into how people function and the willingness to take whatever actions are required.

There are three types of minds. One can think for themselves, second one understand what others are thinking, and third cannot think for themselves or understand others are thinking.

The ideal leader should be a good person who can change his/her behavior depending on the situation. Every scenario is unique and should be treated as such (like the fortune winds & circumstances limits). Another idea mentioned in "The Prince" is Fortuna: an unforeseen event that could be managed if foreseen but can be very damaging if not swiftly managed. A coach cannot anticipate every scenario that may arise off or on the court; however, they can create a sustained framework for dealing with issues involving teachers, players, parents, or spectators.

Machiavelli believed that people only follow the rules because they fear the consequences if they won't follow. A coach does not have to punish players continually, but must at least give the impression that everyone is responsible for their acts. Young people are discovering themselves, and they may not be able to develop responsibility on their own. Choices made based on the likelihood of negative consequences would then eventually get to become good habits.Setting high expectations at the start of the year would build the first-impression prejudice without negatively impacting the team's environment. Players would be swept up in the excitement of the upcoming season &, therefore, will have no qualms about getting penalties.

After that, the rules could be slightly relaxed to deal with unusual situations. A coach could also keep a positive attitude throughout the year by giving out rewards at regular intervals.

Overall, the basketball time should be a positive experience. Coaches must convey the importance of the "happening" (for players) – as well as the value of the "act"(losses & wins). Without knowing the players, no suitable (or effective) decision is made. When a coach tries to modify a young person's philosophy, there will probably be significant conflict. Such a framework should not begin without a thorough understanding of where the student is now, breaking a major development task into smaller goals.

- **Marjorie Special School**

McClure Special School has been a three-to-eighth-grade state special school for children with physical & medical needs and children with multiple to mild learning disabilities. The school has just been last surveyed by OFSTED in September 2014, & it was rated as a good school. Learning Cultures trained their entire staff before inspection, such as teaching assistants & support staff, within principles & skills of coaching.

The Head teacher & senior leadership crew wanted to build a performance management system that focused on what performs well & how teachers & their support personnel should collaborate to learn from one another, share best practices, & portray how their training, intervention, or support affects learning over time.

Lesson observation served as an important aspect of the review procedure.

It was important to modify the perception that analyzing a lesson was all about granting a grade & figuring out what was ineffective or unsatisfying to a system where the teacher was part of the procedure & learned from the reviews given what they required to improvise their teaching & impact.

Lesson observation has evolved and is now a critical component of the school's approach for ensuring a long term & effective continuing professional development (CPD) plan, where teachers select the lessons that they'd like a senior leader to observe, are not ones that they are comfortable with, but rather ones that require the expertise of an even more experienced practitioner, might assist the teacher in making use of new approaches. Lesson observation and the reviews that come with it are now observed as a crucial component of a culture that promotes professional dialogue, reflective feedback, & coaching to enhance teaching and learning.

Chapter: 5 Empathy and Persuasion

We are living in bubbles. The majority of us are encircled by individuals who appear like us, vote like us, earn like us, invest money like us, get similar educations as us, & worship in the same way we do. As a result, we have an empathy deficit, which is the core of many of our issues. It is because of how unified people's social lives have become and the fact that humans are biased by nature. However, researchers have found that, contrary to popular belief, empathy is a learnable skill. People can take steps to recognize their biases & move beyond their viewpoints to try to comprehend those held by others. Also, you will meet new friends along the way.

5.1 What is empathy?

It's about empathizing with others and showing compassion for them. According to neuroscientists, it occurs when two portions of the brain start working together: the emotional site perceives others' feelings, while the cognitive center seeks to grasp why they experience that way & how we could help them.

Empathy is now on the downward trend in the U. S. & elsewhere, according to some surveys that inspire parents, schools, & communities to endorse programs that benefit people of any age improve & preserve their capability to wander in the other's shoes.

Empathy, according to research, makes individuals better managers, workers, & friends & family members, but it has a much broader impact than just the personal effect. According to researchers, we all are in this together, and compassion & connection are crucial for the sustainability and humane future.

5.2 What is the significance of empathy?

Empathy allows us to connect with & help others; however, it might have evolved with a self-centered reason to use others as a "social antenna" to detect threats. From an evolutionary standpoint, developing a mental framework of another individual's intent is crucial: the emergence of an interloper, e.g., could be deadly, thus establishing sensitivity to other people's signals could save your life.

5.3 How to employ empathy to entice and persuade your target audience?

Understanding Others

That is probably what most people think of when they hear the word "empathy": "sensing others' perspectives & feelings, & taking a productive interest in their issues as Goleman puts it. Those who engage in this behavior include:

- Pay attention to emotional cues. They are good listeners who also pay close attention towards non - verbal communication, almost subconsciously grabbing subtle cues.
- Demonstrate sensitivity and an understanding of others' viewpoints.
- They can assist others because they have a good understanding of their needs & feelings.

All of these are abilities that can be made perfect, and only if you want to. To avoid getting overwhelmed by other person's emotions, some people may turn off their sentimental antennae.

For instance, there have been several scandals in the UK's National Health Service, in which doctors and nurses have been blamed for not caring about patients. It's possible that they were overburdened with patients' needs and lacked adequate support, causing them to shut down for fear of not being able to cope.

Developing Others

Others' development entails responding to their needs & concerns and assisting them in reaching their full potential. Individuals who are knowledgeable in this field are likely to:

Reward & praise individuals for their accomplishments & strengths, and give them constructive feedback on how to boost

Mentor & coach others to help people to reach their full potential.

Offer stretching assignments that will aid in the development of their teams.

Having a Service-Oriented Mindset

Possessing a service orientation, this is aimed primarily at work situations, means prioritizing the requirements of customers & seeking ways to improve their loyalty and satisfaction.

People who take this approach would go above and beyond for their customers. Customers' needs are genuinely understood, and they'll go so far out of the way to meet them.

Customers will see them as a "trusted advisor" in this manner, resulting in a long-term connection between the customer & the company. That can occur in any industry or any circumstance.

Mercedes Benz: No More Satisfied Customers

Mercedes-Benz, the car manufacturer, is no longer interested in achieving customer satisfaction.

That does not mean that customer experience is not important to Mercedes. Quite the opposite. It means that customer experience is so important that satisfaction is not enough. Instead, the company wants its customers to feel delighted by their experience with Mercedes.

The company's president and CEO believe that engaging Mercedes employees is key to achieving that. For example, a recent company poll found that 70% of employees had never driven a Mercedes. They are now being given the opportunity to do so, so that they can better empathise with customers, and therefore engage with them more effectively.

Many non-work scenarios require us to assist others along the way, and by focusing on their needs, we may be able to look up to the situation differently & provide more helpful support & assistance.

Leveraging Diversity

Leveraging Diversity implies being capable of creating & developing opportunities through various types of people while also acknowledging and celebrating the fact that we all offer something unique to the table.

Leveraging Diversity doesn't imply that you treat everybody the same way, but rather that you tailor your interactions with others to meet their needs & feelings.

People who have this skill respect & relate well to people from all walks of life. They view Diversity as a chance in general, knowing that diverse teams perform much better than homogeneous teams.

When people see intolerance, bigotry, or stereotyping, those who are good at leveraging diversity address it, resulting in a respectful atmosphere for all.

 The Dangers of Stereotyping

Claude Steele, a psychologist at Stanford University, did a series of tests about stereotypes. He asked two groups of men and women to take a maths test. The first group was told that men usually did better in such tests than women. The second group was told nothing.

In the first group, where people had been reminded about the stereotype, the men performed significantly better than the women. There was no difference in the second group.

Steele suggested that being reminded of the stereotype activated emotional centres in the brain, resulting in anxiety among the women, which affected their performance. This shows how dangerous stereotypes can be, and how they can have a very real effect on performance.

Political Awareness

Many people think of "political" skill sets as manipulative, but "political" in the best sense means sensing & responding to a group's sentimental undercurrents and power dynamics.

Political awareness can assist individuals in successfully navigating organizational relationships, enabling them to succeed where others have previously failed.

5.4 In Action Example of Audience Empathy

By now, you probably have a better concept of just what audience empathy appears like, but seeing a good example never hurts.

Thank You, Mom

Procter & Gamble's campaign "Thank You Mom" has been one of the favorites. The campaign received widespread praise and added $500 million in revenue alone from the London Olympics.

The campaign was a huge success because it reached out to moms (speak about just a sweet spot!) & recognized the important work they do every day.

The campaign did some soft selling by highlighting P&G products that make mothers' jobs easier, safer, and more efficient, among other things.

Finally, P&G established optimistic brand associations with all of their target audience – & probably assisted a few kids to reconcile with their mothers.

5.5 How to Make an Empathy Map?

We can create an empathy map as one starts to bring empathy into practice:

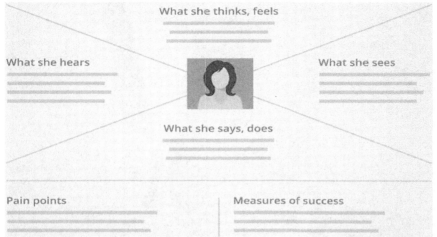

Here's where to begin.

- Make a square with your pencil.
- Make four equal sections out of the square.
- See, Think, Hear & Feel, and Say and Do are the sections to label.
- In the center of the square, put a symbol of the target audience, including a logo or a face. All of the sections should connect to this central point.
- Fill inside each section with your responses to the questions asked.

Chapter: 6 Business Persuasion

Selling oneself may be unsettling at first. On the other hand, your business will flourish if you can successfully sell your abilities and ideas. Every entrepreneur requires the ability to persuade others. What is the reason for this?

When speaking of persuasion just as an entrepreneur, it is not about forcing people to buy your products or invest in your firm. Instead, consider persuasion to be an interpersonal talent that allows you to connect with those around you. Persuasive people have a lot of influence. They're well respected, & able to speak about their accomplishments, objectives, & concepts in a manner that enthuses and inspires others around them.

To put it another way, successful entrepreneurs must be persuasion experts. A compelling entrepreneur can persuade clients to buy and build a solid network of people who want to assist their company.

Persuasion is not a skill that most individuals can learn immediately. When persuasion is employed properly, it might become dishonest or gimmicky, making true connections more difficult. Any entrepreneur, however, can improve his/her persuasiveness with the appropriate strategy and practice.

6.1 Persuasive marketing

"We aren't thinking machines that get thrilled, but emotional machines who think," Damasio said in the 1990s.

As per Havas Media (2019), 58 percent of content produced by the world's top 1,800 brands is bad, irrelevant, and unsatisfactory. In a world where four million recordings are uploaded to YouTube every second of the day & 49,000 photographs are uploaded to Instagram every second of the day, carefully choosing discussion content becomes increasingly important. Consumers today operate as brand multipliers, which is why firms should invest heavily in developing viral content. Conversation stuff ought to follow STEPPS, the six-letter abbreviation for some more persuasive marketing, as Jonah Berger describes it.

SOCIAL CURRENCY	TRIGGERS	EMOTION	PUBLIC	PRACTICAL VALUE	STORIES
People care about how they look to others. They want to seem smart, cool, and in-the-know. So be sure to find the inner-remarkability (Will It Blend?) and make people feel like insiders (Please Don't Tell).	Top-of-mind means tip-of-tongue. So consider the context (Rebecca Black) and grow your habitat so that people are frequently triggered to think about your product or idea.	When we care, we share. Emotional content often goes viral (United Breaks Guitars, Susan Boyle). So focus on feelings rather than function. And kindle the fire using high arousal emotions.	Built to show, built to grow. The more public something is, the more likely people will imitate it. Design products and initiatives that advertise themselves (red bottom shoes) and create some visible behavioral residue (Livestrong bracelets).	News you can use. Useful things get shared. So highlight incredible value (Rule of 100) and package knowledge and expertise so that people can easily pass it on (Corn shucking video).	Information travels under what seems like idle chatter. Stories are vessels. So build a Trojan horse. A narrative or story that people want to tell (Jared from Subway) which carries you idea along for the ride.

Social currency

According to social currency, those who discuss a brand or promote its content must feel unique. As per Berger, it's all about establishing a sense of "social status" / "value" on content sharing. When individuals share material that makes them feel special, intriguing, or unique, it has a greater likelihood of being dispersed, as per Berger. As a result, the aim is to develop content that improves a person's social standing. An American Red Cross generated social currency by encouraging its supporters to share details about the organization.

Triggers

The concept behind 'Triggers' is that what we see, smell, or hear may cause particular thoughts, ideas & conversations. Brands must design and develop these triggers to create quick brand links. This concept is extremely close to the 'Penetration Religion's' features of physical and mental availability and the creation of distinguishing assets. Unlike the 'Influencer Religion,' which aims to start dialogues, the 'Penetration Religion' uses these features as mental shortcuts to increase sales. As a result, 'Triggers' are all about being the top of your mind and on the tip of your tongue.

Emotion

We share when we care. Our emotions have an impact on how we view things (products & experiences). Emotions such as enthusiasm, happiness, or terror are evoked in brand discussions to encourage sharing. Consider how quickly amusing memes spread on social media; the same may be said for things that affect us.

Public

If anything is built to display, it is intended to grow. Another requirement for increasing word-of-mouth should be to make content readily (and publicly) accessible, distributed, & shared by the masses. Because more individuals are exposed to ideas that are expressed in public, they are more prone to become contagious. There's a 'human psychology' component at work: the more apparent something is, much more likely the people are to (want to) participate in that or even mimic it.

Practical value

(Branded) material that is valuable, relevant, and brief is more likely to be shared. People enjoy giving useful information, especially when it is brief and pertinent. Consider how blog posts add up their click rate with titles such as "Three Factors You Didn't Know about X".

Stories

Among the most effective methods to draw a brand into existence is storytelling, which should be a key component of any content strategy. People enjoy stories (see how children cannot go to bed without hearing a bedtime story), but their true strength resides in their memorability. Stories are memorable! They must wrap the branded material inside a tale that could be shared. To ensure brand memory, the brand has to be an intrinsic part of the tale.

Blendtec, a firm that provides professional & home blenders, is an example of a business that has succeeded in creating viral content. According to the narrative, George Wright, a new advertising hire, strolled into the office one day & observed a mound of sawdust upon the floor (which already leads us to the last S in STEPPS). When he inquired about it (presumably after some workplace renovations), his coworkers informed him that it was the consequence of the CEO's everyday activities (& personal challenge) of attempting to smash the blenders. Every day, the CEO did toss an inanimate object into the blender to check whether it would break or not.

A fundamental concept of an 'Influencer Religion' is to create viral content using STEPPS. This school of thought claims that, in the changing media landscape, brands must shift from "marketing to individuals" to "marketing through individuals." Marketers aren't any longer the only owners of a brand.

"A brand isn't any longer defined by what we inform consumers; it is defined by what customers tell one another." - Scott D Cook

Consumers today act as brand amplifiers, communicating their thoughts and feelings with those around them.

Through social listening & dialogue, any brand must feed these conversations and track & comprehend what people are stating.

6.2 Persuasive sales communication

A skilled marketer might persuade you to purchase a fork when everything you required was a spoon. They didn't achieve their goal, by dark magic. A salesperson's ability to interact with - & listen to - the audience allows him to take command of the event and affect the result without you ever knowing.

Before we get into how to be a compelling communicator, let's clear up some common misconceptions about "sales." The tactics we explain below are, first and foremost, valuable for the genuine salesperson. However, you do not need to hold that formal title to be classified as a salesperson.

Take a glance at the below examples:

- A spouse persuades you to spend cash for a new vehicle.
- An employee persuades her supervisor to give her a raise.
- A kid sells the notion of getting the family a new dog.

- To gain fresh work, a customer makes a pitch to a prospect.

Aristotle, a well-known Greek philosopher, defined three types of persuasion proofs: pathos, ethos & logos. Ethos is a sort of persuasion in which someone uses their credibility to influence someone else. A company's brand name is a good example.

If the organization is a well-known, the salesman can leverage the brand name to encourage the client to purchase the product. The argumentation or sales pitch made by the salesperson gains credibility as a result of this. Pathos is a sort of persuasion in which a person persuades another person by using emotions.

Use the power of objections to your advantage.

A salesperson can argue that a given product is user-friendly & that utilizing it will provide the client with peace of mind and comfort.

An emotional argument is that the client would experience something while using the goods or service. Persuasion via logos is a sort of persuasion in which a person employs an argument to persuade another person. For example when a salesperson presents the merits of a service or product to a client & how those

benefits fit the client's needs. The salesman can then logically connect the product's benefits to enhanced sales and decreased client costs.

Example

Consider the following scenario: you are a car salesman, & your customer states to you, "Ah, yes... lovely automobile, but you see that's a little small in size for my needs."

You have two options at that stage: either you go opposing them & say, "No, Mr. Client, it is not that tiny, it is big enough."

No, I don't believe this strategy is very effective.

Or you may also be honest and confess that this automobile is a bit smaller, but capitalize on it by saying something such as, "Ah Mr. Client, I notice you have a keen eye; indeed this automobile is a bit little, I agree."

When it relates to sales, persuasion may be defined as the process of persuading someone to buy some service or product. Salespeople can use a variety of techniques to improve their persuasive communication skills. Here is a handful of the most important:

- Persuasive communication abilities are a unique mixture of ethos, pathos, & logos proposed centuries ago by the Greek philosopher Aristotle. We consider the salesperson's credibility, his emotions, & his logic in this order.

- Learn to provide the client with smooth-flowing information while remaining unconcerned as to how to influence him.

- His background understanding of the issue determines a person's credibility. If an individual who realizes how to educate communication skills wants to spread his expertise, he will check his trustworthiness.

He must demonstrate that he is an effective communicator. His pathos is examined as well as his confidence level. He must reassure his customer that he is trustworthy & that what he is offering would provide him with a positive experience. A logical salesperson is also a knowledgeable salesperson. If the salesman is unsure of what he's doing, he will not persuade the client.Isn't it wonderful to achieve success on both a professional and personal level? This success is based on your ability to interact effectively with your customers. The buyer is looking for a guarantee from the seller. Persuasive communication abilities are a means to a competitive market for salespeople.

Excellent communicators & persuaders are self-assured in their abilities. They understand how to interact with others and how to control their anxiety levels.

The technique of influencing people is one of the persuasive communication abilities of salespeople. Persuasion takes different forms for various people. It's crucial to understand how these personalities act in various situations. To these people, salespeople are just like gurus. They could either create or shatter their reputation in front of the clients. Building a solid link between the salesperson & the client is the only approach to establish a good rapport. Learn how to maintain a competitive advantage without being unethical or disrespectful.

Communication skills help salespeople become more educated and competent. Clients start to appreciate them & pay them greater attention. You discover something new every time you interact with a client. You most likely made a mistake, but you can learn from it and avoid it in the future. Maintain contact with a co-salesperson who can assist you in preventing these blunders. It can be tough to put theoretical communication abilities into practice when you are a novice salesperson working alone. That, however, becomes a launch point for salespeople, since if they experience fear for the first time & manage to conquer it, they will never experience it again.

6.3 Persuasion in Customer Service

People would complain about poor customer service, & you would then lose customers, regardless of how good your product is.

The good news is that we could turn things around. However, transforming the customer service from average to excellent will take time. It requires a real commitment to reform, support personnel, and collaboration across the board.

What is the definition of customer service?

The act of offering assistance to both potential & existing customers is known as customer service. Client service representatives typically respond to customer inquiries via phone, email, chat, & social media interactions & they may also be in charge of developing material for self-service assistance.

Based on the customer service beliefs & the type of help they intend to provide, businesses can also construct their interpretations of customer service. For instance, at Help Scout, customer service is defined as offering timely empathetic assistance while keeping customers' needs at the front of every interaction.

What is the significance of customer service?

Suppose 86% of customers stop doing venture with a company because of a bad experience. In such a case, it implies that every customer service interaction should be viewed as a possibility to retain, acquire or up-sell.

Great customer service seems to be a source of revenue. It provides customers with a seamless, integrated experience that is in line with the company's mission.

According to various studies, poor customer service costs U.S. businesses over $62 billion per year, or even seven out of ten customers say they have paid more to do the venture with an organization that provides excellent service.

Knowing that service to customers laid the foundation of your consumer experience, it allows you to delight & engage customers in new & exciting ways.

Example

The latest study demonstrated how, inside a restaurant, tips to waiters' grow in direct proportion to their attitude toward customers: those who offer customers a sweet at the close of the meal could earn an extra 3%, all who gave two sweets could earn 14%, & those who offered candy, & along with that are also kind and nice could earn up to 23% which is more than their usual pay.

6.4 The connection between persuasion & negotiation

What is the concept of negotiation?

Negotiation is a technique for resolving disagreements. It is a method of reaching a compromise or agreement while avoiding conflict and disagreement.

Individuals seek the best probable result in any disagreement (or maybe an organization they depict). The fundamentals of fairness, mutual benefit, & maintaining a relationship, on the other hand, are critical to a successful output.

Many situations require specific types of negotiation, including international affairs, government, the legal system, industrial disputes, & domestic relationships etc. On the other hand, general negotiation skills can be learned & used in a variety of situations. Negotiation skills could be extremely useful in resolving disagreements between you & others.

Stages of Negotiation

It may be beneficial to pursue a structured framework for negotiation to obtain the desired result. In a working environment, for instance, a meeting bringing all parties concerned together may be required.

The stages of the negotiation process are as follows:

- Preparation
- Deliberation
- Goals clarification
- Pursue a win-win outcome through negotiation
- Agreement
- The implementation of a plan of action

- Preparation

Before any negotiations begin, we must decide when & where the conference will be held to talk about the problem and who will take part. Setting a time limit could also help avoid the conflict from escalating.

This stage entails ensuring that you have all relevant facts about the situation to explain your position. Recognizing the 'regulations' of your establishment, to whom assistance is given and the reasons for such refusals are all examples of this. You may be able to refer to policies in your organization to prepare for the negotiation.

Preparing ahead of time to discuss the disagreement would then help you avoid additional conflict & wasting valuable time during the meeting.

- **Deliberation**

Members or individuals of each side present their case, i.e., their interpretation of the situation, at this stage.

Questioning, listening, & clarifying are important skills to have at this stage.

Taking notes, however, during the discussion stage can be beneficial in recording all points in case if further clarification is required. It is critical to listen, as it is all too easy to render the mistake of simply stating too much & listening too little when there is a disagreement. We should give each side the same amount of time to state their case.

- **Goals clarification**

The goals, interests, & viewpoints, including both parties of the disagreement, must be clarified during to the discussion.

It's a good idea to rank these factors in priority order. It is probable to recognize or create some commonality through this clarification. Clarification is an important component of the negotiation procedure; without it, misconceptions are likely to arise, posing problems & barriers to attaining a favorable conclusion.

- **Pursue a win-win outcome through negotiation**

This stage seeks to achieve the 'win-win' outcome, in which both parties feel they have acquired something positive from the negotiation process & that their viewpoints are being taken into account.

The best outcome is usually a win-win situation. However, this might not always be possible; it must be the end objective of negotiation.

At this point, consider the suggestions for possible alternatives & compromises. Compromises are frequently positive options that can benefit all parties involved more than sticking to one's original positions.

- **Agreement**

Once both sides' views & interests have been considered, we could attain an agreement.

It is critical for everyone associated with keeping a clear head to reach a satisfactory conclusion. Any agreement must be completely transparent so that both parties are aware of what's been decided.

- **The implementation of a plan of action**

Just develop a plan of action from the agreement to carry out the decision.

Strategies for Negotiation

We may not have an option as to whether or not negotiate when doing business. We only have one option: how excellently we negotiate. Every day, we all engage in some form of negotiation. Supervisors employ negotiating skills to encourage employees, set budgets & timeframes, start negotiating for promotions & raises, parents try negotiating with their kids to clean up, & spouses negotiate whenever they decide how to handle their time or money.

Here are six key negotiation strategies that could be used in life or business but are particularly useful in the negotiating process:

Negotiation is a continuous method, not a one-time event

Good negotiating results are the outcome of great relationships, which must build over time. As a result, good negotiators are always looking for ways to improve the relationship & strengthen their place. In certain cases, the negotiation outcome is already known before the parties meet to discuss it.

Think positive

Numerous negotiators undervalue themselves because they do not accurately interpret the power they possess. You have far more strength than you assume for most negotiating conditions. You should believe that another group requires what you carry to the table much as you desire a successful negotiation. Also, make sure your positivity shines through during the negotiation. While communicating with some other party, be conscious of your voice tone & body language, which is nonverbal.

Prepare

The importance of information in negotiations cannot be overlooked. Investigate the other party's history, past problems, and any sensitive issues. The more information you get about the other party's situation, the better place you will be in to negotiate. The practice seems to be an essential aspect of preparation! Negotiation is similar to golf or karate. To execute well, you must practice.

Before you start negotiating, consider the best and worst-case scenarios

When things don't go your way, don't get too fired up. It's a smart time to reassess your position & come back to the table in such situations. In most cases, if you know what each party's highest & lowest expectations are, you could usually find a middle ground in the intertwining areas.

Take and give

Always ensure to get anything in exchange when someone grants something up or admits on a portion of a negotiation. Otherwise, you'll be conditioning another group to request more while diminishing your position & worth. Maintaining the balance establishes equality for both parties.

Build value by being articulate

That is crucial, and it is what distinguishes great negotiators from masters. You would shine once you have a firm belief about what you are negotiating for. Master the art of presenting your ideas & thoughts in such a way that others recognize their worth.

How to Improve Your Negotiating Skills

- Consider negotiation more like a puzzle to be fixed than a war to be won.
- Pay close attention to what's being said and show empathy.
- Make sure the negotiation is a win-win condition, or you'll end up frustrated.
- Rather than focusing on compromise, focus your efforts on achieving your goals.
- Improve your interpersonal and communication skills.
- With family and friends, exercise your negotiating skills & strategies
- Accept & improve your mistakes.
- Recognize your true worth & learn how to say no when necessary.
- Negotiation should be approached as a presentation. Focus on improving your body language to give you a competitive advantage.
- Be strategic and astute. It's said that if you conquer the first negotiation, you will usually be delighted to let you beat the next two or three.

- Define your skills & use them to impress and persuade others.

Being a master of persuasion is a skill. It necessitates the smooth resolution of conflicts & mutually acceptable agreements.

Motivational levers

Psychotherapist Abraham Maslow, a well-named theorist from the behavioral age of management history, developed a motivational concept centered on universal human desires. Maslow believed that everybody would have a hierarchy of human needs that includes physiological, safeness, social, esteem, & self-actualization.

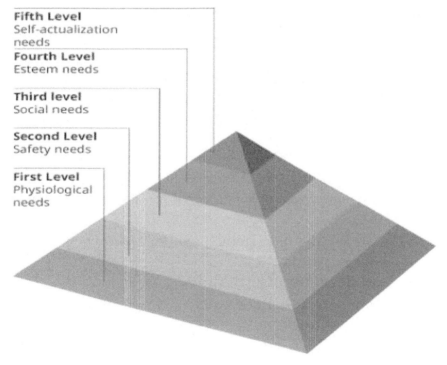

Fifth Level
Self-actualization needs

Fourth Level
Esteem needs

Third level
Social needs

Second Level
Safety needs

First Level
Physiological needs

Physical needs include physiological requirements & safety. Individuals then concentrate on needs involving interpersonal relationships once these needs have been met. Social needs, or the needs for relatedness (acceptance by others) & for giving & receiving love and friendship, are at Maslow's level 3. On the job & off the job, informal social groups assist people in meeting these needs. Esteem needs have been at level four of Maslow's hierarchy, & they include the desire for others' respect and a sense of achievement and accomplishment. Emotions, feelings of self-worth are reflected in the fulfillment of these needs. Managers' & other employees' recognition and appreciation lead to a belief in self-worth.Self-actualization needs for satisfaction and making the most of one's abilities are at the top of Maslow's hierarchy.

Let's pay attention to an example regarding Wegmans supermarkets to get a stronger insight into how Maslow's hierarchy entails in the actual world.

Supermarkets aren't regarded as the best destinations to work because of the long hours, low pay, & high annual turnover—unless one works at Wegmans, which has been on Fortune's "Best Organization to Work For" list.

Wegmans' success is due in part to the company's regard to the needs of its employees at all stages of Maslow's hierarchy. The company is paying above-market wages, so till 2003, Wegmans covered 100% of its workers' medical insurance premiums costs (physiological needs). Wegmans' closest competitor has a staff turnover of around 19 percent, which is nowhere near Wegmans' 5 percent. And over half of Wegmans' store managers started working there when they were still in high school (safety needs). The Wegmans culture had grown stronger & more deeply entrenched over time due to employees staying so long.

Decision-making levers

"The question is whether to be and not to be." Hamlet moaned.

"Now shall I stay, and should I leave right now?" says the narrator. The Clash had inquired.

"In the yellow wood, two roads deviated," Robert Frost observed.

If you're having trouble making a decision, you're not alone. Literature, poetry, & popular culture are all sympathetic to your plight. Unfortunately, while realizing your distress, you may not always just sing you to a correct ending. How could you be certain you're making the best decision possible, whether in business or even in life?

If making decisions were simple, we wouldn't be making music about it. However, researchers have spent as much time studying the decision-making procedure as they have anything else, & they've come up with a variety of ideas & models that could help us know how to make better decisions. Let's look at five of the most well-known decision-making models.

Making Reasonable Decisions

The rational choice-making model suggests that decisions are made after gathering & analyzing objective, orderly, & structured data. The model motivates decision-makers first to comprehend the situation, then organize & interpret the data before acting.

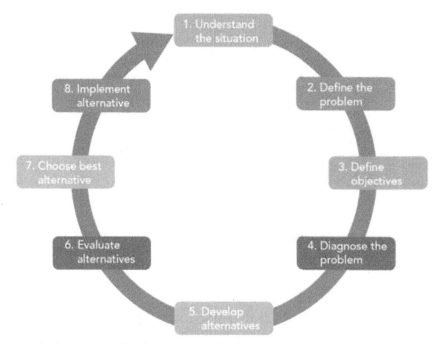

Let's begin with the rational choice-making model.

Recognize the problem

You have a good understanding of the situation. Customers are leaving negative reviews online about their experiences at your establishment. Your team's attempts to create new business will undoubtedly be harmed as a result of this. You must find ways to improve your customer satisfaction ratings.

Define the issue

You and your colleagues sit down & read the most recent 20 or 30 consumer reviews from three different travel sites. Customers' dissatisfaction appears to be linked to the latest rate increase. They don't believe they're receiving better value for money any longer.

Establish the goals

What are the requirements for your solution? You would like to start receiving higher customer ratings. You wouldn't want to have customers on the internet complaining about anything. Your goal is to achieve 100 percent happiness and five-star ratings.

Determine the source of the issue

This is the step in which you try to figure out & understand what's causing you problem. Perhaps you decide that all consumer-facing employees must report on quality problems daily. Also you discuss with operations on bonuses that could be integrated into the guest satisfaction without sacrificing too much profit margin.

Should develop alternative

In the end, you want to make a long list of options and not make a hasty decision. You go over your employees' quality reports. You wait for recommendations on additional perks from operations. You've gathered all of the information.

Evaluate alternatives

Consider your options. You can begin to make a decision when you have all of your options on the table. Each employee recommendation and every operational suggestion should go before you, & you should carefully consider each option.

Choose a different option.

Perhaps one of the employees has recommended adding two more members to the housekeeping department, as the existing staff is having trouble keeping up with rising demand caused by the opening of a new office building down the street. In reply to the rise in business travelers, a representative of your operations department has recommended giving a continental breakfast. Both appear to be good ideas. Which will have a greater impact?

Implement a different strategy

You opt to employ two more housekeeping staff members, knowing that clean rooms & common areas are important to your customers. You have the budget verified and put those two jobs on the market. You schedule a follow-up just at the thirty-day mark and check if the consumer ratings have improved.

6.5 Persuasion in close relationships

Orina, Wood, & Simpson (2002) conducted a study. The researchers taped and analyzed conversations among 123 heterosexual couples around a difference of their opinion in their relationship. These assessments looked at which companion was more determined to persuade another, what tactics each used to convince the other, & how much each companion's opinion swayed in the end. The researchers looked at three different categories of strategies:

Coercion tactics: Include belittling and mocking a partner who disagrees, as well as exhibiting negative emotional states, to force a partner to comply with their wishes.

Relationship Referencing Tactics: Demonstrating the significance of the relationship, highlighting shared relationship consequences, appealing to the partner's love/concern, & using inclusive words (- for example, we, our, us), to convince a partner's agreement are all relationship referencing tactics.

Logic & Reasoning Tactics: Utilizing logic & facts to try to persuade the partner to change their mind.

The findings revealed some gender gaps in persuasion strategies.

To begin, more women (68 percent) than men (32 percent) wanted to influence the change in their companion. Women even used coercive tactics at a higher rate than men. Despite this, men and women have used relationship referencing tactics in roughly equal amounts. Men, on the other hand, were considerably more likely to employ logic & reasoning strategies. Men were also substantially more likely to come around to their female partners' points of view.

Further evaluations revealed reciprocity & correlations among partners' chosen tactics. When women used more coercive tactics, the male companions were more likely to use coercive tactics in response. Men also more probably responded with relationship referencing tactics when women mentioned the relationship.

Chapter: 7 NLP to persuade/influence people

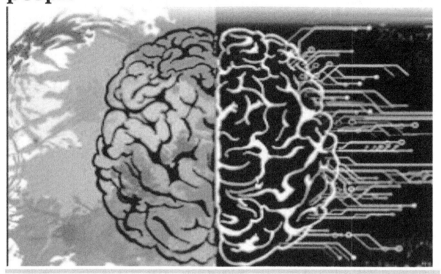

7.1 History of NLP

NLP (Neuro-Linguistic Programming) appears to have two primary parts to the transition or "programming". The neuro or brain component comes first, followed by the language component, which includes speech and gut instinct, five senses and intuition. Dr. Richard Bandler was the first one to coin the term in the 1970s.

He defined it as "the model of interpersonal communication, primarily focused on the relationship between successful behavioral patterns & the subjective encounters (especially thought patterns) underlying them," as well as "a process of alternative therapy which aim to educate individuals for self-awareness & effective communication, & also to change their behavioral patterns." It's a multi-faceted approach that incorporates strategic thinking and an awareness regarding the numerous processes that influence behavior.

NLP was founded at the beginning 1970s by John Grinder, an associate professor (University of California), & Richard Bandler (a student). Bandler & Grinder wondered why some people were more likely to succeed in their endeavors than others, for example, why some therapists were more successful than others. Bandler then set up meetings with the three top persons within the industry to start figuring out what made them who they are & what common thread linked their values. By applying Grinder's linguistic expertise, Bandler & Grinder managed to figure out the therapists' trend. They analyzed patterns of behavior using language-based models. As a result, NLP came into being.

NLP is based on two assumptions:

- We have no idea what the truth is. Our actions are based on our perspectives or even perceptions of actuality. Our limitations are focused on our "neuro-linguistic" layouts of reality, not on reality itself.
- The body, society, & the universe are all intertwined. The methods that occur within & between them are systemically linked. They interact & have an impact on one another.

7.2 Optimizing Performance

The concept of NLP (Neuro-Linguistic Programming) is extremely powerful. Many people believe it contains the most reachable, positive, & useful facets of modern psychology, & as a result, it could be beneficial in practically every aspect of inter-personal & personal relationships. We can use NLP for personal development and businesses & organizations; for instance, it can improve customer service & all different kinds of selling.

NLP allows for better self-awareness & control and a better understanding of the feelings and behaviors of others, which leads to improved empathy & cooperation. NLP enhances comprehension in all one-on-one communications, particularly interviewing & appraisals. NLP plays an important role in facilitative selling. NLP is an enabler of EQ, which is an element of the multiple intelligence concepts. Stress management & the development of self-belief, assertiveness, & confidence can all benefit from Neuro-Linguistic Programming.

NLP's empathic caring principles also help with the practical implementation of moral and ethical considerations (such as achieving objectivity & detachment) and the use of loving & compassionate opinions (such as simply helping other people) in life & workplace. These few examples demonstrate the importance of NLP as an idea for personal & organizational development.

For many people, attending NLP training has been a life-changing experience. Its techniques provide significant benefits to people with the most part in organizations:

- Executives & directors
- Customer care operatives
- Managers at various levels
- Engineering & technical staff
- Salespeople
- Secretarial staff
- Administrators
- HR & counseling staff
- Receptionists
- Trainers

7.3 What are the gains of Neuro-Linguistic Programming (NLP) Technique?

It can teach people how to:

- Set clear objectives and develop realistic strategies.
- Coach new & existing staff members to help them get more satisfaction from their work.
- Recognize and manage stress & conflict
- Improve the development of new customer relationships and also sales performance.
- Improve customer service staff skills & lessen customer loss.
- Enhance people's effectiveness, productivity, &, as a result, profit.

7.4 Operational Principles

NLP is a set of compelling techniques for rapid & effective behavior modification & also an operational philosophy that guides their use. It is comprised of four operational principles that are explained in greater detail below these headings.

- Know what goal you wish to accomplish.
- Have enough sensory acuity (clear understanding) to tell if you're getting closer or away from your goal.
- Have enough behavioral flexibility to change your behavior till you achieve your desired outcome.
- Take action right now.

It's critical to have a clear idea of what you want to accomplish. Individuals may wander their whole life without some kind of a sense of purpose if they do not have defined outputs. The importance of living with a defined purpose is emphasized in NLP. It is essential to speak & act in certain ways to accomplish certain outcomes. NLP teaches a set of linguistic & behavioral patterns which have been proven highly effective in changing other people's beliefs & behaviors

When using any one of these trends, NLP emphasizes the importance of continually calibrating the person you're interacting with to check if what you're doing is effective.

It's important to try something new if it doesn't seem to be working. The concept is to change your behavior till you achieve the desired results.

The systematic implementation of NLP patterns is mandated for variability in behavior. A crucial component of NLP is to take action. In a nutshell, NLP is about observing, thinking, & doing to achieve your goals in life.

Principle 1 of NLP is "Achieving Outcomes."

NLP emphasizes the importance of making progress toward your objectives. Life will become a practice of aimlessly wandering without outcomes. Once you've decided your goal, you can start focusing on achieving it.

NLP specifies a set of requirements that outcomes must meet:

One must state the outcomes in a positive light. This implies that an outcome should be what you desire rather than what you don't desire.

The outcomes must be able to be tested & demonstrated in sensory experience. It is required as a way of assessing progress toward the desired outcome achievement.

Sensory specificity is required for the desired state. You should be able to describe what the outcome would look, sound, & feel like when you have achieved it.

The subject must initiate & maintain the desired outcome or state. This puts the subject in the position of responsibility and control for the outcome rather than someone else.

The outcome is to be contextualized appropriately & explicitly. This indicates that outcomes cannot be stated as absolutes.

NLP aims to give people more options rather than taking away their options or decrease the number of probable responses. The goal is to make options or responses accessible in the right circumstances.

The desired state or outcome should be environmentally sound. That means thinking about the consequences for yourself and others and not pursuing outcomes that will harm you or others.

Principle 2 of NLP is Sensory Awareness

After you've determined your desired outcome, you'll need enough sensory understanding to determine whether you're approaching it or not. NLP teaches how to "read" or calibrate people. That requires recognizing changes in muscle tone, breathing rate, skin color, lower lip size, radiance, & location. An NLP practitioner has to use these & other indicators to evaluate what impact they are having on other people while interacting. This information provides insight into how the other individual perceives you. To accomplish, it is crucial to concentrate one's complete attention externally & on the other individual to notice and "read" the changes.

Principle 3 of NLP is Changing Behavior

The third NLP operational principle is to change your behavior till you receive the desired response. To determine that what you're doing will lead you in the right direction; one should be using sensory acuity. It's a good idea to keep doing what you're doing if it's getting you closer to your goal. However, when, on the other side, your actions are leading you away from your objectives, you should change your path.

Principle 4 of NLP is Time for Action

The final operational rule of NLP is to take action. The logo "Complacency rules" & "I don't care any place here". NLP is all about taking an immediate attempt to improve your behavior for others and for yourself.

NLP Presuppositions

Here are some assumptions that underpin NLP. These all things must be present for the communication to be effective. Each presupposition has been explained in greater depth beneath these headings.

- The response you have is the meaning of communication.
- The territory is not depicted on the map.
- Language is just a secondary means of experience.
- The body and mind are both parts of the very same system & have an impact on one another.
- According to cybernetics (the science of controls & systems in animals, involving machines & humans), in a cybernetic system, having the wide spectrum of variability or behaviors of choice would control the system.
- Adaptive behavior is the goal of human behavior.
- A person's current behavior represents the best option available to them.
- Behavior should be evaluated, appreciated, or modified as needed in the context provided.
- People have almost all of the resources they require to make the desired changes.
- It's only a fact of how 'possible within a world' or 'possible for me,'
- Behavioral data is the most reliable source of information regarding other people.
- It's important to distinguish between self & behavior.
- There appears to be nothing like a failure; only feedback is available.

Presupposition 1 of NLP is meaning equals response

When you communicate, it's generally believed that you're passing information on to someone else. You have information for the other individual that refers something to them, and you want them to understand what you're trying to communicate.

People frequently feel that if they speak exactly what they mean, they will be understood. Effective communicators understand that their job isn't done once they've finished speaking. They understand that what they say is what another individual believes & not what they mean to say.

It's crucial to consider what another person thinks you're saying & how they react when communicating. That necessitates the individual pay attention to the reaction they are receiving. If that is not the reply they want, they'll have to modify their communication until they receive the desired response.

There are several main causes of 'misunderstanding' even in communication:

The first stems from how each person's life experience with words within a language is unique. Often, what one individual implies by a word is not the same as what another individual means by the same word.

The second misinterpretation arises from a failure to recognize that an individual's tone of voice & facial expression communicates information and that another individual may react to these instead of what is being said. 'Actions speak louder,' as the adage goes, & NLP practitioners are taught that the individual should pay much more attention to the actions whenever the two seem to conflict.

Presupposition 2 of NLP is Map & Territory

Good communicators understand that the depictions they have used to arrange their encounter of the world ('map') aren't the world ('territory').It's critical to understand the difference between the various semantic levels.

First and foremost, there would be the world. The second factor is an individual's perception of the world. That is the person's 'model' or map of the world, & it is unique to each individual.

Every person creates their model of a world & thus gets to live in a slightly different reality than the rest of the world. You act on your perspective of the world rather than the world itself. This experience may or not be correct.

The way a person perceives the world & the options available to him/her is determined by his/her experience, model, representation or map of the world. Many NLP techniques require you to alter your mental model of the world & making it more valuable and in line with how the world truly is.

Presupposition 3 of NLP is Language & Experience

Language is the secondary means of experience. What exactly do we mean when we say that?

The semantic level of language seems to be at the third level.

- The first is the stimulus delivered by the word.
- The second factor is the individual's representation of the stimulus's experience.
- The third factor is the individual's verbal description of the experience.

Language is a representation of experience rather than an experience itself. Words are just arbitrary symbols that are used to portray what a person feels, sees or hears. People who talk in other languages use distinct words to depict the same stuff that English speakers hear, see, or feel.

Furthermore, because each person's life experiences, sights, sounds, and feelings are unique, their words have distinct meanings for each of them.

People are eligible to communicate efficiently at such a level that these interpretations get similar. If they're too dissimilar, communication difficulties arise.

Presupposition 4 of NLP is Mind & Body Affect Each Other

The body and mind are both parts of the very same cybernetic system & have an impact on one another. There is nothing as a separate 'mind' or a separate 'body.' Both terms refer to different parts of the relatively similar 'whole' or 'gestalt.' These behave as one & influence one another in quite a manner that there is no distinction between them.

Anything that tends to happen in one portion of the cybernetic system, including a human being, impacts the entire system. That implies that how an individual thinks impacts how they feel, & how they think is affected by their physical body condition. An individual's emotional process, behavioral output, perceptual input, physiological response & internal thought process all happen simultaneously.

In practice, this implies that an individual can alter his/her thinking by changing the thoughts directly or by altering their physiology or other feelings. Similarly, an individual's physiology or emotions can be influenced by how they think. The significance of visualization & mental rehearsal in improving the manner of any activity is one essential result of this that we will discuss later.

Presupposition 5 of NLP is the broadest range of behaviors

In human systems, control refers to the skill to change the quality of one's own and others' experiences in the present and over time.

The individual with the most behavioral flexibility - that is, the ways to interact - will be in charge of the system, i.e., control. It is always favorable to choose over having none, and having more options has always been preferable to have fewer choices.

That also corresponds to the previously stated third general rule of NLP. This principle states that an individual must change his/her behavior till the desired result is achieved. If what you're doing isn't working, switch things up and try something new.

Presupposition 6 of NLP is Behavior & Adaptation

Adaptive behavior is the goal of human behavior. The perspective from where an individual's behavior arises determines that person's behavior.

Your opinions about the world shape your reality. A person's actions are in line with his/her circumstances. All of an individual's actions whether good and evil, are adaptations. Everything is valuable, considering the circumstances under which it is learned. It might not be suitable in another situation. Individuals must be aware of this & modify their attitude when the time comes.

Presupposition 7 of NLP is The Best Option is Current Behavior

Every action has a positive intention. An individual makes the best option accessible to him/her at a certain particular time. Provided who the individual is and relies on all the personal experiences & choices he/she is informed of. If given a better option, they will choose that.

It is important to offer someone other options in an attempt to transform their inappropriate behavior. These additional choices can be provided using NLP techniques. NLP is founded on the notion of expanding rather than restricting options. We simply provide more choices & contextualize the ones that already exist.

Presupposition 8 of NLP is Context of Behavior

You must assess your behavior in aspects and what you're capable of becoming, implying that you must strive to achieve your full potential.

Presupposition 9 of NLP is Resources to Change

People have everything they require to render the changes they want. The goal is to find or gain access to those reserves & make them accessible in the right context. This task can be accomplished using NLP techniques.

In practice, this implies that people don't have to waste time attempting to understand their problems or creating resources to cope with their problems. People already have most of the resources they require to address their issues. All that is required for these resources is to be accessed and transferred to the recent time frame.

Presupposition 10 of NLP is The How of Probability/possibility.

It is probable for you to execute any behavior that any other being has been capable of performing. The method of evaluating 'how' you do this is known as modeling,' &it is through this process that NLP was born.

Presupposition 11 of NLP is Words aren't enough; actions speak louder

Pay attention not only to what people are saying but also to how they act. If there seems any inconsistency between the two, go with the behavior. Instead of focusing solely on their words, go for behavioral proof of change.

Presupposition 12 of NLP is Distinguish Self & Behavior

If we want to create separation among behavior & self, it's helpful to distinguish between the two. For instance, only because somebody 'screws up' on anything does not make them a 'screw-up.' What an individual says, feels or does at any given time is their behavior. That is not, however, a person's self. The self of a person seems more than their actions.

7.5 Techniques & Definitions

NLP is a collection of powerful techniques. The following are some of the techniques, along with their definitions:

Anchoring: The method of equating an internal reaction with an external trigger, allows the response to be reactivated quickly and sometimes covertly by initiating the trigger.

Anchors: These can be found naturally or purposefully placed. They can be found in any representational system and are used to regulate both negative & positive internal states.

Stacking anchors: is a technique for increasing the strength of a subject's reaction to a single anchor by aligning a series of events with that anchor.

Chaining anchors: It creates a set of anchors that lead from an undesirable state to the desired state via a sequence of intermediate states.

Associated state: Being fully present in a state to fully appreciate its kinesthetic. This entails being present in the experience and viewing it through the person's eyes.

Dissociated state: Re-enacting a past event from the viewpoint of a bystander or observer. It implies that instead of experiencing the original emotion, the individual experiences the emotional responses of an observer.

Double kinesthetic dissociation: It is the procedure of witnessing a film of the experience while watching yourself. That is being used in the cases of phobias & severe psychological trauma.

Calibration: It is the method of matching a subject's internal reactions to observable behavioral cues in an ongoing communication

Change history: It uses selective anchoring to guide a subject to re-experience the series of previous incidents. The relevance of past events is modified when resource states are created for each situation & implemented in the participant's repertoire.

Rapport: It is the process of forming a relationship with that of a subject, which is marked by harmony, mutual understanding, & mutual trust. That is accomplished by keeping the perceived distinction at the unconscious stage.

Reframing: It is a technique for separating a troublesome behavior from its positive intention to the internal component responsible for it. New behavioral choices are made that retain the positive intent while do not have the troublesome by-products.

Strategy: A series of overt behavioral and mental steps to accomplish the desired outcome is referred to as a strategy. That is portrayed by a particular sequence of representational frameworks that are used to complete the steps.

Sub-modalities: External experience is classified into subclass referred to as sub-modalities. Decomposition of a sound, image, or feeling into their individual components.

7.6 NLP Modeling

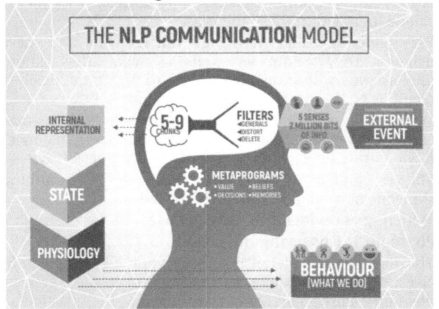

THE **NLP COMMUNICATION** MODEL

INTERNAL REPRESENTATION

5-9 CHUNKS

FILTERS
◄GENERALS
◄DISTORT
◄DELETE

5 SENSES
2 MILLION BITS
OF INFO

EXTERNAL EVENT

METAPROGRAMS
•VALUE   •BELIEFS
•DECISIONS •MEMORIES

STATE

PHYSIOLOGY

BEHAVIOUR
(WHAT WE DO)

The method of re-creating brilliance is known as NLP modeling. By perfecting the physiology, beliefs & specific thought mechanisms (that is, strategies) that sustain under the behavior or skill, we could model any human conduct.

It's all about accomplishing a goal by observing how someone else does it.

When Richard Bandler & John Grinder simulated Virginia Satir's strategies, they attempted to do what several others had failed to do before them. They wanted to see if they could replicate her remarkable results too in family therapy.

Rather than simply copying behaviors, Bandler & Grinder sought out the thinking strategies she was employing. The most difficult aspect of interviewing specialists is that skill sets are often unconscious. For example, we can't describe how we talk, walk, or write. What qualities do you possess as a successful golfer or parent? The expert's concepts explain their success. Irrelevant habits or even superstitions, like sportsmen & their lucky socks, can be included in these theories.

NLP modeling entails trying to transfer what an expert believes they know as well as what they know unconsciously. It entails being able to create the desired result as well as transferring the conduct to others.

Modeling in NLP somehow doesn't necessitate extraordinary abilities. You could, for instance, demonstrate how somebody keeps his/her desk tidy.

The very similar key questions are used to figure out how someone stays depressed or frustrated.

Modeling is divided into three phases

Phase no 1: Observing the model

This includes completely imagining yourself in somebody else's reality via using what NLP refers to as a second position shift. The emphasis is on the particular individual's "what" (physiology & behavior), "how" (internal thinking tactics), & "why" they just do it (assisting beliefs & assumptions).

Direct observation provides us with the "what." Asking good questions will reveal the "how" & "why." Deep trance identification seems to be an effective tool for completing this step. It entails generating more details than could be acquired logically through the use of unconscious clues.

Components of NLP modeling

Modeling success is made possible by NLP Techniques, Skills, & Presuppositions. These include looking at the models:

- Representational Systems
- NLP Techniques
- Physiological factors (such as states & body postures)
- Meta programs, values, & beliefs

- Reference structures provide the required background knowledge.

Phase no 2: Figure out what makes the difference

Traditional learning consists of gradually adding bits of a skill till we have all of that. The disadvantage of this method is that we don't exactly know which parts are critical. On the other hand, modeling is the foundation of accelerated learning, collects all of the components, & then subtracts to look out what is required.

We can figure out what pieces are crucial by systematically removing elements of the system framework behavior. If the procedure still appears to work without that aspect, it is not significant.

The most crucial inquiries are:

- What are the successful person's behavioral patterns?
- How does she/he get the results she/he wants?
- What did she do to get this that a non-successful person would not have done?
- What is the difference which makes the distinction?

You could refine & sequence the model once you get all of the pieces.

Phase no 3: Build a method for teaching the skill

You can't effectively teach a skill till you have most of the necessary pieces & the proper sequence. Many skills are currently taught with additional background knowledge & bits muddying the waters.

It's crucial to practice the skill's natural sequence. It would be disgusting if you attempted to bake a cake without first blending the ingredients. Despite this, we believe we could teach separate skills elements out of sequence & out of context & achieve success.

The NLP model is an excellent technique for speeding up the acquisition of new skills. The foundation of better NLP training involves strong modeling practices.

7.7 Using solution-oriented NLP to solve problems

There are four different approaches to use NLP for addressing problems.

Reframing of Content

When you feel powerless in the face of a problem, it's a very effective technique. Reframing gives you power by transforming a negative experience into something positive.

When confronted with major issues, it's natural to feel panicked or fearful. However, this only serves to exaggerate the issue in your mind. Shifting focus is a more efficient way to fix problems with NLP. It aids in clearing of your mind and making sound decisions.

For instance, if you and your partner break up, it feels as if the world is ending. Now let us reframe it by considering it from a different perspective. What are the advantages of being single?

- Freedom to do whatever you wish, when you want.
- Time to concentrate solely on yourself.
- Valuable lessons for future relationships.
- Ready to embark on a new relationship adventure.

NLP training educates you on how to witness a problem in a new light, one you probably haven't seen before. As a result, you'll have a more positive encounter with the situation.

Rapport

Relationships are the core of the universe. The real root of so many troubles in human interactions is a lack of communication. Wouldn't it be wonderful if you could learn to resolve conflicts more quickly & have better relationships? Individuals who engaged in NLP training frequently report that their relationships have improved significantly.

The sense of being on a relatively similar page as someone is referred to as rapport. There seems to be mutual understanding, trust, & empathy when you have a good relationship with your family, coworkers, & friends. It is made simple to communicate.

You could see other people's viewpoints if you understand their position and have empathy for them.

NLP techniques could assist you in getting along well with almost anyone by helping you establish a strong rapport with them.

Manage Your Emotions

An NLP program would prepare you for the rest of your life. It would instruct one of its most important skills, namely, how to control your emotional state and having a good understanding of how other person's emotions work.

When confronted with quite an angry spouse, for instance, and you lose your cool, the situation will undoubtedly deteriorate. The smarter option would be to acknowledge her or his feelings & then answer back with empathy.

Anger is simply an expression of another problem, such as fear, misperceived injustice, and a lack of rapport. Therefore, before you react, reach into their world, comprehend their perspective, & then respond.

You could significantly reduce conflicts by respecting your spouse's world, which is likely to differ from yours. As you can see, the advantages of NLP are limitless because we could apply it to almost any aspect of life.

Listen Actively

In any scenario, be it personal or professional, active listening is a valuable skill. It aids in the formation of rapport, the understanding of what the other individual requires, and the development of stronger relationships. The advantages of NLP could be life-changing in one's family life.

For instance, dealing with children, particularly teenagers, could be difficult. It's critical to grant them space and time to express their frustration, disappointment, and unhappiness as they go through a phase of immense emotional and physical change.

The desire for children to be heard is strong. They require a secure environment in which they can freely express their emotions. It's crucial not to disturb them. Or, even worse, listen with the intent to refute what they're saying.

Nod at right times to denote you fully comprehend what they're telling. It provides them the certainty that you're listening. Finally, after they've completely explained a problem, ask context clarifying questions for the things you don't understand.

To summarize, we all have problems from time to time. It's a natural part of life. We do, however, have choices. We can discover to solve problems more quickly and effectively. One method is to use NLP to solve problems.

You could even try to avoid a lot of issues if you take it a step further. Clearer conversation with the persons in your life, for instance, can prevent many issues.

7.8 NLP case studies

In about one session, go from a smoker to a non-smoker

For around 30 years, Russ had been a heavy smoker. He smoked 40 cigarettes per day during the week and even more on weekends.

The challenge

Russ smoked all of the time. He used to smoke 40 cigarettes on a typical workday. He smoked more on weekends.

The effect

He had tried various methods to quit smoking, including patches, lozenges, & sheer willpower (most difficult path of all). He got as far as two weeks of "cold turkey," but he was irritable & fidgety. His wife recommended NLP, so he called & made an appointment.

"I didn't recognize what to expect, so I just did enjoy the last few weeks of smoking," Russ explained. When the day arrived, I had already smoked all of my cigarettes before going in, however, ensured I had enough cash with me in a sense if I needed more cigarettes when I got out."

Solution

During the session, his smoking habits have been discussed first. He has explained the process of therapy & what he expected. Russ had just several 'light bulb moments' after explaining the 'conscious' & 'unconscious mind,' as well as other relevant concepts.

He was taught a simple NLP technique because he had earlier used cigarettes to relieve stress and relax. He discovered that he could relax while remaining in complete control.

After that, an hour of therapy was performed. During the session, a variety of hypnosis & NLP techniques were used. Russ found the therapy to be enjoyable & relaxing.

Result

Russ was ecstatic with his outcomes. He could be around smokers, drink a few pints, and still be a non-smoker because old triggers got disconnected. He felt a lot better. His wife was delighted.

Russ followed up with a testimonial a few months later. "I couldn't understand how a 40-per-day smoker, who'd been smoking for around 30 years, can move out from a two-hour session as just a non-smoker. But, wonder what? I succeeded! I used to be a smoker, but after a two-hour session, I felt as if I have had never smoked before. Thanks for the best money I've spent in years!"

A total of £1 million is raised from four sessions and advancement up the batting lineup.

Matthew worked as a partner inside a medium-sized Chartered Accounting firm. He wished to boost his work performance.

The challenge

Matthew worked as a partner in a medium-sized Chartered Accounting firm. He aspired to enhance his work performance & rise through the ranks of the accounting firm. He'd never had any coaching before.

The effect

Matthew's ambition & desire to succeed were the only factors that made the challenge possible. He had a wonderful life and was quite successful. He only wanted to add to it.

Solution

A standard corporate coaching approach has been used, first inquiring Matthew what he wanted (to make him clear), then exploring his options for achieving it & having to agree on action marks each session. He didn't have any limiting beliefs; he was simply a busy person with many demands on his time. He was capable of prioritizing after being helped to be completely obvious regarding his goals &values.

Result

Matthew was a member of a business networking team. When it came time to speak, Matthew and a few other individuals were asked to do testimonials. Matthew stood & said, 'I had four coaching sessions with Jeremy & managed to make £1 million,' In addition, I've gone up to number three in the firm's batting order.'

Chapter: 8 Conversational Hypnosis

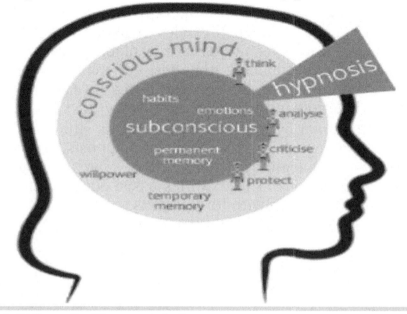

8.1 What Is Hypnosis?

Hypnosis seems to be a trance-like state of mind in which a person's attention concentration & suggestibility are enhanced. While hypnosis is frequently stated as a state of sleep-like, it is more accurately understood as a period of focused attention, increased suggestibility, & vivid fantasies. People appear to be sleepy or zoned out; however, they are hyper-aware.

Hypnosis is indeed a very genuine process that could be used as a therapeutic tool, despite numerous myths & misconceptions. Hypnosis has also been shown to provide medical & therapeutic benefits, including anxiety and pain reduction. It's even been recommended that hypnosis can help with the reduction of dementia symptoms.

8.2 What is Conversational Hypnosis?

Anybody who seeks hypnotherapy wishes to make a positive change in their lifestyles. A hypnotherapist will employ whatever techniques are available to assist their client in accomplishing the desired change. Whereas trance-based protocols seem to be the most effective, a somewhat more indirect strategy is sometimes necessary.

Conversational hypnosis is useful in this situation. This technique, also known as "indirect hypnosis," relies on stories & allegories rather than direct hypnotic recommendations. These stories assist the unconscious mind in coming up with its solutions.

Conversational hypnosis differs from other hypnotic methods in that it can put you in a trance while keeping your eyes open. Many people believe that to be hypnotized, you must close your eyes. That is simply not true.

Hypnosis uses natural trance states that your mind already generates to help you make incredible changes. When we've been driving down the highway, watching a television show, or just procrastinating at work, we've all had moments where we might have zoned out with open eyes.

That is the sensation of conversational hypnosis. The eyes might well be open, however, and your thoughts are elsewhere.

If you've ever simply get lost in a great book, you will be aware of how conveniently the human mind can become engrossed in a good story. Conversational hypnosis is built on this foundation. It absorbs the conscious mind through stories.

While a conscious mind concentrates on the characters & plot, an unconscious mind understands the story's underpinning framework.

Conversational hypnosis is a sort of hypnosis that is both relaxing & free-flowing. The hypnotist may lead the hypnosis session through several topics; words would flow as if they were in a conversation.

Conversational hypnosis is not the same as a regular conversation you would have on the sidewalk. It's chockfull of language trends and metaphors that wouldn't fit anywhere else.

8.3 Why should you be interested in learning conversational hypnosis?

Have you ever been in a situation where you're trying to persuade somebody to do something & they just won't budge no matter what/ how you say? They always dig in their heels deeper, no matter how badly you try. It's a common issue. Many people face this problem, including managers, salespeople, coaches, & therapists. Your efforts are directed toward achieving the best results possible, but the individual refuses to comply, causing the results to suffer.

So, what could you do if you run into resistance again? The simplest option is just to give it up, but this is not the case. Conversational hypnosis is another result-oriented option.

The following are several advantages to learning & using conversational hypnosis:

- Conversational hypnosis would get you with a set of skills that will benefit you & others. A hypnotherapist, who could persuade a client to see things in a new light, resulting in feeling empowered by the results, is extremely valuable.
- When you master this skill, you automatically become the go-to person for solving problems that nobody else has been able to solve.
- Conversational hypnosis teaches you how to employ your voice to influence positively and persuade those

around you in a manner that the client finds irresistible.

- You could think about a client/ situation from multiple perspectives. It allows you to think more freely, allowing you to think outside the box which others cannot.
- Allows you to make instant connections & develop deep relationships with anyone you meet without the awkwardness.
- Among the most rewarding aspects is being able to help others resolve issues that are causing them pain.
- You could overcome your rigidity & finally do what you've always wished to do by understanding conversational hypnosis & the layout of language.
- Allows you to make positive changes in your thinking & behavior with the added benefit of assisting others in doing the same.

8.4 Conversational hypnosis and its ethical implications

There comes great responsibility with great power." - Voltaire

Among the most effective methods of influence is conversational hypnosis. As a result, you must put your abilities to good use.

To put it like this: how do you feel about a man who goes about showing everybody else what and how they must live their lives?

Is this someone with whom you'd want to spend much time? How about the man who simply asks a brilliant question at precisely the right moment to end a crisis? Or who has the uncanny ability to say only the correct thing to stoke your imagination?

The two individuals described may be just the same person.

The distinction among them is not really in their intentions, but how they carry them out and how their actions affect others.

That is the way to develop a moral compass for using the Conversational Hypnosis practice.

Although good intentions are admirable, you must retain yourselves to a relatively high standard due to the tremendous influence that hypnosis could have on people's life.

This exercise is designed to demonstrate that you do own a moral compass. However, it is often only by taking a step back & having the perspective to untangle the knotty issues of what is & is not an acceptable behavior.

However, you should do this long in advance, as you might well get caught up in the moment and not be able to think things.

There are a complete set of ethical instructions that would guide you through the process, including:

- Don't betray your clients' trust (e.g., don't take advantage of them).
- Please don't sleep with the clients.
- Keep the information private you have about your clients.
- Clients should not be lied to (for instance, promise a cure)
- Don't work on issues you're not sure how to solve.
- Give no "health advice." Telling a client to prevent seeing a doctor, for instance.
- Maintain a level of general integrity appropriate to your profession.

These are fairly standard ethical guidelines that are based on common sense.

Even with these guidelines, however, there are subtle disputes that many people are unaware of. For instance, consider the therapist's conflict of interest: he needs the client to return (so he could make a living), but then trying to get the client to stop needing you.

That is a common dilemma that only a few schools address.

That is a massive mistake because we tend to rationalize our actions backward – mostly out of convenience rather than reasoned principles.

8.5 Conversational hypnosis stages

James Braid stated the guidelines and the steps to induce hypnosis in a person.

A 4 Stage Formula is the name given to these steps.

The first stage of the four-stage protocol is to **absorb attention**. The simple term, absorbing attention means capturing your subject's attention.

That necessitates a high level of concentration and the skill to draw the subject into you & keep them pursuing your lead through suggestions & hypnotic language. After you've completed the first stage, you could proceed on to the next.

Bypassing the Critical Factor will be the second phase of a four Stage Formula. In hypnosis, the critical factor is the conscious mind's reasoning that says, "That's not possible."

When a critical factor exists between the subject & their hypnotic state, hostility to hypnotic trance develops. For the subject to reply on an unconscious stage, you must bypass it.

You would be prepared to introduce hypnotic suggestions as in advice form once you bypass this critical factor. The suggestions would align with your subject & the advice would then come out via the conscious mind & take effect as soon as no critical aspect stands in the way.

The third stage is to stimulate an Unconscious Response after you've bypassed those critical factors. You've successfully led the subject into a hypnotic state if you've activated unconscious responses.

Every unconscious response is an indication that you're doing the job properly as a hypnotist. Unconscious responses could take many forms; however, an emotional response would be a good example.

Emotional responses are triggered through an unconscious level, which means the subject has no option for their feelings. They're simply the result of your subject's unconscious reacting to & implementing the thoughts & understandings one already has.

Keep in mind that if you're dealing with someone in a highly elevated state of emotion, such as after a breakup or a recent loss, the person is already in his hypnotic process.

You, as a hypnotist, would have no authority over the subject of a hypnotic treatment if you did not appear to be the process's authoritative figure. They would not pay attention to you or try to follow your recommendations; they are resistant to your logic & require time to awake from the state they appear to be before you can attempt to trigger a hypnotic state over which you have control.

Before you can start to work towards your desired outcome, you should be able to obtain & retrieve a reaction from the unconscious. That draws us to the four stages of the four Stages: leading the unconscious towards the desired outcome.

Once the subject is in a trance-like state and you've completed the first three stages, you'll use suggestions to guide them through their unconscious than to achieve your objectives.

When all steps of the four Stage Formula are completed successfully, you can engage with the subject in what seems like a hypnotic conversational interaction.

8.6 Conversational hypnosis tactics

Assume being capable of influencing nearly everyone you encounter being a conversational hypnotist. So much so that you can easily encourage them to do good things or even change their mindset?

That is the one-of-a-kind "gift" that a wonderful conversational hypnotist can give to the world. But that's just the start.

You can go a long way once you comprehend the tactics & principles. When you enter a room, everyone's eyes light up with delight. And when you say

your adolescent kids do something, they do so without even a hint of reluctance. Just so your customers feel moved to do some more business deals with you.

You'll become irresistible once you've mastered conversational hypnosis. You'll naturally exude charm. You'll gain the ability to make each interaction with other individuals more powerful, meaningful, and harmless.

You'll learn how to influence others by ensuring that they have more enjoyment when they're around you. You'll persuade individuals to do what you desire in a manner that tends to make them sound good.

But first, let's see what it requires to become a conversational hypnotist who can communicate effectively.

Tactic 1: Improve Your Attitude

- **H+**

H+ is probably something you've read or heard about.

H+ is a term that describes your ability to communicate with others from the start of a conversation.

It all comes down to intention: putting your thoughts aside & opinions so you could focus on the individual in front of you.

It is hypnosis plus.

Hypnosis aims to do everything possible to make the other individual's life more enjoyable & fulfilling.

It isn't about you; it's about them. Here's a short story that perfectly illustrates the point:

Case Study: How H+ Helped One Of The World's Most Famous Magicians

*H*oward Thurston was the most famous magician of his time. From the late 19th to the early 20th century he thrilled audiences all over the world. His performances were so amazing, so mystifying, so astonishing, that people turned up in droves to watch him at work.

He was so successful that he was making millions of dollars, which was a considerable amount in the early 1900s.

What was the secret of his success? Dale Carnegie, author of *How To Win Friends And Influence People*, wanted to know.

He interviewed the great man in Thurston's dressing room during one of his final Broadway performances.

Was it education? No. Thurston ran away from home as a boy and spent years traveling like a hobo in boxcars. He taught himself to read by studying passing railway signs.

Was it skill? No. According to Thurston, there were lots of equally talented magicians around, and possibly some that were far superior.

Thurston put his success down to a few key points.

- First of all, he was a master showman who could get his personality across to an audience. He had what we'd call stage presence and a larger-than-life quality that kept people engaged and engrossed.

- Secondly, everything he did was rehearsed in advance down to the smallest detail, timed precisely to the split second. That would naturally have given him even **more confidence** and made what he was doing seem even more **astounding and effortless**.

- Third, and the thing that Thurston said was most important of all, was his **genuine interest in people**. Whenever he went on stage he felt grateful that so many people had come to see him. He appreciated the fact that they were helping him earn a decent living doing what he loved. And because of that, he wanted to give them the best show that it was within his power to give.

Thurston adored his audience, and that **genuine warmth and respect** must have resonated with every person sitting on the other side of the footlights.

Now that's H+.

- ## Going First

Consider smiling at someone while your heartbreaks or attempting to help someone unwind when your mind is racing with images of a tense work situation.

You simply aren't going to manage it, no matter how tirelessly you try. There's a lot of inconsistency between what you think & what you say and do.

In other words, you cannot work toward something if you have conflicting suggestions about that in your head, as your performance will reflect those conflicting ideas.

You can see it in the manner you speak, your body language, your behavior, the tonality of one's voice, & even the way one breathes.

So the tactic is to get into the best possible frame of mind just before engaging in any interaction.

Consider the case of somebody you know who is constantly stressed. After a few mins with you & your conversational hypnosis tricks, they should be feeling much more relaxed. They feel lighter and happier as if a burden has been lifted from their shoulders.

However, if you've stressed yourself, that's unlikely to happen. Maybe it was because you have been in line waiting and someone yelled at you. Perhaps another driver on the freeway cut you off. Or perhaps a coworker is making things difficult for you.

You won't have clarity or peace to use to anybody else if your mind has been packed with such kinds of thoughts.

Tactic 2: Hypnosis Principles That Have Been Proven To Work

- **The ABS Formula**

To perform any type of hypnosis on other person, you must accomplish three things. The ABS Formula is made up of the following three elements:

A – Abbreviated for Absorb Attention

Hypnosis is a natural, intensely focused mental state. It is centered on what is going on inside the unconscious mind rather than what is going on outside.

That is why you must entice the other person to engage you in the hypnotic experience to gain their attention. If you don't get their attention, hardly anything you say or do will affect them.

And how could you expect to bring them in a trance if you don't have their attention?

It's not as hard as it sounds to get someone's attention. It's as easy as this:

- Getting into your H+ mindset
- Establishing eye contact

- Telling them a story, a metaphor, or anything else they'll enjoy
- Taking advantage of something they're speaking and directing the conversation towards a more hypnotic direction
- It's also a great idea to show them an image or diagram.

B – Abbreviated for Bypassing the Critical Factor

It's just a couple of limitations crammed into your head. Because the primary objective is to access the unconscious mind, one must avoid the critical factor & prevent it from interfering. Prevent it from disrupting the other individual so they can break free from their constraints & enjoy new & liberating experiences.

Various tricks can help you do this, including the use of:
- Engaging stories
- Linguistic bridges & powerful words
- Hypnotic themes
- Enticing phrases

S – Abbreviated for Arouse the Unconscious Mind

By now, you've probably figured out where we're heading with this. You began provoking the unconscious mind once you've succeeded in getting the other individuals' attention & bypassed their critical aspect. You've already started the process of inducing a hypnotic state in them.

As you might expect, this is a fluid process. It could take place in a couple of seconds or minutes. It has been split up into steps to deliver you a better idea of what's going on; however, it should flow smoothly in practice.

For example, we could use all of the tactics for bypassing the critical factor mentioned simultaneously. So let us just have a glance at each one individually.

- **Engage Them With Interesting Stories**

Everyone finds it interesting to listen to a good story, regardless of whether they read it themselves, get it to read for them, or watch this on a screen. Stories can carry us to various times and locations. They allow us to take a break from reality & keep our daily lives on hold for a while.

Stories could be about anything that did happen to you, anything that occurred to someone else, or maybe something you read about or heard, like in My Friend John genre.

The other person begins to listen as soon as one begins telling a story. They're curious to learn more. They're interested in finding out what tends to happen, who did everything, how the plot develops, or how things are resolved at the end.

Spicing up can make even the most compelling story more powerful. Metaphors & similes are one way to accomplish this. Instead of telling you had a pleasant dining experience, you could state your steak was just as tender as butter. Then maybe the restaurant was just as opulent as a palace, & the staff greeted you as if you were royalty.

To have a compelling punch, employ power words and linguistic bridges.

Power phrases or words are surprisingly easy to come by. There are dozens of them, but here are the top five:

- Because
- And
- Imagine
- Which means
- Remember

Linguistic bridges make up the first three items on the list. They mix things up. As a result, you could state, close your eyes & relax, though one does not always imply the other thing.

On the other hand, the word generates a linguistic bridge between the two opinions in your head, which is often quiet enough to stimulate the unconscious.

You can do the same with the certain two words to establish a cumulative effect.

So you might tell yourself to close your eyes & relax as that feels better just to let go of that pressure, which means you could relax.

Imagine & remember are two words that perform in a little different way. When you ask somebody to imagine something, their imagination is sparked.

So, where are their inventive ideas? In the back of their minds. When you inquire them to recollect something, the very same thing happens.

Because memories aren't a component of their conscious state, they must go inside to access them.

- **Set the Desired Emotion With Hypnotic Themes**

We've already come up with a couple of hypnotic themes. The key themes of many hypnotic processes revolve around relaxation & comfort. A trance theme is the name given to them, but it's just another means of stating the same thing. Other hypnotic themes include security, peace, unconsciousness, dreams, & hypnosis.

You pick whichever hypnotic theme you would like to focus on & turn it into a smooth & compelling hypnotic conversation using powerful words and linguistic bridges.

You could even speak for a lot longer with just these five power words if you wish to. And using a few similes or metaphors, it's convenient to see just how the easiest of stories could become a gripping adventure that you must engage in.

- **Use hot words to spice things up.**

Words that have been emotionally charged are referred to as "hot words." They have the skill to penetrate through the unconscious mind as they have energy & power built into them.

However, unlike other words, hot words have a secondary function. They elicit a strong emotional reaction that could just come from one spot: the unconscious mind.

You can commence using such a response as a component of the hypnotic method as quickly as one has it.

We can find hot words in a variety of places. Inspirational teachers, politicians, & motivational speakers all use them.

They're all over the front pages of the sensationalist newspaper articles and tabloids. They also appear frequently in advertising you are exposed to on a routine basis.

Hot words are intended to grab your interest, draw you into a story, elicit a reaction, or elicit an emotion. As you could see, that encapsulates the majority of an ABS Formula.

Here's an example of a typical tabloid caption:

"With stolen cash, the company's boss flees the country."

A more conservative media outlet might execute the same story with a less dramatic headline, such as:

"The CEO escapes with the company's profits."

Although both headlines inform the same story, however, the first is more interesting. The words "flees" & "stolen" are straightforward and evocative.

He didn't merely escape the country; he took off running. He didn't simply have the money; rather stole it. So if you read it, you can't help but be moved by the man's greed and his criminal activity, the suppliers & workers who are never paid, the state in which he abandoned his family, & so on.

Everything you've learned so far serves a legitimate purpose. The goal is to generate a hypnotic environment. To put it another way, you want to induce a hypnotic trance in someone so that you could interact with their unconscious mind. But how can you tell if you've succeeded?

Tactic 3: Recognizing Trance Signals

- **If Somebody Is In A Trance, How To Recognize It**

There are a few trance signals to keep an eye out for. Because everyone is different, you will notice that some individuals do one thing while others do another. You will be able to say if someone is in a trance.

However, once you understand the signals, spotting them will be simple. And if you notice them right away, it means the individual's unconscious mind has so far been paying close attention.

Here are some common trance signals to keep an eye on:

- Relaxation of the characteristic
- Breathing patterns change
- Dilation of the pupils
- Dulling of the eyes, almost as if they are losing their focus
- Eyes that want to close
- Lack of ability to move

These are all indicators that someone is entering a trance state. Detecting the signals, however, is only the first step.

You'd define these trance indicators to the individual in an official hypnotherapy session. You might say, for instance, that their breathing has slowed.

And also that their eyes appear to be closing or that they have ceased to move. That results in a feedback loop that reinforces the trance state.

However, if you were simply eating in a restaurant speaking with someone, you would easily recognize that the other individual is entering a trance state (& whatever you are doing is working).

When you first start, having so much information provided to you all in one go can be overwhelming.

However, the key to mastering conversational hypnosis would be to enter the state of H+, then practice using power words, metaphors & stories till they become part of the routine.

You would be in your direction of using conversational hypnosis too in your routine interactions once you attain the confidence to begin things out & find how they work.

And once you've done that, everyone you meet will find your conversations more powerful, influential, and irresistible.

8.7 Ericksonian Hypnosis

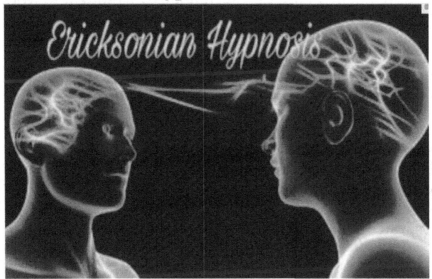

Ericksonian hypnosis has been the term given to a type of hypnotherapy developed & taught by psychiatrist Milton Erickson. The term refers to a specific type of hypnosis. Ericksonian hypnotherapy, unlike traditional hypnotherapy, alters behavior through indirect suggestion, metaphor, & storytelling instead of direct suggestion.

Many consider Milton Erickson to be the "Father of Revolutionary Hypnotherapy." Short-term therapy, NLP & guided imagery have all been influenced by his work.

Erickson is often said to be "The tremendous therapist who has ever lived,"

Hypnotic trance (awareness) comes in many forms & affects all of us in our daily lives. In hypnotherapy, for example, trance is frequently recognized & used to create change. However, these states, such as daydreaming, are something we experience daily without realizing it. The use of such an altered awareness also for therapeutic purposes is known as traditional hypnotherapy. It employs direct suggestions to encourage positive behavior change.

Traditional hypnotherapy techniques are thought to work for several people but not for everyone. Few people, whether consciously or unconsciously, are capable of resisting these suggestions. Indirect suggestions are used in Ericksonian hypnosis since they seem to be more difficult to resist. That's because the conscious mind frequently fails to recognize these as suggestions. The indirect suggestion is usually disguised as a metaphor or story such as: "As you hear to the story, the eyes may become tired; you are permitted to close them & you can. If you close the eyes & begin to relax, you may feel a pleasant & deep feeling of comfort."

Instead of being a straightforward command, a type of recommendation alludes to the likelihood of the client's closing of eyes. Erickson discovered that such a sort of suggestion was effective without conscious opposition. He developed methods of implementing changes with what looked to be a regular conversation. That enabled the subconscious to be somehow aided without the conscious mind's opposition.

Ericksonian hypnosis' essential components

Because Erickson took a novel approach to hypnotherapy, many of his techniques were thought to have died. However, certain aspects of his approach have been identified, analyzed, & refined & are now essential components of Ericksonian hypnosis.

- **Being adaptable in your approach**

Erickson was a very adaptable person who would change his approach depending on the client. He acknowledged that each client would require a unique approach. He'd be indirect & soothing at times, & direct & aggressive at other times. At some other times, his hypnosis was barely discernible as hypnosis.

Erickson was an expert at customizing his sessions. He used to spend time understanding the client to comprehend their situation better and use that knowledge to implement change.

- **Using symptoms to influence change**

Erickson would often see client issues as a process. He believed that the symptoms were a key component of the procedure, so he would concentrate on modifying the symptom (for instance, its location or intensity) to change the problem's overall pattern. For instance, if a client had a compulsive urge to rinse hands, then Erickson would tell them to rinse 100 times, he thought that by doing so, the behavior would shift from an internal obligation to that of an externally enforced chore, making it less compelling to wash hands fifty times a day.

- **Activating the unconscious mind**

Erickson believed that the unconscious mind possessed all of the resources needed to create a positive transition, so he decided to focus on engaging the unconscious mind through any means possible.

He didn't believe in Freud's theory that we should eliminate the source of problems from the past. Imagination & metaphor are the unconscious's languages. Erickson had this idea, so therapeutic stories, jokes, riddles & metaphors were an important part of his work.

8.8 Is NLP a form of hypnosis?

Induction is not a formal feature of NLP. It does not use relatively similar tools & techniques as hypnosis since both the conscious & unconscious minds are involved. However, NLP is not the same as hypnosis.

Chapter 9: Mind Control Techniques

9.1 What does mind control mean?

Mind control is a broad term that encompasses various contentious theories and techniques aimed at undermining an individual's ability to control their thoughts, behavior, emotions, or decisions. Mind control has been referred to as "simply a scientific form for brainwashing,". It is a broader term that can encompass topics like hypothetical neuro-technology that might one day claim to "hack" the human mind.

Researchers had known since the mid-1930s that creating a potential field along the neural cell membrane can end up causing it to fire unnaturally. Experiments with giant ocean squid axons revealed that such artificial stimulation is possible.

Coercion, cognitive dominance, brainwashing, psychological impact, & the malignant usage of social dynamics to alter & manipulate people over time are all terms used to describe mind control. It's a strategy that governments & corporations frequently use to get what they want. Individuals who wish to accomplish something in their businesses or relationships usually use coercion to achieve their goals.

Mind control is like a form of brainwashing behavior used by people who attempt to manipulate everyone into delving deeper into their values & ways of doing things.

That implies a form of deceit intended to persuade gullible people to participate in something they don't believe in. People sometimes take advantage of it for personal gain. Several people are probable to claim that it's all about coercion. That isn't true because, in exploitation, disparities are sometimes overlooked.

9.2 Difference between brainwash & mind control

Coercive persuasion, also known as brainwashing, is a systematic attempt to persuade disbelievers to accept a particular allegiance, command, and perhaps doctrine. It is a colloquial term that refers to a technique used to manipulate human action and thought against the individual's desire, will, and knowledge. By controlling the social and physical environment, an effort is made to abolish allegiances to unfavorable individuals or groups, to show to the person that his or her attitudes or thought patterns are incorrect & must be modified, and to foster loyalty & unquestioning obedience to a ruling party.

The term most commonly is applied to religious or political indoctrination or some ideological remolding program. Brainwashing techniques usually include isolation from closest associates & information sources; a rigorous regimen necessitating absolute obedience & humility; solid social pressures & rewards for cooperation; & psychologically and physically penalties for non-cooperation varying from social ostracism & criticism, lack of food, sleep, & social connections, to bondage & torture.

Steve Hassan, a researcher, makes a distinction between mind control & brainwashing. The contrast lies in that the subject is aware that he or she is being influenced or manipulated. When people are brainwashed, they are aware that they've been manipulated, and their thinking shifts in favor of said manipulator. The victim of mind control, on the other side, is completely unaware of the manipulation that is taking place.

Destructive influencers are now using social media to recruit people through manipulation, deception, hypnotic & subliminal programming, & other methods. Hassan's Influence Continuum seems to be a new model distinguishing between healthy, ethical influence & destructive, unethical influence.

He has assisted thousands of people, or even families, in healing from the effects of undue influence for over four decades (mind control). He is regarded as one of the best-known authorities on political influence, brainwashing, deprogramming, & controlling groups & individuals, for over forty years of experience.

9.3 Techniques of Mind Control to Be Conscious Of

We'll go over several actual mind control in interpersonal relationships and groups techniques used by ordinary people.

Isolation

Physical isolation has a lot of power, but manipulators will usually isolate one mentally if physical isolation isn't possible or practical. It can be accomplished in various ways, ranging from one-week country seminars to criticizing one's family & circle of friends. The overall goal is to limit any other impact by manipulating information flow.

Criticism

Criticism is used to isolate people. The manipulators frequently use "us versus them" vocabulary, criticize the external world, & assert their superiority. Thus according to them, it will help you consider yourself fortunate to be affiliated with them.

Peer pressure & social proof

To brainwash new members, those attempting to manipulate groups would traditionally use social proof & peer pressure. Social proof is indeed a psychological condition in which (some) individuals believe that others' actions & beliefs are appropriate & should be justified since "everyone does it." It is especially useful when a person is unsure of what to consider, how to act, and what to do. In such situations, many people will observe what others are doing and follow suit.

Alienation anxiety

New members to manipulative groups are typically welcomed warmly & form several new friendships, which initially appear much deeper & more worthwhile than everything else they have ever known. If any suspicions arise later, these bonds will serve as an influential tool to keep them in a group. Even if they're not convinced, life in the outer world may appear to be very lonely.

Repetition

Another effective persuasion technique is constant repetition. Although it may appear overly simplistic, repeating the same message over & over again helps make it more familiar & easier to remember. When repetition and social proof are combined, the message is delivered without fail.

One more evidence that repetition projects is the existence of affirmations (as just a self-improvement approach). If you can convince yourself through wordplay, there's a good chance you will be persuaded to think & respond in a certain way.

Fatigue

Physical and mental exhaustion are the results of fatigue & sleep deprivation. You become more vulnerable to persuasion if you are physically exhausted and less alert. According to a study published in the Experimental Psychology Journal, people who had just slept for 21 hours were much more susceptible to recommendations.

Creating a new identity

Manipulators ultimately want to change your identity. They would like you to quit being yourself & become a robot who obeys their commands without question. They would then attempt to retrieve some confession from you employing all of the methods & mind manipulative tactics mentioned above — some acknowledgment that you believe they are nice people doing a great thing (variations are possible). It could be something unimportant at first, such as agreeing that the group's members are fun & loving folks or that some of their viewpoints are valid.

Once you embrace that one small thing, you might be more willing to accept another, & then another. You start to identify as one of the clusters before you realize it, out of a wish to be consistent in what you say & do. It is especially effective if you realize your confessions had been recorded or filmed, as there is concrete evidence of your latest identity in case if you forget.

You might be thinking regarding "groups" in your existence now that you've read this. Are they attempting to manipulate you? Let's pretend you're a member of Greenpeace. It all began with a slight donation, followed by a fun event (many new friends), & before you understand it, you're seated in a small boat rioting Shell's polar drilling while your education & career are placed on hold. What happened here, exactly? Did Greenpeace dupe you into doing this? No, it's not true. They had an impact on you. While Greenpeace may have persuaded you to go and do something you would never have considered doing before, they do not use you for their gain. They asked you to do what they think is correct (though opinions may differ), & you agreed — no personal gain is involved.

Consider a controlling karate instructor who is verbally & physically abusive to his students while expecting complete admiration & obedience in return & who convinces them that they're the ones who are just about to learn some secret special that would place both Rambo & Terminator to shame. Whether his motivations are purely financial or simply a desire to manipulate & feel superior, there is no doubt that he is employing the mind control techniques described above.

Drug use

Drug use can be subtle or overt. The usage of narcotics is not always visible,

But it helps to control the mind.

Hypnosis

Making a victim's mind vulnerable & making the manipulation process easier.

9.4 Who employs mind control techniques?

Anybody who desires to manipulate or to have influence over some other person can use mind control. Furthermore, those who employ these methods have very specific goals in mind, often political, social, and personal. Their main goal is to deprive specific people of their freedom of expression & personal convictions.Mental control is also a common technique used by sects, cults, & religions. They need them to attract new followers & keep their existing ones engaged. These groups' leaders frequently employ mind-control strategies on their followers.

Manipulation & exploitation are masters for psychopaths, sociopaths, narcissists, & others who have little or no empathy. However, some types of mind control can occur in intimate relationships when one of the disputants abuses their power such as those between a teacher & a student, a parent & a child, a boss & a subordinate, & a doctor-patient etc.

9.5 Mind Control Techniques & Their Usefulness

These mind control tools are used in a variety of ways, not all of which are negative. They're useful in some situations, as far as they're not intrusive or forced.Such mind control techniques could be highly beneficial to the lives of such patients when used by conscientious doctors and psychologists. They're effective for overcoming addictions, healing from traumatic experiences, boosting self-esteem, & even calming suicidal or self-destructive ideas.

Mind control is not always a bad thing. If used for self-serving reasons, this technique then can become negative.

Techniques of Mind Control for a Happy Life

Our minds are extremely powerful, but we can use mind control techniques to control them. It is feasible to implant thought in our minds, feel the emotions associated with that thought, & train our minds to respond in the way we want.

Every thinking person strives for happiness and follows her or his direction to achieve it. Individually, we have different ideas about what happiness is.

In our lives, we frequently experience a vague discontent that we will be aware of while being unable to pin down. It is due to our unfulfilled wishes & dreams.

Subconscious mind

Our subconscious mind understands the components of our happiness, and our conscious mind often does not. Our conscious & subconscious brains must work together to reach our full potential.

Our attitudes, emotions, & outlook on life are all governed by our subconscious mind. We can focus on stuff that is important to us by utilizing the subconscious power. Irrational fears prevent us from reaching our full potential. Fear, hopelessness, & a loss of belief in humanity & God are all common negative emotions that keep us from being happy.

We could regulate our mind & free will by harnessing the subconscious power.

Here's a quick rundown of several prevalent mind control techniques which can aid you to live a better life:

Visualization

We train our minds to work forward into success by visualizing ourselves succeeding. It is possible to attract positive energy.

Regardless of how impossible the goal appears to be, positive visualization attracts good fortune! Sports psychiatrists widely use this technique to help athletes achieve peak performance.

Khalil Gibran wrote a couplet that states that the universe gives one whatever one single-mindedly asks for. It is a validation of the strength of positive visualization that Rhonda Byrne also reaffirmed in the latest popular movie "The Secret."

Meditation

Meditation is among the oldest methods for mind control. We allow peace & calm to circulate into our minds by relaxing the mind & emptying it of its thoughts. Meditation calms the jumble of thoughts that flit through our heads & gives one's subconscious a voice.

The alpha waves generated by the mind have been scientifically proven to peak after meditation. These Alpha waves help people think more creatively and positively. Meditation trains the mind to concentrate solely on the present moment.

Mirror talk

Man is both his best friend & his worst foe. Negative self-talk becomes a self-fulfilling premonition. Constantly chatting down to oneself is a surefire way to be looked down on by everyone.

When we start giving ourselves positive strokes & encouragement, on the other side, the mind is fed and focused on what is attainable, & it works toward that aim.

Self-hypnosis

Like meditation, self-hypnosis clears the mind, including all thoughts & focuses it towards a single goal. Alcoholics Anonymous has used self-hypnosis & the repetition of the single mantra to successfully free addicts from self-destructive alcohol addiction.

Goals are to be written down, and self-evaluation is done regularly.

Our objectives take shape when we write them down. Reviewing goals & progress toward attaining them allows you to render the necessary changes. Reviewing your progress also helps you stay focused on your goal and keep your spirits upbeat.

Chapter 10: Brainwashing

10.1 Brief History

Edward Hunter, a journalist, was the first one to raise the alarm. In September 1950, his headline in Miami Daily News read, "Brain-washing Tricks Compel Chinese into Communist Party Ranks." Hunter defined how Mao Zedong used frightening ancient tactics to transform the Chinese individuals into thoughtless Communist automatons within the article & later in a book. He coined the term "brainwashing" to describe the hypnotic process, which is the translation of the Mandarin words "wash" (xi) & "brain" (Nao). He also warned about the potentially dangerous implications.

That wasn't the first time that fears of Communism & mind control had infiltrated the American public consciousness. The United States Chamber of Commerce, deeply concerned about the expansion of Communism, suggested expelling liberals, socialists, & communists from spots such as schools, libraries, newspapers, & entertainment in 1946. Hunter's incendiary rhetoric didn't effect till three years after Korean War until American POWs began admitting to bizarre crimes.

Colonel Frank Schwable has been the top-ranking military officer to meet that destiny. When Hunter was taken down over Korea & captured in 1952, & by February 1953, he as well as other POWs had falsely admitted to just using germ biological warfare against these Koreans, dropping everything including anthrax to just the plague on unwary civilians. The American people were shocked, and they were shocked even more when 5,000 of its 7,200 POWs filed a petition to the US govt to end war and approved statements to their alleged terrible offenses. The ending nail into the coffin was the refusal of 21 American soldiers to be repatriated.

The threat of brainwashing became very real, & it was all around. The US military refused the soldiers 'confessions but could not clarify how they were coerced into making them. Apart from brainwashing, what else could account for the soldiers' actions? Mind control became popular in movies such as The Manchurian Candidate, which depicted individuals whose minds were washed & governed by outside powers. In the book Masters of Deceit, J. Edgar Hoover, FBI Director, mentioned thought-control several times.

The American Psychological Association then gave it faith by 1980, when the Diagnostic & Statistical Manual of Psychological Disorders -III included brainwashing under the "dissociative disorders." Had Communists in China & the Soviet Union discovered a machine and perhaps a method for rewriting men's minds & removing their free will?

However, the simple answer is no; however, that hasn't stopped the US from investing heavily in its fight.

The term was defined in a variety of ways, relying on who had it. According to Melley, Hunter, who turned out to be CIA propaganda operative, described it as a mystical, oriental procedure that the West couldn't comprehend or anticipate. On the other hand, brainwashing was far less mysterious to scientists who investigated the American POWs after they came back from Korea. (Those men had been tormented).

10.2 Coercive persuasion techniques

If you refer to brainwashing as coercive persuasion, you may be able to grasp the concept better.

When by use of force, we persuade someone; this is known as coercive persuasion. This method of persuasion is more powerful and intrusive. This sort of persuasion is used by sects, totalitarian state governments, terrorist groups, & kidnappers, among others.

It's not easy to brainwash someone or use coercive persuasion. To get someone to alter belief structure, thought pattern, or the way they act & behave, you must employ various techniques. There are four different types of coercive persuasion techniques: social, environmental, cognitive, and emotional & those that stimulate dissociative states.

Social, environmental techniques

These techniques control or manipulate the subject's environment or surroundings. The aim is to destabilize the individual's resistance so that they are persuaded more easily. The following are some examples of social-environmental persuasion techniques:

Isolation: This makes persuasion simpler for the subject. It means separating the person from the rest of the world psychologically, socially, and physically. To put it another way, the individual is completely isolated.

Information manipulation & control: Information manipulation & control is a type of isolation with much less information, the person will have fewer options from which to choose. Their ability to think critically is limited as well.

Establishing a condition of existential dependency: This attempt to make somebody else think that their existence depends on someone else. That person is usually a type of leader. In reality, this means meeting someone's primary & secondary needs till they become completely reliant.

Psychophysical debilitation: Psychophysical debilitation is linked to certain types of physical debilitation. As a result, your willingness to oppose persuasion tactics is weakened.

Emotional techniques

Emotional conditioning influences motivation. As a result, if you can control people's feelings, you can manipulate their motivations & behavior.

Emotional pleasure activation: This entails charming people & treating them well. It's used to entice people in & capture their attention.

Fear, guilt, & emotional anxiety activation: Using punishments & rewards to elicit emotional states of fear, guilt, & anxiety. These feelings encourage submission & dependency.

Cognitive techniques

These techniques are based on the two we've already addressed. A person who is physically unfit & feels guilty would be an easy target for brainwashing.

Negation of critical thinking: The perpetrator demonstrates to the victim the folly of following one's thoughts. As a result, they repress their thoughts every time they have an idea.

Deceit and Lies: Deception and lies are used to distort reality by concealing information, by deceiving or lying.

Demanding submission: By asking submission, the concept of a group thinking is established. Individuals are expected to submit to whatever the group decides. We can describe it another way as conformity & submission are being developed.

Group identity: It is necessary to have a collective identity. As a result, people lose their individuality and adopt the identity of the group. Individuals may lose any distinctive characteristics as a result of this.

Controlling attention: Attempting to manipulate what occupies somebody's attention means you can force someone to pay close attention to persuasion efforts.

Controlling language: It has been a way of restricting freedom. One way to avoid certain questions or evaluations is to leave out several words or phrases.

Altering the source of power: When an individual's principle of authority is shattered, they are exposed to totalitarian rule. As a result, such an authority figure gains complete control. Everyone else is required to submit.

A technique that causes dissociative states

Dissociation is a type of trance that occurs when an experience becomes more intense. This state causes a loss of consciousness & identity for a brief period. In totalitarian societies, they are much more common. Followers become more vulnerable as a result of levels of consciousness. As a result, restricting their options & reducing their capacity to evaluate them makes it easier to manipulate them.

When you try to influence somebody's surroundings to weaken them, this is known as coercive persuasion/brainwashing. The manner they feel and think changes as a result of cognitive & emotional persuasion. That causes them to fall into trance states, making them relatively easy to persuade.

Chapter 11: How to Defend Yourself Against Mind Control?

Vulnerability

Every single person is susceptible. You are included in this!

It is false to assume that just weak & vulnerable are susceptible. Believing that "it will never occur to me" renders a person especially vulnerable to mind control techniques because they aren't looking for them!

Understanding how a cult works & the cult tricks used to lure & keep members is the best method to prevent yourself from being lured by a cult (it is a myth that people join cults; they are recruited) &being made a subject to mind control.

Robert Cialdini, for instance, has identified six fundamentals of influence that are referred to as "weapons of influences." These appear to exist in all societies around the world, & they are beneficial in maintaining society's stability and prosperity. He discussed reciprocity, consistency, & commitment, as well as social proof, charisma, authority, & scarcity. He referred them as "weapons of influences" since they operate outside of most people's awareness, & cults use them to influence & manipulate their followers.

Cult experts

Numerous cult experts have studied cult psychology, & while each has its explanation & model of how such groups operate, there are several similarities.

After studying American POWS in China, Robert Lifton, who invented the term "thought reform." defined his eight fundamentals, available inside a thought reform scheme like destructive cults.

Steven Hassan, a former representative of the destructive cult, had already developed his four-point framework, which he detailed in Combating Cult Brain Control.

He explained how deadly cults employ mental control strategies to alter members' identities by controlling their behaviors, emotions, & thoughts & how they further increase their control by restricting direct exposure to information (BITE model).

Margaret Singer explained her six-point scheme in the manuscript Cults in Our Midst. Where,

- The individual is completely unaware that a system is controlling them.
- Their time and surroundings are regulated.
- They are made to be fearful and reliant.
- Previous attitudes and behaviors are suppressed.
- New attitudes and behaviors are instilled, &

- They are introduced with a doctrine that has closed logic.

The results of a one-on-one cult in an intimate relationship with a sociopath, such as a wife & a husband, where all of the attention is focused on one victim, could be very disturbing. The term "complex trauma" is now commonly used to define what happens to kids raised by narcissistic parents or psychopathic.

11.1 Who would be the victims?

Have you ever really heard the phrase "drinking a Kool-Aid"? The Jonestown Massacre was a tragic mass suicide, which occurred on Nov18, 1978; on this day, over 900 persons, led by cult figurehead Jim Jones, attempted suicide by drinking a poisonous drink of cyanide & Flavor-Aid, a cheaper version of Kool-Aid.

Jones cautioned his supporters that vicious outsiders would come & harm them after a session by Congressman Leo Ryan (U.S), who probed into rumors of unfair treatment just at a compound in which the cult's supporters lived. He told his followers that they should commit "revolutionary suicide" by poisoning themselves & others. Cult members first poisoned the children, & parents & nurses then used syringes to inject the poison inside the children's throats.

The events gave rise to the keyword "drinking a Kool-Aid," which is now used to describe anyone who has been brainwashed into accepting someone else's erroneous beliefs.

When we hear stories like these, we wonder who could be so effective & persuasive that individuals would do such unthinkable things. Psychologists are also looking for an explanation, and they spend a lot of time researching how people like Jones were able to have such a strong influence on their followers.

Identifying a victim

The first step is to realize that someone is controlling you.

People who have mental control over you also have emotional control over you. Because your emotions are being exploited, you are oblivious that someone is already controlling you. And, because emotion affects logic, deciding to put an end to it isn't easy.

They explore themes of trust, guilt, hope, &, on occasion, love.

They begin by establishing trust. It is accomplished by making the controller appear vulnerable & in requirement of somebody to trust. Then they'll subtly describe you as the person they're looking for. It presents you (the victim) with a challenge to prove that you are the character they are seeking, & you want to demonstrate that you are capable of exceeding their expectations.

When they (the controller) notice you've slipped into the trap, they'll use it to make you feel guilty. They'll take advantage of the vulnerability they displayed at the start to get whatever they want. They'll also make use of the promise you made to them. A promise you made to the controller that you would prove yourself.

In these kinds of relationships, there will always be an unattainable end goal. It could be a wedding or a marriage, a promotion, money, and social status. The controller is usually the individual who would "grant" these objectives but knows that they will never be achieved or will take a long time.

If you're looking for a friend and if you're the victim, you'll need the help of an outsider.

Once you've realized what's going on, it'll take a lot of effort to stop or walk away. A system of support is required. A complete disconnect from the controller is required.

The next step is to erase them from your mind by forgiving them. It may not be simple, yet it is necessary. Grudges will linger on your mind if you keep them in your heart. You'll reckon of them even more because your anger would then keep reminding you of how much they've wronged you & how much you despise them. Convince yourself that being free has put you in a far better position & that you have a brighter future ahead of you.

11.2 Defusing brainwashing - Solutions
Repetition
Many cults have mantras or songs that members of the cult repeat together in various ways, like singing. This method not only helps to build a group identity but also has hypnotic-like effects. Followers' chants become increasingly true to them, rendering them less likely to believe contradictory logic or opinions.

This technique is often used to brainwash unconsciously.

When we look in the mirror, for instance, we see flaws that lead to negative mantras like "No one would ever consider me attractive."

We go over to work & feel envious of a regarded coworker who is progressing up the career ladder faster than we are, & we tell ourselves, "I merely do not possess what it requires to succeed". We become resilient to logic and opinions outside our realm of perception, just like cult members who are regularly exposed to certain beliefs.

And many of our deeply rooted beliefs are self-actualizing, preventing us from possessing the confidence & courage to be genuinely happy and achieve goals that would result in greater success or self-esteem.

The ideal way to retrain one's brain

- When you have such negative thoughts, set - up stop signs. As a form of self-defense, approach them with rehearsed positive mantras.

- Make a list of your thoughts as opposed to your truths. "I will never succeed," though. "I didn't have the promotion, but my boss prefers me to lead this project and "I have been around for years since my company thinks I have potential and talent."

Isolation

Cult leaders frequently use isolation to get their followers to accept their ideology more quickly.

Brainwashing, either mild or extreme, does seem to be conceivable in large portion due to isolation,", if you only listen to the brainwashed text daily, & rarely (or never) reveal yourself to alternative options, you're getting to be much more inclined to embrace what you listen without thinking."

Our emotions of inadequacy & powerlessness boost when we proceed to assume negative sentiments about ourselves within an isolated environment.

The ideal way to retrain one's brain

- Talk to people you care about & who you can trust. Let them know how you're feeling, even if it's difficult. These people can often assist you in gaining a better understanding of your strengths and accomplishments.

- Talk to other people who are dealing with the same problems as you. Many organizations, for instance, can connect you with other people who share similar feelings. Mental Health America is one of them. This organization has quite a database of groups to join that deal with various issues like anxiety and depression.

- For all those who find it difficult to deal with psychological pain, they have an Emotions

Anonymous organization. According to self, there are also several online assistance groups where individuals connect & collaborate toward healing.

- Take into account counseling or treatment. When we call out to beloved ones with our concerns and receive positive feedback, we frequently dismiss it. We do this because we believe that those concerned about us would lie to safeguard our sentiments. Our thoughts might be a little more open & receptive to various ideas or alternative perspectives if we speak with an impartial outsider.

Fatigue

Almost everyone is aware of the negative consequences of sleep deprivation or exhaustion.

If you find this very hard to acquire the sleep or rest you require maximum performance, the loop of negative thinking will be much more difficult to break.

Ideal way to retrain one's brain

- Enhance your sunlight exposure and other bright light sources. According to Health line, getting enough natural sun rays or sky bright light "tends to improve daytime vitality as well as the quantity and length of nighttime sleep."

- Make your room more conducive to sleep. Room darkening drapes, earplugs, or a noise-canceling fan is all recommended by the Mayo Clinic.

- Near bedtime, do acts that relax you. According to Web MD, take a warm bath for almost an hour before bedtime, read a short book, or listen to relaxing music.

Without Permission, Hypnosis

Many people now use hypnosis to recall memories from their childhood and even past lifetimes. They use hypnosis to aid them in modifying something about them from time to time.

The best way to retrain one's brain

It's quite acceptable to seek alternate therapies. Many people have stated how beneficial hypnotic sessions may be.

Putting one within the hands of an unknown hypnotherapist, on the other side, is risky. You could be setting your life & well-being in jeopardy without even realizing it.

When you don't agree with the efficacy of hypnosis and someone approaches you & claims to take you inside a trance, don't let them make an attempt. You must, at the least, be preceded by somebody you can trust.

Scary Tactics That Trick Your Mind

Threats to obscure mind games are all examples of scare tactics. This mind control technique uses an individual's fear and, without a doubt, is among the most deadly of all.

The best way to retrain one's brain

It's critical to seek support from friends, family, & the appropriate authorities if you feel intimidated in any way. The paranoia alone may cause you to do something you wouldn't typically do under regular conditions.In nature, such mind control brainwashing tactics are practically undetectable.

Conclusion

Dark psychology is a little-known and kind of unofficial branch of psychology. There are no "dark psychology" studies or "dark psychology," & no standardized education classes are available.

That is why, when people look up the topic on the internet, they only find a lot of questionable books and sites.

Dark psychology, on the other hand, acknowledges that people can act darkly without intending to. This field takes a more straightforward & perhaps less hypocritical approach to human behavior than is often said in academic psychology. Dark psychology understands that people can act in harmful, destructive, cruel or antisocial ways for no apparent reason. The part which makes dark psychology such an intriguing field of study is psychology's propensity to experiment with discovering why people behave in this way.

The majority of people research the subject to defend themselves. Knowing how & what motivates, persuaders, & manipulators work is necessary for defending yourself against these dark forces. Because persuasion can have both negative & positive motivations, even those who aren't using dark psychological strategies can benefit from exercising convincing skills.

Dictionary

Abnormal behavior: Personal distress, psychological dysfunction, divergence from social standards, danger to self and others, and societal cost are all factors of this type of behavior.

Abnormal psychology: The scientific study of abnormal behavior with the goal of being able to predict, explain, diagnose, and cure maladaptive behavior in a reliable manner.

Attitudes: People's judgments about objects, ideas, events, or other people.

Avoidant personality disorder: Feelings of inadequacy and greater sensitivity to negative feedback cause a pervasive pattern of social anxiety.

Behavior therapies: Treatment which entail lengthy discussions between therapists and clients with the goal of actively altering maladaptive behavior using learning principles.

Brain: The nerve system's major organ.

Case study: A study method in which a single subject is thoroughly investigated.

Consciousness: The degree to which people are aware about themselves and their surroundings.

Dark adaptation: The process by which light-sensitive receptor cells become more sensitive.

Dark psychology: Attempts to comprehend the thoughts, attitudes, & perceptions that lead to predatory behavior in humans.

Dark Triad: It includes narcissism, Machiavellianism, and psychopathy as personality qualities.

Emotion work: The way of acting on the basis of a feeling that isn't truly felt.

Emotional intelligence: A skill that allows people to recognize, express, comprehend, & manage their emotions.

Hypnosis: A technique through which a person is given advice.

Intelligence quotient (IQ): A person's mental age is calculated by multiplying his or her chronological age by 100.

Machiavellianism: A cynical, manipulative attitude & the idea that the aims to justify the methods.

Narcissism: Excessive self-absorbedness, a sense of superiority& a strong need for others' attention.

Personality disorders: Stable patterns of experience & behavior that diverge considerably from patterns considered normal by a person's culture are characterized by disorders.

Psychological test: An instrument that is used to collect information about personality traits, emotional states, aptitudes, interests, abilities, values, or behaviors.

Spitefulness: Destructiveness & willingness to cause harm to other people, even if one harms him/her self in the method.

Social skills training: A behavioral therapy that targets to increase a client's relationships with other individuals.

Sadism: Wish to inflict mental or physical threat to others for one's own satisfaction or to benefit one.

Values: Perceptions of what is significant in life.

Book 5: Emotional Intelligence 2.0

Improve Your Social Skills & Emotional Flexibility to Achieve Success in Life, Business & Relationships

Introduction

A fascinating phenomenon occurs in the workplaces of the twenty-first century. In this digital world, as we automatize most of our tasks and put our faith in machines to take over responsibilities, we realize the value of emotions and feelings.

Indeed, feelings, and more precisely, emotional intelligence, are involved. Emotional intelligence refers to our capacity to identify and appreciate our own and others' emotions, comprehend their impact, and apply that understanding to our thoughts and behaviors. Since emotionally intelligent individuals get along well with others and are more empathetic and caring, they are more likely to succeed than their peers. And it is for this reason that emotional intelligence is a topic worth studying further.

Emotions play a role in the course of learning. If you have any doubts, consider the joy you felt when you eventually solved a particularly difficult problem or completed a significant report. Recall your fear of entering an interview room when you were uncertain about the information. Without emotion, there is possibly not much learning happening. In a typical long lecture, remember the nodding heads. If feelings are in charge of learning, we can consider how we could use them to help our students learn more effectively. Additionally, it is important to educate students about how their "emotional intelligence" contributes to or detracts from their college success. Luckily, important new insights into how the brain develops emotions and how they influence success in all facets of life have emerged over the last fifteen years.

Emotion is derived from the Latin word "emovere," which implies agitate, stir, or move. As a result, an emotion is regarded as the organism's "stirred up condition." Emotions play a critical role in human biological evolution and adaptation because they affect how we perceive, comprehend, and react to our environment. They play a critical role in the development of learning because it is via our subjective sentimental world that humans create their personality traits and complexities.

Due to the critical existence of emotions, scientists began researching humans' capabilities to reason and comprehend their own feelings, effectively interpret, and regulate their own emotions, and properly regulate them (Salovey & Mayer, 1990). They coined the word emotional intelligence, which has since spread to almost every part of the planet.

Emotional intelligence has become increasingly popular as a criterion for identifying successful individuals and as a means of achieving this achievement. The concept of emotional intelligence explains why two people with an identical IQ can attain inconceivably extraordinary levels of success in life (Goleman,1998), as people are often successful not for their information, but for their ability to interact emotionally and socially with others through the use of charismatic temperament in their interactions (St. Clair, 2004).Without question, almost everyone's life objective is to accomplish and achieve happiness. To excel in this endeavor, regardless of the area being created, emotional intelligence appears critical and should be considered. When constrained by massive asset limitations, military leaders must make quick decisions in environments defined by ambiguity and uncertainty.

The Armed Forces require leaders capable of forming cohesive groups, fostering trust, and cultivating positive environments. Military leaders must establish and communicate a shared vision and specific mission objectives necessary for the firm or department to be effective responders to the call and defenders of the state. They have a critical responsibility to ensure the military's current and potential success (Taylor -Clark, 2015). These requirements are less concerned with the specific abilities of cognitive ability, specialized knowledge, and strategic capacity and more concerned with the sensitive skills and abilities of emotional experience.

The emotionally stable person will be able to predict misfortune and its consequences and suspect how others will respond to difficulty. This understanding enables him to respond appropriately to challenges and resolve issues quickly. Therefore, emotional intelligence has been suggested as a necessary asset to consider in the military because it empowers military personal to understand their own emotions as well as the emotions of others (Sewell, 2011), resulting in increased success in directing the quest to success.

Chapter 1. Origins Of Emotional Intelligence

Wayne Payne reportedly coined the word Emotional Intelligence for the first time (1986). In his research paper, an analysis of emotion: evolving emotional intelligence; self-integration in relation to anxiety, pain, and desire, he coined the term Emotional Intelligence. Payne's paper sought to investigate and discover the essence and attributes of emotion as well as emotional intelligence, and to provide a philosophical and theoretical structure in response to his discovery that the society was suffering from emotional ignorance (p. 23), with many of society's problems being linked to emotional states such as anxiety, addiction, depression, and pain. He recognized that courses devoted to studying the essence of emotions and emotions generally did not exist. Payne's work laid the groundwork for subsequent researchers in this area. His claims were welcomed in a new era of discovery. Payne's dissertation aimed to construct a manual to assist individuals in developing emotional intelligence, as he stated in his work's introduction.

Three major facets of his approach to emotional intelligence can be summarized. The very first area is dedicated to bringing up significant problems and concerns about emotions. The second area would be to provide a vocabulary and context for examining and discussing the questions and issues raised, and the third area would be to explain principles, approaches, and tools for improving emotional intelligence (Payne, 1986, p. 23). Following Payne's work, multiple authors decided to expand on and research the concept.

In 1990, Peter Salovey and John D. Mayer, building on Wayne Payne's work, described 'Emotional Intelligence' as "a subset of social intelligence that entails the capacity to track one's own as well as others' emotions and feelings, to differentiate between them, and to use this knowledge to direct one's thought and behavior" (Salovey & Mayer, 1990, p. 189). They recognized that humans need the ability to handle their own and others' emotions. As a result, those who have developed a high degree of emotional intelligence would benefit themselves and others in several ways in almost every area of life. However, it was not till 1990, with the publication of Daniel Goleman's book Emotional Intelligence: Why EI Matters More Than IQ that the idea of EI became ingrained in society's history and began to be implemented globally (Goleman, 1998).

According to Goleman's website (Goleman, n.d.), his intention for his book was to encounter two strangers have a discussion in which EI was mentioned, and they would both understand what it indicated. As he later acknowledges, he was unaware of the effect EI had. The universal recognition EI and his book received resulted in the bookselling over 5 million copies and being translated into over 30 languages. However, Goleman was taken aback by the book's influence on the world of business, particularly in the areas of leadership and growth that would later be established in this work (para. 14).

According to Goleman, prior to bringing his work to the market, IQ had been developed as the benchmark of greatness in life, but here he was with a novel perspective on the fundamentals of life success (para. 2). According to the Harvard Business Review (as quoted in Goleman, n.d.), EI is one of the most popular business concepts of the decade, being a paradigm-shattering concept (para. 14).

These days, it is reasonable to conclude that emotional intelligence has achieved popularity in nearly every country globally. It piqued the attention of numerous individuals and scholars, prompting the publication of numerous magazines, books, newspaper papers, and research experiments. Additionally, when the term "emotional intelligence" is entered into Google, the search engine returns up to (April 2021) results, demonstrating how EI is ingrained in contemporary society.

Chapter 2. Concept and Theories of Emotional Intelligence

Numerous authors have made significant contributions to the study of EI, but due to the scope of this research, only three approaches will be examined in greater detail. Each of them contributes to our understanding of what EI implies (Spielberger, 2004).

These three are as follows:

Mayer- Salovey's model defines EI as the ability to see, understand, supervise, and use feelings to facilitate thought, as measured by a capacity-based scale.

Goleman's model views EI as a set of abilities and aptitudes that drive management execution and is quantified through a multi-rater assessment.

The Bar-On model depicts a cross-segment of interdependent social and emotional capacities, skills, and facilitators that influence intelligent behavior as assessed by self-report.

2.1. The Model of Mayer and Salovey

Two of the most influential people, Mayer and Salovey, in the field of emotional intelligence, describe it as the ability to reason regarding emotions and the capacity of emotions to facilitate thought. It encompasses the capacity to accurately interpret emotions to access and produce emotions to facilitate thinking, comprehend emotions and emotional intelligence, and regulate emotions reflectively to facilitate intellectual and emotional development (1990, Salovey & Mayer, p. 10). Meaning it is the capacity to comprehend and regulate our own emotions and the emotional responses of others and groups. Additionally, Mayer and Salovey noted that EI encompasses the capacity to be aware of and express emotions, the ability to deliver and navigate feelings, the ability to be mindful of our emotions and emotional intelligence, and the capacity to regulate and monitor our emotions in order to promote intellectual and emotional development (Salovey & Mayer, 1990, p.40).

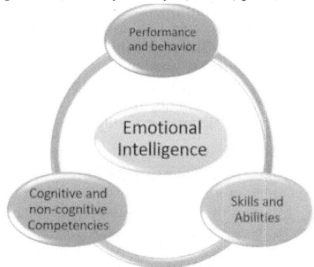

These two writers proposed a model based on four primary capabilities: awareness, assimilation, comprehension, and emotion control (p.10). Emotional perception or awareness is described as the capacity to differentiate and recognize one's own and other people's emotions. On the other hand, assimilation is the capacity to produce, use, and experience emotions required for communicating or engaging in other cognitive processes (Salovey & Mayer, 1990, p. 11). The third skill, comprehension, requires the analysis and understanding of emotional information in order to recognize that multiple emotions can occur concurrently and that they can also alter over time.

Finally, emotion management includes the capacity to remain receptive to feel while still monitoring and manipulating one's own and others' emotions. Additionally, they explained that in order to attain the final skill, emotion regulation, and individuals must have mastered the previous three. In other words, prior to mastering one skill, the preceding abilities must be mastered. This is entirely rational, as a person who is incapable of perceiving his or her own emotions will never be able to comprehend, much less control, them (Fernández-Berrocal & Extremera, 2006).

2.2. Bar-On Model

In contrast to Mayer and Salovey's definition of emotional intelligence, a new model called Bar On was introduced in 1997. This model does not exclusively link emotional intelligence to feelings or intellect. Alternatively, this model requires that EI encompass a wide variety of personality traits that may be associated with professional and daily performance (Schulze & Roberts, 2005, p. 40).

According to the Bar-On model, EI is a set of noncognitive capacities, competencies, and skills that affect an individual's ability to cope successfully with environmental pressures (p. 40). It attempts to determine whether certain individuals have a greater chance of achievement than others. The model revisits EI by examining personal traits that are more closely associated with life achievements, classifying them into five categories: intrapersonal and organizational abilities, adaptability, stress control, and general attitude.

1. Self-esteem, emotional self-awareness, assertiveness, self-actualization, and flexibility all contribute to the development of intrapersonal skills.

2. Adaptability comprises three components: social responsibility, problem-solving, and interpersonal relationships.

3. Interpersonal skills include social responsibility, empathy, and the ability to form and maintain personal relationships.

4. Stress management involves both tolerances for stress and impulsiveness.

5. The term "general mood" encompasses both satisfaction and optimism (2005, Schulze & Roberts).

The Bar-On type demonstrates that EI or emotional intelligence needs an emotional component and a cognitive component.

It is influenced significantly by a solid social dimension (interpersonal skills, stress management, and adaptability related to the social environment). As a result, it establishes the concept of emotional-social intelligence as a collection of interrelated social and emotional competencies, abilities, and facilitators that decide our ability to comprehend and express ourselves, comprehend and relate to others, and cope with daily demands (Bar-On, 2006, p. 14). Without these abilities, the human being will be unable to comprehend and articulate himself (p. 14), communicate effectively with others, cope effectively with daily activities and adversities, and regulate and track our emotions to avoid the reverse situation of emotions controlling us.

To bring the Bar-On model into effect and determine an individual's level of emotional and social intelligence, the Emotional Quotient Inventory (the EQ-i) was created. It has since become the most commonly used indicator of emotional-social intelligence (Bar-On, 2006, p. 15). Essentially, the EQ-I consists of 133 short phrases with five distinct responses ranging from very rarely or not true for me to very often true or true for me (Bar-On, 1997, p.17). The test can calculate the EQ-I based on the individual's answers; this indicates which skills and competencies the individual possesses or, more specifically, how they evolved. Apart from calculating the EQ-I, this method produced some noteworthy results. To begin, they demonstrated that as humans age, their EQ-i increases; in other words, as we age, we become increasingly socially and emotionally intelligent. Additionally, the Bar-On model demonstrates that women are more emotionally conscious, more empathic, have stronger interpersonal relationships, and are more socially conscious than men. On the other hand, men tend to have a higher sense of self-worth, are more self-sufficient, better handle stress, are more adaptable, find it easier to tackle obstacles, and are more confident than women (Bar-On, 2006).

2.3. The Daniel Goleman Model

Daniel Goleman asserts that EI is more important than IQ in terms of acknowledging an efficient and satisfying existence. Achievement factors include diverse indicators such as a promotion at work and maintaining secure and productive relationships with others. According to Goleman's model, IQ is greatly amplified; as one of the chapter topics succinctly puts it, "when smart is dumb."

Daniel Goleman, who earned a Ph.D. from Harvard University, chose to study journalism, and became a columnist for the New York Times. He spent twelve years at the New York Times studying the cerebrum and emotions. Following up on a Mayer and Salovey article on logic, he was inspired to write a book that would achieve literary success: "Emotional Intelligence: Why It Can Matter More Than IQ." Goleman provides a comprehensive overview of EI and its significance to society in the book. His central proposition is that emotional illiteracy is responsible for various social infractions, like emotional dysfunction and instructive dissatisfaction wrongdoing.

Additionally, people at work often fall short of their potential due to an inability to manage their emotions appropriately. Fulfillment and efficiency in the workplace are jeopardized by unnecessary clashes with colleagues, an inability to articulate one's natural needs, and an inability to communicate one's feelings to others. Goleman approaches the subject of insight from a variety of angles.

Goleman's model suggests two distinct divisions for EI. Firstly, components of EI associated with individual capacities (e.g., self-awareness) are distinguished from those associated with social skills (e.g., empathy). Second, those areas of EI concerned with consciousness are separated from those concerned with the management and direction of emotions. For instance, recognizing that someone is distressed is distinct from having the ability to cheer them up. However, both "reading" and "changing" feelings are useful for identifying EI's broader concept.

His first book outlined alluring characteristics such as self-assurance, responsiveness, self-awareness, self-control, compassion, motivation, and social abilities (Paul, 1999):

- **Self-management**: The ability to regulate or redirect undesirable driving factors and temperaments, as well as the predisposition to delay judgment and reflect before acting. Trademarks exemplify dependability and uprightness, as well as comfort with ambiguity and receptiveness to alternate.
- **Self-awareness**: The ability to interpret and comprehend one's own dispositions, emotions, and the effect they have on others. It embodies fearlessness, self-awareness, and a concept of humor. Self-awareness is contingent upon one's ability to monitor one's own emotional state and to identify and name one's emotions correctly.
- **Empathy**: The ability to understand the mental makeup of others. It is the capacity to comprehend

and relate to individuals based on their emotional responses. Hallmarks include an aptitude for developing and maintaining abilities, as well as service to clients and customers.

- **Internal motivation**: A desire to strive for motives other than economic gain and status -external incentives - such as an inner vision of what is essential in life, a sense of accomplishment, or an interest in acquiring. It is a predisposition to pursue goals with zeal and perseverance. Among the trademarks are a strong desire to succeed, good faith in the face of disappointment, and authoritative responsibility.

- **Social skills**: The ability to manage interactions and develop social relationships and the ability to discover mutual opinions and create affinity. Viability in driving transition, enticement and developing skills, and driving groups are all signs of social aptitude.

According to Goleman (1998), the characteristics recorded are emotional skills. In that ability, they could be defined as learned abilities based on EI that result in exceptional performance at work or somewhere else. The concept emphasizes emotional intelligence's dependence on learning. In contrast, psychological theories of intelligence have traditionally described mental capacity in terms of aptitude, a preexisting ability to acquire specific mental aptitudes via learning. Thus, IQ test scores are often viewed as indicators of an individual's capacity to acquire scholastic knowledge rather than acquiring knowledge itself (Jensen, 2005).

On the other hand, Goleman regards emotional intelligence as a collection of educated skills that can lead to success in a variety of social settings, such as the workplace (2010, Boyatzis & McKee, Goleman).

For example, empathy competence enables group leaders to understand their colleagues' emotions, resulting in increased group feasibility. This same skill motivates the sales agent to close further deals by improving their ability to recognize customers' emotional reactions to a particular item. On the other hand, emotionally immature behaviors can be extremely detrimental to associations. Although this seems to be a powerful argument, it is more often false: the primary reason workers leave a company is a bad management—people do not exit companies, they quit managers (2012, p. 269, Zeidner, Matthews & Roberts).

Chapter 3. What Is EI?

Emotional Intelligence (EI) is the capability for perceiving, regulating, and evaluating emotions. According to some scholars, emotional intelligence can be acquired and enhanced, while others assert that it is an innate trait.

While the ability to convey and regulate one's emotions is critical, so is the skill to comprehend, perceive, and react to others' emotions. Picture a world where you were unable to comprehend your friend's sadness or your coworker's anger. Psychologists relate to this capability as EI (emotional intelligence), and several experts argue that it may be more critical than intelligence in terms of overall life performance.

Two of the main scholars on the topic, therapists Peter Salovey and John D. Mayer, describe emotional intelligence as the capacity to identify and appreciate one's own and others' emotions. Additionally, this skill includes using this emotional awareness to make decisions, resolve issues, and interact with others.

Thus, according to Salovey & Mayer, emotional intelligence is classified into four distinct levels:

- Emotional perception
- Emotional reasoning
- Emotional intelligence
- Emotional control

Historically, emotions and intellect were often regarded as mutually exclusive. However, in recent decades, scholars studying emotion psychology have developed an increased interest in affect and cognition. This field examines the interaction and effect of cognitive abilities and emotions on how people think. Consider the effect of moods and emotions such as happiness, rage, anxiety, and sadness on how people act and make choices.

Emotional intelligence (or EI) is defined as the capacity to:

- Understand, recognize, and affect others' emotions.

- Acknowledge, comprehend, and regulate our own feelings.

In realistic terms, this implies being mindful that emotions will influence our actions and affect others (both negatively and positively), as well as understanding how to control our own and others' feelings and emotions.

Emotional control is important in stressful circumstances. For instance, when we are...

- Meeting limited deadlines
- Receiving and sharing feedback
- Not having sufficient funds
- Managing difficult relationships
- Overcoming setbacks and failures in work life
- Adjusting to change

What makes emotional intelligence so significant?

As is well known, the most popular and fulfilled people in life are not the brightest. You are probably familiar with academically talented individuals but socially incompetent and ineffective in their careers or personal interactions. Intellectual capability or intelligence quotient (IQ) is insufficient for achieving success in life on its own. Although your IQ will help you gain college admission, it is your EQ that will allow you to control your stress and emotions as you approach your final exams. E Q and IQ coexist and work best when they complement one another.

3.1. The Importance of Emotional Intelligence

'Emotions precede thought,' it is a scientific reality. When our emotions are running strong, they alter how our brains work. Our cognitive capacity, decision-making abilities, and even interpersonal skills get deteriorated.

Comprehending and controlling our own (and others') feelings enables us to achieve greater success in both our private and professional relationships.

Emotional intelligence is critical; the importance and rewards of improving your EQ are numerous and undervalued in many fields. Emotional intelligence is the key to a more fulfilling and happier life for the following reasons:

- Emotional intelligence helps you to comprehend and control your emotions in order to inspire yourself and foster meaningful social relationships; it is the first step toward realizing your full potential.
- EI possesses enormous benefits and values in terms of family, academic, and professional performance.
- Individuals with high emotional intelligence are less susceptible to the negative effects of stressors while successfully coping with negativity and promoting more positive emotions in their place.
- Intellect is most effective when combined with a high level of emotional intelligence.
- Employing and improving emotional intelligence in the workplace has been shown to increase job efficiency and social skills of employees significantly.

- Emotional intelligence is a valuable skill because it helps individuals avoid making decisions relying on emotional biases. Effective communication and collaboration are inextricably related to high EQ levels.
- Happiness, for example, is a critical EI facilitator that contributes to our self-actualization.

At an individual level, emotional intelligence enables us to:

- Conduct awkward discussions without causing offense.
- When we are anxious or overwhelmed, we may control our emotions.
- Enhance relationships with those that matter to us.
- At work, emotional intelligence will assist us in the following ways:
- Resolve disagreements.
- Others can be coached and motivate.
- Establish a collaborative culture.
- Enhance team psychological safety.

Your EQ can be more important than your IQ, particularly at work.

Daniel Goleman cites Harvard Business School studies in his book "Working with Emotional Intelligence" to demonstrate that EQ matters twice more than IQ and technical expertise combined in deciding who will succeed.

According to a Harvard Business Review 2003 article, Emotional Intelligence accounts for 80 percent of the competencies that distinguish top performers from others. We have learned over the course of our years working with cutting-edge organizations that the brightest people in an organization are not necessarily the most successful. EI is what separates the most active workers from the rest.

3.2. Impact of Emotional intelligence

Emotional intelligence has a positive impact on the following:

Your academic or professional success. A high level of emotional intelligence will assist you in navigating the workplace's social complexities, leading, and motivating others, and excelling in your career. Indeed, when evaluating critical job applicants, many businesses now consider emotional intelligence to be as vital as technical skill and conduct EQ testing prior to hiring.

Your physical well-being. If you are unable to control your feelings, you cannot manage your tension as well, which can result in severe health complications. Stress that is not managed increases blood pressure, inhibits the immune system, increases the risk of cardiovascular disease and stroke, leads to infertility, and accelerates the aging process. The very first step toward increasing emotional intelligence is to learn effective stress management techniques.

Your psychological well-being. Unmanaged feelings and stress can also have a negative effect on your mental health, predisposing you to depression and anxiety. When you are unable to comprehend, accept, or control your feelings, you will also find it difficult to establish solid relationships. It can worsen any mental health issues by leaving you feeling sad and alone.

Your interpersonal relationships. Through comprehending your emotions and learning to manage them, you can more effectively articulate your feelings and comprehend those of others. It enables more efficient communication and the development of better relationships, both at the workplace and in your private life.

Your sociability. Being emotionally aware serves a social function, as it connects you to other life and the environment around you. Social intelligence helps you distinguish between friends and foes, gauge another person's involvement in you, alleviate tension, control your nervous system by social contact, and feel happy and loved.

3.3. Developing Emotional Intelligence - Four Critical Skills to Increase the EQ

Emotional intelligence is an ability that can be learnt at any time. Nonetheless, it is important to note that there is a distinction between reading about EQ and implementing that information into your life. Simply knowing that you should be doing something does not guarantee that you will overcome stress and will be able to trump your best intentions. To permanently shift attitudes in pressure-resistant ways, you must first learn how to manage tension in the moment and in any relationship to maintain emotional awareness.

The following are the critical skills for increasing your EQ and enhancing your ability to control emotions and communicate with others:

- Self-control
- Self-consciousness
- Social consciousness
- Managing relationships

Skill 1. Self-control is the first critical skill in developing emotional intelligence.

To activate your EQ, you should be able to manage your emotions to make rational choices about your actions. When you experience excessive stress, you can surrender control of the emotions and the capacity to behave mindfully and appropriately.

Consider a moment when you were overcome by tension. Was it simple to think logically or make a logical choice?

Most likely not. Once you experience excessive stress, the ability to think logically and correctly evaluate emotions—both your own and those of others—is affected.

Although emotions are vital pieces of information that remind us about ourselves and others, when we are stressed and forced out of our comfort bubble, we could become confused and let go of our emotions. With the skill to handle tension and maintain an emotional state of awareness, one can learn to absorb disturbing news without allowing it to overwhelm your perceptions and self. You will be enabled to make decisions that allow you to handle impulsive attitudes and emotions, take action, keep commitments, and adjust to changing circumstances.

Skill 2. Self-awareness is a critical skill to develop emotional intelligence.

Stress management is just the initial step toward developing emotional intelligence. According to attachment psychology, your present emotional experience is most likely a product of your early life. Your ability to regulate fundamental emotions such as sorrow, anger, fear, and joy is often conditional upon the consistency and quality of your early emotional experiences. If your primary caregiver acknowledged and respected your emotions as an infant, your emotions are likely to have developed into valuable assets in adulthood. However, if emotional interactions were disturbing, threatening, or painful in your infancy, you may attempt to separate yourself from your emotions.

However, the ability to communicate with your emotions—to maintain a moment-to-moment relation with your shifting emotional experience—is critical for comprehending how emotion affects your thoughts and behavior.

- Do you have continuous emotions, encountering one feeling after another as the circumstances change?
- Are you experiencing physical sensations in areas such as your throat, stomach, or chest due to your emotions?
- Do you have distinct feelings and emotions such as rage, sorrow, fear, anger, and joy, all of which manifest themselves through subtle facial expressions?
- Are you capable of experiencing powerful emotions deep enough to catch both your own and others' attention?
- Are you aware of your emotions? Are they an element of your decision-making?

If some of these experiences are new to you, you may have "muted" or "turned off" your emotions. To increase your EQ — and thus your emotional well-being — you must rebond, embrace, and become familiar with your core emotions. It is possible through the practice of mindfulness.

Mindfulness is the deliberate practice of concentrating your mind on the present moment. Though mindfulness cultivation originated in Buddhism, most religions incorporate some kind of specific prayer or meditation practice. Mindfulness assists you in shifting your focus from thinking to the present moment, your emotional and physical experiences, and provides a broader perspective on life. Mindfulness relaxes and centers you, increasing your self-awareness in the system.

Creating emotional awareness. It is critical first to learn how to handle stress, as this will help you feel more at ease, reconnect with intense or negative emotions, and alter how you perceive and react to them.

Skill 3. Social awareness is very important for emotional intelligence.

Social knowledge helps you understand and perceive the primarily nonverbal signs others use to interact with you continuously. These signals reveal how others really feel, how their emotional response changes with time, and what is truly important to them.

When people communicate using similar nonverbal signals, you can read and comprehend the group's power dynamics and mutual emotional experiences. In a nutshell, you are empathic and socially adept.

Mindfulness is a valuable partner in the development of social and emotional awareness. To develop social consciousness, you must first acknowledge the critical role of consciousness in the social system. After all, you cannot pick up on indefinite nonverbal signals if you are lost in your own thoughts, preoccupied with other things, or just zoning out on your computer. Social consciousness involves your presence at the time. While most of us take pride in our ability to multitask, doing so indicates that we will miss the slight emotional shifts occurring in others that may help us truly comprehend them. By putting aside other thoughts and concentrating on the activity itself, you are potentially more likely to advance your social goals.

Following the rhythm of another person's emotional reactions is a two-way street that allows you to be aware of your own emotional changes. Attending to others does not imply a reduction of one's own self-awareness. By devoting time and effort to really listening to others, you will gain some insight into your own emotional state, values, and beliefs. For instance, if you experience discomfort when others share such views, you would have gained valuable insight into yourself.

Skill 4. Relationship management is also a critical skill for emotional intelligence.

Working closely with others is a system that starts with emotional maturity and the capacity to consider and acknowledge the experiences of others. When emotional sensitivity is developed, you will effectively learn extra social skills that will enhance your relationships' effectiveness, fruitfulness, and fulfillment.

Develop an awareness of how well you communicate nonverbally. It is hard to prevent communicating nonverbally with others about your thoughts and feelings. The numerous muscles in the face, particularly those around the eyes, nose, mouth, and forehead, enable you to express your own emotions nonverbally and to read the emotional intent of others. Your emotional part in the brain is active all the time—and even though you overlook its signals, others will not. Identifying the nonverbal signals, you give to others will make a significant difference in the quality of your relationships.

Utilize lightheartedness and play to alleviate tension. Humor, laughter, and play are all normal stress relievers. They alleviate the stresses and assist you in maintaining perspective. Laughter balances the nervous system, relieving tension, winding you down, improving your mind, and increasing the capacity for empathy.

Develop the ability to see conflict as a chance to grow close to others. In human interactions, conflict and disputes are unavoidable. At no point can two people have the same desires, beliefs, and aspirations. That, however, does not have to be a negative thing. Addressing conflict in a positive, productive manner will help people build trust. When disagreement is not viewed as intimidating or abusive, it promotes relationship independence, innovation, and protection.

3.4. Examples Of EI in Daily Life

At times in life, you can look at somebody and ponder, "How is he always so in complete control?" Either it is a boss who navigates difficult work situations without offending anyone or a buddy who instantly makes total strangers feel at ease upon meeting them. The response is found in their emotional intelligence, or their capacity to control their own and others' emotions.

Every day, you see displays of emotional intelligence in action. And, without realizing it, you use your emotional maturity to manage daily circumstances and relationships. For example, a worker who has received a reprimand from the boss may wish to express her feelings to you. You hear empathically, then clarify the potential causes of the boss's rage critically and counsel your friend on preventing this in the future. And you do all of this without causing distress or offense to your colleague. It is a classic illustration of how to apply emotional intelligence in the workplace.

Countless individuals use empathy and compassion on a daily basis to manage social experiences at work. For instance, when one person talks in an office meeting, others listen. It occurs naturally, and such actions are indicators of workplace emotional intelligence. Of course, some people will still disturb others, but we will concentrate on cases of emotional intelligence that are used to improve social interactions in this section.

Examples Of Emotional Intelligence in Practice

Let us examine the science of emotional intelligence (EI). Daniel Goleman, a leading expert on emotional intelligence, identified five main components of emotional intelligence. Self-regulation, Self-awareness, inspiration, empathy, and social skills are the five components.

Goleman asserts that these five aspects of emotional intelligence are critical in developing a successful leader. There are numerous examples of leaders guiding their decisions with their emotional quotient.

- Leaders encourage and are ready and willing to make difficult choices in order to accomplish their objectives.
- Leaders project an air of confidence, sincerity, straightforwardness, and self-awareness.
- Leaders are open and friendly and have a natural ability to communicate.
- Leaders demonstrate empathy for others and the ability to influence their thoughts and behavior.

Consider the following areas of life where emotional intelligence is advantageous:

1. In our everyday lives, we see examples of emotional intelligence:

Successful leaders are self-aware of their flaws. They do, however, have the desire to enhance each day.

Would you still go places if you were stubborn, unable to consider your flaws, or resistant to self-improvement? To grow into a good leader, you must cultivate self-awareness in order to identify and resolve your weaknesses.

On the other hand, would you want to help someone succeed who lacks self-awareness and is highly resistant to criticism and suggestions for development? This type of individual will never mature and is doubtful to become a leader.

Leaders are ones who place emphasis on personal growth, on learning new skills, and on inspiring others through mission delegation and accountability. Such leadership actions exemplify emotional maturity in our everyday lives.

2. At the workplace; an example of emotional intelligence:

True leaders prioritize job and work objectives over all other considerations, including personal desires and conveniences. A business leader develops close relationships with the company's board of directors, partners, other shareholders, and even industry competitors.

When we use the term 'leader,' we refer to someone who views the big picture, communicates that vision to others, and mobilizes their mutual abilities to accomplish that plan.

Leaders have an unwavering view of what must be achieved and need no external motivation to accomplish their objectives. A true leader can communicate the role of each team member in the greater scheme of things. They recognize the critical role that employees play in propelling the company forward.

Both of these are illustrative of leadership that demonstrates emotional intelligence.

You will develop the qualities necessary to become a great leader by fostering vision, inspiring others, responsibility, and social skills.

3. Emotional maturity in leadership is exemplified by the following:

Never, ever is a leader a lone wolf. Only with the help of others will you be a leader. Matter of fact, is it possible for a leader to exist without followers?

Not at all.

Leaders demonstrate exceptional people skills built on a high level of emotional intelligence, which assists them in gaining a following. They have an ability to empathize with others and are prepared to read an individual and a situation in order to react appropriately.

Although they are focused on job objectives, they never overlook that their coworkers and subordinates are people, and they appreciate and accept them as humans first and colleagues second. This empathy assists them in establishing respect and trust.

Chapter 4. EQ versus IQ

The words EQ and IQ are often used interchangeably and incorrectly. EQ and IQ do, however, have some important distinctions. The term "IQ" stands for "Intelligence Quotient," and it refers to a person's relative intelligence. The Emotional Quotient, abbreviated as EQ, is the capacity to recognize and control one's own and others' emotions. For someone who is exceptional in both domains, the sky is the limit.

IQ - The Intelligence Quotient

According to Merriam-Webster, IQ is "a numerical value used to express a person's apparent relative intelligence." Determined by multiplying the mental age (as measured on a standardized test) by the chronological age - or by a score based on one's results on a standard intelligence test in comparison to the average output of those of the same age.

The second definition is "expertise or knowledge in the particular subject." "No one can doubt this fan's football IQ" is an illustration of the second definition being used in a sentence.

A score of less than 70 indicates an intellectual disability, while a score of more than 145 indicates genius or near-genius. Although it is theoretically possible to achieve an IQ of 180 or higher, two-thirds of the world has an IQ between 85 and 115. IQ will fluctuate over time, depending on an individual's tendency to learn new concepts.

The intelligence quotient, or IQ, is a score obtained via standardized intelligence tests. IQ is intrinsically linked to intellectual activities such as the capability to read, comprehend, and apply knowledge to skill sets. The IQ test measures a person's ability to think logically, comprehend words and perform math operations. Individuals with a higher IQ can think abstractly and draw correlations more easily, so generalizations are simpler.

EQ - The Emotional Quotient

The Emotional Quotient (EQ) is characterized as an individual's capacity to perceive, comprehend, and effectively apply the strength and wisdom of emotions in order to promote increased levels of cooperation and productivity. Since the terms emotional intelligence and EQ are synonymous, they are frequently used interchangeably.

Good leaders and high performers demonstrate a high level of emotional intelligence. This enables them to work successfully with a diverse range of people and to adapt quickly to changing market conditions. Indeed, emotional intelligence can be a more accurate indicator of success in performance than intelligence.

Certain assessments are performed to measure EQ. A person responds to a series of questions and receives a score for each of the five sub-categories that comprise EQ, as well as a total rating. As with IQ, an individual may concentrate on particular aspects of EQ and try to enhance their scores.

Emotional intelligence, according to the psychology department at the University of New Hampshire, is the "ability to reason validly with emotions and to employ emotions to improve thinking." EQ relates to a person's capacity to interpret, regulate, assess, and show emotions. Individuals with high levels of EQ are capable of managing their feelings, using their emotions to aid in thought, comprehending emotional meanings, and correctly perceiving the emotions of others. The way an individual interacts with others and retains emotional control contributes to their EQ.

4.1. Can EQ or IQ be Enhanced?

Emotional maturity is best instilled at a young age by modeling behaviors such as sharing, caring about others, placing oneself in other people's place, respecting individual space, and general cooperative principles. There are games and toys available to help children develop emotional intelligence, and kids who struggle in social situations have been shown to do considerably better after participating in SEL (Social & Emotional Learning) courses. Adult EQ may also be improved, but to a lesser degree, by constructive coaching.

Certain disorders, such as Asperger's syndrome or high functioning autism (HFA), can include a lack of empathy as a symptom. Although some researchers have confirmed that adults with Asperger's have poor empathy, others have found that EQ can be improved in people with Asperger's or HFA.

While IQ is largely determined by genetics, there are many ways to maximize a person's IQ through brain-food and mental skill exercises such as puzzles, creative thinking problems, and issue strategies that require you to think out of the box.

4.2. What's More Important — IQ or EQ?

There are divergent views on which is more relevant, EQ or IQ. Many who are in the EQ camp claim "a high IQ can get you through the school, but a high EQ can give you a successful life.

Additionally, some believe cognitive ability (i.e., IQ) is a more accurate predictor of performance than EQ, particularly in emotionally stressful occupations. A meta-analysis of several studies comparing IQ and EQ discovered that IQ was responsible for more than 14% of job success, while emotional intelligence accounted for less than 1%.

IQ was once considered the primary predictor of how well we did in life. Psychotherapists such as Howard Gardner believed that IQ was an oversimplified indicator of an individual's abilities and suggested the existence of multiple intelligences. Daniel Goleman came and proposed emotional intelligence or EQ can be just as significant as IQ; in his pioneering work

Emotional Intelligence: Why it can matter more than IQ. The value of Goleman, especially in the business world, has become widely recognized since the word emotional intelligence became popular. Although the question of which is more significant, IQ or EQ, is frequently asked, the response is very complicated and unhelpful. It is as if you are wondering which organ is more vital: the heart or the arteries. They are both critical, and the more pertinent question might be how critical they are and to what extent they are related.

Our Intellectual Quotient, or IQ, is what defines our capacity for problem solving and reasoning. The Emotional Quotient, or EQ, is a measure of our ability to interpret, identify, and handle our own and others' emotions. Our IQ decides our grades in school, which in turn determines which colleges we will attend, which has a significant impact on our first job. However, the relationship between IQ and achievement becomes murkier after that. Naturally, IQ serves as a gatekeeper in the sense that the roles we have to need a certain degree of competence and expertise.

Daniel Goleman claimed that although our IQ can help us obtain a job, the EQ influences our rate of advancement and promotion. When technical skills are considered, the theory goes, it is our potential to collaborate and communicate with others that decide our level of success at work. Daniel Kahneman, a Nobel laureate in psychology, argues that we buy products from people we like and trust even though the price is higher. This has been shown by studies on the effectiveness of salespeople. A large part of our achievement in life is determined by our ability to communicate with others.

The relationship is defined by our ability to comprehend and efficiently use our emotions while interacting with others on an emotional level. According to a Leadership Team Coach, "the most significant impediment to our professional and personal development and fulfillment is located between our ears." If times are difficult, our feelings take over, and we develop disempowering behaviors and habits. Simply refocusing our attention will alter our truth and outcomes." The coach suggests that shifting attention includes EQ, not IQ.

We feel prior to thinking. This has a scientific basis. When we receive a message for the first time, it is processed by the amygdala, a tiny almond-shaped structure in our emotional brain. Our powerful "thinking brain," or frontal neocortex, takes several seconds to process the message. In this time, we are witnessing events like road rage who lose control of their emotions. When the message hits our neocortex, it is already distorted by the emotional brain's interpretation, which is why first perceptions are critical since they are formed emotionally and are difficult to alter.

By the time we reach late adolescence, our IQ is primarily dictated. On the other hand, our EQ is extremely adaptable, and we can improve it at any stage in life if we are persistent. In the book, The Other Kind of Smart, the relationship between IQ and EQ is explained using the analogy of a race car. Racecar is used as a metaphor for our journey through life. Our intelligence is contained inside the engine and its components. It is the tool with which we have been entrusted. Our EQ is the driver. If we are lucky enough to be gifted a powerful engine and high-quality parts, we can be well on our way to success.

It is more than that, though. The driver (EQ) has leverage over the efficiency with which these parts are used and their ability to interact with one another. We have also heard stories of extremely intelligent people who have burned and crashed due to their inability to perform efficiently. We are also familiar with people who do not achieve so great an IQ test and do not do so well at school, but who do exceptionally well in their lives. Naturally, the fusion of a strong engine and well-designed parts in the hand of a highly qualified driver provides us with a significant advantage. Thus, our achievement in life is highly dependent on our ability to use both our EQ and IQ in accordance with one another.

4.3. Application of EQ and IQ

For a prolonged time, it was assumed that IQ was the supreme barometer of career and life achievement, but recent research indicates a direct correlation between higher EQ and active professionals. Individuals with a high EQ consistently outperform their peers in achievement, collaboration, support, and initiative. Numerous firms and large companies require EQ testing as part of the recruiting process and provide coaching sessions on social and emotional skills. Among academics and even among students, Social and Emotional Learning (SEL) is getting a lot of publicity.

The most frequently used IQ assessments are in the fields of psychology and education. Standardized intelligence assessments are used to identify individuals who are exceptionally capable/gifted as well as others who need additional support in the classroom. IQ is a predictor of academic performance and is often used to assess career opportunities for recent graduates.

Measurement and Evaluation

Numerous tests have been developed to evaluate emotional intelligence. These assessments are usually classified into two categories: self-report tests and ability tests.

The most frequently used form of test is the self-report test since it is the simplest to conduct and score. Respondents rate their own actions in response to questions or comments on such assessments. For instance, when asked to rate a statement such as "I often feel as though I understand how others feel," a test taker may respond as disagree, somewhat disagree, agree, or strongly agree.

On the other hand, ability assessments include making individuals react to circumstances and then evaluating their abilities. Oftentimes, such evaluations enable participants to show their skills, which are then evaluated by a third party.

Although assessing emotional intelligence is highly subjective, there seem to be a number of standardized tests available. If you are undergoing an emotional intelligence assessment conducted by a medical professional, the following steps can be used:

The Mayer-Salovey-Caruso Emotional Intelligence Test (MSCEIT) is a capability-based assessment that assesses the four divisions of Mayer and Salovey's Emotional Intelligence model. This test subjects' tester to a series of problem-solving exercises focused on emotions. Test takers complete tasks that measure their capacity for perceiving, identifying, comprehending, and managing emotions. The score indicates a person's ability to reason with emotional data.

The Emotional and Social Competence Inventory (ESCI) is based on an earlier instrument known as the Self-Assessment Questionnaire. It requires having individuals who are familiar with the individual rate the individual's abilities in many different emotional situations. The test is structured to assess the emotional and social abilities that contribute to a person's ability to be a successful leader.

Goleman's assessment model is based on emotional competencies. The Emotional Intelligence Appraisal or the Emotional Competency Inventory are the two assessments used in Goleman's model. Both experiments have their critics and fans. Theorists also attempted to increase the objectivity of IQ testing.

Since it took age into account, the Stanford-Binet exam was the first genuine IQ evaluation. The score is calculated by dividing the test-mental taker's age by his or her chronological age and multiplying by 100.

David Wechsler, an American psychologist, created three intelligence tests: one for primary and preschool children, one for older kids, and another one for adults. Factor analysis is used to calculate the ranking. The assessment's sub-tests are compared to age-appropriate norms.

The Woodcock-Johnson Test of Cognitive Abilities is another often-used test. The Woodcock-Johnson battery of assessments covers a broad range of cognitive skills. All three measures are still used, though none are widely regarded as the best or most reliable.

Additionally, there are numerous more informal online tools, the majority of which are free, for investigating your emotional intelligence.

The Advantages and Disadvantages of Testing

Both IQ and EQ testing are controversial. Proponents of EQ testing argue that it helps assess job performance and teamwork performance. However, since emotional intelligence contradicts traditional intelligence concepts, testing is not a reliable indicator of professional and academic performance. Thus, although individuals with a high EQ perform well at work, tests do not always accurately determine who has a higher IQ. A portion of the issue stems from the findings' unreliability. Sometimes, people will not reply correctly out of desperation to do well. Consequently, the conclusions are, by definition, subjective.

IQ assessments are widely used in a variety of fields, including education. According to proponents of testing, it is a structured evaluation that demonstrates intelligence transcends class, determines the need for special education, and evaluates the efficacy of special training and services. Additionally, IQ testing will expose previously unknown abilities. However, these tests have a drawback in that they provide insufficient details. They do not assess basic cognitive mechanisms and do not accurately predict job performance because they exclude non-academic intellectual SKILLS. Similarly, unique, or original answers are labeled as incorrect, even though they demonstrate intelligent thought. Knowing a child's IQ score can limit them. Finally, some types of questions on IQ tests can indicate prejudice toward minorities or other cultures.

Chapter 5. Can Emotional Intelligence be Learned?

A frequently asked question is whether humans are born with a high EQ or could it be acquired. While some people are born with more natural abilities than others, the good news is that emotional intelligence qualities can be acquired. (This has to be the case, as emotional intelligence has been shown to increase over time.) To do this, individuals must be personally inspired, practice what they learn thoroughly, obtain input, and reinforce their newly acquired skills.

5.1. Who Amongst Us Is Emotionally Intelligent and Is It Significant?

Emotional intelligence, in general, enhances a person's social effectiveness. The greater one's emotional intelligence, the more positive one's social relationships. My colleagues and I recently defined the emotionally intelligent individual in the following terms in a review: Centrally, the high EI person is more capable of perceiving emotions, incorporating them into thinking, comprehending their meanings, and managing emotions than others. For this person, resolving emotional issues is likely to take less cognitive effort. Additionally, the individual has a slight advantage in linguistic, social, and other intelligence bits, especially if the person scored higher on the EI's understanding emotions section. High-level EI individuals are more receptive and cooperative than others. The individual with a high EI is more attracted to occupations requiring social interaction, like counseling and teaching, than jobs requiring administrative or clerical tasks. Individuals with a high EI are less likely to participate in problematic behaviors and are less likely to engage in self-destructive, unhealthy behaviors such as smoking, binge drinking, substance abuse, or aggressive incidents with others. The individual with a high EI is more likely to have sentimental belongings around the house and to engage in more productive social interactions, even more so if the person performed better on emotional management. Additionally, these individuals may be more adept at articulating motivational goals, objectives, and missions. (p. 210; Mayer, Salovey, & Caruso, 2004). Bear in mind that the particular enhancement that emotional intelligence provides will be subtle and, as a result, will take some effort to recognize. It would not be seen in all social situations.

5.2. EI Is Essential

Certain tasks are performed effortlessly and deftly by some of us, while others are completely incapable of performing them. This is true of the majority of the difficulties we encounter in life. Some of us are excellent chess players, while others struggle to understand how the pieces move. While some of us are natural-born conversationalists, others struggle to say hi.

Now, the planet could survive without chess and without brilliant conversationalists, although it would be a relatively poorer place as a result. Emotional intelligence is a type of intelligence that deals with the ability to distinguish and comprehend emotional knowledge. We are surrounded by emotional information. Emotions convey fundamental emotional states between individuals; they convey urgent impulses such as "let us get united," "I am suffering," or "I am going to harm you."

What skill assessments of emotional intelligence reveal is that only a very few individuals can pick up on, comprehend, and appreciate the subtler versions of such messages. That is, only the person with a high EI comprehends the entirety and complexity of these messages.

Emotional information is valuable. It is among the primary types of information processed by humans. That is not to say that everybody must process it properly. However, it suggests that it is moving around us, and those who are sensitive to it are capable of performing certain tasks exceptionally well that others are incapable of performing. Each of us needs emotional intelligence to get through emotionally challenging days. And if we lack emotional intelligence, we should look to those of greater emotional intelligence for guidance.

Chapter 6. Emotional Intelligence & Personality Psychology

There are many explanations as to why personality and emotional intelligence should be understood in tandem. Emotional intelligence is a component of human personality, which provides the framework for emotional intelligence to function. Emotional intelligence can be thought of as a mental skill that includes the capability to reason rationally with emotional data and the ability of emotions to facilitate thought. Personality could even be characterized as a person's trend of internal observation and social interaction as a result of the interaction of the significant psychological subsystems in that individual.

Among the significant psychological subsystems are emotion, intellect, and the self. There are some critical explanations on why this relationship must be understood:

- To cultivate a more balanced understanding of what emotional intelligence implies (e.g., mental skills inside, or an aspect of, personality). By considering emotional intelligence psychologically—as a component of personality—one may try comparing and contrasting it with other components of personality: those that are identical, those that are linked, and those that are distinct. For example, ability-based emotional intelligence has recently been reinterpreted as a broad intelligence (similar to verbal, spatial, or perceptual-organizational levels of intelligence) that functions within the personality domain of information guidance (see Mayer, Caruso & Salovey, 2016).

- If an individual's ultimate goal is to comprehend a target factor — such as violence or problematic behavior — an understanding of the personality framework as a whole will assist in connecting EI to other related aspects of personality for empirical analysis.

- Recognizing EI as a component of the broader personality system may also lead researchers to which aspects of personality can affect, enhance, or diminish the effects of EI.
- Extensive research has been conducted on the manner in which the components of personality are articulated. Recognizing that EI is a component of personality provides insight into how it will be conveyed.
- Personality psychology is undergoing a revival at the moment.

6.1. Emotional Intelligence and Personality Traits

Emotional intelligence can be employed to forecast positive and fascinating results in a person's life. Regrettably, some false assumptions have been developed about EI and what it indicates, most notably during the concept's popularization in 1995.

In the mid-1990s, several journalists made false statements about the value of emotional intelligence. For instance, one of these false assertions was that emotional intelligence was the best measure for life's success." Our objective is not to shame any journalist(s) with this research, and therefore we have chosen not to mention where my several quotations come from,

We never made such statements about emotional intelligence—in reality, we were first to call such claims into question and criticize them. Along with the aforementioned papers, we spoke out firmly in a number of conversations with journalists to attempt to correct widespread misunderstandings about the field in this reference. Other writers have also attempted to correct the record.

Some promoters of emotional intelligence have voiced concern that we have not been much more outspoken in our support for emotional intelligence's more robust arguments.

6.2. What Predictions Does EI Make?

To comprehend and measure the impact of emotional intelligence, it is essential to understand how the various components of personality affect an individual's life in general.

The majority of personality traits have a gradual but consistent effect on an individual's social experiences and, more broadly, on his or her environment. For instance, a particular personality trait, such as extraversion, usually accounts somewhere between 8% and 15% of the variation in a single act, such as choosing to attend a party. The theory is that since certain personality characteristics are constant over time, they exert control over a person's acts and attitudes over very long periods of time, and over such time periods, they impact the individual's social growth and accomplishments. Psychologists usually measure a personality trait's impact in terms of the percentage of variance that it accounts for in an individual's deviation from the standard. Consider a high school where the average grade level is a B. Assuming a standard distribution of grades, many students often earn B grades. However, sometimes, grades C and A are also assigned (and at times D, and F, too). Assume now that a student earns an A average. The issue is to what extent is the student's higher grade due to general intelligence. To begin, a researcher correlates the students' general intelligence and GPA across all students. A correlation coefficient of, say, r =.50 is obtained. The correlation coefficient is squared (.25) to obtain the ratio of variance described. Once multiplied by 100, the amount of variation in grades explained by general intelligence equals 25%. While this is a small simplification, since one is usually working with the percentage described of squared deviation units, it expresses the general understanding.

6.3. What do people with a high level of emotional intelligence see that so many others miss?

The secret to this is in what those with a high level of emotional intelligence excel at. They excel at developing healthy social interactions and averting disputes, battles, and other social clashes. They excel at comprehending mentally stable living and preventing issues associated with drugs and substance misuse. It is possible that by giving coaching guidance to others and directly intervening in such cases, certain individuals support other groups and individuals into living in greater harmony and gratification. Thus, maybe even more essential than a high score on an emotional intelligence test is understanding one's proficiency in this category of skills.

By determining one's level, one may determine when and to what extent one should be self-reliant in sensitive areas, as well as when to request others' assistance in interpreting the emotional information occurring around oneself. It is probably less important to have a high or low level of emotional intelligence than to recognize that emotional knowledge exists, and that certain people can comprehend it. Knowing this, one may use emotional knowledge by locating those capable of comprehending and reasoning about it. We are living in the information age. We are all reliant on knowledge and its prudent use. The development of the capacity framework of emotional intelligence broadens our understanding of the information that surrounds us; it informs us that emotional data exists and that certain people can perceive and use it. The framework enables us all to make prudent use of emotional knowledge - whether by our own direct comprehension or through the support of those who do.

Chapter 7. Evaluating Your Emotional Intelligence

According to researchers, emotional intelligence consists of four distinct levels: emotional awareness, the ability to reason with feelings, the ability to comprehend emotions, and the capacity to monitor emotions.

Emotional perception: The first step toward comprehending emotions is to interpret them correctly. This will include an interpretation of nonverbal signs such as facial expressions and body language in certain instances.

Emotional reasoning: The next move is to use emotions to facilitate thought and cognitive function. Emotions assist us in prioritizing the things to which we pay close attention and respond; we emotionally react to things that capture our attention.

Emotional comprehension: The feelings we experience may have a wide range of meanings. When anyone expresses angry feelings, the viewer must understand the source of the person's rage and its possible meaning. For instance, if your employer is upset, it could be because they are annoyed with your work, or maybe because they received a ticket for speeding on their way to work that morning, or it could be because they have been arguing with their wife.

Managing emotions: This skill is a critical component of emotional intelligence at the highest level. Emotional control includes regulating emotions, reacting accordingly, and behaving to the emotions of others.

The four divisions of this model are classified according to their complexity, with the more fundamental processes occurring at, the lower levels and the most advanced processes occurring at the higher levels. For instance, the lowest levels include perceiving and transmitting emotion, while the highest levels involve a greater degree of conscious involvement and emotional regulation.

7.1. Impacts of Emotional Intelligence

Recent years have seen an increase in interest in learning and teaching about emotional and social intelligence. SEL (Social and emotional learning) services have become a required component of many schools' curricula.

These programs aim to improve students' health and well-being while also assisting them academically and preventing bullying. There are several circumstances in which emotional intelligence can be beneficial in everyday life.

Think before reacting.

Emotionally intelligent individuals understand that while emotions can be strong, they are also temporary. When an emotionally charged incident occurs, such as being angry with a colleague, the emotionally intelligent approach is to pause before reacting. This enables everyone to regain control of their impulses and think more logically about the various factors at play in the argument.

Improved Self-Awareness

Not only are emotionally intelligent individuals' adept at imagining how others would feel, but they are also skilled at grasping their own emotions. Self-awareness enables individuals to understand the many factors that influence their emotions.

Empathy or compassion for others

A significant component of emotional intelligence is the ability to consider and empathize with the feelings of others. This sometimes requires deciding how you will respond in the same circumstance.

Individuals with high emotional intelligence can consider the perceptions, views, and feelings of others and use this knowledge to understand why they act in such ways.

7.2. Application in Various Life Areas

Emotional intelligence can be applied in a variety of ways in your everyday life. Several different approaches to developing emotional intelligence include the following:

- Acceptance of criticism and accountability
- Being able to say "no" when necessary.
- Being willing to learn from a mistake.
- Possessing the ability to find solutions that work for everybody.
- Being able to communicate your emotions to others.
- Empathy for others
- Understanding why you do what you do.
- Having excellent listening abilities
- Having no preconceived notions towards others

Effective interpersonal communication requires emotional intelligence. According to some experts, this skill is more significant than IQ alone in assessing life success. Thankfully, there are several things you can do to improve your emotional and social intelligence. Understanding emotions will pave the way for strengthened relationships, well-being, and communication abilities.

7.3. Suggestions for Increasing EI

While it is important to be emotionally intelligent, what steps should you take to develop your own emotional and social abilities? Here are some suggestions.

Take note.

To comprehend how other people feel, the first part is to pay close attention. Allow yourself to be receptive to what others are communicating to you, both verbal and non-verbal. Body language is capable of conveying a great deal of information. When you feel that someone is experiencing an emotion, consider the various factors that may be leading to that sentiment.

Empathize

Although recognizing emotions is important, you must also be capable of putting yourself in another's shoes in order to better appreciate their perspective. Develop an ability to empathize with others. Think how you might feel if you were in their shoes. Such exercises will assist you in developing an emotional understanding of a particular situation as well as the long-term development of stronger emotional skills.

Evaluate

Emotional intelligence requires the ability to argue with emotions. Analyze the impact of your own feelings on your choices and actions. When considering how others react, recognize the implications that their emotions serve.

Why is this individual experiencing this emotion? Are there any unidentified causes that may be causing these feelings? What distinguishes your emotions from theirs? When you investigate these issues, you can discover that the role becomes clear that emotions perform in how individuals think and act.

7.4. Potential Drawbacks

Lack of emotional intelligence can lead to a wide variety of possible pitfalls that can impact many aspects of life, including relationships and work.

Individuals with less emotional skills are more likely to engage in conflict, have lower-quality partnerships, and exhibit weak emotional coping skills.

Although having a low emotional intelligence can have a lot of drawbacks, having an extremely high level of emotional skills could also present difficulties. For instance:

- According to research, individuals with a high level of emotional intelligence may potentially be less imaginative and inventive.

- Individuals with high emotional intelligence may struggle to provide negative feedback out of fear of hurting others' feelings.
- According to research, individuals with a high EQ may sometimes be used for misleading and dishonest purposes.

Chapter 8. Emotional Intelligence & Leadership

Your technical abilities may have aided in securing your first promotion, but they do not promise your next. If you strive for a position of leadership, there is an emotional component to remember. It is what enables you to mentor teams effectively, handle tension, provide feedback, and communicate with others. This is referred to as emotional intelligence and is responsible for approximately 90% of what differentiates top performers from peers who possess comparable knowledge and skills.

Emotional intelligence is characterized as the capacity to recognize and control one's own emotions and the ability to recognize and manage the emotions of others.

Goleman first emphasized the role of emotional intelligence in leadership more than a decade ago, telling the Harvard Business Review, "The most successful leaders share one critical characteristic: they all possess a high level of what has come to be recognized as emotional intelligence." That is not to say that intelligence (IQ) and technological abilities are insignificant. They are important, but they serve as the entry-level qualifications for executive positions."

Over time, emotional intelligence—also referred to as EQ—has developed into a necessary skill. According to Talent Smart's research, emotional intelligence is the most powerful predictor of results. Furthermore, recruiting managers have taken note: in CareerBuilder's survey, 70% of employers stated that they place a higher premium on emotional intelligence than on IQ, claiming that staff with higher emotional intelligence are most likely to remain cool under pressure, solve problems effectively, and react with empathy to coworkers.

8.1. The Emotional Intelligence's Four Components

Typically, emotional intelligence is classified as having four main competencies:

1. Self-awareness
2. Self-control
3. Social consciousness
4. Management of relationships

To increase your emotional intelligence, it is critical to comprehend what each component entails. Consider the following four categories in greater detail:

Self-Awareness

All begins with self-awareness. Self-awareness refers to your capacity to recognize not only your weaknesses and strengths but also your emotions and their impact on you and your team's overall success.

According to organizational psychologist Tasha Erich's study, 95% of people believe they are self-aware, but only 10% to 15% really are, which may create issues for the workers. Collaborating with coworkers who are not self-aware can halve a team's effectiveness and, according to Erich's study, result in increased tension and lack of motivation.

To achieve the best of someone, you need to first get the best out of yourself, where self-awareness enters into action. One simple way to gauge your self-awareness is to complete 360-degree feedback, which involves evaluating your results and comparing them to the views of your supervisor, colleagues, and direct reports. You will gain insight into your own actions and learn how you are viewed within the company as a result of this process.

2. Self-Control

Self-management is the capacity to control one's emotions, especially during stressful situations, and keep a positive attitude in difficulties. Leaders who are deficient in self-management tend to respond and have a difficult time reining in their impulses.

A reaction is frequently automatic. That being said, the more in touch you are with one's emotional intelligence, the easier it is to pass from reflex to response. It is worth remembering to pause, relax, compose yourself, and do what it takes to control your emotions — whether that means going for a stroll or calling a friend — so that you can react to shocks and stresses more appropriately and deliberately.

3. Social Awareness

As it is critical to understand and control one's own emotions, it is also critical to be able to decipher a room. Social knowledge refers to the capacity to identify the feelings of others and the dynamics at work in your organization.

Leaders who are socially conscious demonstrate empathy. They make an effort to consider their colleagues' emotions and experiences, which helps them interact and work with them more effectively.

According to DDI, a global leadership development agency, empathy is the most important leadership ability, with leaders who master it achieve more than 40% more in coaching, influencing others, and judgment. According to a separate study conducted by the Center for Creative Leadership (pdf), managers who exhibit greater empathy toward their subordinates are perceived as superior performers by their supervisor.

By engaging with empathy, you can improve your team's success while also enhancing your own.

4. Managing Relationships

Relationship management relates to the capacity for influencing, coaching, and mentoring others and effectively resolving conflict.

Although some tend to avoid confrontation, it is important to fix problems appropriately as they occur. According to research, each unresolved dispute will consume approximately eight hours of work time in rumors and other unproductive behaviors, depleting resources, and confidence.

To maintain a happy team, you must have those difficult conversations: According to a recent survey conducted by the Society for Human Resource Management, 70% of employees rated "respectful management of all employees at all ranks" as the most important factor contributing to job satisfaction.

8.2. Why Emotional Intelligence Is Important in Workplace?

The atmosphere of a company is set by its leaders. If they lack sufficient emotional intelligence, the effects may be more serious, including decreased employee satisfaction and a higher unemployment rate.

While you could thrive at your job professionally, if you cannot easily interact with your colleagues or work with others, those professional skills will get overshadowed. You will continue to develop your career and company by mastering emotional intelligence.

Promoting Emotional Intelligence in the Workplace

The way most companies do business has shifted significantly over the last two decades. Naturally, there are a few management levels, and leadership styles are less dictatorial. However, there has been a deliberate shift toward information- and team-based, customer-oriented work, allowing individuals to exercise greater autonomy on a general basis, even at the lowest levels of the organization.

Since modern companies are constantly striving to enhance quality, they understand that increased emotional intelligence will result in objective, quantifiable benefits. These include increased revenue, improved recruiting and retention, and more successful leadership, to name a few. Naturally, the standards for professional achievement are evolving as well. Staff is also evaluated on new criteria: not only their intelligence, training, and skills, but also how well they interact with one another. And this is heavily based on personal characteristics such as humility, self-control, and interpersonal skills. These new standards are increasingly being used to determine who will be recruited and who would not, who will be kept and who will be cut loose, and who will be promoted or passed over.

Emotional intelligence could be the (long desired) missing link that connects traditional "can do" skill factors of job performance to dispositional factors of job performance. Modern organizations, which are expressly referred to as "emotional maturity" or "emotional intelligence," now provide development and training. As a result, their leaders foster and manage an atmosphere that values versatility, responsibility, accountability, standards, incentives, transparency, and dedication.

Emotional Intelligence in the Workplace: A Review

Emotional intelligence (EQ) has been found to be equally relevant if not more vital than IQ for professional performance. Numerous studies have conducted a comparison of cognitive and emotional intelligence. The initial study was conducted at a leading Asian bank. The findings indicate that EQ is significant. And more important in predicting workplace achievement and success in comparison to IQ (McCauley, 2004).

However, not long ago, many employees, when they allowed emotions such as empathy or compassion towards others into their work, felt it would jeopardize their objectives and accomplishment. Today's market environment is markedly different. Emotional intelligence is now regarded as a primary concern in the workplace (Goleman, 1995).

Businesses also discovered the value of collaboration, communication, listening, and social interaction. Intelligence enables each employee to be more comfortable with his or her job and place where one performs (McCauley, 2004). In the workplace, emotional intelligence operates precisely as emotional intelligence is used in marriage. We examine harsh sarcasm and criticism in the form of personal insults. The sarcastic connotation creates a sense of helplessness and rage in the other person. When individuals are enraged and helpless, they often become less. Inspired to work in a particular situation, such as in a marriage or on the job (Goleman, 1995). Low motivation can result in the sense of failure, which causes people to give up.

Psychiatrist, Levinson, Harry (as cited in Goleman, 1995) proposes the following steps when approaching a worker who is acting inappropriately or needs some improvement. First, be specific; second, propose a solution; and then be mindful, and ultimately, be sensitive. Levinson observes, "is equally vital for praise as for criticism. I would not claim that ambiguous praise has no impact, but it does. not contain much, and there is little to be learned from it " (Goleman, 1995, p. 154

Levinson urges individuals to view criticism as a chance to improve.

As a team, resolve disagreements or issues. Additionally, Levinson will advocate for married couples. To handle their differences effectively as a team, using critique as a means of communication in comparison to a direct insult, develop a healthy relationship (Goleman, 1995)

8.3. 7 Techniques for Developing Emotionally Intelligent Teams

When Daniel Goleman published "Emotional Intelligence" in 1995, no one anticipated that this best-selling book could revolutionize the leadership position. With over 5 million copies sold and the Harvard Business Review describing it as a "revolutionary, paradigm-shattering concept," it is obvious that Goleman hit a chord with corporate executives.

Even so, is it conceivable to form emotionally intelligent teams?

Vanessa Dru skat and Steven Wolff assert in their seminal research findings published in "Building the Emotional Intelligence of Groups" that emotional intelligence underpins the efficient systems of successful teams and that the processes that result cannot be imitated; they should originate from sincere team-level emotional intelligence. Dru skat and Wolff illustrate their argument with the following analogy: "a piano student may be taught to perform Minuet, but he will never become the future Bach without a proper knowledge of music theory and the experience of playing from the heart."

While building effective teams is not as straightforward as replicating the strategies of emotionally intelligent groups of individuals, you can establish the required conditions for team members to improve their emotional intelligence. These three criteria are mutual trust, a shared understanding of group identity, and a shared understanding of group efficacy.

The following seven actions will help you cultivate the three conditions necessary for emotionally intelligent teams to exist:

1. Acquire a ringleader

Until you can begin working on your team's EI, you must first focus on yourself by cultivating the following:

- Self-awareness - Leaders are not only conscious of themselves but also of their feelings.
- Emotional control - leaders, retain their composure.
- Effective communications - leaders, can communicate themselves.
- Social knowledge - leaders should recognize when something is wrong and provide constructive input.
- Dispute resolution - leaders are capable of successfully resolving disputes.

Along with these EI characteristics, leaders can earn the confidence of their team members. It can be achieved by focusing on the following five characteristics of respected business leaders:

- Be courteous and respectful - leaders show common courtesy to others.
- Demonstrate an openness to change - leaders evolve from their errors and weaknesses in order to help you develop.
- Listen - leaders do more than listen; they elicit information from their employees and solicit input from their employees.
- Avoid making excuses - leaders must own up to their shortcomings.
- Assist others - leaders are generally ready to lend a hand to those in need.
- Remember, if you expect your team to develop emotional intelligence, you must first focus on developing your own EI and developing into a leader your team would admire and rally behind.

2. Determine the weaknesses and strengths of team members

Your group members are more than staff or individuals with a certain job title. They are one-of-a-kind individuals with fascinating stories to tell. Additionally, your workers possess a range of skills, abilities, and experience to benefit your overall objectives.

To get the best out of each team member, begin by starting to understand them personally. Ideally, you can become acquainted with them outside of a project so that you can appreciate what they can do beyond their conventional job position or title. According to Dru skat and Wolff, Hewlett-Packard prefers that each employee participates in cross-training. It means that the team considers "how each member should fill in for someone else's work."

Alternatively, you want to focus beyond first experiences, promote creativity, delegate teaching to team members, and reward and recognize team members. If a team member makes a mistake, provide helpful feedback to indicate that the leader gives more value to the workers' progress than just being disciplined for their neglect.

3. Activate passion

To begin, as a leader, you must ensure that you recruit the appropriate team members. I am not referring to individuals who possess the necessary skills or experience. I refer to individuals who suit your organization's culture and are enthusiastic about their careers and your company.

Even if you recruit the right people, they will occasionally lose their zeal. To avoid sagging motivation, you can rekindle passion by implementing the following:

- Recognize the team members' achievements and dedication
- Providing a versatile and stimulating work environment that values teamwork

- Assembling a mission statement for your business to ensure that everybody has a sense of intent

4. Establish team norms

As Dru skat and Wolff and stated in "Group Emotional Intelligence Growth,"

"Emotional intelligence in groups is about small actions that have a major impact. It is never about praising a team member for staying up late to reach a deadline; it is about expressing gratitude for doing so. It is not about going into great depth in exploring concepts; it is about having a brief one-on-one conversation with an anonymous member. It is not about maintaining peace, avoiding conflict, or all members getting along; it is about recognizing when harmony is fake, friction is unspoken, and respecting others."

Remember, when establishing rules, ensure that they are consistent with your beliefs. When these guidelines align with both your company and your teammate's beliefs, they will be more receptive to supporting and adhering to these **laws.**

5. Create novel approaches to stress management

Stress can contribute to employee burnout and can wreak havoc on their overall well-being. As a result, the team must be able to deal with stressful conditions such as commitments and disagreements with colleagues in a healthy manner.

To assist in reducing the employees' stress levels, consider the following strategies:

- Maintain schedules: Rushing and expanding tasks can hurt the team's time management behaviors and capabilities.
- Advice team members to withdraw from work and take breaks: Enable everyone to energize by allocating time to activities that promote relaxation.
- Discourage multitasking: Multitasking is ineffective. Indeed, it can double the time required to complete a

mission. Encourage staff to concentrate on completing a single task at a time.

- Settle disputes: Not everyone can get along in the workplace. However, resolving any problems prior to them disrupting the workplace is a perfect stress reliever.
- Be empathetic: be mindful of the factors that drive your team, as well as any difficulties they might be facing. For instance, if a teammate has recently lost a loved one, you should be sensitive and realize that their mind is somewhere else. You can also inquire about how you can be accommodating of them.

6. Allow team members to speak for themselves

It is important to have outstanding communication skills. You will assist your team members in developing improved communication skills by helping them practice active listening, improving their comprehension of body language, and providing an outlet for their grievances or concerns. However, avoid allowing negative feelings to affect the entire team. Rather than that, approach it constructively so that the team can work together to solve a problem and determine the best course of action.

Additionally, you can have an outlet for your team to share their thoughts. The Hay Group, a consulting company, employs a method called storyboarding,' in which team members produce a small poster representing their ideas. Moreover, ensure that you inquire about and encourage the opinions of your quiet team members.

7. Encourage staff to interact and have fun.

Although spending each waking moment together has its drawbacks, having workers who spend more time together outside of work will potentially benefit the workplace.

Experiences of members from emotional intelligence groups

Stephen Tom states:

"Team members should unquestionably socialize outside of work. It makes teamwork more fun and assists coworkers in remaining motivated during times of stress. These relationships foster open communication, a strong work ethic, adaptability, and a greater understanding of each individual's roles and responsibilities. When the right professionals are hired, workplace drama is minimized."

Vital Group's Davis Roger states:

"Culture is not created solely within the confines of your company. Having workers who enjoy spending time together will help make work more enjoyable and motivate them to put their hearts into the work they do on a daily basis for the company."

Ford Consulting Group's Emma Robert adds:

"Whether you take them to a baseball game several times a season, have a regular Friday afternoon drink with coworkers, or sweat together during business challenge activities, the result is the same: Colleagues who care about one another work harder. You are no longer a group of individuals who come together in an office, but a true community dedicated to the common good."

Factors contributing to a team's success.

EQ specialists Steven Wolff and Vanessa Dru skat tell us that three variables are very necessary to the functioning of a workgroup:

1. Confidence among members.
2. A sense of collective identity
3. A sense of collective effectiveness (2001).

If these three variables seem to be closely correlated with emotional intelligence, you are correct! You cannot have an emotionally mature team without emotionally intelligent participants, but it also requires emotionally intelligent principles and rules, the right team environment, and a willingness to develop team EQ.

To accomplish this, you will need the following:

· Individuals' ability to comprehend and regulate their emotions.

· Emotional comprehension and management at the group level.

· Consciousness of and desired to deal with emotions in settings other than the group.

Maintain knowledge of these three stages as you work.

Chapter 9. Couples and Family Therapy through Emotional Intelligence

"Marital counseling takes a broad view, concentrating on interconnected issues and neurotic relationships between partners. Today's marital therapists focus on the affective, emotional, and behavioral dimensions of the husband-wife partnership within the framework of marriage and family structures" (Goldenberg & Goldenberg, 2004, p 103). Numerous couples pursue family or marital counseling for many reasons, including financial difficulties, divorce-related issues such as mistrust or adultery, difficulties caring for the home or kids, and even sexual issues. These couples seek the therapist's assistance or guidance, but the majority of couples do not believe that a deficiency of emotional intelligence is a contributing factor to a failed marriage (Fitness, 2005).

Emotional intelligence is critical for the success of marriage (Goleman 1995). Goleman defines a handful of emotional skills and competencies, which include the ability to calm one's emotions, empathize with partners, and listen. In comparison to couples who lack empathy and listening skills, couples with these skills are more likely to resolve their differences effectively. "Mastering these skills enables healthy conflict; the good fights that enable a marriage to thrive and resolve the negativities that, if allowed to develop, can ruin a marriage" (Goleman, 1995 p 143). These characteristics, such as empathy and listening, are perfectly aligned with Goleman's components of emotional intelligence and are the two approaches that family therapists may use when dealing with couples (2004, Goldenberg & Goldenberg.)

9.1. A Prosperous Marriage

According to Nash (mentioned in Forgacs, & Mayer, Ciarrochi, 2001), a happy and successful marriage is very simple: couples should learn how and when to confess and apologize when they are wrong; additionally, they should forget and forgive when the other is at fault and consider and learn the appropriate time to say, "I am sorry." Individuals who can accept an apology, regardless of how challenging the situation is, have a high level of EI. One must be able to recognize his or her partner's feelings and desires, exercise self-control, and demonstrate empathic capacity. "What is intriguing about these abilities is how close t are to the ingredients proposed for emotional intelligence" (Ciarrochi, Forgacs; & Mayer, 2001, p. 98).

Most marital relationship study follows a reasonably consistent collection of procedures. Generally, couples enter a laboratory and explore marital problems of low and high tension in front of webcams. Each partner may be connected to tracking equipment that allows for monitoring different physiological parameters such as heart rate, skin conductance (sweating) and muscular activity during the interaction. Following that, couples head to the lab and observe their video-recorded experiences separately. When observing, partners indicate their emotions and thoughts at different points during the talks; they can also attempt to deduce their partners' emotions and thoughts. Finally, professional observers will code the emotional content of a couple's interaction transcripts and video recordings of their nonverbal interactions (e.g., facial gestures, manner of speech, body movements).

In general, these kinds of testing findings have been very consistent (1995, Goleman). Further research revealed that marriage is undoubtedly an emotionally charged environment and that high-conflict relational discussions are emotionally and physically arousing as indicated by physiological measures such as heartbeat, body temperature, and muscular activity. Gottman (as quoted in Goleman, 1995) shows that individuals differ in their ability to correctly perceive and recognize one another's feelings, with certain partners appearing to be oblivious of their partners' emotional signs or likely to correctly identify even the most common examples, such as mistaking depression for aggression. Additionally, individuals tend to differ significantly in their ability to convey feelings clearly, with certain couples sending unclear emotion signs to their spouses, such as frowning and smiling simultaneously. Significantly, researchers have discovered reliable correlations between these differences in people's ability to reliably communicate and understand emotional and marital satisfaction (Goleman, 1995).

When working with couples, it might be necessary for therapists to begin by teaching the couples about the different types of emotions. As research demonstrates, certain individuals are unable to recognize or describe their own feelings (Fitness, 2005). Couples may work with their partner and therapist to practice recognizing feelings in themselves and the partner during the session. Couples who acknowledge that there are additional feelings and emotions besides sadness and anger may be able to accurately identify their personal and others' feelings (Goleman, 1995)

Additionally, the therapist may assist couples in sharpening their communication skills, both verbal and nonverbal. According to research, many couples struggle to communicate with one another. Couples can develop these skills with the assistance of therapists who encourage I-statements such as "I felt disappointed and sad when you forgot our dinner plans. It would not hurt me so if you called me to cancel. "Rather than that, "you jerk, you always forget you do not think about me." (1995) (Carstensen, Gottman, & Levenson). Additionally, therapists can assist couples by highlighting nonverbal communication during the session, such as "I saw after he said that he sighed and stared at the floor; what do you suppose he was feeling then?" When couples grasp the fundamental principles of communication, they can not only practice these skills in sessions with the help of their therapist, but they can also practice and develop these skills at home (Tucker-Ladd, 2000). Another skill that counselors should focus on with partners is the idea of listening. Goleman (1995) asserts that listening is the ability that holds couples together. Certain couples speak over their partners and are unaware of or unconcerned about what others think or do because they are solely focused on themselves. Some people hearing their partner shout or talk may interpret it as an attack (Goleman 1995).

Couples may benefit from therapists or psychologists by promoting sense and reflection. Following one person's talk, the other will interpret and represent the sentiments expressed by the other's language, and vice versa. Couples that can summarize and represent their partner's thoughts and words would be more effective communicators (Fitness, 2005; Tucker Ladd, 2000). Of course, listening involves empathy, which involves genuinely hearing the emotions behind what is said (Goleman, 1995). Empathy is a necessary component of being an emotionally intelligent person in any relationship; thus, if married couples can learn how to use this quality, they can conquer marital obstacles (Ciarrochi, Forgacs & Mayer, 2001; Goleman, 1995). The fundamental components of effective communication, like the I-language, understanding verbal and nonverbal signals, and listening, are how family counselors aid their clients in addressing emotional intelligence and reestablishing a happy marriage (Fitness, 2005).

9.2. Example Counselling Activity

Thanks to Hamachek (2000), there is a few interventions or activities that therapists can offer to or exercise with their clients to ensure that emotional intelligence is implemented both during and outside of sessions. One thing counselor should do in meetings with their partners is role-play scenarios that have occurred between them. The couples must share their experiences, opinions, and words with the councilors in how they occurred at home. The counselor will ask the couple to follow principles of emotional intelligence and will have them respond to the situation using the basic aspects of listening skills and I - statements that reflect principles of emotional intelligence. By helping clients play out the scenario, the therapist will ascertain what was problematic about the encounter and then work with the pair to develop more constructive and effective strategies for resolving conflict or disagreements (Carruthers, 2005; Fitness, 2005).

Along with the role playing, counselors may instruct the couple to maintain a log of their feelings and thoughts about themselves, their relationship, and their interactions with their partner. Couples will communicate and analyze their records with their counselor during meetings and then learn to manage and discuss their records with their partner at home. Couples may develop emotional intelligence with the help of therapists and practice at home, which will improve the quality and connection of their marriage (Carruthers, 2005).

One critical principle for therapists to remember while communicating with different couples on emotional intelligence is not to overlook cultural issues (Bar On & Parker, 2000). Communication and relationships with one's partner vary significantly across cultures. Additionally, therapists must ask clarifying questions to gain insight into the couples' manner of living. It is essential for the therapists not to impose their own ideas and opinions on their patients, but rather to collaborate with them to comprehend and make sense of their relationship'.

Chapter 10. Emotional Intelligence and Children

The times of taking Intelligence tests (IQ) are long gone. Here are several reasons why EQ or emotional intelligence is a more accurate indicator of a child's progress.

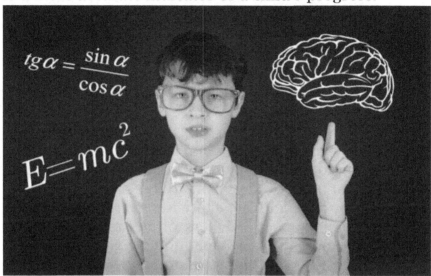

James, 6, gave a toy car he had brought from his home to a special needs boy on the school bus. He would notice that no one would sit next to the kid, as he was frequently obnoxious on the drive. According to James's mother, his strategy worked; the diversion enabled the other child to concentrate and maintain his or her composure. It was his initiative. James is much attuned to other children's feelings and thought of the approach on his own, his mother explained.

The account exemplifies her son's high emotional quotient (EQ). It is a set of skills that has garnered a lot of attention recently, with some analysts and academics asserting that it is more important than your child's intelligence quotient (IQ).

According to psychologist Daniel Goleman, IQ accounts for approximately 20% of the factors that decide life performance, whereas other influences such as EQ, temperament, wealth, family education degrees, and pure luck account for the remainder. Cognitive abilities such as memory, verbal comprehension, processing, and reasoning speed can aid a person academically but will only take them so far in reality. To truly excel, certain IQ characteristics must be complemented by social-emotional abilities such as determination, perseverance, impulse regulation, coping strategies, and the capability to postpone gratification.

Emotional intelligence is a predictor of future relationship success, fitness, and overall quality of life. It has been demonstrated that children with a high level of EQs achieve higher grades, remain in school longer, and make healthy decisions in general (they are far less likely to drink, for instance); teachers often say that high-EQ learners are more supportive and make good classroom leaders. Additionally, there is a connection between bullying and emotional intelligence, with EQ education programs seen as a means of preventing it. Additionally, having good emotional intelligence is a stronger indicator of job performance than getting a great IQ, which means managers value candidates who can complete tasks and work well with others in increasingly collaborative work environments.

10.1. How Do You Evaluate EQ in Children?

A standard IQ test measures cognitive ability by assessing vocabulary, reading understanding and memory, reasoning, and math abilities. Meanwhile, EQ tests measure various facets of emotional intelligence, including communication skills, empathy, intrinsic inspiration, and our ability to manage our emotions. Schools that take a more progressive approach to social-emotional learning are beginning to measure students' EQ to establish a benchmark, just as they do for math and reading r. Many school counselors would recommend an EQ test to a child with social difficulties to decide which skills to focus on.

As with IQ ratings, a score of 100 indicates average EQ ability; 115 indicates exceptional ability, and 85 indicates some difficulties.

Globally, EQ scores are declining, according to the State of the Heart 2020 survey, an annual scorecard generated by Six Seconds, the Emotional Awareness Network, a non-profit organization whose goal is to promote and raise awareness of emotional intelligence through research and education. It uses online assessments to assess the emotional intelligence of 100,000 people across 126 countries. According to some researchers, this downturn is due to elevated anxiety and stress levels, which makes it more difficult to deal with life's comebacks. Another factor contributing to our increasing dependence on social media and the internet for communication is our growing reliance on them. We are not utilizing the fundamental social-emotional development necessary for interpersonal interactions and future professional and vocational performance.

A 12-year-old girl, Anza, defended a boy with a learning disability by stepping up to a bunch of children taunting him in the playground. "How might you feel if anyone addressed you that way?" she inquired. As with James, Anza is able to comprehend another's point of view and then take measures to alleviate the person's distress. Holly, her nine-year-old sister, has autism, and it is possible if her EQ deficiency increased Anza's emotional intelligence. It has frequently compelled her to decipher his emotions by behavioral instead of verbal signals.

However, EQ encompasses more than empathy. Additionally, an emotionally intelligent child is one who can correctly label their own emotions, manage them, and monitor their responses to them; for example, she can express her anger or frustration in words and consider ways to resolve her feelings instead of throwing a book against the walls. Additionally, a child with a higher EI can manage more complicated social interactions and form lasting friendships due to their ability to connect to or empathize with others.

As a child develops into a teenager and then an adult, EQ becomes more and more associated with internal motivation and personality. It controls her decision-making and her ability to channel her thoughts and emotions to deal with tension, solve problems, and achieve goals. For instance, an excellently developed EQ is exemplified by the student who can balance her time effectively enough to complete homework assignments, prepare for exams, work a part-time job, and apply to university while managing multiple peer and family relationships.

When a high EQ child approaches puberty, we begin to see how it has helped him manage all junior high's emotional and social pitfalls and prepared him for life as a young person. Simultaneously, it is concerning for kids whose EQ, emotional intelligence is still developing.

What is the good news? Contrastingly IQ, which remains constant over time, EQ may increase. However, for a child to truly acquire and master these skills, specific instruction and practice may be required.

10.2. Can Children Be Taught EQ?

"There is a dimension that kids are born with; however, a sizable portion is acquired. Nature and nurture are inextricably linked," says Joshua Freedman, a CEO of Six Seconds. Most of the social-emotional component is taught in Canadian schools, where the emphasis on earlier childhood and elementary school education is on emotional literacy and social skills, a concept that refers to the ability to name and manage one's feelings and to respond appropriately to the emotions of others.

"What we are attempting to do with small kids is to emphasize those areas as well as conventional curriculum objectives," says an emeritus professor of education at the University of British Columbia. They have revamped the province's primary education program over the years, promoting empathy via play, particularly in the early years.

In almost any format, story time is also critical, including visual storybooks, oral storytelling, imaginative play, doll role-playing, and allowing children to read independently. "Through storytelling, children develop an understanding of the social world—it teaches them how to react to situations and deal with different emotions in different events," he explains. "It is an effective way for any of them to develop their ability to contextualize circumstances. Kindergarten is about children developing an awareness of their own emotions, the ability to communicate those feelings, the ability to get on with other children, the ability to share, and the ability to be willing to take responsibility -a lot of this is done; in schools."

It may seem elementary, but it is essential for children to learn these concepts to concentrate, act well in class, and form friendships. (No one likes to play with a child who is incapable of sharing or taking turns.)

For the children to advance through the grades, they must learn how to be responsible community members while in school. Children are allowed to put away their textbooks and possessions, to be respectful of the work and ideas of others, and to take on projects that benefit the whole school or society. (For instance, grade six students organizing a campaign to gather winter clothing contributions for a homeless charity.)

These types of social programs are important as they teach children that they are a participant of something greater than themselves. We all are interdependent and must exercise social responsibility in the classroom or the community.

Participating in programs like Roots of Empathy is yet another way for schools to incorporate emotional intelligence into their classroom instruction. This widely implemented Canadian program —teaches empathy through daily visits from a mother/parent and infant. Throughout each session, a professional facilitator directs students' perceptions about the baby's emotions by assisting them in recognizing and naming possible meanings for various facial gestures or vocalizations. The children are then prompted to recall a time when they felt frightened, upset, or sad.

Once children learn that all people, including infants, experience these feelings, they begin to develop empathy, according to Carolyn Parkes, the North American director of Roots of Empathy. Not just that, but as students begin to empathize, it becomes more difficult for them to be cruel to their classmates. "Research on Roots of Empathy indicates a decrease in violence and a rise in pro-social conduct," Parkes explains. "It is very difficult to be hurtful to another person when you recognize their emotions and who they are. Consequently, bullying decreases."

Joshua Freedman advocates for a more holistic, developmental focus on social-emotional learning in classrooms. We want to see schools do it similarly to math or other subjects with a spectrum and series. And we evaluate it, we devote time to it, and we do not do it for an only for a couple of days here and there," says Freedman, although he admits that any time spent creating EQ pays off.

Six Seconds discovered that when a mathematics and science teacher focused time on SEL (social-emotional learning), the remainder of the more conventional math lessons were simpler to complete (compared to classes without the EQ component). One lesson per week was devoted to emotional intelligence. She began by asking students how they were coping and then went on to an EQ exercise, such as watching the video clip about a tough decision and discussing what made it difficult afterward. Finally, the instructor instructed students to compose about a similar scenario or dilemma they were currently experiencing and then find solutions. The instructor compared the results—improved math learning over three months due to EQ exercises—to improved relationships, communication, and context for problem-solving in the classroom. "It is a truly lovely situation," Freedman says. "By devoting some time to social-emotional learning, we will actually advance academically.

10.3. EQ Modelling Starts at Home

From infancy on, parents start teaching their children emotional literacy. A few of the things in the early years that are so critical are that children should be able to identify how they feel and verbalize those feelings rather than act out. Physical violence in children peaks between the ages of two and five, just before they begin school. It is a period when children pull, beat, or bite because they lack the language to properly express themselves. However, their disruptive behavior creates a chance for parents to educate them to name those emotions and guide them on getting along with other children by play or moderating their interaction with other children.

According to the director of parent education at Six Seconds, parents should examine their own emotional intelligence. It begins through our self-awareness. Parents who attended EQ workshops have stronger family relationships, according to the organization. When your children are sad or disappointed, have you ever told them to "suck it up"? Or have you ever told a crying girl, "You are good," or "Do not be sad"? That is not supportive. The aim is to slow down and be more critical about how our children are feeling.

Norman, a father of two adolescents, believes that parents ignore their children's emotions because they do not know how to handle those feelings themselves—their emotions are so large and intense that we choose to turn on the happy function as soon as possible.

When our children show intense emotions, we become overwhelmed. However, one of the most important lessons you can remember is that you are not required to do something much of the time. Children scream, and you want to console them. Rather than that, simply sit. Shut your tongue in your mouth. You may affirm or reflect their emotions, but ultimately, it is their responsibility to figure out how to fix it. You will assist them by providing on-the-spot coaching.

10.4. A High EQ Is Required For Landing a Good Job

Employers recognize that employees who demonstrate high levels of emotional intelligence can perform their jobs and better qualified to read organizational conditions, communicate with coworkers, and solve problems.

"Today's employers value individuals with a strong EQ. We are collaborating with companies such as Google,

American Express, and FedEx—and it is a top priority for them while they are hiring," says Steven Stein, CEO of Multi-Health Systems, a test-publishing company that invented the EQi, one of the first measures of emotional intelligence. Testing potential employees as part of the overall interview process—is legal, he says, if the test is relevant to the position for which they are applying.

"When we pick people, we depend on some fairly hard data," says Stein, who is also the author of The EQ Edge: Emotional Intelligence and Your Success and Emotional Intelligence for Dummies.

Employers assessing candidates' emotional intelligence demonstrate a significant transition in thought, which is even more reason you should start to nurture your children's emotional intelligence. Together with their IQ, their EQ will help smooth the way for potential success in all areas of life.

Chapter 11. Developing Emotional Intelligence

Emotional intelligence is a collection of skills that can be developed by practice. EI or EQ is one of the most powerful predictors of business performance. According to a report conducted by Johnson & Johnson, the top leaders in the workforce have exhibited a higher level of emotional intelligence. Additionally, Talent Smart reports that 90% of achievers in the industry have a high EQ, whereas 80% of poor achievers have low Emotional intelligence. Simply stated, emotional intelligence plays an important role.

Many our clients come to us upset with their bosses, on the verge of quitting due to their tense relationship with their employer. Once we get to know what is said, we often notice that these leaders lack emotional maturity. Do not let it be you! Do not let that be you!

Being an astronaut is perhaps the most difficult work on the planet to obtain. NASA selects approximately half a dozen applications per decade from tens of thousands. The application process is strenuous and time-consuming. To apply, you must be an absolute warrior. You must possess extensive knowledge of science and technology. You must have a minimum of 1,000 hours of piloting training. You must be physically strong and fit. And, most importantly, you must be a slick badass.

Ness Sharp embodied both characteristics. She earned a master's degree in aerospace engineering and a postgraduate degree in astrophysics from the United States Naval Academy. For over five years, she flew air services in the Pacific for the US Navy. Being one of the very few who were chosen to be an astronaut in 1996 was a lucky occurrence for her.

Clearly, she was as sharp as a tack. However, in 2007, after learning that her boyfriend was with another woman, Lisa traveled 15 hours straight from Houston to Orlando, wearing a diaper, to threaten her boyfriend's new crush in an underground car park. Lisa was armed with zip ties, pepper spray, and large garbage bags and had devised an ill-conceived scheme to abduct the woman. However, before Lisa might even get the person out of her vehicle, she suffered an emotional breakdown, which resulted in her arrest.

EI is a term coined by scholars during the 1980s and 1990s to describe why smart folks like Lisa often do extremely dumb things.

According to the statement, just as general intelligence (IQ) is a measure of your capacity to process knowledge and make sound judgments, emotional intelligence (EQ) is a measure of your capacity to process emotions—and make sound judgments.

Some individuals have an abnormally high IQ but a poor EQ—think of your eccentric professor who does not see the point of showering or does not match his socks or. Some men have an exceptionally high EQ but a low IQ— think of the street hustler who cannot even say his own name but convinces you to hand over your shirt.

11.1. Emotional Intelligence Defined

Emotional intelligence is comprised of five critical components:

1. Self-control
2. Self-awareness
3. Compassion
4. Inspiration
5. (Adequate) values

The path to emotional intelligence is essential to discover or construct these five elements within oneself.

If this all sounds a little abstract and vague, and if you have never met a street hustler who convinced you to strip naked on the street (are not you fortunate?), consider someone in your experience who:

- Accepts responsibility for their choices rather than blaming others for any mishap
- Maintains a relaxed demeanor while remaining in charge of stressful situations
- Takes the time to listen to you and makes you feel respected
- Genuinely thinks about the environment and works to improve it in their own unique way
- Expresses their feelings rather than subside them

That is a person who is emotionally intelligent. And if you are not already one, you may become one.

What is remarkable about emotional intelligence is that it infiltrates every part of your life. Emotional intelligence has been linked to professional and academic achievement, as well as financial stability. Satisfactory relationships, increased life satisfaction, and improved mental and physical wellbeing.

Every undertaking in life involves decision-making. And if you repeatedly allow your emotions to cloud your judgment, you are unlikely to go very far. Even a single emotional gaffe—cue Ness and her 15-hour abduction spree—can devastate an entire career. Therefore, organize your life through developing emotional intelligence and avoid being a nitwit like Ness.

11.2. Enhancing EQ

Here are a few ways to start doing it.

Develop Self-Awareness

As is the case with many emotional tasks, you cannot improve at them until you understand what the fuck they are. When you lack self-awareness, attempting to control your emotions is akin to sitting in a small boat without a sail on top of a sea of your own emotions, utterly at the mercy of the tides of whatever is happening at the time. You are unsure of your destination or how to get there. And the only thing you can do is scream and yell for assistance.

Self-awareness entails comprehending oneself and one is actions on three levels: no.1) what one is doing, no. 2) how one feels about it, and no. 3) the most difficult aspect, determining what one does not know about oneself.

Understanding What You are Doing

You might think this would be straightforward, but the reality is that most people in the twenty-first century have no idea what the heck we are performing half the time. We are running on auto mode—checking email, texting BFFs, checking Instagram, watching YouTube, checking email, texting BFFs, and so on.

Eliminating distractions from your life—for example, sometimes turning off the mobile and interacting with the world around you—is a good first step toward self-awareness. While seeking out spaces of quiet and solitude can be intimidating, they are important for our mental wellbeing.

Other sources of diversion include work, television, video games, drugs/alcohol, and bogus online arguments. Schedule time away from them in your day. Avoid listening to music or webcasts during your morning commute. Simply look at your own life and think about it.

Consider how you are feeling. Ten minutes in the morning should be set aside for meditation. Try deleting social media from your device for a week. You would be shocked by what happens to you when you try it on a regular basis.

These are the distractions we frequently use to suppress a lot of unpleasant feelings, so eliminating them and reflecting on how you act without them will sometimes expose hidden emotions you were not aware of. However, avoiding distractions is also important because it pushes us forward to the next level.

Recognize Your Emotions

At first, paying attention to your feelings can stress you out. You may discover that you are often very depressed or a bit of an unpleasant person to several people who come across you. You may notice that there is a great deal of anxiety happening and that the entire "phone addiction" aspect is just a way to calm and divert yourself from that stress. It is critical at this level not to pass judgment on the emotional responses that arise.

You might be compelled to think along the lines of, "Ugh!" Anxiety! What the hell am I doing wrong?" However, this worsens the problem. Whatever the emotion is present has a valid reason for being there, even though you are unaware of it. Therefore, refrain from being too critical of yourself.

Recognize Your Emotional Inflexibility

If you become aware of all the icky, unpleasant sensations you are feeling, you will begin to gain an understanding of where your own little crazy lives.

For starters, I am extremely sensitive to interruptions. When I am attempting to talk, and the person I am talking to is distracted, I become irrationally angry. It is personal for me. And while sometimes it is simply them being rude, there are moments when this happens, and I eventually wind up looking like a complete idiot because

I cannot stand going 2 seconds without having every word, I say respected. That is a portion of my emotional inflexibility. And it is only through awareness that I will ever be able to react against it.

Self-awareness by itself is not enough. Additionally, one must control their emotions also.

Deal with the emotions and issues

Individuals who assume that emotions are completing life often pursue methods of "controlling" their emotions. You cannot. You have no choice but to respond to them. Emotions are simply signing that something requires our attention. We can then determine whether the "something" is significant and determine the right plan of action to take—or not take.

There is no such concept as a "good" and "bad" emotion; rather, "positive" or "negative responses to your emotions exist.

Anger may be a harmful emotion if it is misdirected and causes harm to others or to oneself. However, it may be a helpful emotion if used to right wrongs and/or defend others or oneself. When you can control and reduce your negative feelings, you reduce your chances of being overwhelmed.

It is easy to say but hard to do, is it not? Consider the following: If someone is causing you distress, avoid making assumptions. Rather than that, encourage yourself to examine the situation from many angles. Refrain from becoming angry as much as possible and keep an impartial viewpoint. Take advantage of workplace mindfulness and notice how the outlook changes.

When something positive happens, joy can be a beautiful feeling to share with everyone you care for. However, it can be a frightening emotion if it is obtained from inflicting harm on others. This is the process of emotion management: identifying what you are feeling, determining if it is an acceptable feeling for the situation, and behaving appropriately.

The point of this is to develop the ability to channel your feelings into what psychology refers to as "goal-directed actions" or, putting it simply getting your act together.

Develop Your Ability to Motivate Yourself

Have you ever been totally absorbed in an activity? As in, you begin something and become absorbed in it, and when you awaken from the quasi-hypnotic state you have induced in yourself, you realize few hours have passed, but it seemed like fifteen minutes? It sometimes happens to me as I write. When I struggle to figure out ideas in my mind and place them into sentences, I lose the sense of time and experience this wave of subtly layered emotions. It comes like a mixture of curiosity and slightly irritated excitement, accompanied by tiny doses of dopamine whenever I feel like I have just come up with a brilliant line or a funny joke. This feeling inspires me to continue writing, and I love these emotions.

Point to be noted that I do not wait for the emotions to emerge before I begin writing. I begin my work, and the sensation builds, which encourages me to continue writing, and the sensation develops a little more, and so on. I call this the "Do Something Principle," which is a very simple but extremely magical trick. The Do Anything Principle asserts that motivation is a result of and a source of action.

Many people seek inspiration first, then take decisive action and transform their lives and circumstances. They attempt to energize themselves mentally and then eventually act on it. However, by the following week, they have lost momentum and are back at it, bouncing off to some other "method" of inspiration. But try flipping it completely on its head. When you need motivation, simply do something remotely relevant to the task at hand, and then action breeds motivation, which breeds action, and so forth.

When I am not in the mood to write, I tell myself I will only focus on the outline for the time being. Once I have done so, it frequently prompts me to consider something interesting I had not considered previously that I would like to add, and then I write it down. I am a quarter of the way through a draught in a split second, and I am not even dressed yet. The argument is that to use your emotions to pull yourself together successfully, you must take action.

If nothing motivates you to feel, do something. Do something. Create a sketchbook, enroll in a free online programming class, engage in conversation with a stranger, practice a musical instrument, gain knowledge about a particularly difficult topic, volunteer in your neighborhood, go salsa dancing, create a bookshelf, or write a poem. Keep an eye on your feelings before, during, and then after whatever you are doing and use them to direct your potential actions.

Additionally, keep in mind that it is not only "healthy" feelings that inspire you. At times, I am irritated and very angry that I cannot precisely express what I am trying to convey. At times, I am fearful that what I am writing will not strike a chord with readers. However, for whatever excuse, these emotions often serve only to motivate me to write more. I enjoy the challenge of grappling with something just out of control.

Recognize Others' Emotions to Build Healthy Relationships

All we have discussed so far has to do with managing and directing one's own emotions. However, the primary goal of emotional intelligence development should be to cultivate healthy relationships in one's life.

And successful relationships, familial or friendship-based—begin with an acknowledgment and respect for each other's emotional needs. Accomplish this by empathizing with and engaging with others, by listening to others and expressing yourself openly with them—in other words, by being vulnerable.

Concentrating on non-verbal and verbal signals will provide useful insight into the coworkers' or clients' emotions. Concentrate on others and put yourself in their shoes, even if only for a moment. Although empathic comments do not justify unacceptable conduct, they serve as a reminder that everybody has their own set of problems.

To empathize with others does not necessarily imply that you comprehend them fully, but rather that you consider them as they are, particularly when you do not. You learn to appreciate their life and to treat it instead of as a tool for something else. You recognize their anguish as your pain and grief- as our mutual pain.

A relationship is where the emotional experience connects with the proverbial pavement. They draw us out of our comfort and into the physical world. They help us understand that we are a portion of something far bigger and more complicated than we are.

And finally, relationships are how we determine our values.

Incorporate Values into Your Emotions

When Daniel Goleman's book "Emotional Intelligence" was published in the 1990s, the term "emotional intelligence" became a common buzzword in psychology. To inspire their employees, CEOs and managers read workbooks and attended retreats on emotional intelligence. Therapists attempted to increase their clients' emotional sensitivity to assist them in gaining control over their lives. Parents were advised to instill emotional maturity in their children to prepare them for a shifting, emotionally charged environment.

However, much of this line of thought misses the point. That is, emotional intelligence is irrelevant in the absence of values orientation. You may get the most emotionally mature CEO on the planet, but if he is using his abilities to inspire his workers to sell goods produced through poor people's exploitation or environmental destruction, how is emotional intelligence a virtue in this case?

A father may teach his son the principles of emotional intelligence, but if he has not also taught the values of integrity and respect, he may develop into a ruthless, lying little hypocrite -one who is emotionally intelligent!

Conmen possess a high level of emotional intelligence. They have an excellent understanding of feelings, both their own and those of others. However, they end up manipulating people for their own personal benefit. They place self-importance above everything and put other people at risk. However, if you value little beyond yourself, things can get ugly.

Despite her brilliance and experience, Ness Sharp was incapable of managing her own feelings and put a high emphasis on the wrong items. As a result, she allowed her emotions to propel her off the proverbial cliff, from outer space to imprisoned space.

Eventually, whether we are aware of it or not, we are still doing what we value. And our feelings can enact certain ideals in some way by motivating our conduct. You must know what you really value to guide your emotional energy to your life goals. And developing an understanding of what you value—not just what you claim to value—is perhaps the most emotionally intelligent ability you can acquire.

Be careful of your vocabulary

Make sure to use the right words. Concentrate on improving your communication skills at work. Emotionally intelligent people prefer to use more precise language that enables them to express shortcomings more effectively, and then they work immediately to correct them. Have you had a tense session with your boss? What led it to be so terrible, and what would you do to prevent it from happening again? When you can find the source of the issue, you have a better chance of resolving it rather than stewing over it.

Recognize the sources of stress

Make note of what causes you stress and take constructive steps to reduce it in your life. Avoid being disturbed at night if you feel that opening your work email just before bed will cause you to become overwhelmed; check it in the morning. Even better, leave it till you arrive at the office.

Recover from adversity

Everybody faces difficulties. It is your response to these obstacles that will either set you up for success or send you into full-on meltdown mode. You are also aware that constructive thinking will get you a long way. To assist you in recovering from hardship, cultivate optimism rather than complaining. How can you take away from this experience? Pose constructive questions to ascertain what you can get from the situation at hand.

Emotional intelligence can develop over time if there is a desire to do so. Everyone, obstacle, or circumstance presents an excellent opportunity to assess your EQ. It requires practice, but you will instantly begin reaping the benefits.

Having a high degree of emotional intelligence can benefit you in all aspects of your life, including relationships, work, and personal life. Who would not want such a thing?

Chapter 12. Quick Ideas for Enhancing Your Emotional Intelligence

Emotional intelligence drives both your professional and personal success, but it begins with you. Understanding and controlling your own emotions will help you achieve success in all aspects of your life, from trust, empathy, and motivation to social skills and self-control.

Regardless of your professional career, whether you run a team of two or twenty, or only just yourself, assessing your capacity to maintain your overall emotional energy is a great place to start. Because emotional intelligence is not taught or tested in schools, then what is it, where did it show up, do you have it, and is it so important?

Thankfully, emotional intelligence is an ability that can be acquired, and we have compiled a detailed list of tips to assist you in assessing your own degree of emotional intelligence and developing critical emotional intelligence abilities that can be applied in daily life. We follow a few of these ideas personally, while others were revealed to us by our incredible clientele who understand how to empower and inspire their teams and themselves.

12.1. Initial Tips for Starters

Although detailed examples are given in previous chapters, we recommend beginning with these initial eight quick tips; they serve as an excellent springboard for establishing the basis of emotional intelligence.

#1) Get in the habit of analyzing your feelings.

Sometimes we lead busy, hectic lives, and it is too common for us to lose connection with our emotions. Set a timer for different points in the day to reconnect. When the timer sounds, take deep breaths and assess your emotional state. Keep an eye out for where your emotional response manifests as a physical sensation in your body, and then locate and describe the sensation. Practice makes perfect.

#2) Accept responsibility for your emotions.

Your feelings and behavior are entirely your responsibility; if you take responsibility for your feelings and behavior, it will positively affect every aspect of your life.

#3) Pay close attention to your actions.

When you are perfecting your emotional sensitivity, take a moment to observe your behavior as well. Observe your behavior when you are feeling specific feelings and how this affects your daily life. Controlling out feelings becomes easier as we become more aware of our reactions to them.

#4) Do not overlook the negative.

Reflecting on unpleasant emotions is almost as necessary as focusing on the positive. Comprehending why you feel upset is critical to developing into a well-rounded person capable of dealing with negative situations in the future.

#5) Discuss your ideas.

It is all too quick to get trapped in an 'opinion bubble' in today's hyper connected world. It is a state of being in which your own beliefs are continually reinforced by those who hold similar beliefs. The importance of checking out all sides of the story cannot be overstated (even if you still feel they are right). This will aid in your comprehension of others and make you more open to new ideas.

#6) Set aside time to appreciate the positive.

Celebrating and focusing on good moments in life is a critical component of emotional intelligence. Positive feelings make people more resilient and increase their likelihood of having fulfilling relationships that help them overcome adversity.

#7) Do not forget to inhale and exhale.

Life presents us with a range of situations, and many of us deal with tension daily. Do not forget to relax while this happens to help you control your feelings and prevent outbursts. Take a timeout and wash your face with cold water, go outside for some fresh air, or have a drink – something to help you maintain your composure and give yourselves a chance to process what is unfolding and how you might react.

#8) A life-long practice

Recognize and recall that emotional intelligence is an ability that must be developed and refined over time; it is very much a lifelong activity.

12.2. Tips For Enhancing Self-Perception

Self-perception is a critical component of emotional intelligence since it enables you to recognize and appreciate your own persona, moods, and feelings, as well as their impact on others. It involves a rational evaluation of your capabilities – your abilities and limitations – as well as an understanding of how others interpret you. It will illuminate places for personal growth, enable you to learn how to respond best, and reduce false assumptions.

#9) Recognize and accept the emotional causes.

Self-aware individuals can identify their feelings when they arise. It is important to be adaptable to your feelings and to adjust them to your circumstances. Do not refuse your emotions time but also avoid being rigid with them; allow time for your emotions to process before expressing them.

#10) Develop the ability to look at yourself critically.

It is difficult to know yourself fully, and it is almost difficult to look at yourself critically, so feedback from those who understand you well is essential. Inquire about your weaknesses and strengths, jot down their responses, and compare them. Keep an eye out for trends and try not to disagree with them – they are not necessarily correct; they are merely attempting to assist you in evaluating your experience from another's perspective.

#11) Recognize what motivates you.

When starting a project, everybody has a primary inspiration. The challenge is remembering this guiding power as adversity arises. Far too much, people begin a project then struggle to finish it because they lose inspiration. Take the time, figure out what motivates you, and use it to propel you to the finish line.

#12) Do not expect others to trust you (if you cannot trust yourself).

It can be difficult to establish trust in others, and once trust is lost, it is even more difficult to get it back. Bear in mind that humans are fallible and can make mistakes. By extending your confidence, you are encouraging others to do the same.

You have the option of overreacting or remaining calm in response to a situation. However, it is entirely up to you.

#13) Have faith in your instincts.

While you are still undecided about which direction to follow, go for your gut instinct. After all, the subconscious has been figuring out which direction to take your whole life. You will master self-management until you have mastered self-awareness and how the feelings function. This includes accepting accountability for your own actions and well-being and managing emotional outbursts.

#14) Foresee how you would act.

Consider a scenario you are about to enter to foresee how you would feel. Practice identifying and acknowledging your emotions - naming your emotions keeps you in balance. Rather than just responding to the emotion, try to pick an apt response to it.

#15) Create a schedule (and commit to it!)

Maintaining a schedule and adhering to it is critical if you want to accomplish things effectively. When you schedule arrangements in your planner, you are telling yourself, "I am going to do A, B, and C by X date, and it will take Y hours. When you make this vow, it becomes more difficult to procrastinate.

#16) Snap yourself out of it

Changing your sensory feedback is an important way to hold your feelings in balance - motion, as the old cliché says, determines the mood. So, shake up your physical body by going to a fitness class, or consider channeling your distracted mind with a game or a book - something to interrupt your current routine.

#17) Keep a journal.

Writing a journal is an excellent way to have an accurate sense of yourself. Begin by jotting down what occurred at the end of each day, how it affected you, and how you deal with it. By documenting such information, you will better understand what you are doing and identify potential sources of error. Review your comments on a regular basis and take notice of any patterns.

#18) Stop for a while to relax.

Emotional outbursts will arise because we do not take the time to calm down and evaluate how we are feeling. Allow yourself a pause and make an intentional attempt to meditate, do meditation, or read - a little escapism will do wonders. And then, the next time you experience an emotional response to something, practice pausing before reacting.

#19) Do not get angry.

Transform your emotional energy into something useful. It is acceptable to hold overwhelming emotions inside, particularly if it is not right to express them. Once you do, though, rather than venting your frustration on something pointless, channel it into inspiration. Avoid being enraged; instead, strive to improve.

#20) Show an interest.

A critical component of self-management and emotional control is making a deliberate effort to be involved in the subject matter, both business and personal.

#21) Eat healthily.

It may seem easy but controlling what you drink and eat can significantly impact your emotional state, therefore trying to maintain a healthy diet.

#22) It is all up to you.

When it comes to reacting to a scenario, you have the freedom to choose how you respond: You can overreact or stay calm. However, it is your decision.

12.3. Tips For Enhancing Inspiration

Self-motivation is a personal ability component of emotional intelligence. It refers to our inner drive to accomplish and strengthen our dedication to our goals, our willingness to act on incentives, and our overall enthusiasm.

#23) Positivity

It is important to cultivate a constructive and optimistic outlook to stay motivated. See challenges and defeats as opportunities for growth rather than failures, and avoid negative people favoring optimistic, self-motivated people – they will positively impact you.

#24) Personal objectives

Personal priorities may include long-term guidance as well as short-term inspiration. So, take out a paper and pen and dream of where you see yourself and create some goals. They should be based on your abilities, important to you, and, eventually, exciting, and attainable. This mission alone is sufficient to inspire you immediately!

#25) Assist and support.

Never be afraid to seek assistance if you require it, or vice versa. If someone else needs assistance, do not hesitate to provide it. Observing others excel can only serve to inspire you.

#26) Continual education

Both awareness and information are critical for feeding the mind and maintaining a sense of curiosity and motivation. And, with knowledge so readily available, you could refuel your beliefs and passions with a single click!

#27) Get up and stretch your legs.

A 10-second burst of motivation is easier to obtain with these steps: Stretching out helps you raise your level of motivation. You will be in the proper mindset when you go to your desk, which means you will be able to work.

#28) Be willing to step outside your comfort zone.

The most significant impediment to reaching your full potential is failing to challenge yourself often enough. If you are willing to step beyond your comfort zone, amazing things will come to you, so do as much as possible.

#29). Be rational.

Before setting a new target, defining some simple objectives that lead up to that final goal is important. You must also accept that significant change is an unavoidable part of daily life. Performing well at something helps you gain confidence, and self-confidence is a prerequisite for succeeding in something new.

12.4. Tips For Enhancing Compassion and Empathy

Simply put, empathy is the capacity to comprehend the feelings of others. Recognize that everyone has unique emotions, expectations, causes, and fears. By becoming empathetic, you allow their experiences to align with your own in to react appropriately emotionally. It is a lifelong ability and the most critical for relationship navigation, and while it does not come easily, there are a few approaches to cultivate it.

#30) Viewpoint and perspective

We are all familiar with the expression "put yourself in other's shoes," and this is precisely what we are doing here. The best way to gain some insight the next time a problem or circumstance occurs is to put yourself in the other party's shoes and really consider what is going on from their perspective. Often there is not wrong or right. However, you can understand enough yet to draw a conclusion or give helpful advice.

#31) Pay attention.

To empathize with others, you must first understand what they are thinking, which means that listening is at the heart of empathy. It entails allowing them to speak without interference, preconceptions, skepticism, and pausing your own concerns to absorb their situation and understand their feelings before reacting.

#32) Allow yourself to be vulnerable.

One of the simplest ways to demonstrate genuine exchange or empathy is listening to someone's experiences and relating them to your own. Do not be embarrassed to be vulnerable; it may be the beginning of a wonderful and enduring relationship.

#33) Make an effort to be approachable.

If you are the team leader of a team or collaborate on a project, someone strives to maintain an approachable and open demeanor.

#34) Understand what others are saying.

A helpful technique is to use 'I understand' and 'I see' to demonstrate that you listen while somebody is speaking but only say these things when you are listening.

#35) Develop an interest in strangers.

Highly empathic individuals have an unquenchable curiosity about strangers. As we interact with people who are not part of our immediate social group, we gain knowledge of and better understand their perspectives, attitudes, and lives that differ from our own. Therefore, the next time you are on a bus, you will know exactly what to do...

#36) Become immersed in a new culture.

Even in our ever-shrinking world, the old phrase 'travel broadens the mind' remains valid. Occasionally, the best way to expand your mind is to board a plane and travel to a totally different place.

12.5. Tips For Enhancing Social Abilities

In terms of emotional intelligence, social skills refer to the abilities required to effectively manage and manipulate others' emotions. It encompasses a broad spectrum of skills, from communication and conflict resolution to adapt to transformation, meeting different people and developing relationships, and it encompasses nearly every aspect of our lives, from work to romance. It is not very easy and requires the application of nearly every point we have discussed so far, but here are some pointers for you.

#37) Perfection comes with practice.

While practicing your interpersonal skills can seem odd, practice makes better as with everything else in life.

#38) Starting up!

To jump-start, your social skills growth, concentrate on one ability you want to improve. Doing so narrows your focus, which helps you stay motivated. Daniel Goleman, a well-known international psychologist, recommends focusing on someone you know who excels at that particular ability, watching how they behave and manage their feelings, and then adapting and applying that experience to yourself.

#39) Put on another person's shoes.

No, it is not literal! Everybody has heard the expression 'walk a mile in another person's shoes,' but how often people really do so? Give it a shot; you never know what could happen.

#40) Total abstinence from social media

We are not trying to make you feel old but frequenting face-to-face social settings and getting involved in real-life situations can provide several social skill opportunities for you. Therefore, the next time you are tempted to instant message your best friend, arrange to meet for a beer! Emotional intelligence does not develop under the constraints of (un)social media.

#41) The unidentified

The most effective way to develop your social skills is to go out and be sociable. It may sound elementary, but you cannot improve your social abilities without engaging in social interactions! Join a community or network that is not part of your normal circle; this is ideal for putting all of our ideas into action.

#42) It is not what you say but how you say it that matters.

We are discussing the value of a nonverbal expression and how it can influence how someone perceives you. Body language, eye contact and tone of voice all play a role in communicating your emotional state to others. Therefore, once you have stabilized your feelings, consider your physical appearance.

#43) Improve your networking skills.

Attending local networking activities is an excellent way to improve your social skills. The wonderful thing about these activities is that anyone who attends has a common purpose.

12.6. What Not to Do!

Individuals with a high EQ very rarely exhibit the following characteristics, which you should be aware of.

#44) Negativity

Emotionally intelligent individuals can stifle negative feelings. They recognize that negative thoughts are merely that – thoughts – and draw conclusions based on reality, as well as their ability to silence or filter out any negativity.

#45) Drama

Individuals who are emotionally intelligent listen, give sound guidance and extend compassion to others in need, but they do not allow the lives and feelings of others to influence or rule their own.

#46) Making a complaint.

Complaining indicates two conclusions: One, that we believe we are the victims, and two, that we do not believe there are any possible remedies. An emotionally intelligent person rarely feels victimized, and even less often does he or she believe that a solution is out of reach. Instead of focusing on who or what to blame, they think of a solution, dissolve it in private, and accept the responsibility themselves.

#47) Selfishness

While a certain amount of selfishness is necessary to succeed in life, an excessive amount may damage relationships and create disharmony. Avoid being too greedy and consider the needs of others.

#48) Excessive criticism

Nothing lowers a person's morale more quickly than being excessively critical. Bear in mind that people are just like you and tend to have the same incentives (and limitations). People need to learn about others before they can articulate their desired improvement.

#49) Capitulating to peer pressure

Simply because someone else is doing something does not obligate them to follow through if they do not wish to. They think differently and never adhere to the wishes of others.

#50) Fantasizing about the past

Many with a high level of emotional intelligence prefer to learn from their mistakes and decisions and, rather than focusing on the past, live in the present moment.

By comprehending and effectively using emotional intelligence, you, too, will maximize your potential and accomplish your goals.

Chapter 13. Signs of Low Emotional Intelligence

Have you encountered someone who is perpetually out of control of their emotions? Maybe they are frequently doing or saying the incorrect thing at the incorrect time. Or maybe they are always criticizing others but have a difficult time acknowledging criticism. If this fits someone you know, the likelihood is that this person has low emotional intelligence. Emotional intelligence, or emotional quotient (EQ), is a trait that, like general intelligence, differs between individuals.

As per the theory of emotional intelligence (EQ), people use this form of intelligence in the following ways:

- Comprehend and manage their own moods and emotions.
- Understand how others feel and empathize with them.
- Resolving issues and ensuring that their needs are addressed.
- Empower others.

Individuals with low emotional intelligence cannot correctly identify feelings, recognize how others feel, and express and honor emotional needs. And these tendencies can wreak havoc on relationships. However, having lower EQ does not always make you a terrible person. Furthermore, it would be best if you focused on strengthening your emotional muscles.

13.1. What Is Emotional Intelligence Deficit?

Low emotional intelligence is described as the inability to interpret emotions accurately (in oneself and others) perfectly and allow that knowledge to direct one's thoughts and behavior.

Emotional intelligence (a.k.a. "emotional quotient" or "EQ") is essential for virtually every aspect of life. Indeed, many experts now agree that EQ is more important than IQ in predicting overall life performance. As such, having a low EQ or emotional intelligence may have a detrimental effect on interpersonal relationships and your physical and mental health.

13.2. Significant Characteristics of Low-Intelligence Individuals

In general, poor emotional intelligence means that you often struggle to:

- Comprehend and control one's own feelings
- Have an awareness of how others feel

Weak or poor emotional intelligence can manifest itself in many ways. Most of these manifestations have an effect on the individuals around you, and you can experience difficulties maintaining relationships.

Several critical indicators include the following:

- Difficulty comprehending the source of certain emotions
- A pattern of tantrums or mood swings
- Difficulty expressing one's views or asserting one's authority in a situation
- A lack of interest in developing novel methods for resolving problems
- Reluctance to receive criticism, whether positive or otherwise
- Difficulty communicating thoughts or making a point
- An inclination for doing the incorrect thing at the incorrect time
- Certain blindness to others' emotional signals
- A tendency to dwell on errors rather than learning from them and moving on
- Pessimism and a lack of motivation in the aftermath of setbacks

The following are classic indicators of low emotional intelligence, explained.

They must always be 'right.'

You are probably familiar with someone who is perpetually in conflict with others. Friends, relatives, coworkers, and even total strangers become entangled in disagreements with these acrimonious individuals.

Individuals with low EQ also argue an argument to death while not willing to listen to anyone else. Even if you demonstrate that they are incorrect, they will insist that your arguments are incorrect.

They are determined to win at any cost and are incapable of actually "agreeing to disagree." It is especially true if others are dismissive of the individual's inability to comprehend what others are experiencing.

They are ignorant of other people's emotions.

Most individuals with poor EQ seem to be indifferent to the feelings of others. They can be taken aback that their partner is unhappy with them or that their colleagues dislike them. It is not just that; they even get irritated because people believe they understand how they feel.

They act imprudently.

Generally, individuals with poor EQ lack the ability to say the appropriate thing. Additionally, they may be unable to distinguish between right and wrong timing while speaking.

For instance, they could make an offensive remark at a funeral or crack a comment immediately after a traumatic experience. If you respond negatively to their out-of-character answer, they will assume you are excessively sensitive. Due to their difficulty in comprehending others' emotions, it is unsurprising that they are unable to perceive and react adequately to the emotional tone and environment.

They place the blame for their problems on other.

Individuals with a low EQ do not know how their feelings can cause problems. The one thing that a person with poor emotional intelligence will not do is take responsibility for their behavior. If something bad happens, their first instinct is to point the finger at something or someone else. They could argue that they had no choice but to act in a certain way and that others clearly do not understand their situation.

For instance, if they read your messages, you are responsible for keeping your phone unlocked. If they miss an assignment, break a lock, are not hired, or burn dinner, they will find a way to blame someone else.

They possess substandard coping skills.

The inability to deal with emotionally charged circumstances is a sign of low EQ. For those with poor, emotional intelligence strong emotions, either their own or that of others, are hard to decipher. These people often flee these circumstances to avoid dealing with the emotional consequences. It is also very normal for people to conceal their true emotions.

They often exhibit emotional outbursts.

Emotional intelligence involves the ability to control one's emotions. But individuals with a low EQ often fail to comprehend and control their feelings. They can lash out defensively, unable to articulate what they are truly feeling and why they are so upset.

An individual with low EQ can also experience unexplained emotional tantrums that seem out of control. The slightest provocation sends them into a frenzy that can last minutes, if not hours.

They face relationship difficulties.

Individuals with a low EQ sometimes have a small circle of close friends. This is because close relationships include reciprocal give-and-take, emotional bonding, kindness, and emotional support, all of which are usually lacking in low-EQ individuals. Rather than that, individuals with low EQ often come across as abrasive and indifferent.

They steer discussions towards themselves.

People who are emotionally unintelligent sometimes dominate the conversation. And when they seem to be listening attentively and asking questions, they still find a way to redirect the conversation back to them. Generally, they must demonstrate that they have had it worse or better than what you are experiencing.

Whatever you say, they have been there and done that. Have you been involved in a car accident? They have as well...and their pet died. Are you planning to climb Mount Everest? They reached the summit of Mount Everest five years ago. They will even give you a list of suggestions if you are so like!

A lack of emotional intelligence can manifest itself in a variety of areas of your life. Fortunately, there are a lot of ways to improve your emotional intelligence. Enhancing your abilities can help you build stronger professional and personal relationships.

13.3. How does emotional intelligence affect our daily lives?

Emotional intelligence encompasses a broad range of abilities that has personal and professional advantages.

When you can correctly recognize emotions, you can find it simpler to cope with negative emotions that can influence your performance or mood. Successfully managing emotions, in turn, will help you build stronger relationships and increase your chances of career success.

Example

You have recently suffered a romantic setback. You contact your best friend for comfort, hurt, depressed, and lonely.

"Why do not you drop by? We are about to order takeout and watch a video," the short response states. The bid attracts you, but you note the word "we," which indicates that their friend will also be present. You are aware that spending time with the happy couple would almost certainly make you jealous, and you do not wish to vent your frustration on them.

"I believe I am just venting to you," you explain. "Let us meet up tomorrow. "You opt for a stroll instead. When you return, you curl up with a favorite book to de-stress.

In this case, emotional intelligence enables you to:

- Restrain impulsive behavior
- Exercise self-control in the face of confrontation and stressful circumstances
- Maintain a positive and motivated attitude toward targets, even in the face of setbacks

Empathy, or the capacity to consider how others feel, is often associated with emotional intelligence. Numerous experts believe Empathy is a critical element of leadership. Certain hiring managers look for emotional maturity in a new hire. Also, emotional intelligence has been linked to increased overall health and a higher standard of life and work satisfaction.

On the other hand, poor emotional intelligence often results in problems relating to other people or processing one's own emotions.

You can have difficulty resolving conflicts or sharing ideas to coworkers, colleagues, and family members.

When you are angry, you can want to suppress your emotions, but this avoidance may increase stress and can lead to mental health symptoms such as anxiety or depression.

With all this in mind, it is easy to see that many people regard low emotional intelligence as a disadvantage.

However, here is another angle to consider: Increased emotional intelligence facilitates the ability to influence others. Occasionally, there is no risk in that.

If you notice your brother is depressed after his job loss, for instance, you might focus on a quest to improve his mood by assuring him that he will soon find employment. You motivate him to apply for his dream work and provide assistance with rewriting his resume.

But on the other hand, if you are aware that your partner wishes to see you happy, you will choose to highlight a slight disappointment or a bad day in order to elicit affection and convince them to do something good for you.

Individuals in positions of power or who wish to assert authority over others could potentially abuse their emotional intelligence by playing with and manipulating the emotions of others for personal gain.

To summarize, emotional intelligence does not always equate to "exemplary human being." Furthermore, someone who lacks emotional intelligence is not an "evil guy."

13.4. What factors contribute to a person's lack of intelligence?

Numerous factors may influence the development of emotional intelligence.

Parenting styles and upbringing

Early in life, emotional sensitivity and Empathy start to develop. As you grow, your parents or caregivers assist in developing these skills. Children grow up with better EQ. When their main caregivers:

- Act promptly in response to their needs
- Extend affection and comfort
- Exemplify effective emotional management skills
- Allow them to discuss and share their emotions in meaningful ways

Emotional intelligence deficiencies can also run-in families. Children with parents who lack emotional intelligence can struggle to control their own emotions, as they have less opportunities to develop healthy coping mechanisms.

Additionally, you could have lower EQ emotional intelligence if your parents were inconsistent in their love and warmth, never let you communicate your emotions, or disciplined you for expressing them.

Moreover, research has established a correlation between low emotional intelligence and negative parental demands, which may include the following:

- Efforts at exerting power
- Excessively severe discipline
- Erratic discipline

Psychiatric disorders

Difficulty detecting and controlling feelings may be a symptom of a range of mental health disorders, including depression and borderline personality disorder. Inadequate emotional intelligence can also contribute to social anxiety.

When you have difficulty knowing how others feel, you can find interactions frustrating and fear doing something that may enrage others. Continual social anxiety will ultimately lead to social avoidance and lead to feelings of hopelessness or desperation.

Additionally, research indicates that alcoholism and other drug use disorders are associated with lower emotional intelligence. This link is bidirectional: Addiction can alter the way your brain processes feelings and urges, impairing your ability to perceive and control them.

However, if you already struggle in these areas, you can turn to alcohol or other drugs to help you cope with difficult emotions or manage difficult social situations more easily.

Alexithymia

This disorder manifests as an inability to recognize and communicate emotions. Alexithymia patients can also have difficulty empathizing with others. They can place a higher emphasis on logic and specific facts than on creative or emotional thinking.

Alexithymia can be caused by a variety of factors, including the following:

- Traumatic experiences during childhood
- Traumatic brain injury
- A stroke

This problem interpreting feelings can also manifest itself temporarily in some mental health disorders, such as depression, and then subside along with other effects until therapy is initiated.

Additionally, research connects alexithymia to autism, implying that up to half of all autistic individuals have alexithymia.

Most people believe that autism is synonymous with low emotional intelligence, but the existence of alexithymia alongside autism can make emotional communication and Empathy difficult for others.

13.5. How to deal with people who have a poor or low EQ?

Are you interacting with someone that you suspect lacks emotional intelligence? They can find your emotions approach as perplexing as you do with their inability to manage emotions.

These tips will assist you in meeting in the center and facilitating more fruitful interactions.

Acceptance of an offer

Bear in mind that everybody brings something unique to the table. Consider and admire their distinctive personality characteristics and attributes rather than concentrating exclusively on their emotional abilities.

You cannot change anyone. However, you may inspire them to focus on their own emotion management. When it comes to assisting others with their reform efforts, gentle motivation still trumps criticism.

Inquire as to how they feel if they seem stressed.

Set a good example for others by remaining calm and demonstrating compassion. Include them in practicing regulation techniques alongside you, such as going for a stroll or attempting some deep breathing.

Attempt to pay attention.

It is normal to become angry when you believe no one is hearing what you are saying. The majority of people have been in this situation at some stage in their lives. However, it will be harder to work through such pain without effective coping mechanisms in place. Assist them in feeling heard and acknowledged by consciously listening and concentrating on what they are saying:

Avoid any misunderstandings by asking clarifying questions.

Summarize or focus on what they have said (rather than merely repeating it back) to demonstrate that you have considered the context of their comments.

Adhere to logic.

When anyone prefers rational over emotional methods, using rationality in your own communication will help you connect more effectively. Concentrate on reality rather than emotions. It means you can explain an incident in its entirety rather than omitting critical information to highlight its emotional effects.

Clarifying your own thoughts and expressing exactly what you think, rather than relying on your sound or body language, will also contribute significantly to good conversations.

Chapter 14. The Disadvantages of Extreme Emotional Intelligence

Though meanings differ, EQ often includes interpersonal and intrapersonal abilities, notably adaptability, sociability, flexibility, and prudence. However, any human characteristic has drawbacks.

The disadvantages of having a higher EQ include a reduced capacity for creativity and innovation. Individuals with a high EQ are often excellent at relationship building and collaboration but may miss the required levels of nonconformity and unconventionality to question the status quo.

Due to their higher interpersonal sensitivity, people with a high EQ have trouble giving negative reviews, and their cool-headedness and optimism also make receiving it difficult. They will be hesitant to ruffle people's feathers, putting them at a loss when forced to make unpopular decisions or effect change. Individuals with a high EQ can also have an excellent capability for manipulation. They run the risk of exaggerating their social abilities by concentrating exclusively on the emotional dimensions of communication and ignoring rational arguments.

Finally, these workers can exhibit a higher degree of conscientiousness and thus be averse to risk. While EQ is an undeniably attractive and highly adaptable characteristic, obsessing over it will result in an excessively diplomatic workforce incapable of driving innovation and change. Let us examine this case through the lens of an example.

Sofia is an incredibly loving and compassionate person. She is very sensitive to the feelings of others and is both kind and thoughtful. Sofia, on the other hand, is very hopeful. She is always cheerful and optimistic, even in the midst of bad news. Her coworkers adore her because she is a symbol of harmony. Regardless of the level of stress and pressure at work, Sofia is upbeat and confident and never loses her composure.

Sofia's boss loves working with her because she rarely complains, is dependable and demonstrates excellent organizational conduct. Indeed, Sofia is an exemplary ethical and trustworthy person. Additionally, Sofia's personality ensures that she is usually motivated to work, even If her manager is not handling her well.

Who does not want Sofia on their team? In several respects, she seems to be the perfect employee, someone who has exceptional potential for a management career.

If this strikes a chord with you, you are not the only one. A lot of folks will consider Sofia's personality to be an advantage, and not just in a professional sense. The primary explanation for this is Sofia's high emotional intellect (EQ), which accounts for all of the characteristics mentioned above.

Thousands of research studies have examined the significance of EQ in a multitude of spheres of life, demonstrating the persuasive benefits of high EQ in the areas of work, wellbeing, and relationships. For instance, leadership, job efficiency, career progression, happiness, and health are all positively associated with EQ (both physical and emotional). Additionally, EQ is associated with destructive job habits, psychopathy, and a penchant for stress.

However, is increased EQ always favorable? Even though the downside to increased EQ is largely unknown, several reasons are skeptical of a one-size-fits-all or higher-is-always-better approach to EQ. Some things are best in moderation, and every human characteristic has a downside.

Let us return to Sofia and consider some of the less desirable consequences of her high EQ.

Reduced capacity for imagination and innovation.

There seems to be a negative association between EQ and many personality characteristics associated with creativity and innovation. For centuries, creativity has been correlated with characteristics associated with low EQ: creative moodiness, nonconformism, aggressive impulsivity, and a hyperactive ("up-and-down") attitude. Although it is probable for talented artists to be emotionally intelligent, but the more typical trend for individuals like Sofia is to excel at following procedures, evolving relationships, and cooperating with others but to be lacking the requisite levels of unconventionality and nonconformity to motivate them to question the status quo and come up with something new.

Difficulty communicating negative reviews and accepting them.

Upon first glance, higher EQ individuals such as Sofia can appear to excel at both sending and receiving input, as both require social interaction. However, scratch the surface, and you may discover that Sofia's good interpersonal awareness and empathic concern will make it difficult for her to give constructive or negative input to others. Additionally, high-EQ individuals such as Sofia may be so well-adjusted and level-headed that they may be oblivious to critical feedback they get indeed, since they are usually so relaxed, adjusted, and optimistic, high EQ levels can be difficult to shake.

Afraid of ruffling people's feathers.

One of the primary reasons for Sofia's popularity is that she embodies many characteristics we seek in followers. While individuals like Sofia are mentally well-suited for entry-level or middle management positions, senior leadership positions will often demand the ability to undertake unpopular decisions, create significant change, and prioritize results over employee relations. Moreover, senior leaders and managers will have a significant effect on their companies only if they are entrepreneurial in their pursuit of innovation and development. This involves unpopular choices, which are less likely to be made by individuals like Sofia, who may be more concerned with getting along than with getting ahead.

A **highly developed capability for manipulation.**

Sofia's higher EQ can allow her to empathize with her audience and convey a message that feels authentic to them, which is often positive. When taken too far, however, it can escalate into coercion. The danger of abusing one's social skills is that one can concentrate exclusively on the emotional elements of communication while ignoring rational arguments and other transactional aspects. In that context, the evil side of EQ is that it enables individuals with malicious intent to be excessively convincing to gain their desired outcome. Like charisma, we prefer to consider EQ as a positive trait; nevertheless, it can accomplish both immoral and ethical objectives.

Fear of risk-taking.

Many creative projects necessarily require a delicate balance of risk-taking and risk avoidance. Individuals like Sofia are often more likely to take calculated risks and avoid making bold decisions. It is because a higher EQ correlates with greater conscientiousness. Meaning, the higher your Emo Quo, the more likely you are to fight desires and make rational choices. However, increased EQ equates to increased self-control; excessive self-control results in destructive perfectionism and avoiding risks.

Clearly, Sofia is an incredibly desirable employee, yet her exceptionally high EQ qualifies her for positions that require self-regulation and the ability to sense and respond to the emotional demands of others. All salespeople, real estate agents, customer service representatives, counselors, and psychologists profit from Sofia's EQ. By comparison, Sofia's profile can be damaging, if not detrimental, to jobs that require imagination, innovation, leading reform or taking risks. It is not to suggest that Sofia should not strive for a senior leadership position. She may, but it would take considerable self-coaching. For instance, she will need to begin seeking out and seriously considering negative feedback, abandon her preoccupation with avoiding conflict, and dismiss the status quo (or employ and care for those who do.)

Without a doubt, EQ is a beneficial and highly adaptive feature, and, logically, we prefer a high EQ over a low EQ. On the other hand, obsessing over high EQ would breed a workforce of emotionally healthy, content, and diplomatic individuals who will harry along and happily obey laws rather than stimulating change and creativity. They can make excellent followers and administrators but do not expect innovative leaders or reform makers from them.

Chapter 15. Activities & Exercises for Emotional Intelligence

As the name implies, emotional intelligence exercises and activities are intended to help individuals develop, improve, and maintain their emotional intelligence, which is frequently referred to as EI or EQ for Emotional Quotient.

Numerous individuals are motivated to improve their EI for a variety of reasons.

Several of the most frequent reasons to focus on your EI include the following:

- Desire to succeed in a leadership position.
- Attempting to integrate into a new organization or team.
- Making an attempt to expand your network and meet new people or contacts.
- If you are starting up a new business and want to strengthen your customer service.

And, indeed, many people want to improve their EI simply to understand better themselves and the people with whom they interact. There are no negative consequences to developing emotional intelligence, and the benefits can be multiple.

If you are looking to improve your EI, you are not alone! Continue reading to learn how to accomplish your goal.

15.1. Exercises for Developing and Improving Emotional Intelligence

These exercises are designed to assist individuals in developing emotional intelligence, and they are especially beneficial for leaders looking to improve their EI/EQ.

Leaders' Emotional Intelligence Assessment

Leaders have a significant job in any organization: they must shape, interact, and add value to the organizational vision. Emotional intelligence, of course, plays a significant role in this role.

It is a self-assessment activity for leaders that is the first step toward improving their emotional intelligence.

This activity includes ten characterizations of vision-killing behaviors that a leader may involve in, as well as a scale for rating your own involvement in each behavior on a scale ranging from very rarely' to very often.'

Among the behaviors that destroy vision are the following:

1. Adhering to the old saying "Do as I say, not as I do," and failing to set an example.

2. Treating people badly—for example, by failing to demonstrate concern, failing to say thank you, failing to respect others, and failing to make others feel valued.

3. Excessive focus on the task at hand and disregard for the people.

4. Concentrating on an excessive number of things simultaneously.

5. Failure to accept accountability; for failure

6. Concentrating exclusively on the details and failing to communicate the "whys" or the full picture.

7. Providing inconsistent guidance.

8. Inability to provide clear direction.

9. Permitting individuals who are not performing their jobs to remain.

10. Demonstrating a lack of personal dedication to the vision

If you frequently engage in these behaviors, this is a sign that your leadership EQ is low. Focus closely on the three behaviors you engage in most frequently and commit to reducing or eliminating them completely.

Analyses of Personality or Temperament

Temperament analysis is another excellent assessment activity. It was created to assist participants in learning about temperament, comprehending their own, and learning how to deal with it.

To begin, remember that our temperament is comprised of tendencies and emotions that are affected by four aspects or parameters:

- Genetic Inheritance
- Personal Experiences
- Physical Characteristics
- Environmental Factors

To begin, complete the temperament questionnaire:

1. Three adjectives to describe your temperament. Choose the ones that most accurately describe you.

2. Suggestions for three adjectives used to describe your temperament by others

3. Examine each of the adjectives listed in the preceding two questions and determine whether or not each one is a result of (or is influenced by) Genetic Inheritance, Physical Attributes, Life Experiences, or Environmental Conditions.

4. How does every temperamental trait affect you personally?

5. How does each temperamental component affect your performance in a leadership role?

6. Which of these variables would you like to alter and why?

Consider each question carefully and consider discussing them with a friend to maximize the learning opportunity.

Assume you are the Fog (Regulating Your Emotions)

Accepting criticism can be extremely difficult for many of us, even more so when it triggers strong emotions. This straightforward exercise will teach you how to "be the fog" and control and modify your emotions in a stressful situation.

What to do

"Pretend to be a fog! Consider yourself to be a fog. You absorb the stone without flinging the stone back when somebody hurls a stone at you. It is a very simple and efficient method for people who repeatedly criticize you."

For instance, if someone says to you:

- "You simply do not comprehend."
- "You are slothful."
- "You are constantly late."
- "You have no sense of responsibility."

Reply with:

- "Yes, I simply do not understand."
- "Yes, I am occasionally slothful."
- "Indeed, I was late."
- "Yes, I do not accept responsibility."

When you embrace criticism (without taking it personally), you will discover that you disempower the person who is criticizing you. To practice, ask a trusted friend to criticize you rapidly, one after the other, and counter with the fogging technique.

15.2. Group Activities for Emotional Intelligence

You are in luck if you would want to assist a group in developing their EQ or improve on your own EQ in a group environment. There are numerous group activities devoted to cultivating, boosting, and sustaining emotional intelligence.

Consider the following:

Emotional Acceptance

This activity can assist you in developing one of the most basic aspects of emotional intelligence: the ability to comprehend and accept one's own emotions. Although this activity requires a group of people, it could easily be modified to work with just a pair. How to accomplish this is as follows:

- Distribute your team into pairs and assign them seats that are sufficiently apart from one another to provide a sense of privacy.

- Assign who might go first to each pair.

- Inform group mates that they all will have the opportunity to share a moment when they felt victimized. Once a partner has described the experience, the other partner should describe how they felt as a consequence of it in as much level of detail, focusing on their specific emotions at the time and how they felt afterward.

- Allow approximately 15 minutes for the first partner to share and the pair to discuss before reversing roles.

If you are conducting this activity in a group, gather everyone together and lead a group discussion around the following questions:

- What were your initial thoughts when told to communicate a traumatic experience with another person?

- How did you share it with others? How did it make you feel to share it with another person?

- How did you feel understanding your emotional acknowledgment and acceptance?

- Does this activity assist us in accepting the way certain experiences make people feel and understand that it is acceptable to feel a certain way following negative experiences?

- Did you get more at ease after acknowledging your experience-induced emotions?

- Would you regard using this activity to help you evaluate and accept your emotions following negative experiences?

Making Eye Contact

As the exercise's title implies, it entails making eye contact to better understand our own emotions and how we emotionally interact with others.

Distribute index cards to your participants and instruct them to distribute them evenly throughout the room. Encourage them to envision themselves in an art museum or gallery.

Following that, instruct them to proceed through the following stages:

First Stage

a. Assume that your participants are in a public space and avoid making eye contact with anyone else. They should be prepared to improvise and act the part. Give this section one minute.

b. Bring everyone to a halt and instruct them to record their emotions on their cards.

Second Stage

a. Ask your participants to make eye contact as they move around the room during this round. They should, however, break eye contact and look away as soon as they have established it. This section should take approximately two minutes.

b. Bring everyone's attention to their cards and ask them to record their emotions.

Third stage

a. For this round, instruct your participants to make eye contact with anyone and to pair up with that person immediately upon making eye contact. They should stand parallel to one another and avoid eye contact with others. Give this section two minutes.

b. Bring everyone's attention to their cards and ask them to record their emotions.

c. Reunite everyone and discuss.

Allow for approximately ten minutes for group discussion. The following are a few discussion starters:

- How did you feel as you progressed through the phases of the exercise?
- How did you feel when you were forced to break eye contact?
- How did you feel when you made eye contact with the person and approached them to pair up?
- If you were slow to find someone to pair up with, how did it feel to search for someone with whom you could make eye contact?
- Was it easy to maintain eye contact with someone?
- How comfortable do you feel when you maintain eye contact with someone?
- What pre-conditioning governs our behavior when it comes to initiating and maintaining eye contact?
- How do these statistics compare across societies?

This exercise will demonstrate how critical eye contact is to emotional connection for you and your group.

Self-Awareness-Building Exercise

A stack of 3 x 5 index cards is all that is required to begin developing your self-awareness in a group setting. And, of course, a crowd!

Instructions are as follows:

First:

1. Ask the attendees, "How do you feel?" If possible, consult each participant individually rather than as a group.

2. Because the majority of people will likely state that they are fine, prepare to begin the exercise with the following: "How come we almost always state that we are fine, even when we are not?"

Continuing the conversation by asking questions such as:

a. "Do you find it easier to express your emotions?"

b. "What makes it difficult for you to express your emotions?"

c. "Are you capable of intentionally shifting your emotions?"

Second:

1. Discuss the need to understand the whole spectrum of human emotions to fully understand oneself and others and give yourself the ability to manage your emotions.

2. Ask the group to generate as many feelings as possible and record them on each card.

3. Arrange the cards on a table to assist the group in avoiding duplication.

4. Gather all of the cards and place them face down on the table.

5. Distribute two cards randomly to each person.

6. Instruct participants to disclose their cards and describe how they would transition from one feeling to the next.10

Allow other participants to give their own explanations after the participant's explanation.

Conclude with a conversation using questions such as:

a. Do you believe you generated a large number of emotions?

b. Was it simple?

c. Are you shocked by the variety of emotions?

d. Was it simple to transition from one emotion to the next?

Conclusion

While "rational" intelligence is necessary for success in life, emotional intelligence is necessary for developing positive relationships with people and attaining your objectives. Many individuals feel that emotional intelligence is as least as essential as conventional intelligence, and many businesses now conduct emotional intelligence tests when hiring new employees.

Emotional intelligence is the knowledge of one's behaviors and emotions - and the impact they have on others around one. Additionally, it implies that you regard people, are attentive to their goals and needs, and are capable of empathizing with or identifying with them on a variety of levels.

Bear in mind that you must channel your emotions in order to propel things and people ahead rather than allowing yourself to get swept away. As a leader, you must always strive for self-improvement and maximize the potential of your team members in order to accomplish greater objectives.

The fundamental premise of emotional intelligence is that success and happiness in life have nothing to do with IQ. Because emotional intelligence is not a permanent characteristic, you may take efforts to develop your emotional awareness and improve your ability to recognize emotions in yourself and others.

Developing emotional intelligence may aid in the development of better connections and relationships. Additionally, it may help you build strength in the face of setbacks and enhance your capacity to cope with stress and other unpleasant emotions.

While developing the ability to regulate your emotions may seem challenging, you really have a variety of possibilities. Once an emotion has been acknowledged, momentary diversions might assist you in putting it away. Grounding exercises may assist you in improving your ability to cope with challenging emotions in the present. Meditation may aid in the development of total emotional awareness and regulating abilities, which may result in longer-term advantages.

While everyone has sentiments, not everyone is capable of acknowledging and comprehending them. While increasing your emotional intelligence may need some work, it is entirely feasible. Are you having difficulty getting started on your own? A therapist is always available to provide advice and support.

Book 6: Gaslighting

A Comprehensive Guide on Recognizing Psychological Abuse, the Signs & Tactics of Gaslighters, and Ways to Save Yourself

Introduction

Gaslighting is a form of abuse or manipulation that can happen in any relation or anywhere. It is a sinister, concealed form of emotional abuse, in gaslighting the abuser makes the other person question their reality and judgment of the situation around them. We can say, in the form of psychological brainwashing. The gaslighter will persuade the victim by saying their memories are false or they remember the event wrong or overreacting to a situation. The gaslighter will tell his memories as the true form or the actual event. Thus, making the victim question their reality or make them lose their mind.

Gaslighting can happen in your close relationships, or groups, or even in parent-child relationships. Victims of Gaslighting feel exhausted, confused, and anxious as they cannot trust their thoughts, memories, or reality anymore. In relationships, Gaslighting happens so one partner can have more control over the other or inflict emotional and psychological damage in any way they want. It will make the victim question their reality. If Gaslighting keeps happening in the relationship, this pattern can take the form of physical abuse and coercive control. The victim slowly loses control of his life, and the abuser gains all the control.

It is not easy to see the signs of Gaslighting. As it is a slow process, the victim cannot believe in himself, often think they cannot trust their thinking, hence losing control of reality. Gaslighting can lead to

- Depression
- Anxiety
- Psychological trauma
- Isolation

In the long run, gaslighting can have adverse effects on the victim's emotional and psychological health. Makes it difficult for the victim to leave the abusive situation as they cannot trust their judgment.

Chapter 1: What Is Gaslighting?

YOUR thoughts, feelings AND Emotions ARE MINIMIZED

The stigma of mental illness makes it easy for people to minimize our emotions and get away with it. You're too sensitive. You're too emotional. When you express your emotions, you are rejected and unsupported. You always feel the need to apologize.

In the dialect, the expression "to gaslight" depicts falsifying other person's memories, facts, reality, and the environment around them to abuse them psychologically. Gaslighting is a form of emotional abuse. Victims are manipulated in a way that they stop trusting themselves, their emotions, and their thought process and start to depend on the abuser and turn against their cognition. Gaslighting is common in an abusive relationship, whether romantic or platonic and is not uncommon in workplaces, friendships, between parents and children. Gaslighting is a common form of abuse. According to CDC, 43 million women & 38 million will experience gaslighting from their intimate partner in their life.

Gaslighting happens gradually; people who are narcissists or toxic manipulate others to gain control and power over their lives. Victims can feel powerless and or confused at all times. If Gaslighting continues for a long time, it can cause depression, trauma, anxiety, and more. In 1944, the movie Gaslight was released. The movie shows an abusive husband who dims and brightens the lights around the house and convinces her wife that she is hallucinating. This manipulation and Gaslighting in the form of denying her sanity causes her to lose her faith in herself. Later, she discovers the truth, and the term "gaslighting" came from this movie. The term "gaslighting" first appeared in the academic journal about socializing of women. According to experts, back in the 1980s, women were made to think they needed romantic connections and relationships to survive. This need made them vulnerable to the gaslighters, which could take advantage of them by manipulating them and providing them with a connection.

Gaslighter makes the victim believe their senses, memories, or feelings are not accurate and do not align with their true feelings or memories, and the victim believes they are not mentally stable to take any action, or the mind is playing tricks. Thus, leading the victim to be dependent on the abuser as they cannot trust their judgment. The gaslighter achieves his purpose by manipulating the other person to the extent that their only choice is left to ask for help from the gaslighter. The classical sign of gaslighting is they say you are overreacting to the event to undermine your feelings.

Gaslighting is often elusive at first. Such as, if you are telling the story, the gaslighter will challenge one small detail, you will admit you can be wrong. You may argue back, often. They will further manipulate you into thinking they are right and you are wrong. Bit by bit, the gaslighter will try to convince you your whole memory is not serving you right; events did not happen in that way you remember. Eventually, there will come a day where you would not believe your memories. As every encounter with gaslighting is so insignificant at the start, you cannot look for a specific reason to be this uneasy. But, with time, you will start questioning your reality, your emotions, and your memories. Often seeking the Gaslighter's help to make you remember correctly. The gaslighter will definitely take advantage of this "trust."

If you have not properly researched gaslighting, many people will tell you it's a man hitting or abusing his wife. But, this is not the case. Gaslighting can be in many forms and situations, from the workplace, groups, romantic or platonic relationships. Anyone is at risk. According to a psychologist, although gaslighting may not be clearly seen when an outsider does so, but when a loved one falsifies your emotions, feelings, and memories, you feel crazy, inadequate, and bad at all times.

1.1 Why is Gaslighting So Dangerous?

Abuse does not have one shape or form, and it can take many forms and is present in any race, culture, sexual orientation, and religion. Abuse can be financial, mental, sexual, physical, or emotional. Withholding one's money and resources is also abuse. If the abuser hits, yells, or constantly puts the other person down, it is a severe form of abuse. All of these can be seen, heard, and felt instantly.

On the other hand, Gaslighting cannot be detected so easily. As it happens gradually and often comes from people we trust to challenge our judgment. Victims feel uneasy and overwhelmed. The self-doubting takes them long to realize what the abuser is doing and when they should seek help. They cannot believe that a loved one will do so. The signs are so subtle at first, almost no significance in them for the victim, then eventually their whole world starts crumbling down. According to a psychologist, the process of questioning yourself and the relationship with the gaslighter for the victim is the most hurtful. The victim has left with no sense of confidence, no self-esteem, and faces dreadful consequences in the long term. By the time the victim realizes what is happening, they either are back at square one of the relationship or trapped in a toxic situation with no way out.

In other ways, If the gaslighting continues for a long time. According to a psychologist, the victim does no longer trusts his perception. Instead, he trusts others' perceptions better. This can cause a feeling of being dependent on others, brain fog, helplessness, anxiety, PTSD, memory problems, and inability to make decisions. These conditions may not even go back to normal after the person has left the gaslighting situation. Gaslighting can leave permanent damage, but professional assistance is always there to help you recover. The victim maybe once was confident, self-assured, but the gaslighting leaves them with nothing. If you have experienced gaslighting, you can think about how your thought process has changed since then. A trained therapist will help the victim understand that what they experienced is not their fault. Therapists can also help them to set firm boundaries and get control of their lives back. The victim does not have to do all of this by themselves; they should get help.

Gaslighting never brings positive results, and it instills fear and distrust in others. It makes communities disperse, develops unfaithfulness among people, separation, and drives wedges. As the gaslighter has to tear down their defenses, get them alone to get them to listen to him and manipulate them. The gaslighter's number one weapon is to isolate the person, no matter if it in the form of a narcissistic spouse, boss, a marketing campaign, a treacherous politician, a scam, a criminal's defense, or a sales pitch.

Gaslighting works by tear down a person's defense, removing their original thoughts, emotions and replacing them with the gaslighter's objectives and ideals to gain complete control over another person's life. But we must learn to distinguish between negativity and gaslighting. Not all negativity or disagreement is gaslighting.

Gaslighting is the main part of the world's main ideologies and dictatorial ones. From communism to being alone, the world's elites tell us what we should believe, who our enemies are, as the population cannot decide for itself what should happen next. When this much pressure exists and people cannot rebel, they choose obliviousness rather than looking for the truth. Gaslighting and ignorance go perfectly with each other.

NDVH (National Domestic Violence Hotline) tells of few ways that an individual can gather proof if he suspects someone of gaslighting him.

Pictures: taking pictures can give them visual evidence of reality. Such as, you can take pictures of where you leave your keys or other belongings, so the gaslighter will not tell you, you left them somewhere else. If your mobile is not a safe place, buy a disposable camera.

Voice recordings: recording your phone conversations will give an advantage of what you said and how you remember it, or if someone else is trying to gaslight you by telling the conversation wrong. Try buying a voice recorder and keep it safe.

Written proof: you can keep a journal and write important things, dates and events so no one can gaslight you, or in case of gaslighting, you can confirm it for yourself if the abuser is lying.

Emailing: If the victim cannot hide the camera, journal, or pictures, they can store it online or email it to a trusted friend or family so they can keep it safe. You can gather the proof and send it via email, erase it from your side, not to make matters worse.

1.2 What's the psychological need Behind Gaslighting others?

Gaslighter's behavior comes from his need to gain control over people's lives, emotions, or things that could benefit them without working for the benefits and avoiding the consequences. Some narcissists who gaslight others often think they are doing you a favor and should be appreciated, and they may feel anxiety over losing you; hence they are doing what they are doing. Psychologically, their need to control the situation or the other person with manipulation and control is ingrained rather than with care or love.

Whether a person intentionally or unintentionally gaslights you, this behavior is destructive, and you should seek help as soon as possible. Gaslighters do not want you to have a personal life, have friends or make decisions for yourself, and they want you to be dependent on them. Making yourself and your mental health a priority is not possible. They want full control of your life and are not afraid to get it. Even your significant other can be gaslighting you; yes, although it sounds disturbing, it is possible.

Gaslighters' main purpose is to get control; that can only happen when you start to doubt yourself, your beliefs, convictions, and thoughts. It works by turning a confident person into an unconfident, confused person. Gaslighters instill this thought that every time you are wrong, you are the problem. They make you believe everyone else also thinks the same, and you should trust them above all. Such as, when a politician works the opposite of what his slogan is, he is making the country worse but argues he knows best. He pretends the country is doing great or at least better than before. The public is confused about what they should believe, what they see, or the politician's version of progress?

According to a psychologist, gaslighting behavior makes the abuser more in control and powerful. A gaslighter does not have the ability to sit and think about what they are doing or self-reflect. They can have low self-esteem, and they do not want to deal with this fact. Often, psychologists identify a gaslighter as a narcissist who does not have any remorse for what they are doing to their partner or others. As gaslighting can be done unconsciously or consciously. No matter the circumstances gaslighting cannot be justified, even if they do not realize they are doing it. Some people's only control is to gaslight others to gain control over their partner's life, thoughts, or emotions. Some psychologists also explain some people gaslight so much that it has become their second nature, and they have to work hard to change themselves.

Psychologists also compare gaslighting in relationships to social issues. According to them, gaslighting and white supremacy, misogyny is related or at least intersect in a manner. These behaviors are often encouraged and excused by people who are in power, and gaslighting is a behavior that keeps oppressed people oppressed as they do not have any access to help, resources, or change, and it keeps powerful positions in power place. In relationships the same manner can be seen, the one who gaslights have more control over the others' life and emotions. It becomes their new normal or correct behavior. The one in control overlooks the other person's emotion and feelings, keeping their position as they are.

1.3 Gaslighting & Narcissism

Not all gaslighters are narcissists, but all narcissists are gaslighters to some extent. Individuals who gaslight others can also have a narcissistic personality disorder. But, as said before, the person Gaslighting is unacceptable and abusive. There are psychologically many reasons why people abuse or gaslight others.

A narcissist, along with different tactics, can also use gaslighting as a weapon. So, before calling a gaslighter, a narcissist one has to look at their overall behavior. Do they have no remorse? Or no empathy? Or is their behavior exploitative? Do they act as they feel entitled? Is the abuse consistent? Or worsen over time without any reason? But again, all these factors do not matter much. What matters is if one person is horribly treating you, or you feel less of a person than before, or your confidence is shaken, or the other person puts you down. If you are constantly suffering from someone's behavior, it is time to accept they are an abusive person, whether a narcissist or a gaslighter. The bottom line is you are suffering, and it should not be that way.

Individuals who are narcissists think so highly of them whether they are being diagnosed with the NPD (narcissist personality disorder) or not. They like to abuse others as they are self-centered and do not have an interest in others' wellbeing until or unless it benefits them somehow. They cannot feel other's pain or care for them. A narcissist likes praise and attention, can demand if you do not act right (the way they want). They use manipulation and gaslighting as a way to achieve control over and undermine other lives, their feelings, and their emotions.

If you are not sure, the abuse is gaslighting or narcissism. Here are few signs for you. A narcissist will

- Respond with anger when criticized
- Thinks so highly of themselves
- Overstates their goals
- For their personal gain, they will use others
- Becomes easily jealous as they should be the one having 'that' or envious
- Very critical of others
- Think they deserve special treatment
- Gaslights others to gain control

The list does not end here, but you should recognize gaslighting if it happens to you or others around you. Seek professional help or help others in finding professional help. If you are the one doing gaslighting intentionally or unintentionally, and you want to change yourself. Seek professional help, and it is never too late to turn a new leaf.

Chapter 2: Process Behind And Signs of Gaslighting

GASLIGHTING RED FLAGS

You apologize without knowing what you did wrong. Sorry

There is an imbalance of power.

They give you affection... then abruptly yank it away.

They assign motives to your actions that are the opposite of your intentions.

When you try to explain how you feel, they're dismissive. You are "overreacting" or "too sensitive."

Most interactions leave you feeling small or ashamed.

They insist it didn't happen that way. Yes. Maybe. I don't Know.

You find yourself questioning your beliefs & opinions. If your point of view doesn't match theirs, it's wrong.

You edit every word before you speak it, changing any thought that they could possibly misconstrue.

Gaslighting is a manipulative tactic that changes the victim's whole perception of reality. The victim will start second-guessing everything, from their emotions, feelings, events, and perceptions to their own self-worth. If the victim talks with the gaslighter, the gaslighter will make sure the victim cannot see what is going on and instead thinks of himself as the problem for everyone, thus choosing to isolate.

Gaslighting tactic can make you confuse, lose your grip on reality, and makes you question your mental health. This is a close look at how someone can gaslight you. Observe others if you have a suspension on them, or look around you if someone is gaslighting the other person.

2.1 How Gaslighting Works?

Here are few tactics you should look out for.

Lying

Individuals who are gaslighting others are pathological and habitual liars. Gaslighters will lie to your face without backing down or changing the story. Asking for proof of their lie is not enough to make them back down. Lying is the basis of their gaslighting behavior. Even though you tell them, 'I think you are lying.' They are still convincing and tell lies with conviction that your truth might start to sound like a lie. You will be left with self-doubt as to did it think it wrong, and maybe they are telling the truth.

Dishonoring

Gaslighters will spread gossip and rumors about you. They will show that they care for you, but on the other hand, will tell others you are very emotionally unstable or suspect others of lying. This is such a powerful manipulative dark tactic that instead of clearing the rumor up with you, people will avoid you in order not to make you go off on them. People will be on the gaslighter's side as he seems to know how to handle you. At the same time, the gaslighter will tell you others think you are crazy. Although these people may have never said anything bad about you, he will make sure that you know they think you are crazy.

Diverting blame

If you ask a gaslighter about something they did or when they lied. They will change the subject by asking you another question or diverting your attention to another important matter; you will forget about it for the time being. Or when asked, they will lie with calmness and say: "you remember it wrong, that is not the way things happened" thus, they are not the ones to blame for this matter. You will be dazed as to what just happened?

Overlooking your feelings & thoughts

For gaining control over your emotions, the gaslighter will minimize your emotions. They will often say during arguments, "you are overreacting," "calm down," or "why are you so emotional?". All of these declarations minimize what you are feeling, thinking, or wants to communicate. Making you feel you are doing something wrong when you are just expressing your feelings. You are dealing with a gaslighter who does not recognize your beliefs, thoughts, or emotions. You start questioning yourself if you are overreacting? You will never feel understood or validated, as it is extremely difficult to live with a gaslighter

Shifting Blame

This is another tactic of gaslighters. In every argument or even in the discussion, you are the one to blame for anything that has happened. In some cases, where you just want to talk about what they make you feel, they will end up blaming you for their behavior. They are great manipulators in every situation. Gaslighter will even tell you are the reason for how they behave, appalling, I know. According to gaslighters, if you behave differently, they will have to treat you like this.

Overlooking their wrongdoings

Gaslighters and abusers are famous for overlooking and denying anything they do wrong. They do not want any responsibility; thus, no consequences for their bad choices. This way, the victim feels extremely hurt as they gaslight and never admit what they did wrong, no acknowledgment of hurting you. The overlooking or denying their own mistakes makes it hard for the victim to move on or heal from this experience.

Saying Compassionate Words as Weapons

In some situations, when a gaslighter is questioned, they will say loving and kind words to defuse the situation as calmly as possible. They will say, "you know how much I care for you; how can I do this?" I know you would like to hear these words, but they do not hold true meaning, especially when the hurt is happening for the hundredth time. If you are in such a situation, try to seek help as you are gaslighted. The person is manipulating you for their own benefit. Pay attention to what they say and what they do. Do their actions match their words? The gaslighter will not love you, only just say the right words.

Reframing & twisting dialogue

If something has happened in the past, gaslighters will twist the dialogue when discussing it in the present. Such as, if your spouse shoved you against the door and now you are discussing it, they will change the situation and say they did it to save you from falling, as you were about to fall, so they shoved you. You will not be able to wrap your head around it. You remember the story differently. As it will happen any time, if not every time, and you will be the one to blame each time, you will start to doubt your sanity that if you remember events wrong. Your second-guessing and confusion is their success.

2.2 Gaslighting Tactics to Watch Out For!

Gaslighting can happen in many ways, and sometimes it is about manipulating the environment or surrounding behind the victim's back. On the other hand, gaslighting can completely emotional and verbal abuse. Gaslighters become skilled at pushing your buttons, as they have control over your vulnerabilities and sensitivities, using these against you. Slowly they will make you question your sanity, your beliefs, and your memories.

These are some famous tactics of gaslighting.

Withholding: In this case, the gaslighter will refuse to understand what you are saying or does not want to listen. This way, they do not have to reply or engage in a conversation they do not feel like. Some examples of a gaslighter saying, "This is so confusing, I do not understand." "I have no idea what you are talking about." "I do not have any time to listen to your nonsense."

Diverting: in this case, the gaslighter will not listen to what one has to say. Instead, they will change the subject or question your sincerity and not listen to the content. This is also known as blocking. One example is "this is one of your friends' crazy ideas." Or "have you been talking to your mother again? She always gives you stupid ideas".

Forgetting or denying: in this classic tactic, the gaslighter will forget something happened or deny that it never happened or forgets part of it. If you accuse them of something they did in the past, the gaslighter will say, "you are just making things up." Or say, "What are you talking about? I never promised anything like this".

Countering: in this case, the gaslighter will question your memory just to make you confused even though you remember the details correctly. They will say things such as, "you do not have a good memory. Or are you sure?" Or "you are unable to remember anything correctly." Making you conscious of yourself. They will say," you often do this; this is not how this happened."

Trivializing: In this scenario, the gaslighter will act as if your emotions or feelings are irrational or unimportant. Your concern for yourself is your overthinking. Disregarding or belittling your feelings. The gaslighter will say, "Why are you so sensitive? Everyone else laughed; my joke was funny and did not belittle you".

Stereotyping: according to one study in American Sociological Review found, a gaslighter will consciously use negative stereotyping. Gaslighter will use anyone's nationality, age, gender, sexuality, race, or ethnicity and tell them people think you are crazy if you seek therapist help (if you are a female).

2.3 Situations of Gaslighting

Between parents and child, these situations can show gaslighting.

As a parent, gaslighting tactic will sound like: "you are not hungry; you just ate lunch." According to a psychologist, parents challenge their child's feelings or reality in a subtle way so that the kid will obey them, but the long-term consequences are dangerous. One example is when a child and a father are playing in a park. The father has instructed his child not to go anywhere, but the kid ran away. He tripped and fell, hurting himself. Rather than comforting the child, the father will say angrily, "why did you do this? Look at this mess you have made." Accusing the child, he did it on purpose. From this example, according to a psychologist, we can see, the issue is not the boy who ran away. Instead, the father's behavior made the child feel like his feeling of being hurt is invalidated or wrong. Instead of being careful the next time, the child learned there is something wrong with him.

In a romantic situation, the gaslighter will say: "I did it because I love you."

This statement is supposed to show you love. Some abusers or gaslighters think they are doing what is best for the other person by manipulating them, thinking they know better, and feeling they know the victim better than the victim knows himself.

One example is when a woman applies for a job and is very excited and has succeeded in 2 to 3 interviews, and 1 or 2 sessions remain. She is working hard and proud of herself; all of a sudden, the company stops responding or contacting her. Her husband tells her he does not think this is the right position for her, or this job is not good enough for her. So, without consulting with her, he contacted the company and told them she is not interested. When she contacted the company, she was informed her husband said she is not interested. When she confronts her husband, he will tell her, "I know you better than yourself, and I knew you would not be happy there."

As these incidents happen, after some time, the victim will start questioning herself if the abuser knows her better than she knows herself? Eventually, she will stop making decisions for herself and letting the abuser control her life, more and more with each incident.

In another situation, the gaslighter will say, when asked about cheating: "you are so paranoid; I am not cheating."

According to a psychologist, gaslighters love to change the reality of others by denying their feelings. They will make the victim a problem instead of changing their attitude. Despite cheating on their significant others, many gaslighters will tell their partners they are sensitive or are too jealous or insecure when asked about their inappropriate relations. And when caught red-handed, the gaslighter will say he did it because their partner is too frigid. When asked him why he is not emotionally available to his partner, he would say it is all of his partner's fault, as the victim did not give him what he needed, and all of a sudden, the discussion is about how incompetent his partner is rather than his cheating. This way, the partner will eventually blame herself rather than the husband.

In another scenario, the gaslighter will say to isolate you: "no one will ever love you but me."

According to a psychologist, isolating you is the number one goal on the domestic abuser's list, and it is achieved by gaslighting you. Your trusted family and friends are the ones who can see the situation for what it really is. Thus, the gaslighter does not want you to be connected to them, so no one can tell you what the gaslighter is doing, so by controlling your thoughts, feelings and by breaking you down, they get to isolate you.

One example is a gaslighter boyfriend who instructed his girlfriend not to go with her friends by saying her friends did not like him and talk bad behind her back. He can go as far as to delete texts or calls by making his girlfriend feel no one can love her like him or the only person who loves her. Gaslighter just does not want to be the main relationship. Instead, the gaslighter wants to be the only relationship for her girlfriend. But the gaslighter will maintain his outside relationship but will isolate you. When you feel alone, the gaslighter will tell you they are with you, and no one else is.

When they abuse you, the Gaslighter will tell you they you made them do this.

If the gaslighter gives you the silent treatment or becomes extremely angry with you. These are the two ways the gaslighter will punish you for gaining control over your life. Such as, when one couple goes on a vacation with their kids, they get in a fight on the first night. After a shrieking match, the husband gets out and stays out the whole night. The next morning, he returns and behaves alright with the kids but does not acknowledge his wife, completely ignores her for the rest of the trip. After few days, the wife is so frustrated with his behavior that she will apologize for anything even when it is not her mistake in the first place, will beg for his forgiveness. According to experts, silent treatment is the crucial gaslighting tactic that denies your existence or your reality and makes you frustrated.

Gaslighters, when acting like a narcissist, will say, "you are too sensitive."

Some gaslighters, gaslights others because this is the only way to know how to behave. They were raised in a dysfunctional family where gaslighting was common, and they use gaslighting to achieve anything. When in adult life, the gaslighters get their high when gaslighting others, and this is the most familiar feeling for them, and it brings them pleasure. It can be seen in many ways, such as in close friendships where one friend needs love, affection, adoration, and gifts. This person will gaslight the other friend, so they keep providing for them.

One more example is two friends from childhood, and one would always belittle the other, tell him he is not good at anything, is ugly, and has bad social skills. After a long time, when they go to different colleges, the victim would realize all of this was never true. The gaslighter belittled him so that he would keep being his friends rather than friends with other people. In reality, he was jealous of his potential, so the gaslighter kept him from seeing his own value and so make himself feel better; he disparages the victim.

According to a psychologist, most gaslighters are narcissists. Thus, they need constant attention. Even if one provides them with a hundred percent of care and love, it will never be enough, and they will find a way to make you feel you are not good enough.

2.4 Signs You're Being Gaslighted

Some signs of being gaslighted are:

- You will start second-guessing your reality or feelings, and you tell yourself this person's behavior is not that bad. Maybe I am just sensitive. According to a psychologist, this is one of the major signs of gaslighting. The abuser will challenge your feelings, your thoughts, your behavior, and much more. One of the alarming signs is you will feel confused as to what you see is not what it is, and what you are experiencing is not real.

- You do not believe your perception or judgment; you feel like there is no point in speaking your emotions, as you are wrong at all times. Sharing any opinion just makes the gaslighter mad, so you decide to stay quiet.

- You are always being lied to. Lies are a great tool for gaslighters to manipulate. Gaslighters are always lying, making you feel wrong. The lies are persistent. Do you catch the other person lying often? Chances are they are gaslighting or at least manipulating you.

- By breaking down your spirit, the gaslighter makes you feel insecure. Just to have full control over you, the gaslighter will make you feel insecure. According to a psychologist, if someone is breaking you down, you can ask yourself. What they are saying is making you feel bad? Do they always criticize one thing that is your weakness, and they know about it?

- Around the gaslighter, you have to walk on eggshells. Anything you do or say can be taken out of context. You have no self-confidence in yourself as to what you are saying is true or not. You feel insecure.

- A gaslighter will try to isolate you from people who care about you. According to one psychologist, gaslighters do this because they want to control your life. They want to isolate you so the people who love you would not be able to tell you the truth.

- You feel there is no one around you who understands you. Furthermore, people around you think you are unstable, crazy, strange, as the gaslighter has told you. You feel powerless, alone, or trapped.

- Sometimes you think, you may be crazy or stupid. The gaslighters' words make you feel uneasy, insane, or inadequate. Often you find yourself agreeing to these things that you are insecure, crazy, or stupid.

- Once, you used to be strong and assertive, but now you may hate yourself or at least do not like yourself. You have become disappointed in yourself; it feels like a failure.

- You always feel confused as you cannot get the details right, or at least the gaslighter tells you so, you cannot remember events, their actions do not match their words.

- You feel you are too sensitive, the gaslighter's words hurt you, or their behavior is insensitive to your needs, and they justify it by saying, "I am kidding." Or "why have you become too sensitive."

- You have anxiety, and you always feel something bad will happen when you are around the gaslighter. You can never do anything right. You can also feel threatened or on edge without any reason.

- You apologize a lot, like all the time. Even when it is not your mistake, you find yourself apologizing. You apologize to others also as you sense they can see you do everything wrong.

- You feel you are never enough. You can never live up to the demands and expectations of your gaslighters, although these demands are maybe unreasonable.

- As you feel inadequate, you have stopped sharing your details with others, as the gaslighter has convinced you, your details are always wrong. Things never happen as you remember them. You feel worried about sharing with others.

- Sometimes you think, "what is wrong with me?". Others are not like me; they are so confident, but you think something is seriously wrong with you. You are going crazy, and nothing makes sense anymore.

- You do not want to make a decision, as they can be wrong. You want the other person who has control over your life to make decisions for you, or you never want to make decisions.

Gaslighting Statements

In a toxic or abusive relationship, gaslighting happens slowly. At first, you meet a gaslighter, and they look like everyone else. But with time, they say statements like these.

- You always imagine things.

- You are so sensitive.
- Do not overreact again.
- I do know what you are talking about.
- I did not say that.
- Why are you trying to confuse me?
- After trying to minimize your feelings, they will say, "Now you are going to feel sorry for yourself."
- Telling you lies, your friends do not like you or talk behind your back by saying, "you have no idea, but your family talks about you and thinks you are going crazy."
- Saying one thing and later denying they said it, such as, "I never agreed to deposit the money in the bank; it was your duty. Thanks to you, now we do not have enough money."
- Manipulating your environment behind your back and then saying, "you cannot find your keys again, shocking how many times you forget stuff."
- They will keep on insisting on the lies they are telling by proving you wrong, "we never went to that show; if I were, I would remember."

Often it is not easy to tell you are experiencing abuse. A psychologist also advises not to discuss being gaslighted by the same person you suspect is gaslighting you. If the person is in authority, you may not feel comfortable talking to them about this, as they are more likely to dismiss you. Or things can get out of control, try to seek professional help, or confined to someone who you trust and the person who listens to you calmly and does not put you down.

Gaslighting can happen in any environment. According to a piece of writing in "Politics, Groups, & Identities," Racial gaslighting can also happen; when people speak against racial oppression, they are labeled as deluded, crazy, or irrational.

Some examples of racial gaslighting are:

- Downplaying any racist accidents
- Completely Denying how events took place
- Immigrants are more likely to encounter racial gaslighting

Gaslighters will criticize how a person is expressing his opinion rather than listening to his message. If an individual has just arrived in a different country and, of course, he is not familiar with its culture, laws, and language. Thus, it is easier for a gaslighter to lie to this person about his legal rights and tell what is normal or what is not. One example is when an immigrant gets a job and is not fully aware of his rights, and his superior might tell him he has no right to protest in this working environment. One more example is the gaslighter will tell the immigrant that authorities are keeping an eye on him for no reason to confuse or make him second guess his choices.

According to NDVH (National Domestic Violence Hotline), if someone is being gaslighted, they will:

- Ask themselves if I am sensitive?
- Does not socialize or becomes withdrawn
- Keep apologizing to the gaslighter
- Defend the abuser's attitude & behavior
- Confused & second guess themselves
- Cannot make decisions for themselves
- Lie to their friends, family to avoid arguments about the abuser
- Feel insecure, joyless, incompetent, or hopeless

2.5 Why & how Gaslighting Happens?

According to a psychologist, initially, abusers do not start gaslighting with full force; if they will, the victims will know exactly what is happening and leave immediately. Instead, the gaslighter starts slow, and this is where the unreality of the victim's situation and confusion comes from. In most cases, the gaslighting relationships start as fairy tales.

In the beginning, the gaslighter will "love bomb" you, meaning they will give you gifts, attention, affection so that you will trust them. As they have built this bond with you, it is easy to move past your defenses, know your vulnerability, and criticize you. The first red flag you can see on the first date is they will ask many personal questions, try to get intimate with you very quickly, declare they love you, shower you with gifts.

According to a psychologist, people want to control a relationship, whether platonic or romantic, for a number of reasons. Some of them are listed below:

Gaslighter believes it is the only method to keep the relationship. They will go to any length just to keep that person around, even if it is abuse. They think there is no other way this person would be with me; it shows their low self-esteem.

Gaslighters feel better about themselves when they have control over someone else's life. They feel if I can control someone's life, I am good at what I do. They feel powerful, and this negative use of power comes out in relationships.

Gaslighters like having control and power. According to research, gaslighters and some people find pleasure in having control and power over others.

According to NDVH (National Domestic Violence Hotline), this is a checklist you should look out for. It will guide you to make the right choice about your circumstances.

- Do you keep second-guessing yourself?

- Do you have no hope?
- Do you think you have become too sensitive after being with the person (gaslighter)? Or do they make you feel you are too sensitive?
- Most of the time, you feel like you are going crazy?
- Do you have to lie to avoid other's criticism?
- Do you feel like a failure who cannot do anything?
- Do you feel insecure, like you are not good enough?
- Are you always apologizing or upsetting the gaslighter?
- Do you feel like making no decisions?
- Do you not feel happy even when you have so much?
- Are you always making excuses for the abuser?
- Is confusion a daily thing for you?
- Do you have this overpowering feeling that something is wrong and have no idea what it is?
- Do you find yourself withholding information for your close friends and family so you do not have to lie?
- You used to be relaxed, happier, confident, and more fun-loving before starting this relationship/ job/ or friendship.

2.6 Personal Signs of Gaslighting

If you think you are a victim of gaslighting, these are some signs you should look for within yourself.

You are focused on your shortcomings: gaslighting works to make you think less of yourself. To change your perception of yourself and make it a negative one. So, one may find themselves obsessed with their negative traits or how they cannot do one thing. They will believe that something is wrong with you or your shortcomings makes you unlovable or unlikeable. The gaslighter does this so you will think less of yourself and stick with them as they are the only one who puts up with you, no one else would love you or want to be your friend.

Your self-confidence is at rock bottom: You can see where this is coming from; you will notice you have such low self-esteem that you accept disrespect from others and the gaslighter. You do not believe in yourself or your abilities, and you believe you cannot get happiness or deserve happiness. So, you turn down new openings for your career, make new friends, to socialize with others because you believe you are so unlovable.

You keep second-guessing yourself: you actually now forget things; where did you put the milk? In fridge or cupboard? So you have to double-check. You do not believe your memories or your ability to do simple tasks, so you think something is wrong with yourself, or you are going crazy. Yes, the gaslighter has achieved his goal of making you feel that way. Now, it is easier to manipulate further by denying your feelings, calling you crazy, insecure, and you will believe it.

You feel very confused: you feel confused all the time about every matter in your life. It varies from general issues to specific issues, and now you do not want to make the gaslighter angry by doing something wrong. So the anxiety or constant state of fear is permanent.

You cannot make any decisions: with all this second-guessing and confusion, you cannot decide for yourself. You are dependent on the gaslighter to make any sort of decision. You do not believe in your decision-making abilities. The gaslighting happens in a way, so you sought out the gaslighter for everything. They created this mess, and then they present themselves as the ultimate problem solver. You are so grateful to them because you have no idea what would you do without them or who would you turn to?

You are always apologizing: you feel something is wrong, and it is because of you, so who ends up apologizing for the mess? Yes, you. It has been fed to you that you cannot do anything right by the gaslighter. No matter who is at fault, you are to blame, and then you have to apologize.

The gaslighter does not take any responsibility for their actions or their behavior. If their behavior is bad, it is because of you.

In your mind, you are a disappointment: you always feel people do not like you, or they think you are not worthy of love. You feel you are the source of disappointment, as you do not even believe in yourself. Again you are focused on your flaws, and you feel your shortcomings are so many than your good traits. In simple words, you are not good enough. Thus, stems your need to apologize all the time.

You barely remember the person you once were: in the back of your mind, you can remember but very little of the person you once were, confident, full of life, so sure of themselves. But now, you are just a shell of a person you once were. You cannot recognize yourself. You feel disconnected from that beautiful past, and it does not match with who you are now. When you look back, it feels like a different life of a different person but not you.

You make excuses for the abusive person: when others see the gaslighter behaving with you in a bad manner. You then make excuses for them and tell people it is not how it looks. Indeed, it is worse. You always defend their behavior even in your head because you believe you deserve this, and they have a total right to treat you this way.

You always lie to others & yourself to avoid conflict: you now feel anxiety about confronting anyone because the gaslighter has trained you that you will be defeated and blamed during any argument. So you lie to avoid arguments and do not call people out on their bad behavior. You do not have the power to say no you always agree on things you do not like. You do not even question them anymore; you just agree. Things can go as far as acting against your beliefs and morals.

You think you are so sensitive: as you spend most of the time overthinking and thinking negatively about yourself.

You think you are so sensitive. You think you overreact to small things and events; even if you feel the gaslighter or other people are rude, you do not complain and probably think you are just sensitive.

Whenever you are around the gaslighter, you feel anxious: as soon as the gaslighter enters the room, you feel tense. This is your subconscious mind's effect on the psychological and emotional abuse you have encountered. Your body prepares flight & fight response in case more gaslighting is coming.

You feel anxious like something is wrong, but you cannot point it out: your subconscious mind knows this person is not good for you. But, you are too deep in the gaslighting to see things. Clearly, your mind knows the issue but does not know how to address it. Because the gaslighter has made you believe in this relationship, romantic or platonic, that you are to blame or things are bad because of you.

If you feel any of this, remember you are not alone. You can always reach out to trusted family or friends, and they will listen to you. If you do not feel safe talking to them, make sure to reach out to a therapist or professional help even if you think this is not gaslighting and you are just confused, there is no shame in seeking help.

Chapter 3: Recognizing a Gaslighter

WARNING SIGNS OF GASLIGHTING

1. DENYING WHAT THEY PREVIOUSLY SAID AND ASKING YOU TO PROVE IT, SO YOU START TO DOUBT YOUR MEMORY

2. CRITICIZING WHAT YOU LOVE TO THE EXTENT THAT YOU START QUESTIONING YOUR IDENTITY

3. OBVIOUSLY LYING TO YOUR FACE IN A DEMEANOR THAT MAKES YOU UNSURE OF ANYTHING THEY SAY

4. OCCASIONALLY DOING NICE THINGS FOR YOU SO YOU STAY CONFUSED

5. PROJECTING BY ACCUSING YOU OF THE THINGS THEY MIGHT BE DOING (I.E. LYING) SO YOU ARE CONSTANTLY TRYING TO DEFEND YOURSELF

6. SAYING SOMETHING COMPLETELY DIFFERENT THAN WHAT THEY ARE ACTUALLY DOING

Gaslighting is hidden manipulation that is very effective and successful at making other people lose their mind and their reality. Anyone can become a target of gaslighting. These gaslighting tactics are present in history and used by cult leaders, domestic abusers, narcissists, dictators, manipulators who still use them. The most successful gaslighter is the one that is very difficult to detect; you can only tell they are a gaslighter by looking at the victim's mental health and his actions. If you want to protect yourself, you have to know much about gaslighters. What they say, how they behave. How can you recognize them? So, you can steer clear of them.

3.1 Who becomes a gaslighter?

People who do these gaslighting tactics most of the time have a personality disorder. It can be psychopathy, NPD (narcissistic personality disorder), dark manipulators, or others. Many manipulators will show one face to the victim and another better face to the world. They make sure that the victim knows if they asked for help from others or tell others that they have been emotionally or mentally abused, no one would believe that they did this, as everyone knows them as the good guy. Gaslighters have the same pattern of abuse in many relationships.

What's the dissimilarity between gaslighting & manipulation or narcissism?

The key part of gaslighting is manipulation, but manipulation is a common technique in itself. Everyone is capable of manipulating others. Not all manipulators are gaslighters. Kids manipulate their parents to get what they want from the very beginning. Businesses do the manipulation to make you buy stuff that you do not need. On the other hand, gaslighting is a mental or psychological abuse with the intention not only to influence them but get complete control of their life after isolating them.

On the other hand, a narcissistic personality has to gaslight others, as he possesses some of the traits of gaslighting personality. But gaslighting does not envelope his whole narcissistic personality. Anyone who is a narcissist feels good about themselves, by self-promoting and feeling superior, gaslighters shakes other person's reality and make them question their own self-worth.

Individuals who use these tricks or tactics become gaslighters.

Trick no. 1: they take control of your reality.

At its core, gaslighting is dominating the other person's reality that they are not able to trust themselves or start questioning their judgment. The control of reality has a different level, from minor scale telling your child they do not feel sad because they just watched a movie, denying the child's feeling. To a larger scale of control, when in 2015, a man got married and posted his wedding pictures on social media then told his long-term partner that it was a creation of her imagination. According to gaslighters, if you tell a lie often enough, it becomes a truth or someone's reality.

Trick no. 2: they do not want to damage you (according to them); they want to feel in control.

What a gaslighter wants to psychologically challenge you, put you in a mindset where things are easier for them to control, and they will do as they please.

For the very same purpose, gaslighting may not always be intentional. It stems from one's need to control the other person and situation psychologically. They gaslight so you cannot challenge them, so the situation can proceed as they want. They do not want to be accountable, or think of consequences or take any responsibility.

Trick no 3. Gaslighter's motives are often driven by sexism.

Yes, gaslighting can happen to anyone from anyone; it is not always driven by gender. But, in most cases, gaslighting is used as a weapon to abuse women emotionally, and it works because of the crazy, jealous, incapable stereotypes against women. In 2014, at Indianan University, a paper published by a female student discovered that the other male students ranked the women based on their attractiveness. When she told them how inappropriate the list was, she was told, "you are too sensitive," or she is keeping a strict eye on innocent talk among male friends; she is insecure about where she is on the attractiveness list, she totally is insecure. Just so the men could keep acting how they wanted, they labeled her a "crazy, insecure woman."

Now, you see what happened there. If any woman tells others about sexist conduct, gaslighters will use the stereotyping method to gaslight her feelings, label her crazy, jealous, or insecure. Rather than actually listening to her, each of her complaints may be looked at as too sensitive or dismiss as trivial misinterpretation. In this way, sexist people do not have to correct themselves or hold themselves accountable, just like gaslighters. They will just say she is one of these overly emotional women who is just insecure; we do not have to listen to her.

Trick no. 4: they will make arguments impossible.

Once gaslighters have undermined you, any disagreement from your side is not important to have a conversation about. They will make you feel you are losing your mind, being crazy, are unstable, a liar, or a failure, so anything you say goes against you. Thus, you are not in a position to disagree; the more you will try to prove yourself right, the more you will fall into their net of gaslighting.

Trick no. 5: they will make you agree with their perception of things.

Any gaslighter would like to be in control and would like people to fit according to their principles. They need the victim of their gaslighting to agree with them. If they sexually harass someone, and in their mind, it is just two people having fun. They will want the victim to agree with them that it is just for fun, so they will undermine the victim's feelings and change her reality, making her agree with him. If the victim does not agree, she is crazy, too sensitive, or just insecure or wants attention.

3.2 What a Gaslighter Will Say?

These are some of the famous phrases gaslighters loves to say, and when they want to gaslight you, they will say these:

- You are just too sensitive.
- You are overreacting
- You are always telling wrong stories
- If you were listening...
- Only if you were paying attention...
- Now, I have to tell you again, and you are incapable of remembering details
- You always make a big deal of things when it is nothing
- You are never paying attention
- You do not make any sense right now
- You do not know how to listen.
- You are too emotional
- We discussed this; you always forget.
- You always imagine things
- Why cannot you communicate clearly?
- You are irrational
- You do not know how to take a joke
- You are always jumping to conclusions
- Stop being so sensitive all the time
- Do not take me so seriously all the time.
- Are you even listening to yourself right now?
- I tell you how it is.
- You are the only one who argues with me on this topic
- You are paranoid like always
- I know what you are thinking
- Do not read too much into this, and it is not that serious

- You always get upset when I am joking.
- You are acting crazy
- You never think clearly
- You always make yourself the victim. Instead, I should be mad.
- I was kidding, and you always take things personally
- You know you are talking absolute nonsense, right?
- This is not what happened, or this is not what I said
- I do not believe you, and you are always lying.
- This is not a good time to talk
- If you say something like this, what does it say about you?
- Everyone will think you are crazy.

Will you notice the main theme in their statements? They will start the dialogue with you because gaslighters are well aware of your insecurities and would love to undermine your feelings so that the fight will leave your system, and you would believe what they have to say without even acknowledging their own actions and how it is affecting others or you. Becoming aware of gaslighting and psychological abuse is a necessary step of moving forward or healing, even if you are not a victim of gaslighting. You should be able to differentiate between arguing and gaslighting.

3.3 The Warning Signs of Gaslighting

The following behavior and traits will suggest a person is trying to gaslight you or another person. Gaslighting is much common in relationships.

White lies

If a person is telling you a white lie that you know is false. It is a possibility they might be gaslighting you. Yes, it is true that not all white lies are equal, but the gaslighter must tell white lies for gaslighting. It will be a transparent false statement as compared to a confused mistakenness.

One example of this is if you are at the louver observing the famous Mona Lisa, and your partner tells you that the Mona Lisa is painted by Donatello, but you know this is not the truth because it was painted by Leonardo Da Vinci. It is because your partner is mistaken. But if your partner is insistent that your favorite painting is The Starry Night instead of the Mona Lisa, and you know your favorite painting is the Mona Lisa, but your partner keeps insisting, and you have told her before this is not the case. It is a white lie and form of gaslighting. Your partner's insistence will actually weaken your reality.

Denying the proof

Denying when the proof is present is one of the classic signs of gaslighting. Gaslighters will be insistent that they are telling the truth, even if you have proof. Gaslighters do this to change your perception of reality and to make you doubt yourself.

One example is when a wife tells her husband to take the trash out before going to work. He hears her but goes right to work without taking the trash out. The wife also goes to work. When she comes home, she sees he hasn't taken the trash out; she gets angry takes the trash out herself. When he comes home, she asks, why did you not take the trash out? The husband would insist that he took the trash out, and the wife is saying she did just now. But the husband is lying despite the proof, and it is shaking the wife's reality after a while.

Manipulating your feelings

A gaslighter will twist and manipulate your feelings towards the things you like or towards people. With this tactic, they reduce their competition or the people who can actually see the truth. This way, the person will be dependent on the gaslighter. One example will be if your partner likes to disrupt your relationship with your parents as you are close with them, which is an example of gaslighting. The gaslighter will lie to you, manipulate your feeling towards your parents so you will not be contacting them. He will say your mother does not like him or says something mean to him. When you ask your mother if she said something mean to him, she will deny it. Now your partner will say she is also a liar. He will say everyone is a liar except for him; by saying this, they challenge your reality, feeling, identity, and being. He has successfully gaslighted you and your reality.

They tear down your defenses

This is one of gaslighting tactics that makes it so dangerous. As it happens gradually and the effects are long-lasting on the victim's psychology, perception, reality, conscience by wearing down your defenses. One analogy is when you remove a single grain of sand from a heap of sand, it does not affect the heap. But over time, all of the grains will be gone, and there will be no sand left.

Actions & words do not match each other

When someone gaslights you, but you are not sure. It is crucial to observe if their actions and words match, observe what they tell you, and show you. The gaslighting only work if you listen to what they have to say instead look at their actions. Words have the power to shatter your reality. Gaslighters are using their words to distract you from their actions.

One common example is when politicians make big promises before an election. After winning the election, they will do against the thing they promised. When asked about it, they will make more other promises and gaslight all of their followers.

3.4 Signs of Gaslighting in A Relationship

The most common gaslighting happens in a couple who is romantically involved. Gaslighter and the victim will show the world that their relationship is perfect but is it indeed not. Gaslighting blows true love and affection out of the relationship.

Your reality does not seem real

Yes, every relationship is different, and everyone faces different challenges. Most of the time, it also means looking at your own behavior. But, when you keep second-guessing your reality to the point where you think anything you see is a lie, and no matter how hard you try, you feel like you are losing it. It is a classic sign of gaslighting. According to a psychologist, the most damaging thing about gaslighting is it makes it hard for the victim to trust themselves. It can happen slowly; the victim cannot immediately spot it; however, you keep feeling like you are losing it or keep thinking what you feel is valid. It is a major sign of gaslighting.

Your partner trivializes your feelings

When one partner shares their feelings or expresses concern, the gaslighter; the other partner will convince them they are overthinking or they are mistaken. If this relationship were healthy, one partner would have listened to the other calmly and address them. He will make sure his partner feels at ease or mentally does not have any conflict. According to a clinical therapist, gaslighters often tell their partner that they are so sensitive or they do not have a right to feel this way. Some of them will go that far as even to deny their feelings.

During a conflict, the gaslighter does not let you talk.

If you find yourself in the middle of a disagreement with a gaslighter, you will find they are continually cutting you off. You will not get a chance to explain yourself. If you keep finding yourself writing long texts or emails explaining your point of view because face to face, you will get a chance to explain yourself. Chances are your partner is gaslighting you.

When a gaslighter hurts you, they will not apologize.

If your partner hurts you, you express it to them; they lack empathy and do not listen to you or apologize. This is one big red flag. On the other hand, if your partner convinces you that what you are feeling is wrong or is not right, you have no right. This is a sign of gaslighting. According to a psychologist, if you are making yourself crazy or exhausting yourself to justify what you feel is valid to your partner. If you have to work hard just to get yourself listened to, you are being gaslighted.

Your partner will blame you or other circumstances instead of taking responsibility.

Most of the time, if your partner blames you whenever you disagree or blames outside factors or actions, it is a sign of gaslighting. According to a psychologist, when complaining to a gaslighter, they will change the topic instead of addressing the issue at hand or discussing what they have done. Some partners may start belittling you and tell you "you are so sensitive" to avoid conflict.

You will feel your efforts are going to waste

If you are in a relationship with a gaslighter, at one point, you will start feeling no matter what you do, and it is not enough. Your efforts are futile. The gaslighter has minimized, denied your efforts. Always the blame is on you whenever you try to voice your concerns. With each passing incident, it becomes your true feelings that you are the one who is at fault. In healthy relationships, both partners will make mistakes and apologize when wrong. According to psychologists, if the blame is always one-sided, it is a sign that the relationship's theme is based on control and power.

If you use your voice, you often feel guilty

In a gaslighting relationship, at one point, sharing your feelings becomes extremely difficult, or it always has been. According to a therapist, if even the thought of telling a concern or telling your actual feelings to your partner makes you feel guilty, it is a sign of your relationship. It is based on control, and that is a key factor of gaslighting. You should pay attention to it; feeling voiceless in the relationship is a sign of being suppressed; it is gaslighting.

Some other examples of gaslighting in a relationship are:

In every gaslighting relationship, there is an avoidance of taking responsibility for the gaslighter.

One example is a couple who become a couple after being friends. As soon as they started dating, partner A started complaining that the other person is not spending enough time with her. When outside with other friends, Partner B will treat partner A platonically and flirt with others. It will make partner A confused, and she initiated a conversation with her partner about their developing relationship. When partner A brought up her worries of flirting with others and asked partner B to spend more time with her, partner B was upset. As he is a gaslighter, he will say, "you always act like I do not care about you" or "is it my fault if I want to make new friends." Partner B made partner A feel she is wrong for demanding an explanation for her valid concerns.

3.4.1 Stop gaslighting in a relationship

Always seek professional support to validate your experience

According to therapists, seeking support from reliable people outside of the relationship is vital to validate your experience of abuse and the psychological trauma that you went through. It will help you feel affirmed in your experience. Gaslighting is so damaging and manipulating, empathy and support are deeply required. If you cannot access a professional therapist, a trusted friend or family member is needed.

One can choose to confront their gaslighting partner

There is a possibility that your partner is maybe unintentionally gaslighting you. According to an expert, in that case, it can be helpful to let your partner know what gaslighting is, how they are doing it to you, and how does it make you feel. Although it puts pressure on you to teach about gaslighting, give them proof of it, and let them know its consequences. But it can be worthwhile if your partner is willing to change him or herself. Shift their ways and remove toxicity from your relationship.

If someone is dealing with a narcissist gaslighter, confronting them is a waste

According to a psychologist, it is not likely for a manipulative, toxic person to admit or take responsibility for their action. In order to have control, they will deny these claims. It is in your best interest to take yourself out of the gaslighting situation. Do not interact with them. Gaslighters will not be interested in your feelings or how they make you feel. It will take more of your energy to deal with them.

If gaslighting keeps happening, leave the situation.

Even If you have told your partner about their gaslighting ways, and it keeps happening. Confronting them again is not an option anymore. You should consider leaving this relationship. According to an expert, if your partner becomes extremely angry or you are in danger with them. It is necessary to think about ending the relationship immediately. Yes, it is not easy, but your safety, your mental and physical health, peace of mind should come first.

Look for your patterns

According to a psychologist, no matter what you decide about leaving or staying with a gaslighting partner. Recognize your attachment patterns. Most of the people who end up in toxic relationships can look back and see they may have overlooked all the gaslighting, toxic behavior, red flags just to receive love and feel the connection with someone. Have you done this? Then, it is time for a better chance.

It is not your duty to stop the gaslighting

All the experts agree on this statement: if something bad happens to you, it is not your fault. Yes, we all have relationship patterns, but your partner's gaslighting is not your wrongdoing. Yes, it is a solid chance that your toxic partner has convinced you that their gaslighting behavior is because of you, but you know deep down this is not the case. It is not your responsibility to stop the gaslighting or modify their behavior. All you can do is save yourself. In a strong and healthy relationship, both partners are responsible for their own behavior, and if someone is gaslighting the other, they have to make a conscious effort to change.

If someone feels like they have been gaslighted, the first thing is to get validation. Make a trusted friend or family your confidant, tell them how you feel, what the other person says to you. It will help you to be honest with your friend or family. Do not make excuses for the gaslighter; tell the situation how it is.

However, if someone is experiencing gaslighting for a very long time, it is reasonable that you cannot tell the truth from gaslighting; you may not even be able to tell who you can trust or who you cannot. That is why you can always seek professional help tell them what you are going through, even if it is not gaslighting. You still will get much-needed help, and they will guide you in what direction you should go. With support groups and treatment, you will become self-aware of your situation. You will get your trust back, your self-confidence, and you will start trusting your judgment more.

3.5 How to Know if You're Gaslighting Others?

Gaslighting is harmful behavior, even if done unintentionally. The victim feels challenged about their reality; it affects their self-esteem and makes them lose confidence. Even if a person does not intend to put the other person down, you may have done it sometimes or are doing it. As you know, a relationship does not have to romantic for gaslighting to happen, and it can be platonic, family members, coworkers, or anyone. These are some signs that you may unintentionally be gaslighting others.

As someone expresses their opinion that does not match your beliefs, you immediately tell them they are wrong. Every human being can have a different opinion about a different situation. Instead, take your time; if you still do not agree, let the point go. Yes, some behaviors are wrong and morally ill that a person needs to call the person out. Gaslighting happens when you refuse to accept that other people have their own thinking and have a right to do things differently. You feel you must make them think like you or do as you do.

Do you find it difficult to keep your opinion to yourself that can easily hurt someone else? But you think you know better than them? Are people afraid to disagree with you? or maybe they find themselves in a position where they find it difficult to respond to your talk? If you think, yes, it happens often, then you are emotionally abusing people. It is a tactic of gaslighting. One example is when a superior gaslights their employees during an argument. The superior will stray from the point at hand and discredit, distract or even confuse them to such an extent they are afraid to say anything and feel guilty for even bringing that up or thinking about that issue. As a superior, you do not have to be right at all times, but you should keep in mind everyone else is a human with real thoughts and feelings. It is important that you encourage them rather than discourage them, so your team would know you care for them, and they can discuss any issue with you.

You believe lying is okay. Yes, we all do tell lies sometimes to get ourselves from a sticky situation. But, if you find yourself lying all the time just to hide your mistakes, you need to ask yourself if it affects the other person. If yes, then how? Do you make commitments and promises to someone and then lie about forgetting those so you can be free from accountability? Or you completely deny saying a thing. Then the person confronted you, and you lied again just to get out of that situation? You may think it is better this way to lie and get out of any situation. Although it affects the other person, they think they remember it wrong or start doubting themselves that they cannot remember details correctly. In this case, you are the gaslighter.

You downplay others' emotions, and you know it. When someone tells you that you have hurt them or said something that caused them pain, your response is to tell them that they are overreacting and they should not be sensitive. This reaction of yours will make them feel their emotions or feelings are not valid. If you do this often, this is you gaslighting the other person. Gaslighting goes as far as nullifying other individual's feelings and emotions. It is way more damaging than one can think. It tells the other person they should not feel what they want to feel. Gaslighting further makes the other person believe they do not, in reality, feel that way. These things or patterns can affect someone's health for a long time. It can cause them anxiety, paranoia, and a lack of confidence in themselves.

3.5.1 Why should you stop gaslighting?

If you find these gaslighting qualities in yourself, or you are guilty of gaslighting. It is time to change. Gaslighting can have long-term consequences on the victim's mental or physical health, confidence, and self-esteem. Your relationships will suffer the strain, whether it be platonic or romantic. If you do not stop yourself from gaslighting others, it can cause them feelings of helplessness, PTSD, depression, and they can live in a constant state of brain fog, where it can cause the inability to make a decision. Thus, you need to make a conscious effort and stop your gaslighting behavior.

Yes, changing yourself is hard but not impossible; it is possible, and you can do it. The first step is to recognize your gaslighting behavior and admit you are the one at fault. Now that you have recognized the problem in yourself. You should do these things.

- Do not make excuses for yourself
- Do make amends
- Recognize your manipulative patterns and what triggers your behavior
- Seek professional help if necessary; there is no shame in seeking help

Eventually, the cure of gaslighting is feeling empathy for others. If you do not have empathy for others, you can start developing it. It is never too late to change yourself. Practice empathy in a romantic, platonic or working environment.

Chapter 4: Stages of Gaslighting

Gaslighting is a form of manipulation and abuse concentrated on making someone doubt the reality.

Blatant lying or constant cover ups

Denying conversations and events ever happened

Manipulating others to see you differently

Actions contradict words. Broken promises.

Your self-esteem slowly erodes away & you begin to question what is real. You start to think your

Gaslighting generates a subtle but biased power dynamic in any relationship, where a person is subjected to a Gaslighter's micro-aggression, their unreasonable judgment, their scrutiny instead of their fact-based behavior. Pathological gaslighters make a severe form of psychological abuse and mind control for the other person. Gaslighting can envelop a relationship, workplace, or an entire society.

Here are some situations where gaslighting can happen.

4.1 Gaslighting in Romantic Situations

Individuals in romantic relationships are often a victim of gaslighting, few of the situations have been discussed in the relationships section in the previous chapter. Gaslighters will make the other person believe what they know is not true. What they feel is not how they feel; they are always overreacting or too sensitive to their jokes. Their emotions and feelings are negated and minimize. Gaslighting will make the other person question their sanity and everyday reality. It is because no matter how hard they try, they feel they can never remember details right and cannot trust themselves. A gaslighting partner will accuse you of things that are crazy or irrational so that other people would leave you and you would leave them. There will be no confidence left in you, making it easier for them to control you. one example is a gaslighter will keep telling you that you forget everything. There would come a time where you cannot actually remember anything.

Some individuals find it hard to leave a gaslighting relationship because they may have a fear of abandonment. Each day is a struggle for them; they are psychologically abused, but they cannot find the courage to leave a relationship, and they love the person more than themselves. It is an extremely valid fear. Leaving a part of your past behind or someone is not easy, especially if the other person has made you dependent on them for so long and you cannot decide for yourself. It has left you with no self-confidence or self-esteem. In most relationships, gaslighting happens in union with other kinds of manipulation and abuse to make sure the victim knows gaslighting compared to other abuses is not "that bad." In reality, it is worse.

According to a psychologist, once you have accepted them as your significant other, the victim will go through 3 phases of gaslighting. These are the signs your relationship is a toxic one.

Disbelief

In the beginning, phase, as the gaslighter is slowly trying to change your reality, you will tell them they are wrong, or they do not understand the situation, or you do not believe them.

Defense

As the gaslighting has progressed, so the questioning of your reality. You will think that maybe they tell the truth, or you do not actually remember what happened. But you still have some fight left in you. As your defenses are coming down, you will try to reason with them or provide some explanation on how they are wrong.

Depression

As much time has passed, you are surviving with gaslighting. You start to believe the gaslighter, and especially they are criticizing your insecurities. The more they gaslight, the more you feel it is true. You will start believing they are telling the truth. A point will come where you have no confidence left in yourself, and you do not trust your judgment. The gaslighter has achieved his goal: making you feel dependent on them, making you doubt your sanity and mental health. Keeping you isolate, letting them control you and your life.

Here are the stages a gaslighter will make you go through.

Exaggerate & lying: the gaslighter makes a negative story about the other person, that something is wrong about them, or wrong with them. They make up this scenario in their mind, as it is not based on facts, objective, or verifiable things. Instead, it is based on false accusations, presumptions, and their own mind. Thus making the other person feel they have to defend themselves.

Some examples are, a gaslighting husband will say, "my wife is a crazy, jealous person, and she needs to know it." A gaslighting manager would say, "the work around here is a waste of space and our money. How can you even justify your right to have employment?". A gaslighting mother will say to her child, "I absolutely hate it when you put away groceries like that; I have told you many times before I hate it."

One partner will slowly start controlling the other, and it will happen quite early in the relationship. One example is when you both agreed to do something on

Saturday. When you meet them or call them to remind them about this, they will tell you, "no, I never said Saturday, I said Sunday. I am busy on Saturday". This happens fairly quickly in the new relationship, but you are too interested in them to notice anything else, or you think you just heard them wrong. Yes, it is a possibility that you misheard them if there are no other signs of gaslighting present. Or they mistakenly said Saturday instead of Sunday. But, if this becomes your normal, you have to take a hard look into the relationship and start asking questions about it. As it keeps happening, one may notice other inconsistencies in what they say and repeat to you. Such as, they told you they love Chinese food. You take them to a nice Chinese restaurant. But, they will respond, "I do not like Chinese; we should go try Mexican food." Now, you must be thinking, am I mistaken? Did I imagine it? Was it someone else who likes Chinese food? Or have they just gaslighted you? But if you for sure that they said Chinese food. Then it is an effort on their part to make them shame or make you think you are never present or paying attention.

Repeating themselves: gaslighter will repeat their behavior, their talk, or insults so that it will ingrain in your mind, and a time will come where you would not even question them about it. They do this in order to control the conversation, have power over the other person. Now the gaslighting is taken to the other level, and the gaslighter will accuse you of not following up with what you have said earlier. In each situation, somehow, the blame comes on you. They may not directly call you out but make you feel bad about your choices. One example is

Person: "My family is excited to meet you as you are coming to the Easter lunch."

Gaslighter: "what are you talking about? We agreed to wait a little longer before meeting the families."

Person: "but, you said the other day you would be happy to come to the lunch."

Gaslighter: "I said it would be nice to meet your family, but we decided to do it in the future. You agreed with me, but now you have already told your family the damage is done, so I guess I will have to go". In this scenario, you did not hear it right, now you have made them go, and they are doing you a favor by agreeing to go with you.

When challenged, things will escalate: when you call the gaslighter out on their lies. He will double or triple down the attacks, deny the proof blatantly, take the argument in another direction, challenge your credibility, make you confuse, and back down. Such as, if someone catches their significant other cheating and you have proof, they will deny the proof and tell you, you imagined the whole thing as you are crazy and jealous.

Now the gaslighting tactics have gone up a notch. They lie to you and in the form that you said something, but you did not say anything in reality. Such as the gaslighter will say, "don't you remember, you said I could borrow your credit card? Now I have ordered a new jacket, I will pay back soon". This time, the gaslighter took your permission to do as they please, when you never agreed to anything in reality. They know you never agreed, but if you confront them, they will tell you a web of lies and something like you were busy, so you said I could take your credit card. Again you will start doubting yourself that did I really agree to this? Now they are slowly taking control of your life.

Wear out the other person: by doubling down the blame and staying on the offensive, a gaslighter wears down his victim as the victim becomes resigned, debilitated, discouraged, self-doubting, pessimistic, and fearful. The victim starts to question his own sanity, identity, and reality.

Now your defenses have started to come down, and the gaslighter will do more obvious lying and deception on you. a gaslighter will tell you that they did not do something. Indeed, they did or vice versa. Some examples are, you have prepared a bath for yourself, and you go out of the bathroom to get something for yourself. They will immediately take your place in the bath and start relaxing. Now you are mad and asking them why they did? They will reply, "you imagine things. I came in here to open taps and run a bath for myself. You must have heard me and thought of taking a bath for yourself". Yes, this sounds ridiculous and far away from reality. Every time it happens, the victims start losing their minds, and their self-confidence is diminishing.

Forming codependent relationships: codependent relationships happen when one partner or both are extremely psychologically or emotionally reliant on the other. In a gaslighting relationship, as the gaslighter provokes anxiety and insecurity in the other person, removing their identity, getting complete control over their lives, making them dependent on the gaslighter. The gaslighter now possesses control to grant respect, security, acceptance, safety, and approval. The gaslighter threatens the other person with this power. This codependent relationship is based on marginalization, vulnerability, and fear.

Giving false hope: gaslighter as manipulation will sometimes treat the victim with superficial kindness, mildness, moderation to give them false hope. In such times, the victim will think, "maybe this person is not that bad," "looks like things are becoming better," or "I can give it one more chance."

Use your judgment: This kind of behavior is just temporary; it is a calculated manipulation technique to make your stay for another round of gaslighting, kicking your defenses down. Making you dependent on them for much longer.

Dominating & controlling: the ultimate goal of gaslighting is to make sure the gaslighter controls the other person's life. Dominating them, controlling them, and taking advantage of them with gaslighting. By keeping a constant supply of coercion, lies, humiliation, minimizing feelings & thoughts, the challenging reality on each turn will give the victim doubt, fear, depression, and anxiety. This is how a gaslighter will take complete control over another person's life.

4.2 Gaslighting in Friendships

This form of gaslighting can look a little different than other gaslighting, such as in a romantic relationship. Gaslighter friends love to gossip behind one's back. They use any kind of information they can get and use it against the person. The reason they gossip is so they can get other information about that person from others. Gaslighter friends also enjoy creating drama, and no, not that type of some drama here and there. They love creating drama to extreme extents.

If you have a friend who gossips all the time, you should limit your interaction with them or the amount of information you give to them. Chances are they will use it against you. If you are the one on the listening end, this time about how the other friend reacted and did this and that. Next time you will be under the toxic microscope, do not think they will not do this to you. After one of the other friends tells what they said about friend A, friend A will disclose what they said about friend B, and friend B will tell what they said about friend A. You will see the gaslighter has created a lot of drama for no reason. The gaslighter's goal is to start a fight and generate conflict just because he or she can.

Frequently, if the gaslighter friend cannot find any information to get the fight started, they will make something up. So if you know someone who does this all the time, next time if they tell you something, you may want to think again before believing them, especially when this information can cause a fight as they could not fight any valid fact to gossip about anything will work. Now is the time to learn how to deal with a toxic or gaslighting friend, if you have a friend like this or you may get a friend like this in the future.

Look out for the gaslighting friend, making friends with your other friends or your partner: They plan to gossip about you with them, on how you are not a competent friend or partner, that you may have relationship issues. This gaslighting person will create unnecessary drama between you and the other person, as they love drama so much.

Stage 1

Pay close attention to small things: If one of your friends is a gaslighter, small things can turn into huge arguments. Such as kitchen cleaning duty among roommates can develop into huge arguments. If one roommate has made dinner and you ask them to clean the kitchen as it is their duty to clean the kitchen today, they will deny and say they never made this mess. Now, the responsibility is on the other friend to clean up the mess that they did not even make. Another example is being left out of plans. A gaslighting friend will invite everyone else but not you to the party they are hosting. They will give invites to each and every one in front of you, except for you. When confronting them about this behavior, they will deny and say, "it was nothing. You are very sensitive like always".

But let me tell you, you are not too sensitive. This is rude, unkind behavior, or even mean for doing something like this to anyone. If you felt hurt, your feelings are valid, and they need to be respected, just like you respect everyone's feelings.

Laying the basis: As you already know by now, a gaslighter who is practiced will not jump in the game right away. They are such smart people or manipulative people who know how to lay the basis of gaslighting so the other person will not suspect a thing. They will prepare the ground for you to fall. It starts with exaggeration and lying in order to make you estrange from your reality. They have to make surroundings in which you feel unstable or come across as unreliable. They will make sure that you know how unstable you are so that you will lose your confidence.

Stage 2

Root & repeat: The gaslighters' goal is to get complete control over you and your reality. They will need time and preparation, and they do not want to make any mistakes after they have gotten you where they want you. The next step for them is to repeat their tactics, their lies, with much greater frequency and intensity, till you are no longer sure of your emotions or feel any reality in your everyday life. They will keep repeating themselves, so a time will come when their saying humiliations are intact in your brain or have become a part of your thinking.

Stage 3

Escalating the build-up: Now that you are in their control, they will up their manipulative tactics. In this stage, you can see how their poor behavior is impacting you. Instead of coming up clean for their smaller lies, they will raise the stakes and tell bigger lies with more manipulation. They will escalate their gaslighting. Sometimes the bad guy will be you, if not all time. The more you try to get out of this phase by fighting with them, the more it will fuel them.

Work angles tiresomely: Gaslighting is no rocket science; you do not have to be a narcissist to gaslight others. Average people gaslight others all the time. Gaslighting more than anything else is all about consistency. In order to keep you in their control, to tear your defenses down, to separate you from the rest of the group, and to muddle your reality. They will never miss an opportunity to degrade you, to shift the blame on you whenever you try to confront them. There will come a time where the fight will leave your system, and it is much easier for them to do as they please.

Stage 4

Creating co-dependency: Gaslighting friendships are riddled with anxiety and insecurities. Even if you were not an anxious person before, you are in a constant state of the doubt after befriending this gaslighting friend. You doubt your feelings, your thinking, and even your experiences. This thing is making you dependent on the gaslighter. The more you will doubt yourself, the more this gaslighter will come to your rescue being a good person, but in reality, it is far worse.

False hope: Gaslighters are much smarter. Although they may not be aware of their behavior, they are mindful of its effects on other person's life. They know if they push too far too quickly, they lose, and you will get scared, probably run for your life. So sometimes, they will behave nicely, kindly. Just like a car, if the fuel runs out, the engine will overheat. You are useless for a gaslighter if they cannot control you. So false hope, false kind behavior is their way to keep you in this situation for much longer.

Stage 5

Dominate & overcome: This is the final stage of gaslighting in friendships. This is where your friend will gain complete control over you and back you into the corner. The fight has left your system, and you feel powerless. You completely believe what they say about you, you believe their lies, you have accepted they know better, and what they do is not wrong. The fear and anxiety in your life are constant, and this overwhelming feeling never goes away. If you recognize yourself at any of these stages of gaslighting. It is advised that you seek professional help or get yourself separated from that gaslighting friend as soon as possible.

4.3 Gaslighting between Parents & Children/ Family

In the family dynamic, a famous form of gaslighting is between parent and child. This is especially unfortunate because their worldview is mainly influenced by what their parents do and say. A child holds the central position for one or both parents and their aggressive behavior, and children are punished, told off, and blamed for. One example is when a parent and child are late for school, and it is not the child's fault. But the parent is insistent that this is the child's fault. They will say, "you are going to be late now because of all the time you wasted. Why cannot you just listen to me and do as I say?". Yes, it happens most of the time that a kid wastes time here and there and will be late for school, but when it is not any fault of the kid and parent is still insistent that they are the reason for going to school late, this is gaslighting. This teaches the kid they are disobedient and troublesome, but in reality, they are just like any other kid. These kids make some ad beliefs about themselves.

If one's parents gaslight them or used to, it is a very difficult situation to be in. If your parent were narcissists, they would have created a dynamic of power play in the household, and they loved to maintain control. The love from them is conditional and only benefits them. Gaslighting parents will use gaslighting to control or shame their children. Will accuse their children of being so sensitive all the time. Minimize their feelings, belittle them. Gaslighting parents will not remember their child's childhood memories or remember them wrong.

By nature, kids will assess the boundaries set by caregivers or by authority figures. It happens with every child, and from a young age, it is necessary to teach children accountability and self-control. Creating boundaries by parents is necessary and reasonable, but gaslighting parents takes it really hard if a child tries to break even one boundary. Even a little carelessness is met with a harsh attitude. Saying such as, "you are so mischievous, and I have no idea what I am going to do with you." This kind of sayings only tells kids that they are not good enough or something is wrong with them. It diminishes a child's curiosity to explore more because he will remember how a little carelessness is met with such a harsh attitude. He does not want to repeat the incident all over again. And there is something wrong with them. These kinds of things stay for a long time with a kid and influence their future behavior.

If your parents were gaslighters, there are two cases you must have experienced. One is the golden child; this child cannot do anything wrong in the gaslighters' eyes. They will not be punished at all. They are glorified and praised, and yes, they were the favorite. Another case is of the scapegoat child; this child probably has been gaslighted the most by parents. This child is not good enough, no matter what they do. Their feelings do not matter, and most of the time, this child has been beaten down mentally to the extent that they lose their self-worth in their own eyes. This scapegoat child will feel they are born without a purpose, feels lost, and is not sure of what they want to do in their life. This behavior is because of all the gaslighting that their parents did; the manipulation and invalidation. This child experienced has ruined their self-worth. They do not believe in themselves, so how can they trust themselves. If a parent is a gaslighter, they will want you to believe their memories rather than your own. This is also true for opinions; gaslighting parents' their child's opinion does not matter much. These parents will want you to trust and shadow them thoughtlessly, and if they say no. they will get punished for it.

Parents' needs come first. A gaslighting parent feels their wants and needs come before their kids or anyone else's, such as, if they are feeling sad or down, they will let everyone know so they can get sympathies. But, when the child goes through the same sadness or depression, they are dealt with, "you do not feel depressed, suck it up. Stop being sensitive". A gaslighting parent have the impractical expectation, and they control your feelings, what can you like what can you not like, and the parent is right all the time, and you are wrong at all times. If you try to confront them about this behavior, they will get extremely defensive and shift the blame on you.

According to them, they are being good parents or doing tough love, but in reality, they are destroying their child's personality forever and damaging any future relations they make.

4.4 Gaslighting in The Workplace

This gaslighting situation is extremely sensitive and tricky. Experiencing gaslighting in the household is different but in the workplace is a completely different situation because, with your mental health, your career is in difficulty. A gaslighter can be a colleague or your superior. Gaslighting in the workplace is all about gaining power and control; it will leave you feeling helpless. One example is when your boss asks you to do one thing after completing it, and you report back. They reply, "why did you waste your time on this thing? When I asked you to do the other project?". You will feel frustrated and try to defend yourself, and the boss will reply, "you are overreacting, don't you think?".

Or in another instance. You were promised a raise after an x amount of period, and when you bring it, you are told by your boss, "I never promised you that. I said I would decide after reviewing your performance, and to be honest, it remains somewhat missing". He will say, "I have heard your superior is not happy about your latest report; looks like someone is not getting a raise." Or "oh, you are not in that email? I guess the boss does not want you to give you that information". Or "I just said, you need to work a little harder, you are so sensitive today, take a chill pill."

If you have a gaslighter in the work environment, they would want you not to succeed at all. They will take credit for your efforts and disrupt your efforts. They will blame you for any failures they cause, so they do not have to take responsibility. One instance, if your supervisor or boss is a gaslighter and they harass you sexually or physically. When confronted, they would say, "you cannot even take a joke" or "why are you so sensitive? Others are not". "I did not mean it like this." Or, "you are lying; it never happened." If this has happened before or still happening, make sure to write your experiences down. Write down everything, conversation, emails, documents, and save in a place where they cannot reach, possibly not on work property.

If you want to confront the gaslighter, calmly confront them not to set them off, or they could become hostile or defensive. If they become hostile or defensive and try to deny any actions (gaslighting you more). Take the matter to HR or another supervisor with proof. One does not have to sacrifice one career for anyone, especially for a gaslighter.

Gaslighting in the workplace can be with actions and words. Sometimes, the gaslighting person will switch off your computer screen when you go away for a minute or two, or they move your things around behind your back. These things will make you confuse and doubt your reality and lower your self-confidence.

4.5 Other Gaslighting Situations

These are some forms of gaslighting that occur in different situations, and they are not non-existent but may be rare.

Medical gaslighting

As per the Complex Post-Traumatic Stress Disorder foundation (CPTSD), this type of gaslighting happens.

When a doctor dismisses a patient's health concerns by telling them they are mentally ill. For example, a medical professional will tell the patients that their symptoms are in their head or imagine them. As per one study in 2019, most doctors will attribute CHD's (coronary heart disease) symptoms in women of middle age to the condition of their mental health than middle-aged men.

Political gaslighting

According to a study, this form of gaslighting happens when a politician or a political group uses manipulation, lying, denying the information to lead people in their chosen direction rather than what is good for people. One example would be a gaslighting politician who will hide or downplay the wrong things their government did. They will doubt their opponent based on their credibility, their mental instability and ignore the controversy and the message. Distract people's attention from important events.

Racial gaslighting

As per a study, this form of gaslighting occurs when individuals do gaslight to a group of individuals based on their ethnicity or race. Such as, an individual will deny that a specific group experiences any discrimination, despite the proof present. Gaslighters will criticize human rights protestors for being so sensitive and emotional and undermine their message.

Institutional gaslighting

In the Journal of Perinatal and Neonatal Nursing, research published that gaslighting occurs in organizations and companies. The company will hide or deny certain information, will lie to the workers about their rights. People who speak against such issues will be labeled mentally ill or incompetent by these organizations.

4.6 The Secret Ingredient of gaslighting

The main purpose of Gaslighting is to confuse a person's life to the extent that they doubt their reality, their feelings, emotions, and much more. The gaslighters will talk you down, make you feel powerless, inadequate, insecure, and weak. If this happens seven days a week, the victim will someday see right through their manipulative behavior. But this secret key ingredient is that the gaslighter will behave completely opposite to how they usually behave; they will be charming, superficially kind behavior, love you. This is necessary to keep the victim around, to keep their hope alive that someday things will get better. To show them it is not all that bad.

It serves as a purpose to further confuse the victim and make the gaslighter more powerful. This on, off, aggressive, then kind, then aggressive again behavior will make the victim nervous as to what will happen next. The victim will forever remain unsure of what is next, and it creates instability in their mind. They cannot decide for themselves or cannot even go to anyone for help. They have no idea when they wake up, who they will be greeted with a cruel partner or a kind one?

4.7 How to protect yourself in gaslighting situations?

If you recognize someone gaslighting you, it is necessary to take steps for your physical or mental wellbeing. You have to protect yourself from your abusive gaslighter. For doing that, you need to build enough confidence to do what needs to be done in this situation.

Get clear on the actions

Before taking any action or making any claim about someone gaslighting you, you must take time to question and process the reality and where you stand. Abusive relationships are not that easy to make sense of. You are dealing with and trying to make sense of your emotions and feelings. On top of that, you have to look at the gaslighter too. You need to make sure you have a clear handle on things, which is difficult as you already have a lot on your plate. You have to make sure that the other person is gaslighting you, or their behavior is just another form of abuse. It must be difficult for you to make sense of the situation if the other person is gaslighting you. Talk with a trusted friend before confronting the gaslighter or taking any action.

Write everything in a journal, your feelings, your thoughts, keep a record of other person's manipulation or gaslighting. Write down each encounter that makes you feel insecure, unstable, or anxious. How the gaslighter/abuser makes you feel. What does he or she say to you? Record each and everything. Do not make excuses, and the clearer one will be in keep records, the easier it will be for them to make sense of it all.

Try building self-confidence

Gaslighting is only effective because a gaslighter will tear down your defenses, make you lose your confidence, separate you from everyone else and ruin your sense of self-worth. To make someone their puppet, they have to make that person flexible. Thus, to beat the gaslighting, it is necessary to build your self-confidence again. When you start loving yourself more than you love them, you will start getting less manipulated or gaslighted. Do not let the gaslighter ruin your self-esteem. Stand up for yourself, get to know your true self, so if a gaslighter is putting you down. You will be able to separate lies from the truth about yourself. Spend time with yourself, focus on your mind, body, and spirit. Celebrate your strength for coming so far, thinking of taking a step in the right direction, polish your skills. Fall in love with yourself. Love your body that has carried you this far.

Most importantly, believe in yourself, prioritize your happiness. If you cannot separate yourself from the gaslight, do not permit them to infiltrate your happiness. Loving you for who you are, is the way to save yourself from further damage.

Get a support system

This is a key part of recovering when it comes to making new and huge changes in your life. You will need their perception of things and their motivation to keep you going in the right direction. In gaslighting, one loses one sense of self. Our support system should be there to guide us and anchor us. People who want the best for you for no reason. Yes, finding your support system might be difficult at first but not impossible. Do not be afraid to ask for help. Tell them what is really going on and how you feel about it. Their advice will be valuable if you do know, you can trust yourself or not. If you are confused again or cannot decide for yourself. The support system will be there for you. Open up to trusted people, people who are not connected to the gaslighter, since he will try to separate you from them. Professional help is a must, but a support system is also necessary. These are the people who will help you stand up for yourself and choose a new, better path for your life.

Set up boundaries

Every successful relationship has one thing in common; boundaries. Boundaries are the backbone of any relationship, romantic or platonic. Gaslighters also know this; this is why they try their hardest to push your boundaries away and away with each experience. To protect yourself from all this manipulation and to gaslight, you have to draw a line and don't let anyone cross that line. Everyone deserves to be happy, but one has to fight for happiness when dealing with a gaslighter. Draw a line between what makes you happy and what you will not tolerate. Do not make excuses for the other person, and they know what they are doing. Stay strong and do not give in to false hope or superficial kind behavior. Also, others have a total right to behave how they want, but you do not have to deal with it. Discuss with the gaslighter what you would not allow anymore. If they cannot respect them, which will probably be the case, seek professional help, get yourself separated from the gaslighter, and seek support from trusted friends and family.

Think of a long-term plan

Now that you have to think of going in a new direction, or at least save yourself from further gaslighting. You have to make some serious changes in your life. We may not change the gaslighting behavior, but we can change whether we choose to stay with them or not, especially when you have told the gaslighter what you will tolerate and what you won't. You have to ask yourself it this what you deserve? A gaslighting partner or friend or a colleague. Is your life going according to the plan? Think and plan again for your future or present. It is never too late. If it is a romantic relationship, or your spouse is gaslighting you, and you have done everything to make them realize what you will not tolerate, now it is time you believe they might not change themselves. You do not have the power to change them, but you can take yourself to a better environment. So now make a plan. Take a look at the gaslighting person's behavior. Are they making any genuine effort to make their behavior right? Have they started listening to you? Do they include you in their life? Do they take responsibility for their actions? If you cannot answer any of these or the answer is yes, then you have to separate your ways from them. Yes, you still can have that amazing future, but you have to take the first step for that. Move slowly but keep moving.

Chapter 5: Tactics Used by Gaslighters

You're overreacting. You need help.

I didn't do that. **You're upset over nothing.**

You must be confused again.

Just calm down. **You're so dramatic.**

I never said that. Why are you so defensive?

What are you talking about? It's your fault.

You twist things.

You're so sensitive.

I never said that. Stop imagining things

I was just joking.

Gaslighting happens in various forms. Often it involves manipulative tactics to make the other person confused, such as messing with one's environment behind their back. Or gaslighting can be in the form of emotional, verbal or psychological abuse. These are the most common tactics of gaslighting.

It is necessary to know about gaslighter's tactics, so you can identify them and save yourself and others around you.

5.1 Lying & Denying

Lies are everywhere. One who is a constant liar; chances are he is also a gaslighter. They will lie, lie and lie. The biggest weapon of gaslighters is denying and lying. They abuse people psychologically by lying and denying the truth until a time comes when the victim starts to question their own reality that maybe the gaslighter is telling the truth all along. Gaslighter wants the victim to get so confused that they even doubt their own worth, lose confidence in themselves. They tell a lot of lies, even when you know that they are telling a lie. Why would a gaslighter do this? They are setting up an example. Because the next time they tell another big you do not know about. So they want to keep you guessing whether it's a truth or a lie? This is the goal; to create confusion.

This constant confusion and double-guessing lead the victim to desperate for transparency which may never come from them because the only person the victim asks clarity for is the gaslighter. It becomes a cycle of emotional abuse making the victim more defenseless with each passing day. This will often happen in the gaslighting relationship. When they say they would do something and you clearly remember hearing it. Then they completely deny they said anything and convince you that you imagine this. The more a gaslighter does this, the harder it is for you to trust your judgment.

5.2 Projection

Gaslighter's signature tactic is projection. What the gaslighter does, he will say you do these things. They have a negative mindset; they manipulate, lie and cheat. Whatever the gaslighter will do wrong, it will be assigned to you that you did this instead of them. Gaslighters do this tactic to distract the victim from their abuse as the victim starts defending himself that they did not do whatever they are accusing them of. Such as, if they use drugs or cheat on you, they will accuse you of using drugs and cheating on them. They will check your phone, go crazy if you are 20 minutes late from work, keep asking you questions. Instead of questioning their behavior, you are too busy answering them. Or if you know they are cheating, and you confront them about this, they will say you are the one cheating, that is why accusing them of doing so.

You will be so appalled and confused that instead of accusing them, you will be busy defending yourself. If the gaslighter is in your work environment. He will write in your performance review that you always come late, just because he is always late. The complete opposite is true. You are punctual at your job. Or if it's a colleague, he will say you are always looking into their computer when you have caught them lurking around your screen. Or, if they are stealing things from your desk, they will accuse you of stealing.

But why do gaslighter project on you or others? It is because this project tactic comes in handy to deflect the blame and take no responsibility. Furthermore, it makes you question your reality and keeping you confused. With accusing you, they buy themselves some time. Meanwhile, you are busy trying to defend yourself. According to a study, when one feels they have behaved in a specific manner or have traits that the gaslighter is projecting on them, it is called projective identification.

What can you do in a situation when a gaslighter is projecting on you? You have to tell yourself that just because the gaslighter has accused you of something does not mean you have done it or have those qualities. Do not give them the power over you. Do not give them any reaction when they accuse you of doing certain things. You just have to say, "oh, really," or "I am very confused about what you are talking about" it will stop them for a while. Or you can literally show you are confused. If you pretend to be confused as a part of you will actually be, and then just keep quiet. Why will it work? Because the gaslighter wants a fight and you are not giving them, do not give a gaslighter the satisfaction of your reaction. If you show you are deeply hurt or want to explain yourself, it is like adding fuel to the fire.

5.3 Congruence

There is no similarity between what a gaslighter says and what he does. Their actions and words do not match with each other. The gaslighter would love to make commitments and promises, will not follow through as they mean nothing to him. So, next comes the action time, and they are absent. When asked about their actions, they will use superficial kindness and love to smooth things over. Whenever you confront them, they will say, "love, you already know how much I love you; I cannot even think of doing this to you." Yes, when hearing these, it looks so authentic, but it never is. You need to pay attention to what one is saying and what the gaslighter do next. Yes, it can happen once or twice. But if it is a regular thing in your relationship, it is gaslighting. What they say is not the problem because they will be using kind words here and there; it's the action you should look for because they can be mean and downright abusive.

5.4 Refusing to Listen

Whenever you talk to a gaslighter, and you have some concerns to share, they will not listen to you and pretend to understand you. after a while, the victim will start to question their sanity and feel bitter. When confronted, the blame will be shifted on you, or they behave this way because of you. Now, you have two problems on your own, and you have to defend yourself for something they did.

5.5 Challenge Your Memory

To create confusion in one's life. The gaslighters will question and challenge your memory. They will deny this is not how the events happened, or you never said that, or they never said that. This kind of manipulation psychologically abuses the victim, and he falls further into the rabbit hole of gaslighting. With denying comes the next step, adding false details and memories when the victim questions it. According to the gaslighter, they can never remember anything right or forget important details.

5.6 Changing The Subject

This is also a classic, and you can see it happening in politics also; the gaslighter will divert your attention to some other thing or another issue rather than talking about the subject at hand. When you ask a question, they will ask another question instead of answering your concerns. They will lie, twist and divert the conversation where they are not accountable for anything. Or, instead of answering, they will question your credibility.

5.7 Isolating The Target

A gaslighter will not be as successful at what he does if he could not isolate the victim. In order to isolate the victim, he will feed him lies such as you are crazy, and you are worthless, nobody will love you when they know how crazy you are. They will make the victim question their self-worth, their sanity. As we discussed before, the victim will search for clarity from the gaslighter whether he is causing the confusion on purpose. He will call you crazy, and after listening to it for a while, you will believe it. They will make sure that you know others also think you are crazy and cannot go to anyone for clarity. They will spread rumors and gossip about you to your friends, family and about them to you, so you will not be contacting each other. They will pretend to be so worried and upset about your behavior and tell others how you seem to be losing it. Or your mental health is deteriorating, and you cannot remember anything. If you try to find the courage and tell your friends and family, some of them decide to believe the gaslighter, so reach out to help from those people who are not in contact with a gaslighter. Or look for professional help.

Gaslighters also show traits of irrationality, narcissism or paranoia. They make the power dynamic by presenting themselves as insignificant, generous, kind and caring. This causes a false sense of familiarity and haven. When thought of them as manipulators, it just adds to the confusion. So the gaslighter will innocently tell you they do not know anything. The confused victim will probably be more confused by this innocence. Thus, the door to confronting the gaslighter closes as they already proved their innocence or they already shifted the blame to someone else, and life goes on as before. Isolating you can happen in many ways, either by telling lies about you, telling lies to you about others, and telling not to believe anyone else they are lying. Gaslighter will do all these, and they will tell you, your family talks behind your back, or they say bad things about you. You know they do not do this, but with all the confusion going around, you would think they are actually telling the truth, and if you confront your family, the gaslighter already told them you are going crazy and are not thinking right, they will put this experience in that crazy box. This is the gaslighter's plan to make you believe their incorrect information, so you will not even question them next time.

5.8 Breaking It Down

I am sure you have learned a lot about gaslighting yet. As gaslighting is a form of sneaky manipulation, it cannot be easily detected right away. It is a complex subject to wrap your head around. Let us discuss how a successful gaslighter is made.

Slow & steady: A gaslighter will subtly undermine you. Gaslighters work so subtly. One of the key factors of gaslighting is their subtleness because if they show all their cards at once, people will run away. A small lie here and there, a mean comment here and there till it starts happening quite often. Even the smartest people will be sucked into the gaslighting hole. Yes, it is that subtle. It is the same as a frog in the pan. Slowly and steadily, the heat is increased, so you do not know what is happening.

In order to make your stay and go through gaslighting, the manipulation is subtle. At first, you will not even consider their tactics as gaslighting or manipulation.

They will say things such as, "you must be imagining it because I know you did not sleep well last night." You will probably agree to these comments, and you will feel so cared for that this person knows intimate details about you.

Gaslighters repel objections & arguments: this is their second key factor to deflect. If the target has started coming to their senses and they confront the gaslighter about it. The gaslighter will easily write them off by saying, "you are so sensitive." "stop overreacting." "I see; your ex has made you so insecure." "you seem tired, so I assume you do not know what you are talking about." It will make you feel crazy, like there is nothing to worry about, but you are still losing your mind.

Furthermore, cementing this fact that according to them, you are going crazy. Now you have one more thing to worry about. Are you actually going crazy, or are you really that insecure?

They make you question everything: gaslighting is a manipulation to the extent that a person may just lose their mind. Gaslighting happens on larger, smaller or medium scales. A gaslighting significant will deny your reality by saying, "you slept a lot. There is no way you are still tired." This is such a small example. A larger-scale example would be when a politician refuses to believe people how the country is getting worse day by day.

They attack your weak points: If they know your identity is important to you or you love your kids. They will attack in those places by telling you and you should not have had these kids. Or, in the case of your identity, they will tell you a long list of negative traits that you may not even have just to confuse you or strip you of your identity. Make you lose self-confidence by attacking the things near and dear to you. A gaslighter will attack your foundation.

Superficial kindness & false hope: false hope and gaslighting go hand in hand. This gaslighting person who was constantly telling how you are unworthy, unlovable and has a long list of negative traits is suddenly so good to you, kind to you and even love. A part of you is happy, but a bigger part of you is confused. This confusion will generate more confusion later on when things go back to the new abusive normal. Again, you will think he has bad times just like anyone, he will be good again, and yes, he will be because this is all a part of the plan. This is yet another attempt on how to confuse your reality even more.

Chapter 6: Dealing & Saving Yourself from Gaslighting

HOW TO FACE GASLIGHTING AND WIN

1. Educate Yourself On Gaslighting

2 Get Some Outside Advice

3. Reconnect With Your Intuition

4. Don't Confront Them Directly

5. Write It Down

6. Consciously Affirm Your Self

7. Prepare For A Struggle—And Leave If You Have To

Gaslighters know that normalcy and stability are the two most preferred things in one's life. Their objective is to make you question each and everything in your life so you will not be able to look at the important things in life. They will present themselves as the most stable one or the one you can depend on, but they are the ones causing confusion in the first place.

6.1 How to Deal with Gaslighting?

There is no immediate solution to gaslighting that will stop the gaslighter in his tracks. All you can do is make multiple efforts on different fronts and create boundaries. That was broken in the gaslighting process. Yes, I know that it is extremely difficult to go from being gaslighted to fighting the gaslighting, but one day has to come where you think of making the right choice. Let us discuss what you can do every day when you have realized that you want to fight the gaslighting.

This is the first thing. You should make sure that you know that you are gaslit. Yes, this is the hardest part to come to this realization. It is sad, but it is true.

You should write everything. In a journal or a safe space, keep a record of your conversation with the gaslighter so the gaslighter will not be able to confuse you any further. This way, the gaslighter would not be able to make you feel like you imagine things; you will be able to separate truth from lies. Having everything is written where the gaslight would not reach you is necessary.

Try to feel your feelings. It is a length, difficult process. You will have to do a lot of work by feelings all your feeling, each and every feeling is valid, and you are not being sensitive or overreacting. For a long time, the gaslighter may have you believed that you are so sensitive, or your world is upside down, or your reality is always not what it seems. Yes, it is going to be difficult to believe yourself again. Let yourself feel, cry if you need to, go through your emotions. Talk to a trusted friend/family. Or what you feel right, but do not seek the gaslighter out for comfort. Do not focus on your feelings being wrong or right. Feelings are feelings. It will be hard for you to think what you feel is okay because the gaslighter told you, you are not to feel it. Do not feel bad about what you are feeling. Do not second guess yourself. If your gaslighter gets a hint of what you are trying to do, they will try their hardest to ruin things for you, but do not give him permission in your mind. Know, you are right; what you feel is valid. You should just focus on your healing.

Include your friends & family. Talking is a necessary part of healing; talking to family and friends you trust will make you feel validated. They will assure you this is not all in your head. They will be your support system.

Keep strong. Do not give in to the gaslighters' tactics again. Stay strong, and this will help you know what you feel is real. You feel what you feel, and no one can tell you otherwise; try to distance yourself from the gaslighter as soon as possible.

Accept the fact that the gaslighter may never apologize. Yes, it is a sad reality. Gaslighters, manipulators or narcissists may never apologize, just to make them feel superior. They will never apologize because they think they have done nothing wrong. Gaslighters think people's reaction to their activities is not a problem. They think the other person is at fault. Their logic is different, such as, if they step on your foot, they will say, "your foot should've not been here." They can never be accountable, and the blame is always on others. This means they will never realize they did anything wrong. So, the closure is not coming, and you have to move on and heal without getting a much-needed apology.

It is a painful experience to go through gaslighting. But you have to stay strong and fight this battle.

6.1.1 Dealing with Gaslighting in Relationships

In relationships gaslighting becomes extreme and quite difficult to manage because you live with the abuser. Or, in some cases, people do not even realize that their partner is a gaslighter for a long time. When you find that out, it can turn your world upside down.

If you are in a relationship with a gaslighter. It is best for you to leave this situation as soon as possible and seek counseling to deal with emotional trauma. But, yes, in some cases, it might not be as simple to up and leave the relationship. So in those cases, you can do these:

Write your thoughts and feelings in a journal. If the gaslighter has isolated, you make sure to confide in a trusted friend (a friend, gaslighter does not know about, or if they do, you know they will not talk to the gaslighter).

It will be quite impossible to change the gaslighter's behavior. So, all you can do is protect and strengthen yourself. It is necessary to understand whatever the gaslighter says, and it is no fault of yours. Their attitude or behavior is also not your fault. Set boundaries again, and do not let the gaslighter break them again. Yes, the gaslighter will manipulate you that you are crazy for needing boundaries or that if you love them, then there are no rules in love. Stay strong, and do not get sucked into these manipulative tactics again. According to research, even online therapy can help you by reducing the symptoms of trauma caused by gaslighting.

Outcomes of Online Therapy for Trauma

A study published in the *Journal of Anxiety Disorders* found online therapy to be **effective in reducing trauma-related symptoms**.

made significant progress immediately after treatment

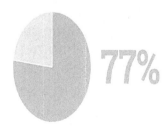

made significant progress at three-month follow-up

6.1.2 Dealing with Gaslighting at Work

Dealing with a gaslighter at work is the worst-case scenario. You may feel like not even going to work on some days. Gaslighting behavior, their insults, jabs, questions can make each day turn into a whole year. Insulting your work abilities even when giving your 100 percent can depress you if you are not strong or likes to overthink. You should keep in mind many gaslighters feel inferior to you, so in order to make themselves feel better, they put down others.

When dealing with a gaslighter at work, set boundaries and do not let them cross those boundaries, get help from co-workers, or supervisor or any other trusted person(s).

Again, make sure you are writing every conversation or every encounter in a journal. If a gaslighter gives you instructions for something, either make sure someone else is present with you or ask them to send via email for record. If you have important information, keep it to yourself. Try not to argue with the gaslighter as they will not acknowledge your point and cause you frustration.

Remember you being a target at work is no fault of yours. Your only responsibility is to take care of yourself emotionally and physically, do not get sucked into gaslighters' manipulative tactics.

6.2 Gathering Proof

It is necessary for you to gather proof if you live with an abusive person. Make sure it is stored in private space, or if you search for something in abuse or gaslighting or storing proof, make sure to erase the history. You can

- Store evidence in a safe location
- Get a second phone or cheap camera, make sure they are password protected
- Keep it with a trusted person, make copies and delete if you can

- If the gaslighter becomes physical when he is angry, according to NDVH (National Domestic Violence Hotline). Think of a safety plan that will save you from emotional and physical abuse before, during, after leaving the relationship/gaslighting situation. These points should be included in the plan.
- Remember contact details of someone you will call for help if needed
- Escape points & safe places
- A plan to safely leave the situation
- Activities for self-care to help you cope

6.3 Things to Say When One Is Being Gaslighted

When the gaslighting is refusing to acknowledge your feeling, you should say:

- "This is how I see this, even if you disagree with me."
- "I do not imagine stuff. Your perspective is just different from mine".
- "Calling me 'insert hurtful names' hurts me; it is difficult to hear you when you talk like this."
- "I know you feel so strongly for this, but my feelings also matter."
- "I want some space because I feel like I am not being understood/heard."
- "I know your intention was just to joke, but it has hurt me."
- "I am making this decision for myself."
- "This is how I feel; my feelings are valid."
- "This is MY understanding, and these are my emotions."
- "I realize that this is what good for me."
- "I understand this is what I need right now."
- "I will not be responding to that."
- "I have a right to change my mind."

- "It is very hard for me to keep discussing this"
- "I would like to take a break from this discussion."
- "I know; I have heard your viewpoint many times, but I still do not agree with this."
- "I understand you are mad, but I am mad too."
- "I do not like how hard I have to try to prove my point. Could you let this go?"
- "I want to understand it myself."
- "It is difficult for me to keep conversing; I have said no one too many times."
- "I do not care who is wrong or right, you are aggressive/abusive right now, so I would not continue this conversation."

But, if you know the gaslighter will be physical towards you if you stand up to them, just walk away from the situation/relationship.

6.4 How to Fight Gaslighting?

The first step is to acknowledge that, yes, gaslighting is happening. Once you accept it, things will be easier for you and manipulation will be hard for the gaslighter. If you cannot leave the relationship right away because you are financially dependent on them or you two have children together. Then here are some tips you can use to defend yourself.

Do not take accountability for gaslighters' actions. Gaslighter will try to tell you that you triggered them to abuse you. Even if you avoid doing those things that trigger them, they will develop new excuses to abuse you.

Do not sacrifice your feelings for the gaslighter. Even if you devote your whole life to them, they still will not be satisfied or happy with you. They are trying to fill a void in themselves, and you are not the solution.

Remember your reality. Just because the gaslighters present themselves as so sure of themselves does not mean they are telling the truth. They are not equipped to see your side of the story. Their opinions do not define your reality, and only you can feel your feelings

Try not to argue with them. If the gaslighter is going to tell lies, it is unlikely that you will have a productive argument. You can spend all your energy trying to tell them what is right and what is wrong. Even if they win an argument does not mean they are right and you are wrong.

Make sure you are safe. Gaslighting works by making you second guess about your gut feelings. But, if you feel you are in danger, you should leave the situation immediately and no, you are not overreacting. You do not need to prove the treat with police coming in, but you have to trust your gut.

Above all, you are not alone. Talk with trusted friends or family; talking about your experience will be your validation, and their support will make you feel loved.

Try to go to therapy, and it will be your safe place where you can talk about your emotions and feelings with no judgment. A therapist will help you differentiate between unhealthy and healthy patterns; you will learn to resist psychological abuse. In extreme cases, a therapist will teach you a safe plan to leave the situation.

6.5 Techniques to Manage & Stop Gaslighting

Dr. Robin Stern is an expert in treating people who suffered gaslighting and is a psychoanalyst. He has described many useful tips such as. These are some techniques that can help the victims of gaslighting, and there are many steps one can take to stop the gaslighter and bring relief to your life.

Journaling is important to differentiate between truth from false and illusions from reality.

To reframe the mindset, use positive imagination/visualization and mental exercises. Such as, how does your best self look like and feel like? And what can you do to reach there?

To deal with anxious thoughts, use relaxation techniques.

Tell yourself, and it is okay to end a long term abusive relationship (gaslighting or others)

Notice if there is a power dynamic between the victim and the gaslighter.

Identify or reconnect again with trusted friends and family, use them as your emotional support

You should know, you cannot control others' emotions and their feelings.

Do not get into who is right or wrong; focus on your feelings and feeling them.

Try to have self-compassion, learn new self-care techniques, and spend time doing what feels good and healthy.

Do not treat yourself as a victim, yes you have suffered through something difficult, but you are strong enough to build a new life or start new. Focus on your strengthens rather than shortcomings.

Recognize your gaslighter, their patterns, thoughts. What triggers them (can be anything or nothing) so you will be prepared for what is coming next. It will not be a surprise you would know what they are saying is not true.

You will be constantly lied to

Gaslighter will turn others against you

You will be criticized for being weak, sensitive or crazy

They will turn your friends and family against you

They never acknowledge your feelings

You have to stay strong through all of this and know what bad stuff they say about you is not true.

If you feel something is not right, trust your gut and act accordingly.

Do not lose touch with trusted friends and family, and they will help you differentiate between truth and lying.

Do not keep believing the gaslighter when they are saying mean stuff about you. You know better than that; you are worthy of love and being treated with kindness.

Do not try to strike back. The gaslighter will not back down and seek revenge afterward, and the cycle will never be broken.

Do not give them a reaction. Do not show you are upset or afraid. The more this bully sees you being affected, the more he will act on it.

If possible, try not to interact with the gaslighter. Yes, in the majority of the cases, it might not be possible but try to have a world of your own with solid boundaries.

6.6 Recovering from Gaslighting

Gaslighting flourishes on uncertainty and gaslighters know this. Thus, he will try to increase the feeling of mistrust and confusion in your life. As a survivor, you need to get validation for your experience.

If you have experienced gaslighting, know that it is a sinister form of abuse. It will leave you feeling unsure, disoriented about yourself, about others and in general. If you do not seek help, it will leave a long-lasting effect on your physical and mental well-being. Yes, it is also possible after gaslighting, you may feel you cannot have a normal healthy relationship again, but this is not true. With help, guidance, and recovery, everything is possible. If you have been gaslighted and you want to heal from it, reach out to your mental health professional or primary care provider. Do not make excuses or lie to them. Tell them the whole truth. It will give you strength and compassion for yourself, and you will be able to explore your feelings and move toward a healthy life. With better help, you can think for yourself again, make decisions, reach out to friends and family.

When you start recovering from gaslighting, it should start with your commitment to breaking the abusive cycle. Do not give the gaslighter permission to ruin your plans to recovery because he will be trying his hardest to manipulate you more now. Be prepared, and try to stay one step ahead of them as you already know your gaslighter's nature. Try to remain as distant as possible.

These are some tips to help you through. You must seek help from a third person. The help should come from outside of the relationship. It is not advised to talk to the gaslighter because they will shut you down as soon as possible. To maintain control, he can go to any limit. Talk to a trusted family member, friend, co-worker to experience your feelings. It will not be easy, but you have to do this. If you have been isolated for a long time, this will be particularly hard for you.

Focus on old trusted friendships and family members. The gaslighter may have fed you that nobody will believe you if you tell anyone, do not let this stop you. Your support system will help you get through this difficult time. Treat your recovery like a steady walk. Speaking to a trusted friend or family is therapeutic. So, you need their love and guidance in this trying time. They will help you separate illusion from reality. They will make sure you do not get sucked back into the cycle of abuse. Do not rush to be all moved on and free. Healing takes time, and there is no definite amount of time assigned to healing. Take as much time you need. Trust from others will reduce your feelings of shame. Through a social circle, you will be able to learn to trust yourself and others around you.

If you still want to work with your partner and your partner is also willing to leave gaslighting and listen to you. Try couple's therapy. Regular, long-term therapy is needed in order to make your or your partner's life better again. Things cannot be patched up in one therapy session. Even if you want to build a separate life from your abuser, therapy is a must and should happen. A therapist will be a neutral third party who will tell things as they are and reinforce your sense of reality. The therapist will also help you deal with other issues caused by gaslighting, such as anxiety, depression and PTSD. If your self-doubt too much, it can also be a sign of Obsessive-compulsive disorder; your therapist will help you overcome that.

Make yourself your priority. Do not lose yourself again; yes, even the gaslighter was not a romantic interest but a platonic relationship. Sadness comes easy but does not let it stay. It is necessary to leave your couch before it becomes your routine. According to a psychologist, create space within yourself emotionally and mentally, then outside of yourself by interacting with people you trust.

Reclaim your individuality and get out of the rut. It can be done by participating in things you love or once liked. Try new hobbies you might end up loving, go hiking, write in a journal, take cooking classes, try stitching, find your niche and do it often. Turn towards those relationships that took a bad position during the gaslighting period. Meet new people also by joining new classes, retreats, workshops and more. Talk about a shared interest.

Yes, it is going to be difficult for a while to remain positive but not impossible. Try self-regulation and emotional awareness, and these are the best antidotes to gaslighting. Build confidence and self-confidence in your reality. You do not need anyone else to validate your feelings or your reality, and you can do that for yourself. Learn to manage those uncomfortable feelings of staying in your company, as the gaslighter made you hate this. If you need a significant shift in your reality of mindset, you will need therapy.

From different therapies, according to some therapists, these are the things that have helped their patients. You can try and see for yourself.

Recognize the problem. Know the situation between you and the gaslighter; name it for your ease. Do not make excuses; accept it for what it is.

Write the conversation down and take an objective look at it. Look for where the conversation is directing off the path, where the gaslighter takes it? Does he make you feel bad? Or how do you feel when conversing with that person? If you have denied the truth, now is the time to face it.

Look for a power struggle in your relationship. If one is having the same conversation with a person over & over again and they do not listen to you or understand you. they are gaslighting you.

Take part in mental exercise. It will encourage you to have a better mindset. Think of yourself without the gaslighter. It may be your closest relationship but do it even if it does not feel good. If you do not have an identity right now. When will you have it? When will you have your own reality? Your life and when will you stand on your own?

Feel what is happening or has happened. Accept your feelings for what they are, and it is okay. It is better to track your feelings, notice the shift. Notice the patterns and look for mood shifts? What triggers you and what helps your mood.

Give yourself permission to give something up. It is okay to leave a toxic and abusive person behind. Yes, it can be your spouse, best friends, mother or siblings. Anyone who causes you mental health has to go. No matter how committed you feel to that person, if they are making you anxious, gaslighting you or abusing you in some other way, their leaving is the healthy thing for you.

Talk to trusted people. Ask their brutally honest opinion on your relationship with the gaslighter. Do not let them hold back. Do a reality check.

Most importantly, do not steer your feelings in one specific direction. Feel your feelings. Do not let them be wrong or right. If after talking to someone you feel down or negative or unhappy, pay attention to that. In a relationship, emotional & psychological wellbeing is important rather than who is wrong or right.

You can control only your opinion. No matter how hard you try, if the gaslighter does not acknowledge your opinion, they never will. Do not push too hard and spend your energy convincing them; you are not responsible for them.

Above all, have compassion for yourself. After enduring gaslighting for a long period of time, it is difficult to give yourself the kindness, love you deserve. But have compassion for yourself; you are building a new life for yourself. Now is the time for self-care.

Trust your instinct. From now on, learn to pay attention to your instinct or your gut feeling. Make a promise you will not question your thoughts, perceptions, feelings from now on. Tell yourself nobody is allowed to tell you the story. In some other words, believe yourself. Your feelings, memories and thoughts should not be up for debate.

If you decide to leave the gaslighter once and for all. Make sure your plan is safe, and there is a friend and family member to help you; even if you have nobody, please ensure you will not be putting yourself in more danger; involve your therapist if seeking therapy. Once you leave completely, cut that person out of your life. Do not go back and forth. Know you are strong enough to change your life.

6.7 When to Seek Help?

CDC (Centers for Disease Control) recommends a set of preventions in case of emotional abuse, domestic relationships, gaslighting or any other sort of abuse.

Gaslighting can turn into physical abuse. Anyone who is experiencing any form of abuse should seek professional help and support.

Any individual can contact an organization for domestic abuse for help and advice on how to create a safety plan.

From a mental health perspective, talking about your experience will help you heal and move on from experience and have compassion for yourself. Especially in an abusive relationship, it is necessary to seek help.

Chapter 7: Psychological Effects of Gaslighting

1. YOUR MENTAL ILLNESS IS USED

against you

A diagnosis of mental illness is easily used as a platform for blame. When your mental illness is at fault for every problem that arises in your relationship, you could be a victim of GASLIGHTING.

Imagine a long-term relationship where one felt respected and loved by their partner. But, over time, things have changed into something you do not recognize. Now their partner has started making fun of their parenting skills, question their memory, mocked their ability to do things. Now the person starts to think if something is actually wrong with them? When they tell your partner that their hurtful comments and statements are actually hurtful, they just laugh and tell the other person to grow up. Now their relationship has started failing with the children because they cannot keep up with things or mental fog is too much to deal with something else.

This kind of cruel, sinister behavior creeps up on a person, and they do not see it coming. In their mind, things were good one minute and not good the next minutes, but if they look closely, they will see things have not been okay for a while. The small issue here and there, your partner putting you down always, making fun of you in front of kids, denying your feelings, telling you; you do not feel a certain way, or things did not happen in this way, can affect your psychological health in a bad way. The person experiencing gaslighting will have low self-esteem, low self-confidence in themselves as a parent and a partner, loneliness, isolation and no joy seems to be their fate. The chronic stress of gaslighting can also reduce work efficiency, health problems, depression, anxiety, PTSD or even suicidal tendency.

7.1 Anxiety & depression

As the gaslighter will constantly make you feel that your perception is wrong or you are always wrong, it will have a negative effect on your mental health. In this case, this negative mindset leads to depression and anxiety. Gaslighting targets your self-esteem, so problems like anxious thoughts are common, making the victim falling harder in the trap of gaslighting. As you know, the process of gaslighting is gradual. It can cause

- Low self-esteem
- Second-guessing yourself
- No trust in one's judgment
- Feeling stressed out
- No confidence
- Social withdrawal & isolation
- Inability to make decision

7.2 Isolation

People who face gaslighting prefers to be alone all the time because they feel they cannot trust their memories, feelings and instincts. So they will end up spending time alone away from once trusted friends and family, just being dependent on the gaslighter. As a result of isolation, they get sucked in gaslighting traps and a negative mindset. Their confidence is low, and self-esteem is non-existence. They feel they are not good enough.

7.3 Delusions

Delusions are the root of all problems, happened as a result of gaslighting. The victim starts to believe the gaslighter in what they have to say; all negative talk told by the gaslighter is true. They get brainwashed into thinking that their memories and feelings are not correct. The way things happened is of the gaslighters way the victim is deluded at this point and will believe what the gaslighter says. These delusions contribute to other mental issues and isolation. Victims may also believe that they have dementia or schizophrenia when, in reality, they are healthy and just being gaslighted.

7.4 Mistrusting yourself

The victim will start mistrusting himself. The change in behavior will be drastic from this. A third person will feel they apologize too much, or stay quiet in social settings, or avoid going with their old friends or family members. One reason for this changed behavior can be the gaslighting they suffer from their partner, and they do not trust themselves. The victim will feel that their opinion has no value, is too sensitive for others, or feels like losing their minds. Although none of these are true, the victim cannot differentiate between their feelings and reality. Now they keep second-guessing themselves instead of taking a decision and sticking with it.

7.5 Psychological trauma

Gaslighting will cause psychological trauma for years to come if a person does not seek therapy. Even if a person recovers from mental abuse, the level of trust they have to gain again is quite difficult. Getting intimate relationships can also be difficult. Making new friends at work or otherwise can be problematic. It is also possible that the victim will feel confused and disoriented even after getting out of the gaslighting situation. They will feel difficulty in speaking their opinion, sticking by their judgment. No matter how much time has passed, the victim can still feel helpless, so do not delay your therapy or professional help.

Gaslighting becomes more dangerous the longer it happens. First, the victim feels okay after getting out of a gaslighting situation, but slowly the perception starts changing. The effects can be very damaging, especially when it comes to building trust and love again in intimate relationships because the victim's subconscious knows love and trust are the way to manipulation and lies. So, emotional unavailability can stem from this gaslighting. Gaslighting damages one's sincerity to love again. If the gaslighter were abusive verbally, the victim would keep hearing their words for a long time to come and find it hard to believe others and continue to blame and judge oneself. As many gaslighters make the victim dependent on them by saying," you will never find someone as good as me." "you are so unlovable or unworthy of love." Statements like these destroy a person's mindset for years.

Recovering from gaslighting is more difficult when people have been in denial about gaslighting or their partner's behavior for a long time. Such as one woman will get engaged to her boyfriend despite knowing he is a gaslighter because she loves the charmer and hates the abuser. To connect and receive love should not be your only goal. You have to find someone who respects you, your boundaries above all. Even a little gaslighting is still gaslighting. Therapy can help you and your partner if you both want to work together, but still, the relationship has changed to a great degree.

7.6 Overcoming the Effects of Gaslighting

First & foremost, you need to get rid of all things that remind you of your abuse. Yes, it includes the abuser (if possible). Now, you do not have to care how close you were to them. No one deserves to be treated this way, and the damage it causes is lasting. If your gaslighter knows you are recovering and moving on, they may try once again to pull you back no matter how sweet they have become or say they love you. Know you deserve better, and if they have not agreed to therapy or professional help, do not go back.

Learn to trust yourself more and more each day. To leave the effects of gaslighting in the past, you need to trust yourself again. Always tell yourself, yes, some bad people may want to deceive you, but your instinct will never guide you wrong. Then, get a therapist's help to overcome those past bad feelings. Or join a support group; you would be surprised to see how many people are trying to overcome the same thing as you and how they are willing to support you.

Count your bad experiences as teachers. Learning from your experience will help you gain strength, self-love will be easier, and you would be ready to face the world again. These are some ways to learn from your experience. Make sure you have enough evidence on what you say is happening, so if someone is betraying you, you can look at the previous signs and leave the situation. Write in journals, take pictures, voice notes to yourself to make sure you perceive it correctly without making you confused. There are always some red flags that say a loved one, coworker, friend, or spouse is gaslighting you. These signs don't need to happen after some time. These can happen at the beginning too. Regardless of the timings, signs are always present.

One will question their perception. If someone is lying to you on occasion but seems very confident, and once again you have started questioning yourself whether he is telling a lie or I remember it wrong? Such as, if your co-worker cannot submit a project on time and when it's time for submission, he turns to you and says, "you were assigned to this project, not me." This co-worker has never done this before, but what is your reaction going to be? Do you deny? Or they told a lie with so much conviction that you are not sure if the project was assigned to you. Gaslighters are tricky like that.

You will not feel under attack when someone is demeaning or insulting you. One's healthy. The natural reaction to being insulted should be upset. If you are not going to let anyone be cruel to kids, why are you letting them talk to you like this? If you start accepting that if a person is being mean to you, telling you that you are worthless or do not deserve love, you are experiencing gaslighting again. These attacks will start slowly and gradually increase in intensity, so make sure you are not there anymore to receive them.

Someone is trying to discredit you. They are discrediting you in a way; not only are you confused, but others believe them also. Such as your co-worker A will tell you casually, you are so incompetent that co-worker B does not want to work with you anymore. A friend will suggest, "I do not know how your siblings stick with you; they are saints." These kinds of statements make you feel alone once again and listen to your gaslighter more.

Make sure if you are experiencing signs like these again, leave the situation immediately. If the situation is friendship or romantic, cut all contact. If it is a workplace, create strong boundaries and keep the contact to a minimum. In any abusive situation, you must limit the contact. Get some distance between yourself and the gaslighter and prepare yourself for emotional healing.

You can always start from the beginning. Look for things you like and dislike about yourself without asking anyone's opinion. Such as, you like that you feel emotions so deeply that minor things move you. Or you love your voice, how soft it is when you speak to others/ or how deep it is. Or you do not like when you get jealous in romantic relationships. Or you want to lose some weight, or gain some weight, set your goals, work on yourself, empower yourself emotionally and physically.

As we discussed before, therapy and professional help are necessary. Therapists are skilled at helping you find more objective, detached ways of observing your life and give you options on how you can make your life better for yourself. If you do not have the courage to go out, you can try online therapy from the comfort of your home.

7.7 Questions to ask yourself to know if gaslighting is recurring?

If the doubts are creeping up again and you are confused if this is gaslighting or not. Or things just do not feel okay. Here are some questions to consider:

- Do you feel you cannot do things the right way?
- Is there confusion and mental fog?
- You are not sure what you have become?
- Are you taking the blame for others' actions/responsibility?
- Is the abuser keep boasting about himself?
- Is the gaslighter a constant liar?
- Are you feeling powerless or trapped?
- Are you feeling alone?
- Do you think you are too sensitive?
- Are you saying sorry too much?
- Your feelings and emotions do not matter to the potential gaslighter?
- You feel others turning against you?

- Do you doubt your memories?
- Is stress more and joy is less in your life?
- Are you again making excuses for the abuser/ potential gaslighter?
- Is the potential gaslighter breaks promises?
- Do you feel like you are losing your mind/ feel stupid?
- Is your self-confidence going down?
- Is making a decision hard again?
- The potential gaslighter asks for respect but does not respect you?

If the answer to most of these questions is yes, then you may want to reassess the situation. Put distance between you and the potential gaslighter, get help and get out of the situation as soon as possible.

Chapter 8: Gaslighting in Groups

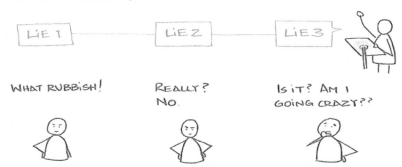

GASLIGHTING

LYING OR DECEIVING UNTIL PEOPLE START TO DOUBT THEIR OWN REALITY

Gaslighting is far more common than any other kind of abuse and is present in our daily lives, from one-on-one interactions to group situations.

8.1 Gaslighting in a corporate environment

In these situations, a gaslighter can be a business competitor, negative manager, biased workgroup, or devious coworker. There is a difference between a manager who keeps you on your toes or a gaslighting manager. A gaslighter would not want you to succeed in any situation or sabotage your success. Corporate gaslighting can be a result of negative media coverage, biasness, or systemic groups. A gaslighter can target individuals or groups. According to psychologists, these four characteristics differentiate gaslighting at work from other difficulties on the job:

- A difficult work circumstance is built on insistent negativity, biasness, and solid proof, established cases, proven data, or strong facts.

- A difficult work situation makes a negative narrative about the victim suffering from gaslighting (opposite to evidence) and ruins the victim's professional or personal reputation.

- The victim's exploitation keeps happening for some time, despite the victim's positive accomplishments, contributions and collaborations.
- When confronted by the gaslighter, he becomes defensive, evasive, dismissive or contentious instead of solving the problem with facts. He may become more aggressive, stone wall or passive-aggressive.
- This gaslighting is based on false accusations, than facts and credibility.

If the gaslighter keeps spreading gossip about you, it is also a practice of passive-aggressive behavior. Gaslighting can also happen online, face-to-face, in meetings and otherwise. All of those negative remarks are designed to damage the target's credibility. This can also happen in comparison with other employees.

8.2 How HR Can Identify a Gaslighter?

According to a psychologist, a gaslighter will exhibit these traits often:
- He will tell lies often and inclined to exaggerate
- A gaslighter never admits to having flaws
- He breaks social rules & violates the boundary
- He guilt trips others and emotional coercion
- Manipulates to gain pleasure or self-worth
- Becomes extremely aggressive or diverts when criticized
- Projects a false personality
- A gaslighter will not turn in your project
- A gaslighter will keep saying racist and sexist things to you, especially when others are not present. When you report to HR, they deny these claims and say you are who said those things.

According to a psychologist, if you see a high turnover rate beneath a specific manager, the people who left do not shed light on 'why they left.' It indicates gaslighting the employees. People work overtime to prove their worth, yet they have no idea what is expected of them because of gaslighting supervisors. A potential gaslighter also wants to be the victim, and It is another sign of gaslighters. One good example is when you are having a difficult time in your life or need to go to the doctor for some reason and when you tell the reason to the gaslight supervisor. They will make up a lie or tell you even worse fake condition about themselves and turn it around onto themselves. As an employee, you will feel sorry and keep working without leaving for your issue. Then, to further drive the lie home, the manager will start taking time off work to validate his lie.

A gaslighter at work is quite incompetent, and their behavior is used as a way to distract others from their incompetence. Gaslighters are intense and dramatic. They can escalate things from zero to 100 quite quickly. If your manager is a gaslighter, it isn't easy to call them out on their performance. When confronted about their job performance as to why they have not submitted the project or finished it yet, they will attack the person questioning them. Now you have to defend yourself, and you will forget the reason why you questioned them in the first place. One example is a pregnant lady who goes to work, and the gaslighter supervisor calls her in for performance review and says, "everything is a mess, and it is not really your fault; I have talked to the team, and the problem is definitely you." The next day she raises a question about his feedback. The boss denies everything and says he never said a word and I am happy with your performance, and we left the meeting happy yesterday, remember? Maybe these pregnancy hormones are your heady cloudy.

Gaslighting in the workplace can have a ripple effect; it can affect the people who are not involved. If the team is cracking, everyone will feel it. According to a psychologist, gaslighting at work creates an unpleasant, tense, unsafe, toxic environment for everyone who is involved indirectly or directly.

8.3 Advice for Gaslighting Work Environment

According to an expert, if you feel you are being gaslighted at work, immediately inform the Human Resources department. For saving themselves, the target should record interactions, messages, emails, or conversations with the gaslighter, keeping this proof safe with themselves or with a trusted friend. Look at the proof to make sure it is really gaslighting or just another difficult work situation. If you are a manager and some beneath you are a gaslighter, it is a tricky game. Gaslighters are good at shifting blame, and it can be difficult to know if they are dealing with someone who is a gaslighter or gaslights others. Gaslighters are not afraid to gaslights co-workers, superiors or other workers.

Managing gaslighters is quite difficult because they can become harsh. Gaslighters may claim harassment or discrimination, hold some information for ransom or threaten other employees. If your HR department is not skilled, it can be a bigger fish to fry. According to experts, gather as much information as possible before confronting the gaslighter about their behavior. Yes, they will deny, but you have proof. Show them evidence and give them time to respond, do not get sucked into their lies again.

8.4 Gaslighting in Marketing & Politics

Evildoers and criminals use gaslighting to change other people's perceptions of their actions and behavior. Gaslighting suffocates the discussions as it attacks a person's knowledge and surety of their beliefs. Unfortunately, science can be utilized to gaslight others.

Tabaco and Cigarettes industries use gaslighting tactics to promote cancer-causing smoking. Many other medical businesses also do the same. They tell the customer that their knowledge might not be true, as these products are not as bad, unhealthy or immoral. Once an individual is gaslit, it spreads like wildfire.

Marketing claims unconfirmed benefits, negative compromises to sell their products. It all is gaslighting, but how will you know what is not gaslighting? If there are verifiable facts available, then it is not gaslighting. We all have seen gaslighting in politics when two political parties are at each other's throats, and instead of backing their claims on facts, they are questioning other's credibility, presenting themselves as the good guy. For gaslighters, the goal is about control and power. Be harshly spreading misinformation, continuously assaulting their victims with mean messages and propaganda, the Gaslighter's objective is to subdue society psychologically. Then the gaslighter will exploit people or groups individually.

Chapter 9: How to Stop the Narcissistic Gaslighter?

WHEN POSSIBLE, DON'T ENGAGE

'WE REMEMBER THINGS DIFFERENTLY'

'I HEAR YOU. THAT ISN'T MY EXPERIENCE'

'I'M STEPPING AWAY FROM THIS CONVERSATION'

'IF YOU CONTINUE TO SPEAK TO ME IN THIS WAY, I'M NOT ENGAGING'

'I'M OPEN TO DISCUSSING A SOLUTION WITH YOU. I'M NOT OPEN TO DEBATING MY FEELINGS'

These are some effective tips to take control back in gaslighting situations:

Read the room: know when the gaslighter is about to go off, be prepared. Gaslighters are good at twisting truths, covering lies, so trust your judgment. Listen to your body; is it becoming stressed when this gaslighter has changed its demeanor. Are you going up and down to be accepted by this person? Realize you have the power to change your circumstances. No matter how much mean stuff they say, it is not true. You can always take your power back. When they start their drama, do not engage them, do not feed their evil energy with your innocence.

Reclaim yourself: you need to remember gaslighting is not personal. You are the target not because something is wrong with you. Instead, there is something wrong with them. Remember, during gaslighting encounters, instead of feeling powerless, know you can decide what happens next. You can always decide not to be drawn in any more manipulation. Trust yourself and know your perception.

Put some distance: during a gaslighting encounter, one does not need to make rash decisions. Try not to confront the gaslighter as they flourish on your emotional reactions. Step back, put some distance between you two, start being less available.

Take the high road: if a gaslighter is spreading lies about you or gossiping about you, do not waste time defending yourself. People who truly know you will know something is wrong with this situation will ask you or at least not believe the gaslighter. Walking away with dignity and silence can speak volumes. So keep moving, do not believe all the mean things. Leave those people who do not have your back.

Value yourself more: self-empowerment is the key factor in fighting against gaslighting. Respect and value yourself, do not look for external validation. Make new commitments to yourself. Write in a journal what you are grateful for. Every day write three things you are thankful for and what you like about yourself. Reconnect with your true version of yourself and create a life you want to live every day and not run away from. People may be gaslighting in social circles because they see your potential when you do not see it and want to dim your light. When you realize your true worth, a gaslighter can't gaslight you. Be you in a world full of someone else; people who love you genuinely and care for you will walk with you.

Know yourself, and do not let a gaslighter brainwash you. Do not let them do whatever they want. They will want to make you in a version that suits them best. It is your duty not to let it happen; yes, you cannot control gaslighters' behavior, but you can tell yourself the truth. One way is to remember exactly what happened, no matter how much brain fog you think you are under. You know something bad or abusive happened, do not let the gaslighter tell you otherwise. Or they will start doing it again and again, do not lose yourself in their games and manipulation.

If you do not trust your memory yet, write things down, take pictures for evidence, be strong for yourself and fight for your rights. The gaslighters want you to submit to them, to listen to them whatever he says. He wants to gain control or power. If they are not physical, talk to them calmly about your boundaries and how they are breaching them.

One person having control of the relationship is not healthy. Instead, it is toxic. Do not let a toxic person have control over you. Hold the gaslighter accountable, and do not let them blame you for what they did. If they keep insisting, just walk away. Do not spend your leftover energy on them proving your point.

Start telling the gaslighter to respect you, do not let him treat you like a doormat. You are better than that. You deserve to be treated with kindness and care. If you do not feel like having a conversation with your gaslighter or feel uncomfortable with the topic, do not discuss that; walk away.

You might have experienced this; at the beginning of the relationship, the gaslighter love-bombed you, pretended to be the best listener. That is how they hooked you, and they were everything a person can want in a partner. But with time why things changed because they have started showing their true face. You wonder if this is your fault if you did something bad or wrong. The second time when they will pretend to listen to you is when you are leaving them. This is their attempt to hook you back into the toxic relationship only if they have not found someone to replace you with another target. Sadly, none of it because they love you. They are trying to fill their narcissistic void. This void is not filled, and games never end. You have the power to say no.

Remember, the confusion of gaslighting stems from not acknowledging your feelings once you have realized the gaslighting pattern. Therefore, it cannot affect you as much.

As gaslighters are insecure people, they need doormat people to make them feel superior, do not give in to their games and manipulation. To feel safe, ironically, they will like to have the upper hand.

Remember, it is highly unlikely to change a gaslighters behavior. Their behavior and manipulation is the only way they know how to behave. To change a gaslighter, their will to change themselves should be high.

If gaslighting is at work, try to look for another job yes, it is not easy, but money cannot worth more than your mental peace.

Regardless of what a gaslighter says, you are loveable and capable of love. You are worthy of every good thing coming towards you. Never forget it always gets better; you just have to stay strong, keep your head high and work on new you.

Conclusion

Gaslighting is an attempt to gain control over someone's life, thought process, and memories and is a form of psychological abuse. The victim starts questioning their reality and cannot trust their judgment. It is a common manipulative tactic of sociopaths, dictators, narcissists, domestic abusers, and many cult leaders. As Gaslighting happens by isolating the victim, isolation can make the victim lose their concept of reality, and the control will go to the abuser; he can do as he pleases.

Gaslighting happens progressively so that the victim loses their sense of reality and depends on the abuser as isolation has already happened. In the beginning, the abuser's behavior seems fine at first but will time, in the victim's depression, anxiety can instill, thus losing their confidence and keeps relying on their abuser's patterns of Gaslighting, with no way to escape.

If you know you are a victim of Gaslighting, make sure to seek professional help and realize what is happening. As one has suffered domestic and emotional abuse, the help should also be professional to get that person out of the psychological manipulation. Professional help will make them realize that they can trust themselves again, their memories are correct. Their perception of reality is accurate; the victim will reestablish their confidence in themselves, in their situation. If someone wants to save their relationship with the gaslighter, both partners must seek professional help and be willing to change and work on themselves. Often the victim will choose to end their relationship with the abuser, as the abuser is wired to make certain types of decisions that cannot be healthy for the victim.

Made in the USA
Coppell, TX
13 November 2021

65711327R00420